WITHDRAWN FROM STOCK

NATIONAL COLLEGE
LIBRARY

RN
RN 6359

D0585101

WITHDRAWN FROM STOCK

Introduction to work study

NATIONAL COLLEGE
RN 6359
LIBRARY
OF INDUSTRIAL RELATIONS

WITHDRAWN FROM STOCK

Introduction to
work study

Third (revised) edition

International Labour Office Geneva

Third (revised) edition copyright © International Labour Organisation 1979

Publications of the International Labour Office enjoy copyright under Protocol 2 of the Universal Copyright Convention. Nevertheless, short excerpts from them may be reproduced without authorisation, on condition that the source is indicated. For rights of reproduction or translation, application should be made to the Publications Branch (Rights and Permissions), International Labour Office, CH-1211 Geneva 22, Switzerland. The International Labour Office welcomes such applications.

ISBN 92-2-101939-X

First published 1957
Second edition 1969
Third (revised) edition 1979
Third impression 1986

Barcode No: 390060104637/60
Dewey No: 658.542
Date Input: 27/07/12
Price:

The designations employed in ILO publications, which are in conformity with United Nations practice, and the presentation of material therein do not imply the expression of any opinion whatsoever on the part of the International Labour Office concerning the legal status of any country, area or territory or of its authorities, or concerning the delimitation of its frontiers.
The responsibility for opinions expressed in signed articles, studies and other contributions rests solely with their authors, and publication does not constitute an endorsement by the International Labour Office of the opinions expressed in them.
Reference to names of firms and commercial products and processes does not imply their endorsement by the International Labour Office, and any failure to mention a particular firm, commercial product or process is not a sign of disapproval.

ILO publications can be obtained through major booksellers or ILO local offices in many countries, or direct from ILO Publications, International Labour Office, CH-1211 Geneva 22, Switzerland. A catalogue or list of new publications will be sent free of charge from the above address.

Printed in the German Democratic Republic   ZIM

Preface

to the third (revised) edition

Writing a book on work study which can be used all over the world by persons trained in different countries with different systems and different terminologies is no easy task. To make this book as widely acceptable as possible, therefore, it has been felt advisable to present the subject-matter in a reasonably simplified manner and to enrich the text with numerous examples of work study practice, a large number of which are based on the experience of ILO management development advisers engaged in work study in many countries.

The original version of this book, published in 1957, was intended mainly for use by persons attending courses in work study at management development and productivity centres in the numerous developing countries to which ILO technical co-operation missions were attached, and to provide basic teaching material for members of the staff of these centres. Since 1957 the book has met with considerable success, easily topping the list of best-selling books published by the ILO. To date, over 200,000 copies have been sold in English, French and Spanish, three of the working languages of the ILO, and the book has been translated into a number of other languages, including Arabic, Japanese and Korean. Although originally intended for use in developing countries, it has become a standard introductory textbook in many institutions in developed countries as well.

Some ten years after the original edition was published, an enlarged and revised edition was produced; this aimed at strengthening certain aspects of the book, particularly the part on work measurement. However, the original intention that the book should be an introductory text for use mainly for educational purposes was adhered to.

Some 20 years after the publication of the first edition, the present completely overhauled and revised edition has been prepared. The basic aims of this revised edition are to bring the contents up to date, to modify the book's purely introductory character, and to make it equally useful for the work study practitioner and for the teacher and student, whilst retaining the simplified approach to the explanation of complex problems. To this end, the chapter dealing with working conditions has been completely rewritten to take account of current advances in knowledge in this field. Similarly, the part dealing with work measurement has been radically modified to accommodate new ideas, and new chapters have been added to deal with work sampling, with predetermined time standards and with standard data. Finally, as a corollary of this new approach, work study has been examined in the light of modern developments in work organisation which aim at reconciling productivity with

V

job satisfaction, thus scotching the notion that the only use of work study is to increase productivity. A chapter on new forms of work organisation has therefore been added. This is the first time that any book in this field has shown that work study has a contribution to make towards making work more human as well as towards raising productivity.

The original edition of the book was prepared by the late C. R. Wynne-Roberts, at the time Chief of the Management Development Branch of the ILO, in collaboration with E. J. Riches, former Treasurer and Comptroller to the ILO. Several members of ILO management development teams helped to prepare very detailed and valuable comments, among them Hans Fahlström, L. P. Ferney, Hy Fish, C. L. M. Kerkhoven, J. B. Shearer and Seymour Tilles. Several others contributed valuable criticisms and commentaries, particularly F. de P. Hanika and Winston Rogers, and the late T. U. Matthew.

The second (revised) edition was prepared by R.L. Mitchell, then an official of the ILO Management Development Branch, who, as chief of ILO missions to India and Turkey, had used the original version extensively in teaching work study and was therefore able to perceive the extent of the revisions needed. The revision also benefited from the advice and collaboration of J. B. Shearer, who also at that time was an official of the ILO Management Development Branch.

The third (revised) edition has been conceived and edited by George Kanawaty, the present Chief of the ILO Training Department, who has also written several parts of the new material. Acknowledgement is also due to John Burbidge, Fred Evans, Rolf Lindholm, Luigi Parmeggiani and Peter Steele for their valuable contributions, all of which have helped to ensure that this book, in its expanded and updated form, retains its function as a basic text on the principles and techniques of work study.

Contents

PART FIVE. APPENDICES

FIGURES

TABLES

Part one
Productivity
and work study

Chapter 1
Productivity and the standard of living

1. The standard of living

By **standard of living** is meant the degree of material well-being available to a person or class or community which is necessary for sustaining and enjoying life.

The standard of living of the representative person or family in the different countries of the world varies greatly from country to country and even, within each country, from community to community. Today, in spite of the immense efforts that have been made, both at the national and at the international levels, a significant proportion of mankind continues to eke out an existence in conditions of acute poverty. In too many parts of the world the ordinary man is still hardly able to satisfy his basic needs.

2. Requirements for a minimum satisfactory standard of living

What are the basic needs that must be met in order to attain a minimum decent standard of living?

Principally, they are—

☐ *FOOD*
enough food every day to replace the energy used in living and working;

☐ *CLOTHING*
enough clothes to permit bodily cleanliness and afford protection from the weather;

☐ *SHELTER*
shelter which is of a standard high enough to give protection under healthy conditions and which is equipped with certain household equipment and furniture;

☐ *SECURITY*
security against robbery or violence, against loss of the opportunity to work, against poverty due to illness or old age; and

☐ *ESSENTIAL SERVICES*
such as safe drinking-water, sanitation, medical care, public transport, and educational and cultural facilities that would enable every man, woman and child to develop to the full his or her talent and abilities.

Food, clothing and shelter are generally things which a man has to obtain for himself. In order to have them he must pay for them, either in money or work. Security and essential services are generally matters for governments and other public authorities. The services of public authorities have to be paid for, generally by individual citizens, so each man must earn enough to pay his contribution to the common services as well as to support himself and his family.

Each nation or community must, in the long run, be self-supporting. The standard of living achieved will be that which the representative citizen is able to achieve through his own efforts and those of all his fellow citizens.

The greater the amount of goods and services produced in any community, the higher its average standard of living will be.

There are two main ways of increasing the amount of goods and services produced. One is to increase employment; the other is to increase productivity.

If in any community there are men and women who are able to work and who want work but who are unable to find work, or who are able to find only part-time work, the output of goods and services can be increased if full-time productive work can be provided for them, i.e. if employment can be increased. Whenever there is unemployment or underemployment, efforts to increase employment are very important and should go hand in hand with efforts to increase the productivity of those who are already employed. But it is with the latter task that we are here concerned.

We can have—

☐ more and cheaper **food** by increasing the productivity of **agriculture;**

☐ more and cheaper **clothing** and **shelter** by increasing the productivity of **industry;**

☐ more **security** and **essential services** by increasing **all** productivity and earning power, leaving more from which to pay for them.

3. What is productivity?

Productivity may be defined as follows:

Productivity is the ratio of output to input

This definition applies in an enterprise, an industry or an economy as a whole.

Put in simpler terms, productivity, in the sense in which the word is used here, is nothing more than the arithmetical ratio between the amount produced and the amount of any resources used in the course of production. These resources may be—

☐   *LAND*

☐   *MATERIALS*

☐   *PLANT, MACHINES AND TOOLS*

☐   *THE SERVICES OF MEN*

or, as is generally the case, a combination of all four.

We may find that the productivity of labour, land, materials or machines in any establishment, industry or country has increased, but the bare fact does not in itself tell us anything about the reasons why it has increased. An increase in the productivity of labour, for example, may be due to better planning of the work on the part of the management or to the installation of new machinery. An increase in the productivity of materials may be due to greater skill on the part of workers, to improved designs, and so on.

Examples of each type of productivity may make its meaning clearer.

☐   *PRODUCTIVITY OF LAND*
If, by using better seed, better methods of cultivation and more fertiliser, the yield of corn from a particular hectare of land can be increased from 2 quintals to 3 quintals, the productivity of that land, in the **agricultural** sense, has been increased by 50 per cent. The productivity of land used for **industrial** purposes may be said to have been increased if the output of goods or services within that area of land is increased by whatever means.

☐   *PRODUCTIVITY OF MATERIALS*
If a skilful tailor is able to cut 11 suits from a bale of cloth from which an unskilful tailor can only cut ten, in the hands of the skilful tailor the bale was used with 10 per cent greater productivity.

☐   *PRODUCTIVITY OF MACHINES*
If a machine tool has been producing 100 pieces per working day and through the use of improved cutting tools its output in the same time is increased to 120 pieces, the productivity of that machine has been increased by 20 per cent.

☐   *PRODUCTIVITY OF MEN*
If a potter has been producing 30 plates an hour and improved methods of work enable him to produce 40 plates an hour, the productivity of that man has increased by $33^1/_3$ per cent.

In each of these deliberately simple examples output—or production—has also increased, and in each case by exactly the same percentage as the productivity. But an increase in production does not by itself indicate an increase in productivity. If the input of resources goes up in direct proportion to the increase in output, the productivity will stay the same. And if input increases by a greater percentage than output, higher production will be being achieved at the expense of a reduction in productivity.

In short, higher productivity means that more is produced with the same expenditure of resources, i.e. at the same cost in terms of land, materials, machine

5

time or labour; or alternatively that the same amount is produced at less cost in terms of land, materials, machine time or labour used up, thus releasing some of these resources for the production of other things.

4. Relationship between increased productivity and higher standards of living

We can now see more clearly how higher productivity can contribute to a higher standard of living. If more is produced at the same cost, or the same amount is produced at less cost, there is a gain to the community as a whole, which can be used by members of the community to acquire more and better goods and services and to improve their standard of living.

5. Productivity in industry

The problems of raising the productivity of the land and of livestock are matters for the agricultural expert. This book is not concerned with them. It is mainly concerned with raising productivity in industry, especially manufacturing industry. The techniques of work study described in it can, however, be used with success wherever work is done—in factories or offices, in shops or public services, and even on farms.

Cloth for clothes, many parts of houses, sanitary ware, drainage and waterworks equipment, drugs and medical supplies, equipment for hospitals and for defence are all the products of industry. So are many things necessary for living above the level of bare existence. Household utensils, furniture, lamps and stoves generally have to be made in workshops, large and small. Many of the goods necessary for running a modern community are too complex and too heavy to be made by cottage or small-scale industry. Railway engines and carriages, motor trucks, electric generators, telephones, computer equipment, all require expensive machines to make them, special equipment to handle them and an army of workers of many different skills. The greater the productivity of the establishments making these things, the greater are the opportunities of producing them abundantly and cheaply in quantities and at prices which will meet the requirements of every family in the community.

The factors affecting the productivity of each organisation are many, and no one factor is independent of others. The importance to be given to the productivity of each of the resources—land, materials, machines or men—depends on the enterprise, the industry and possibly the country. In industries where labour costs are low compared with material costs, or compared with the capital invested in plant and equipment (as in heavy chemical plants, power stations or paper mills), better use of materials or plant may give the greatest scope for cost reduction. In countries where capital and skill are short, while unskilled labour is plentiful and poorly paid, it is especially important that higher productivity should be looked for by increasing the output per machine or piece of plant or per skilled worker. It often pays to increase the number of unskilled workers if by doing so an expensive machine or a group of skilled craftsmen are enabled to increase output. Most practical managers know this, but many people have been misled into thinking of productivity exclusively as the productivity of labour, mainly because labour productivity usually forms the basis for published statistics on the subject. In this book the problem of raising productivity will be treated as one of making the best possible use of all the available resources, and attention will constantly be drawn to cases where the productivity of materials or plant is increased.

6. The background of productivity

To achieve the greatest increases in productivity, action must be taken by all sections of the community: governments, employers and workers.

Governments can create conditions favourable to the efforts of employers and workers to raise productivity. For these it is necessary, among other things—

to have balanced programmes of economic development;

to take the steps necessary to maintain employment;

to try to make opportunities for employment for those who are unemployed or underemployed, and for any who may become redundant as a result of productivity improvement in individual plants.

This is especially important in developing countries where unemployment is a big problem.

Employers and workers also have vital parts to play. The main responsibility for raising productivity in an individual enterprise rests with the **management.** Only the management can introduce and create a favourable climate for a productivity programme and obtain the co-operation of the workers which is essential for real success, though this requires the goodwill of the workers too. Trade unions can actively encourage their members to give such co-operation when they are satisfied that the programme is in the interests of the workers, as well as of the country as a whole.

7. The attitude of the workers

One of the greatest difficulties in obtaining the active co-operation of the workers is the fear that raising productivity will lead to unemployment. Workers fear that they will work themselves out of their jobs. This fear is greatest when unemployment already exists and a worker who loses his job will find it hard to get another. Even in the economically developed countries where employment has for years been at a very high level, this fear is very real to those who have already experienced unemployment.

Since this is so, unless workers are assured of adequate assistance in meeting their problems, they may resist any steps which they fear, rightly or wrongly, will make them redundant, even though their period of unemployment may only be a short one, while they are changing jobs.

Even with written guarantees, steps taken to raise productivity will probably meet with resistance. This resistance can generally be reduced to a minimum if everybody concerned understands the nature of and reason for each step taken and

7

has some say in its implementation. Workers' representatives should be trained in the techniques of increasing productivity so that they will be able both to explain them to their fellow workers and to use their knowledge to ensure that no steps are taken which are directly harmful to them. Many of the safeguards mentioned above can best be implemented through joint productivity committees and works councils.

Chapter 2
Productivity
in the individual enterprise

It was said in Chapter 1 that there were a number of factors affecting the productivity of an enterprise. Some of these, such as the general level of demand for goods, taxation policy, interest rates and the availability of raw materials, suitable equipment or skilled labour, are outside and beyond the control of any one employer. Certain other factors can be controlled from inside the enterprise, and it is these that we are now going to discuss.

1. Resources at the disposal of an enterprise

Productivity was defined as "the ratio of output to input" in an enterprise, an industry or an economy as a whole.

The productivity of a certain set of resources (input) is therefore the amount of goods or services (output) which is produced from them. What are the resources at the disposal of a manufacturing company?[1] They are—

☐ *LAND AND BUILDINGS*
Land in a convenient location on which to erect the buildings and other facilities necessary for the operations of the enterprise, and the buildings erected on it.

☐ *MATERIALS*
Materials that can be converted into products to be sold. They include fuel, chemicals for use in the processes of manufacture, and packing materials.

☐ *MACHINES*
Plant, equipment and tools necessary to carry out operations of manufacture and the handling and transport of materials; heating, ventilating and power plant; office equipment and furniture.

☐ *MANPOWER*
Men and women to perform the manufacturing operations; to plan and control; to do clerical work; to design and to research; to buy and sell.

---

[1] This discussion of productivity applies equally to non-manufacturing fields. The proper use of manpower, equipment and other resources is just as important in running a railway, an airline or municipal services as in running a factory.

9

The use which is made of all these resources combined determines the **productivity** of the enterprise.

The resources consist of "real" things and services. When they are used up in the process of production, "real" costs are therefore incurred. Their cost may also be measured in terms of money. Since higher productivity means more output from the same resources, it also means lower money costs and higher net money returns per unit of output.

2. The task of the management

Who is responsible for making sure that the best use is made of all these resources? Who is responsible for seeing that they are combined in such as way as to achieve the greatest productivity? The **management** of the enterprise.

In any concern larger than a one-man business (and to some extent even in a one-man business) the work of balancing the use of one resource against another and of co-ordinating the efforts of everyone in the organisation to achieve the best results is the job of the management. If the management fails to do what is necessary, the enterprise will fail in the end. In such a case the four resources become uncoordinated—like the efforts of four horses without a driver. The enterprise, like a driverless coach, moves forward jerkily, now held up for lack of material, now for lack of equipment, because machines are badly chosen and even more badly maintained, or because employees are unable or unwilling to do their best. The key position of the management may be shown by a diagram (figure 1).

This is not the place to discuss the activities (listed in the figure) by which the management achieves the transformation of the resources at its disposal into finished products. (The titles of some textbooks on management will be found in the book list at the end of this volume (Appendix 5)). It may not be out of place, however, to say something about the term "motivate".

To "motivate" means to provide a motive or reason for doing something. Used in the context of management it means, in effect, to make people **want** to do something. It is of little use the management carrying out the other activities of getting facts, planning, and so on, if the people who are supposed to carry out the plans do not want to do so, although they may have to. Coercion is no substitute for voluntary action. It is one of the tasks of the management, and perhaps its most difficult task, to make people want to co-operate; the management can only succeed fully by enlisting the willing and active participation of workers at all levels.

3. The productivity of materials

The relative importance of each of the resources mentioned above and shown in figure 1 varies according to the nature of the enterprise, the country in which it is operating, the availability and cost of each type of resource and the type of product and process. There are many industries in which the cost of raw material represents 60 per cent or more of the cost of the finished product, the balance of 40

Figure 1.   Role of the management in co-ordinating the resources of an enterprise

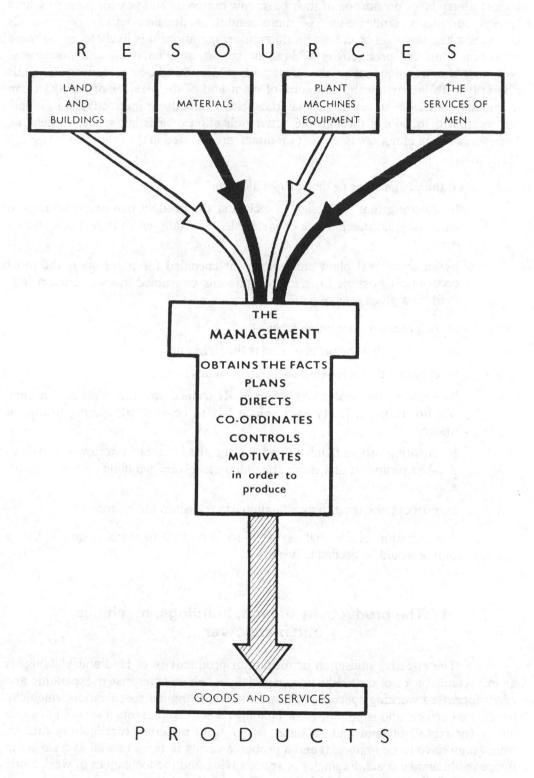

per cent being divided between labour and overhead costs. Many countries have to import a very large proportion of their basic raw materials and pay for them in scarce foreign currencies. Under either of these conditions the productivity of materials becomes a key factor in economic production or operation; it is likely to be far more important than the productivity of land or labour or even plant and machinery. Although the technique of work study, with which this book is concerned, deals primarily with improving the utilisation of plant and of the services of labour, it can frequently contribute to savings in materials, either directly or indirectly, as in saving the erection of buildings through the better utilisation of existing space. In general, however, savings in materials, direct or indirect, are effected in the following ways:

☐   **at the design stage or time of specification—**

by ensuring that the design is such that the product can be manufactured with the least possible use of materials, especially when they are scarce or dear;

by ensuring that plant and equipment specified for purchase is the most economical possible in terms of materials consumed in its operation (e.g. fuel) for a given level of performance.

☐   **at the process or operation stage—**

by ensuring that the process used is the right one;

by ensuring that it is being operated correctly;

by ensuring that operatives are properly trained and motivated so that they will not turn out faulty work which has to be rejected, leading to loss of material;

by ensuring proper handling and storage at all stages from raw materials to finished products, first eliminating all unnecessary handling and movement; and

by proper packaging to avoid damage in transit to the customer.

The question of material saving is so important to many countries that a separate volume would be needed to discuss it.

4. The productivity of land, buildings, machines and manpower

The effective utilisation or maximum productivity of land and buildings is an important source of cost reduction, especially when an enterprise is expanding and needs increased working space. Any reduction in the original specification which can be effected before land is purchased or buildings erected represents a saving in capital outlay (or rental) of land and buildings, a saving in materials (particularly fittings, which may have to be imported) and a probable saving in taxes as well as a saving in future maintenance costs. Examples of space saving and the techniques of work study employed to achieve them will be found in Chapters 9 and 10.

12

We now come to consider the productivity of plant, machinery and equipment and of the services of men and women. Let us take another look at the nature of productivity, which in simple terms was described as the "arithmetical ratio between the amount produced and the amount of any resources used in the course of production". To do this we have to start thinking in terms of **time,** since it is the output of good production from a machine or from a worker in a given time which is used in calculating productivity. Productivity is frequently measured as the output of goods or services in a given number of "man-hours" or "machine-hours".

5. How the total time of a job is made up

☐   **A man-hour** is the labour of one man for one hour.

☐   **A machine-hour** is the running of a machine or piece of plant for one hour.

The time taken by a man or a machine to carry out an operation or to produce a given quantity of product may be considered as made up in the following manner, which is illustrated in figure 2.

There is first—

the basic work content of the product or operation[1]

Work content means, of course, the amount of work "contained in" a given product or process measured in man-hours or machine-hours.[2] The basic work content is the time the product would take to manufacture or the operation to perform if the design or specification were perfect, if the process or method of manufacture or operation were perfectly carried out, and if there were no loss of working time from any cause whatsoever during the period of the operation (other than legitimate rest pauses permitted to the operative). **The basic work content is the irreducible minimum time theoretically required to produce one unit of output.**

This is obviously a perfect condition which never occurs in practice, although it may sometimes be approached, especially in processing industries. In general, however, actual operation times are far in excess of it on account of—

excess work content

The work content is increased by the following:

A.   **Work content added by defects in the design or specification of the product**

This occurs primarily in manufacturing industries, but the equivalent in service industries such as transport might be the specification of a bus service which demands operation in a way that causes unnecessary additional transit time. This additional work content is the time taken over and above the time of the basic work content due to **features inherent in the product** which could be eliminated (see figure 3).

---

[1] The words "or operation" are added throughout because this picture applies equally to non-manufacturing industries such as transport operation or retail selling.

[2] This definition differs slightly from that given in the B.S. *Glossary* (British Standards Institution: *Glossary of terms used in work study* (London, 1969). See note at the bottom of figure 2.

Figure 2. How manufacturing time is made up

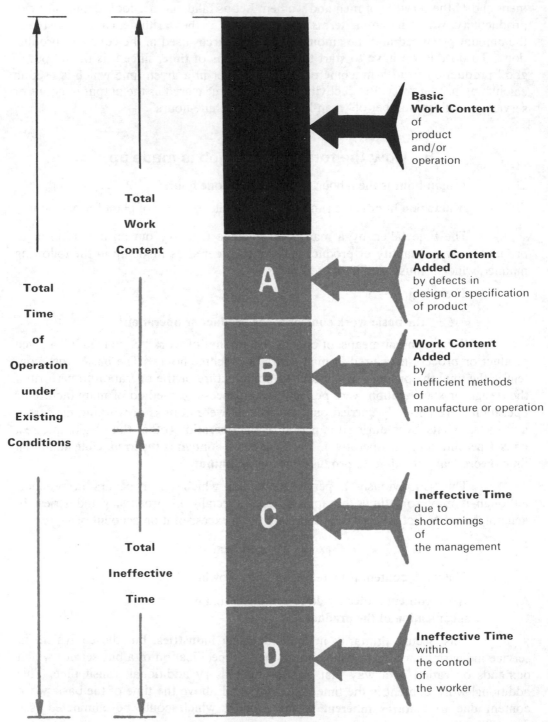

Basic Work Content of product and/or operation

Total Work Content

Total Time of Operation under Existing Conditions

Work Content Added by defects in design or specification of product

Work Content Added by inefficient methods of manufacture or operation

Total Ineffective Time

Ineffective Time due to shortcomings of the management

Ineffective Time within the control of the worker

Note: In the B.S. *Glossary* the terms "work content" and "ineffective time" are accorded precise technical meanings which differ slightly from those used here. The *Glossary* definitions are intended for use in applying work measurement techniques, and are not strictly relevant to the present discussion. In this chapter and the next, "work content" and "ineffective time" are used with their ordinary common meanings, as defined in the text.

Figure 3.   Work content due to the product and processes

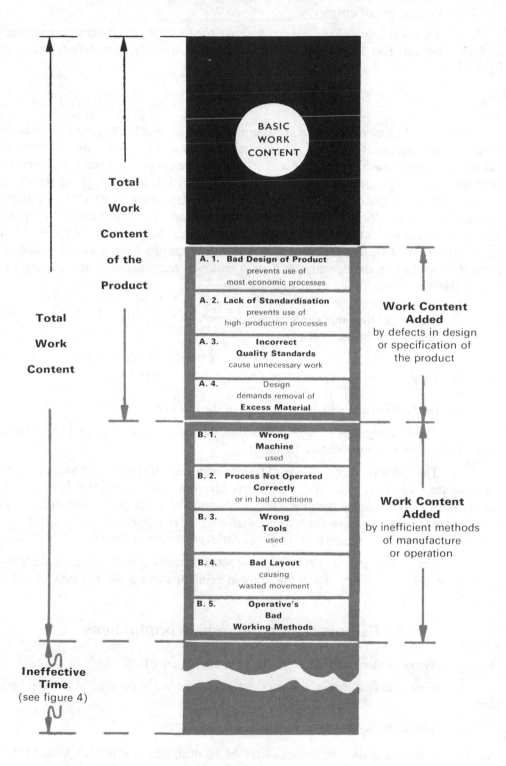

B.   **Work content added by inefficient methods of production or operation**

This is the time taken over and above the basic work content plus A, due to **inefficiencies inherent in the process or method** of manufacture or operation (see figure 3).

*   *   *

The basic work content assumes uninterrupted working. In practice, however, uninterrupted working is exceptional, even in very well run organisations. All interruptions which cause the worker or machine or both to cease producing or carrying out the operations on which they are supposed to be engaged, whatever may be the cause, must be regarded as **ineffective time** (see note at bottom of figure 2) because no work effective towards completing the operation in hand is being done during the period of the interruption. Ineffective time reduces productivity by adding to the duration of the operation. Apart from interruptions from sources outside the control of anyone in the organisation, such as a power breakdown or a sudden rainstorm, ineffective time may be due to two causes—

C.   **Ineffective time due to shortcomings on the part of the management**

Time during which man or machine or both are idle because the management has failed to plan, direct, co-ordinate or control efficiently (see figure 4).

D.   **Ineffective time within the control of the worker**

Time during which man or machine or both are idle for reasons within the control of the worker himself (see figure 4).

The relative sizes of the different sections of figure 2 have no special significance and will vary from operation to operation and from undertaking to undertaking even for the same operation. The application of work study has often made it possible to reduce operation times to one-half or even one-third of their original values without by any means exhausting the possibilities of further reduction.

Let us now examine each of these sets of causes of excess time (excess work content or ineffective time) in turn and look in detail at some of the reasons for them.

6. Factors tending to reduce productivity

A.   **Work content added due to the product (figure 3)**

How can features of the product affect the work content of a given operation?

There are several ways in which this can happen—

(1) The product and its components may be so designed that it is impossible to use the most economical processes or methods of manufacture. This applies especially to the metalworking industries and most particularly where large-scale production

is undertaken. Components may not be designed to take advantage of high-production machinery (example: a sheet-metal part may be so designed that it has to be cut out and riveted or welded instead of being pressed in one piece).

(2) Excessive variety of products or lack of standardisation of components may mean that batches of work have to be small and cannot be put on special-purpose high-production machines but have to be done on slower general-purpose machines (see also C 2).

(3) Incorrect quality standards, whether too high or too low, may increase work content. In engineering practice close tolerances, requiring extra machining, are often put on dimensions where they are quite unnecessary. There will thus be more rejects and a corresponding waste of material. On the other hand, material of too low a quality may make it difficult to work to the finish required or may make additional preparation of the product, such as cleaning, necessary to make it usable. The quality of material becomes especially important in connection with automation.

(4) The components of a product may be so designed that an excessive amount of material has to be removed to bring them to their final shape. This increases the work content of the job and wastes material as well (example: shafts with very large and very small diameters designed in one piece).

The first step towards raising productivity and lowering the cost of the product is therefore to eliminate as far as possible all features in its design and specification that are likely to cause excess work content, including non-standard products demanded by customers where a standard product would serve as well.

B. Work content added due to the process or method (figure 3)

How can inefficient operation of the process or inefficient methods of production or operation affect the work content of the job?

(1) If the wrong type or size of machine is used, one which has a lower output than the correct one (examples: small capstan work put on a turret or centre lathe; narrow cloth put on too wide a loom).

(2) If the process is not operating properly, that is at the correct feed, speed, rate of flow, temperature, density of solution or whatever conditions govern its operation, or if the plant or machine is in bad condition.

(3) If the wrong hand tools are used.

(4) If the layout of the factory, shop or workplace causes wasted movement, time or effort.

(5) If the working methods of the operative cause wasted movement, time or effort.

It should be noted that the idea of work content in terms of time is based on the assumption of operation at a steady average working pace. The additional time taken as a result of a slowing down of the working pace might be considered as ineffective time, but this is unimportant for the present discussion.

Optimum productivity from the process will be reached only if it is operated with the least waste of movement, time and effort and under the most efficient condi-

17

tions. All features which would cause the worker to make unnecessary movements, whether around the shop or at the workplace, should be eliminated.

It will be seen that **all** the items in the excess work content may be attributed to deficiencies on the part of the management. This is true even of bad working methods on the part of the operatives if these are due to failure by the management to see that operatives are properly trained and supervised.

C.   Ineffective time due to the management (figure 4)

Let us now consider the ineffective time in the manufacturing or operating cycle. How can shortcomings on the part of the management affect it?

(1) By a **marketing policy** which demands an unnecessarily large number of types of product. This causes short runs of each type, and machines are idle while they are being changed over to manufacture different products. The workers do not have the opportunity to acquire skill and speed in any one operation.

(2) By failing to standardise component parts as far as possible between products or within product. This has the same effect—that is, short runs and idle time.[1]

(3) By failing to ensure that designs are properly developed or that customers' requirements are met from the beginning. This results in changes of design, causing stoppages of work and loss of machine- and man-hours as well as waste of material.

(4) By failing to plan the flow of work and of orders, with the result that one order does not follow immediately on another and plant and labour are not continuously employed.

(5) By failing to ensure a supply of raw materials, tools and other equipment necessary to do the work, so that plant and labour are kept waiting.

(6) By failing to maintain plant and machines properly. This leads to stoppages due to machine breakdowns.

(7) By allowing plant and machinery to be operated in bad condition so that work is scrapped or returned for rectification and has to be done again. Time spent in rework is ineffective.

(8) By failing to provide working conditions in which the operative can work steadily.

(9) By failing to take proper precautions for the safety of workers. This causes lost time due to accidents.

D.   Ineffective time within the control of the worker (figure 4)

Finally, how can action (or inaction) on the part of the workers themselves cause ineffective time?

(1) By workers taking time off work without good cause: by lateness, by failing to start work immediately after clocking in, by idling at work or by deliberately working slowly.

---

[1] Like "work content and ineffective time", the term "idle time" is given a special meaning in the B.S. *Glossary*. The *Glossary* meaning is not relevant here.

Figure 4.   Ineffective time due to shortcomings on the part
of management and workers

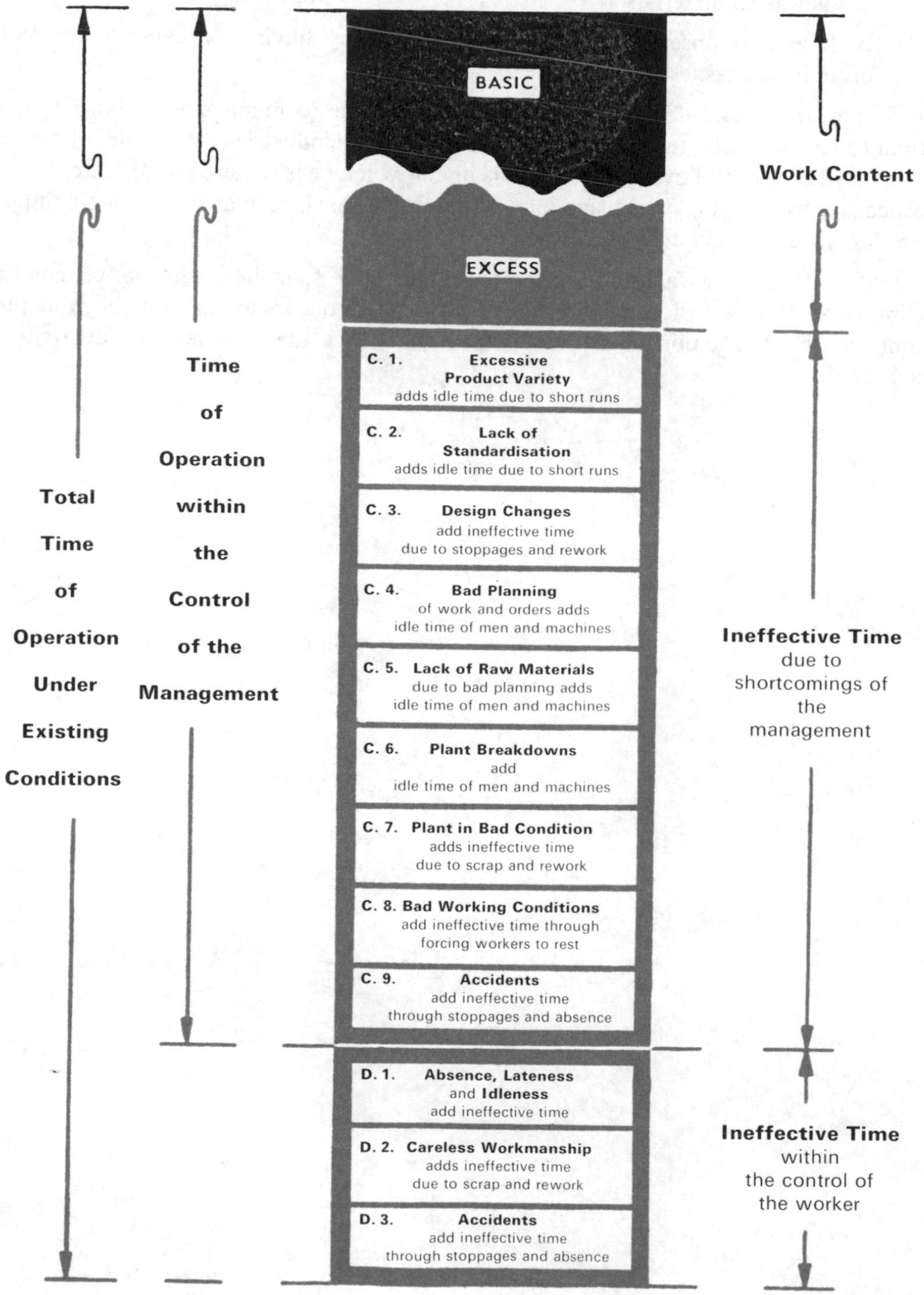

BASIC

Work Content

EXCESS

C. 1.	**Excessive Product Variety** adds idle time due to short runs
C. 2.	**Lack of Standardisation** adds idle time due to short runs
C. 3.	**Design Changes** add ineffective time due to stoppages and rework
C. 4.	**Bad Planning** of work and orders adds idle time of men and machines
C. 5.	**Lack of Raw Materials** due to bad planning adds idle time of men and machines
C. 6.	**Plant Breakdowns** add idle time of men and machines
C. 7.	**Plant in Bad Condition** adds ineffective time due to scrap and rework
C. 8.	**Bad Working Conditions** add ineffective time through forcing workers to rest
C. 9.	**Accidents** add ineffective time through stoppages and absence

D. 1.	**Absence, Lateness** and **Idleness** add ineffective time
D. 2.	**Careless Workmanship** adds ineffective time due to scrap and rework
D. 3.	**Accidents** add ineffective time through stoppages and absence

Total Time of Operation Under Existing Conditions

Time of Operation within the Control of the Management

Ineffective Time due to shortcomings of the management

Ineffective Time within the control of the worker

Note: "Idle time" is used here in the ordinary sense of the term, not that defined in the B.S. *Glossary*.

(2) By careless workmanship causing scrap or making it necessary for work to be done again. Work which has to be done again means wasted time, and scrap means wasted materials.

(3) By failing to observe safety regulations and by having or causing accidents through carelessness.

In general, far more ineffective time is due to management shortcomings than to causes within the control of workers. In many industries the individual worker has very little control over the conditions under which he is required to operate. This is especially true of industries using a lot of plant and machinery and making a complex product (see next chapter).

If all the factors enumerated under the four headings above can be eliminated (the ideal situation which, of course, never occurs in real life), the **minimum** time for the production of a given output and hence the **maximum** productivity is achieved.

Chapter 3
Reducing work content and ineffective time

How can **maximum** productivity with **existing** resources be approached? In every case it must be as a result of action by the management, with the co-operation of the workers, together with, in some cases, extra technical or scientific knowledge. This action should aim at reducing work content and cutting down on ineffective time.

1. Reducing work content due to the product

If the design of the product is such that it is not possible to use the most economical processes and methods of manufacture, this is usually because designers are not familiar enough with these processes; it is especially liable to occur in the metalworking, furniture and garment industries. The weakness can be overcome if the design and production staffs work closely together from the beginning. If the product is to be produced in large quantities or is one of a range of similar products produced by the firm, improvements to make it easier to produce can be introduced at the **product development** stage, when production staff can examine the components and assemblies and call for changes before money has been spent on production tools and equipment. At this time also, alterations in design can be made to avoid making it necessary to remove too much material, and tests can be made in running the product to ensure that it meets the technical specifications demanded. The equivalent to the product development stage in the chemical and allied industries is the **pilot plant.** In transport (a non-manufacturing industry) the equivalent is the experimental service or the proving flights which are carried out on airliners.

Specialisation and standardisation, which are discussed more fully in section 4, are the techniques by which the variety of products or components can be reduced and batch sizes increased so that use can be made of high-production processes.

If quality standards are higher than are necessary for the efficient functioning of the product, the time taken to manufacture it will generally be greater because of the extra care required; unnecessary rejects will also result. Customers sometimes make demands for tolerances or finishes of higher standards than necessary. On the other hand, neglecting quality, especially the quality of materials purchased, may prolong the time of manufacture because the materials may be difficult to work with. Quality standards, on the other hand, must be geared to requirements. They should be set neither too high nor too low, and they should be consistent. The management must be sure of the requirements of the market and of the customer, and of the technical requirements of the product itself. The first two may be established by **market research** and **consumer research.** Where the quality level is set by technical considerations, **product research** may be necessary to establish what it should be. Ensuring that quality requirements are met in the production shops is the concern of the **quality control** or **inspection** function. The men who perform this function must be properly informed of the quality level required and should be able to advise the designers which quality standards can safely be altered to achieve higher productivity.

Figure 5 shows the effect of applying these techniques to reduce the work content of the product. (In the figures in this chapter, as in the last, no special significance attaches to the sizes of the various rectangles; the figures are for illustration only). Yet another technique, which is used also to reduce the work content due to the process or method, is **value analysis,** the systematised investigation of the product and its manufacture to reduce cost and improve value.

2. Reducing work content due to the process or method

If the proper steps are taken to remove features that cause unnecessary work in the product **before** production actually starts, effort can be concentrated on reducing the work content of the process.

In industries which have developed their practice from engineering, it is usual nowadays for the **process planning** function to be responsible for specifying the machines on which the product and its components shall be made, the types of tools necessary and the speeds, feeds and other conditions under which the machines shall be run. In the chemical industries these conditions are usually laid down by the scientists in the research department. In all types of manufacturing industry it may be necessary to carry out **process research** in order to discover the best manufacturing techniques. Proper **maintenance** will ensure that plant and machinery is operating properly and will prolong its life, so reducing capital expenditure. Process planning combined with **method study** will ensure the selection of the most suitable tools for the operative.

The layout of the factory, shop or workplace and the working methods of the operative are the task of method study, one of the two branches of **work study** which form the main subject of this book. As method study will be discussed in detail in Chapters 7 to 12 nothing more will be said about it here. Coupled with method study is **operator training** as an aid to improving the working methods of the operative.

Figure 5 shows the effect of these techniques when applied to reducing the work content of the process.

3. Reducing ineffective time due to the management

The responsibility of the management for the achievement of high productivity is always great, especially in the reduction of ineffective time. Ineffective time can be a source of great loss even where working methods are very good.

Figure 5.   How management techniques can reduce excess work content

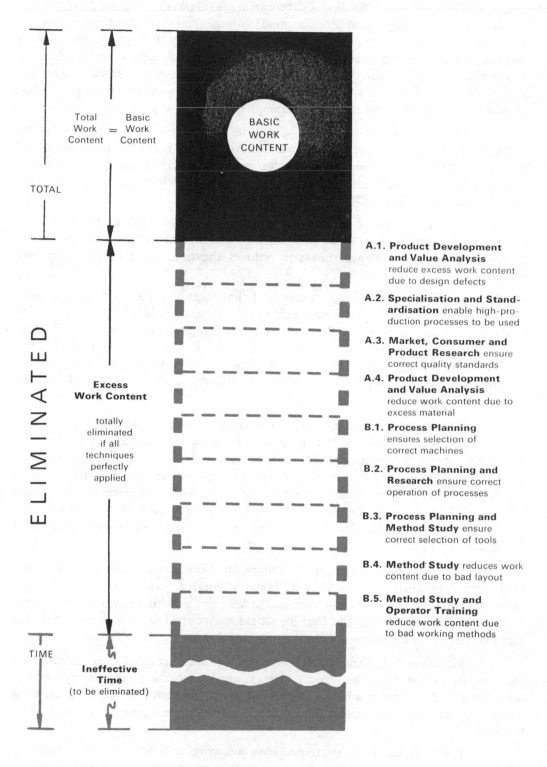

Total
Work   = Basic
Content   Work
            Content

BASIC
WORK
CONTENT

TOTAL

ELIMINATED

Excess
Work Content

totally
eliminated
if all
techniques
perfectly
applied

TIME

Ineffective
Time
(to be eliminated)

**A.1. Product Development
and Value Analysis**
reduce excess work content
due to design defects

**A.2. Specialisation and Stand-
ardisation** enable high-production processes to be used

**A.3. Market, Consumer and
Product Research** ensure
correct quality standards

**A.4. Product Development
and Value Analysis**
reduce work content due to
excess material

B.1. Process Planning
ensures selection of
correct machines

**B.2. Process Planning and
Research** ensure correct
operation of processes

**B.3. Process Planning and
Method Study** ensure
correct selection of tools

B.4. Method Study reduces work
content due to bad layout

**B.5. Method Study and
Operator Training**
reduce work content due
to bad working methods

23

The reduction of ineffective time starts with the policy of the directors concerning the markets which the firm shall try to serve (marketing policy). Shall the firm specialise in a small number of products made in large quantities at the lowest possible price and sell them cheaply, or shall it try to meet the special requirements of every customer? The level of productivity that can be achieved will depend on the answer to this question. If many different types of product are made, this means that machines have to be stopped in order to change one type to another; workers are unable to gain speed on work because they never have enough practice on any one job.

This decision must be taken with a full understanding of its effects. Unfortunately, in many companies the range and variety of product grows unnoticed because of attempts to increase sales by meeting every special demand for variations, most of which may well be unnecessary. Specialisation, therefore, can be an important step towards eliminating ineffective time.

Standardisation of components will also reduce ineffective time. It is often possible to standardise most of the components in a range of models of the same type of product; this gives longer runs and reduces the time spent in changing over machines.

Much ineffective time is caused by failing to ensure that the product is functioning correctly or meets the requirements of the customers before it is put into full production. Consequently, parts have to be redesigned or modified, and these modifications mean wasted time, material and money. Every time a batch of parts has to be remade there is ineffective time. The function of product development, mentioned in section 1 above, is to make these modifications **before** work begins in the production shops.

The planning of proper programmes of work so that plant and workers are kept supplied with jobs without having to wait is known as **production planning,** and the control of that programme to ensure that it is being carried out is **production control.** A proper programme can be worked out and applied only on the basis of sound standards of performance. These are set by the use of **work measurement,** the second technique of work study. The importance of knowing accurately how long each job may be expected to take is discussed at length in the chapters on work measurement (Chapters 13 to 23).

Workers and machines may be made idle because materials or tools are not ready for them when they are needed. **Material control** ensures that these requirements are foreseen and fulfilled in time, and at the same time that materials are bought as economically as possible and that the stocks maintained are not excessive. In this way the cost of holding stocks of materials is kept down.

Machines and plant which break down cause idleness, reduce productivity and increase manufacturing costs. Breakdowns can be reduced by proper maintenance. Plant and machinery in bad condition will turn out bad work, some of which may have to be scrapped. This takes time, which must be regarded as ineffective time.

If the management fails to provide good working conditions, ineffective time will be increased because workers will have to take more rest to overcome fatigue or the effects of heat, fumes, cold or bad lighting. If the management fails to take the proper precautions for the safety of the workers, ineffective time will be increased owing to loss of time through accidents and absenteeism.

It will be seen that, even where the work content of the product and process has been reduced as much as possible under the existing conditions, it is still possible for there to be a great deal of waste simply through failure to use time properly. Much of the responsibility for this rests with the management.

Figure 6 shows how this excess time can be reduced by applying the management techniques mentioned.

4. Reducing ineffective time within the control of the worker

Whether the available time is fully used also depends on the workers. It is widely believed that someone doing a manual job can work faster or slower according to his choice. This is true only up to a certain point. Most people who have been doing a job for a long time have a certain pace at which they work best and at which they will normally work. Usually, a worker trained at and accustomed to his job cannot actually **work** much faster, except for short periods, and equally feels uncomfortable if forced to work more slowly than his natural pace. Any attempt to speed up the rate of working, except by proper training, will tend to increase the number of errors made. The worker can save time mainly by reducing the amount of time when he is **not** working, that is, when he is talking to his fellow workers, having a smoke, waiting to clock off, late or absent.

In order to reduce this ineffective time he must be made to **want** to reduce it, and it is the business of the management to create the conditions that will make him want to get on with his work.

First, bad working conditions make it difficult to work for long stretches at a time without frequent periods of rest and produce an attitude of mind in the worker which makes him feel that he does not want to try.

Second, if the worker feels that he is simply looked upon by the management as a tool of production without any regard being paid to his feelings as a human being, he will not want to make a greater effort than he has to in order to keep his job.

Third, if the worker does not know what he is doing or why he is doing it, if he knows nothing of the work of the firm as a whole, he can hardly be expected to give of his best.

Fourth, if the worker feels that he does not receive justice from the management, the feeling of grievance will hinder him from doing his best.

The willingness of the worker to get on with the job and reduce this ineffective time depends very much on the **personnel policy** of the management and its attitude to him. Personnel policy involves the whole relationship between the management and employees; if this relationship is not a good one, it is very difficult to make any management techniques work satisfactorily. To create the right conditions for good relationships is part of the art of management. A sound personnel policy includes the training of managers and supervisors of all ranks in proper attitudes to and relations with the workers.

25

Figure 6.   *How management techniques can reduce ineffective time*

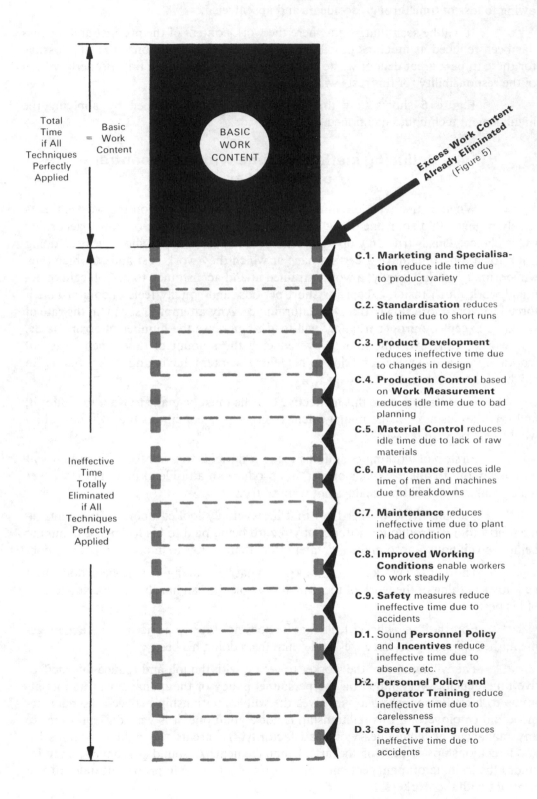

Total Time if All Techniques Perfectly Applied

= Basic Work Content

BASIC WORK CONTENT

Excess Work Content Already Eliminated (Figure 5)

Ineffective Time Totally Eliminated if All Techniques Perfectly Applied

C.1. Marketing and Specialisation reduce idle time due to product variety

C.2. Standardisation reduces idle time due to short runs

C.3. Product Development reduces ineffective time due to changes in design

C.4. Production Control based on **Work Measurement** reduces idle time due to bad planning

C.5. Material Control reduces idle time due to lack of raw materials

C.6. Maintenance reduces idle time of men and machines due to breakdowns

C.7. Maintenance reduces ineffective time due to plant in bad condition

C.8. Improved Working Conditions enable workers to work steadily

C.9. Safety measures reduce ineffective time due to accidents

D.1. Sound **Personnel Policy** and **Incentives** reduce ineffective time due to absence, etc.

D.2. Personnel Policy and Operator Training reduce ineffective time due to carelessness

D.3. Safety Training reduces ineffective time due to accidents

A motivating climate, a job that allows for variety and a soundly based wage structure, including, where appropriate, **incentive schemes,** can motivate the worker to reduce ineffective time and hence will make for high productivity.

Careless workmanship and the carelessness which leads to accidents are both the results of bad attitudes of mind on the part of workers. These can be overcome only by a suitable personnel policy and proper training. It will be seen, therefore, that management has a very great responsibility for reducing the ineffective time due to the action or inaction of workers.

This reduction is shown diagrammatically in figure 6.

5. Inter-relationship of the various methods used to reduce ineffective time

None of the methods discussed can properly be applied in isolation. Each one has effects on others. It is impossible to plan programmes of work properly without the standards provided by work measurement. Method study can be used to simplify the design of the product so that it is both easier to use and easier to produce. Production planning will be made easier if a sound personnel policy and a well applied incentive scheme encourage workers to perform reliably. Standardisation will make the job of material control easier by demanding less variety of materials to be bought and held in stock. Process research, by eliminating features of the plant that are likely to break down, should make it easier to apply a proper system of maintenance.

Modern production management aims at increasing the efficiency of production operation. It does so by looking at several aspects of production, such as product design and material utilisation, quality control, layout and material handling, production planning and control, maintenance management and work study. Modern production management also deals with the systems by which these activities may be carried out in a rational way, singly or in combination, in the enterprise. Work study is a powerful tool in this process.

* *
*

It will be seen that in our discussion in this chapter we have gradually moved from a study of the question of productivity in the enterprise as a whole to the productivity of a certain part of it, namely the productivity of the plant and labour—machines and men. We have looked briefly at some of the methods which can affect that productivity so as to show the many different ways in which problems of productivity can be attacked. In the rest of the book we are going to concentrate on one of those methods, namely work study.

Chapter 4
Work study

1. What is work study?

What is **work study,** and why should it be selected, from among the many techniques discussed in the previous chapter, as the main weapon of attack on the problem of increasing productivity and as a special subject for this book?

> **Work study is a generic term for those techniques, particularly** *method study* **and** *work measurement,* **which are used in the examination of human work in all its contexts, and which lead systematically to the investigation of all the factors which affect the efficiency and economy of the situation being reviewed, in order to effect improvement[1]**

Work study therefore has a direct relationship with productivity. It is most frequently used to increase the amount produced from a given quantity of resources with little or no further capital investment.

Work study was widely known for years as "time and motion study", but with the development of the technique and its application to a very wide range of activities it was felt by many people that the older title was both too narrow and insufficiently descriptive.

2. Work study: a direct means of raising productivity

We have already seen that the factors affecting the productivity of any enterprise are many, that they vary in importance according to the nature of the activities undertaken, and that they are dependent on one another.

---

[1] The definition given here is that adopted in the B.S. *Glossary,* op. cit.

Let us now look at this problem from a different angle. So far, in discussing the use of various techniques to increase productivity, there has been no mention of major capital expenditure in plant or equipment. It has been assumed that productivity would be raised by using **existing** resources. Productivity can almost always be greatly increased by heavy investment of money in new and improved plant and equipment. How much can we expect to gain by using techniques such as work study to improve the use of existing resources as against investing capital in new plant? Any comparison made in general terms will only be a rough guide. It is convenient to do this in the form of a table (table 1).

It will be seen that one of the effective ways of raising productivity in the long run is the development of new processes and the installation of more modern plant and equipment. However, such an approach usually requires heavy capital outlay, and can cause a drain on foreign reserves if the capital equipment cannot be produced locally. Furthermore, to tackle the problem of improving productivity mainly through the continuous acquisition of advanced technology may hamper efforts aimed at expanding employment opportunities. Work study, on the other hand, aims at approaching the problem of increasing productivity through the **systematic analysis** of existing operations, processes and work methods with a view to increasing their efficiency. Work study therefore usually contributes towards increasing productivity with little or no extra capital expenditure.

3. Why is work study valuable?

There is nothing new about the investigation and improvement of operations at the workplace; good managers have been investigating and improving ever since human effort was first organised on a large scale. Managers of outstanding ability—geniuses—have always been able to make notable advances. Unfortunately, no country seems to have an adequate supply of competent managers. The prime value of work study lies in the fact that, by carrying out its systematic procedures, a manager can achieve results as good as or better than the less systematic genius was able to achieve in the past.

Work study succeeds because it is systematic both in the investigation of the problem being considered and in the development of its solution. Systematic investigation takes time. It is therefore necessary, in all but the smallest firms, to separate the job of making work studies from the task of management. The factory manager or the foreman, in their day-to-day work, with its many human and material problems, are never free from interruption for long. However capable he may be, a manager can rarely afford to devote a long time, without interruption, to the study of a single activity on the factory floor. This means that it is almost always impossible for him to obtain all the facts about what is happening in the course of that activity. Unless all the facts are known, it is impossible to be sure that any alterations in procedure which are made are based on accurate information and will be fully effective. It is only by continuous observation and study at the workplace or in the area where the activity is taking place that the facts can be obtained. This means that work study must always be the responsibility of someone who is able to undertake it full

Table 1.   *Direct means of raising productivity*

Approach	Type of improvement	Means	Cost	How quickly can results be achieved?	Extent of improvement in productivity	The role of work study
Capital investment	1. **Development of new basic process** or fundamental improvement of existing ones	Basic research Applied research Pilot plant	High	Generally years	No obvious limit	**Method study** to improve ease of operation and maintenance at design stage
	2. **Install more modern or higher-capacity plant or equipment** or modernise existing plant	Purchase Process research	High	Immediately after installation	No obvious limit	**Method study** in plant layout and to improve ease of of operation when modernising
Better management	3. **Reduce the work content of the product**	Product research Product development Quality management **Method study** Value analysis	Not high compared with 1 and 2	Generally months	Limited—of the same order as that to be expected from 4 and 5. Should *precede* action under those heads	**Method study** (and its extension, value analysis) to improve design for ease of production
	4. **Reduce the work content of the process**	Process research Pilot plant Process planning **Method study** Operator training Value analysis	Low	Immediate	Limited, but often of a high order	**Method study** to reduce wasted effort and time in operating the process by eliminating unnecessary movement
	5. **Reduce ineffective time** (whether due to management or to workers)	**Work measurement** Marketing policy Standardisation Product development Production planning and control Material control Planned maintenance Personnel policy Improved working conditions Operator training Incentive schemes	Low	May start slowly but effect grows quickly	Limited, but often of a high order	**Work measurement** to investigate existing practice, locate ineffective time and set standards of performance as a basis for— A. Planning and control B. Utilisation of plant C. Labour cost control D. Incentive schemes

time, without direct management duties: someone in a staff and not a line position.[1] Work study is a service to management and supervision.

We have now discussed, very briefly, some aspects of the nature of work study and why it is such a valuable "tool" of management. There are other reasons to be added to the above. These may be summarised as follows:

(1) It is a means of raising the productive efficiency (productivity) of a factory or operating unit by the reorganisation of work, a method which normally involves little or no capital expenditure on plant and equipment.

(2) It is systematic. This ensures that no factor affecting the efficiency of an operation is overlooked, whether in analysing the original practices or in developing the new, and that **all** the facts about that operation are available.

(3) It is the most accurate means yet evolved of setting standards of performance, on which the effective planning and control of production depends.

(4) The savings resulting from properly applied work study start at once and continue as long as the operation continues in the improved form.

(5) It is a "tool" which can be applied everywhere. It can be used with success wherever manual work is done or plant is operated, not only in manufacturing shops but also in offices, stores, laboratories and service industries such as wholesale and retail distribution and restaurants, and on farms.

(6) **It is one of the most penetrating tools of investigation available to the management.** This makes it an excellent weapon for starting an attack on inefficiency in any organisation, since, in investigating one set of problems, the weaknesses of all the other functions affecting them will gradually be laid bare.

This last point is worth further discussion. Because work study is systematic, and because it involves investigation by direct observation of all the factors affecting the efficiency of a given operation, it will show up any shortcomings in all activities affecting that operation. For example, observation may show that the time of an operative on a production job is being wasted through his having to wait for supplies of material or to remain idle through the breakdown of his machine. This points at once to a failure of material control or a failure on the part of the maintenance engineer to carry out proper maintenance procedures. Similarly, time may be wasted through short batches of work, necessitating the constant resetting of machines, on a scale which may only become apparent after prolonged study. This points to poor production planning or a marketing policy which requires looking into.

Work study acts like a surgeon's knife, laying bare the activities of a company and their functioning, good or bad, for all to see. It can therefore "show up" people. For this reason it must be handled, like the surgeon's knife, with skill and care. Nobody likes being shown up, and unless the work study specialist displays great tact in his handling of people he may arouse the animosity of management and workers alike, which will make it impossible for him to do his job properly.

---

[1] A person in a "line" position exercises direct supervisory authority over the ranks below him. A "staff" appointee, on the other hand, is strictly an adviser with no power or authority to put his recommendations into operation. His function is to provide expert information.

Managers and foremen have generally failed to achieve the saving and improvements which can be effected by work study because they have been unable to apply themselves continuously to such things, even when they have been trained. It is not enough for work study to be systematic. To achieve really important results it must be applied **continuously,** and throughout the organisation. It is no use the work study man doing a good job and then sitting back and congratulating himself, or being transferred by the management to something else. The savings achieved on individual jobs, although sometimes large in themselves, are generally small when compared with the activity of the company as a whole. The full effect is felt in an organisation only when work study is applied everywhere, and when everyone becomes imbued with the attitude of mind which is the basis of successful work study: **intolerance of waste in any form, whether of material, time, effort or human ability;** and the refusal to accept without question that things must be done in a certain way "because that is the way they have always been done".

4. Techniques of work study and their relationship

Earlier in this chapter it was indicated that the term "work study" embraced several techniques, but in particular method study and work measurement. What are these two techniques and what is their relationship to one another?

> **Method study is the systematic recording and critical examination of existing and proposed ways of doing work, as a means of developing and applying easier and more effective methods and reducing costs**[1]

> **Work measurement is the application of techniques designed to establish the time for a qualified worker to carry out a specified job at a defined level of performance**[1]

Method study and work measurement are, therefore, closely linked. Method study is concerned with the reduction of the work content of a job or operation, while work measurement is mostly concerned with the investigation and reduction of any ineffective time associated with it; and with the subsequent establishment of time standards for the operation when carried out in the improved fashion, as determined by method study. The relationship of method study to work measurement is shown simply in figure 7.

---

[1] These definitions are those adopted in the B.S. *Glossary,* op. cit.

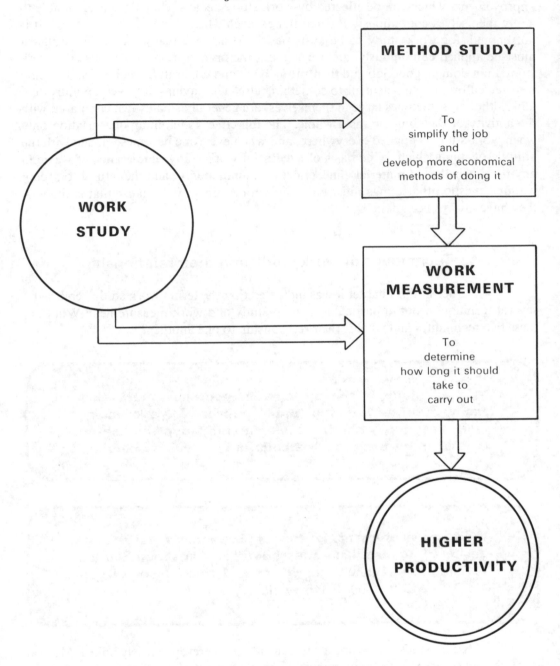

Figure 7.   Work study

As will be seen from later chapters of this book, both method study and work measurement are themselves made up of a number of different techniques. Although method study should precede the use of work measurement when time standards for output are being set, it is often necessary to use one of the techniques of work measurement, such as work sampling (see Chapter 14), in order to determine why ineffective time is occurring and what is its extent, so that the management can

34

take action to reduce it before method study is begun. Again, time study (Chapter 15 ff.) may be used to compare the effectiveness of alternative methods.

These techniques will be dealt with in detail in the chapters devoted to them. For the present we must consider the basic procedure of work study which applies to **every** study, whatever the operation or process being examined, in whatever industry. This procedure is fundamental to the whole of work study. **There is no short cut.**

5. Basic procedure of work study

There are eight steps in performing a complete work study. They are—

1. **Select** the job or process to be studied.
2. **Record** from **direct observation** everything that happens, using the most suitable of the recording techniques (to be explained later), so that the data will be in the most convenient form to be analysed.
3. **Examine** the recorded facts critically and challenge everything that is done, considering in turn: the purpose of the activity; the place where it is performed; the sequence in which it is done; the person who is doing it; the means by which it is done.
4. **Develop** the most economic method, taking into account all the circumstances.
5. **Measure** the quantity of work involved in the method selected and calculate a standard time for doing it.
6. **Define** the new method and the related time so that it can always be identified.
7. **Install** the new method as agreed standard practice with the time allowed.
8. **Maintain** the new standard practice by proper control procedures.

Steps 1, 2 and 3 occur in every study, whether the technique being used is method study or work measurement. Step 4 is part of method study practice, while step 5 calls for the use of work measurement.

These eight steps will all be discussed in detail in the chapters devoted to method study and work measurement. Before doing so, however, we shall discuss the background and conditions necessary for work study to operate effectively.

Chapter 5
The human factor in the application of work study

1. Good relations must be established before work study is applied

Because of their preoccupation with pressing and important problems, some managers often forget that the people who work with them, particularly those under them, are as much human beings as they are, subject to all the same feelings, although they may not be able to display them openly. The man at the bottom of the ladder, the most humble labourer, resents an injustice, real or imaginary, as much as any other man. He fears the unknown, and if the unknown appears to him to offer a threat to his security of employment or to his self-respect he will resist it—if not openly, then by concealed non-cooperation or by co-operation that is only half-hearted.

Work study is not a substitute for good management and never can be. It is one of the "tools" in the manager's tool kit. By itself it will not make bad industrial relations good, although, wisely applied, it may often improve them. This has been the common experience of ILO management development and consultancy missions everywhere. If work study is to contribute seriously to the improvement of productivity, relations between the management and the workers must be reasonably good before any attempt is made to introduce it, and the workers must have confidence in the sincerity of the management towards them; otherwise they will regard it as another trick to try to get more work out of them without any benefits for themselves. Of course, in certain conditions, especially where there is widespread unemployment in a country or an industry, it may be possible to impose work study, but things which are imposed are accepted reluctantly. If the conditions should change, the application will probably break down.

2. Work study and the management

It was said in Chapter 4 that one of the principal reasons for choosing work study as the subject for this book is that it is a most penetrating tool of investigation. Because a well conducted work study analysis is ruthlessly systematic, the places where effort and time are being wasted are laid bare one by one. In order to eliminate this waste, the causes of it must be looked for. The latter are usually found to be bad planning, bad organisation, insufficient control, or the lack of proper training. Since members of the management and supervisory staffs are employed to do these things, it will look as if they have failed in their duties. Not only this, but the increases in productivity which the proper use of work study usually brings about may appear to emphasise this failure further. Applying work study in one shop can start a chain-reaction of investigation and improvement which will spread in all directions throughout the organisation: to the plant engineer's department, the accounts department, the design office or the sales force. The skilled worker may be made to feel a novice when he finds that his methods, long practised, are wasteful of time and effort, and that new workers trained in the new methods soon surpass him in output and quality.

Any technique which has such far-reaching effects must obviously be handled with great care and tact. Nobody likes to be made to feel that he has failed, especially in the eyes of his superiors. He loses his self-confidence and begins to ask himself whether he may not be replaced. His feeling of security is threatened.

At first sight, this result of a work study investigation may seem unfair. Managers, foremen and workers, generally speaking, are honest, hard-working people who do their jobs as well as they can. They are certainly not less clever than work study specialists. Often they have years of experience and great practical knowledge. If they have failed to obtain the most from the resources at their disposal, it is generally because they have not been trained in, and often do not know the value of, the systematic approach which work study brings to problems of organisation and performance of work.

This must be made clear to everybody from the very beginning. If it is not made clear, and if the work study man is at all tactless in his handling of people, he will find that they will combine to obstruct him, possibly to the point where his task is made impossible.

If the application of work study in an enterprise is to succeed, it must have the understanding and the backing of the management at all levels, starting at the top. If the top management, the managing director, the managing agent or the president of the company does not understand what the work study man is trying to do and is not giving him his full support, it cannot be expected that managers lower down will accept and support him. If the work study man then comes into conflict with them, as he may do in such circumstances, he may well find that he will lose his case, however good it may be, if an appeal is made to the top. Do not forget that in any organisation **people lower down tend to take their attitudes from the man at the top.**

The first group of people to whom the purpose and techniques of work study must be explained is therefore the management group, the managing director or managing agent and, in large companies or organisations, the departmental heads and assistant heads. It is the usual practice in most countries to run short "appreciation" courses for top management before starting to apply work study. Most work study schools, management development institutes, technical colleges and work study organisations run short courses for the managers of companies who are sending staff to be trained as specialists.

Here it is necessary to give a word of warning. Running even the simplest and shortest course in work study is not easy, and newly trained work study men are strongly advised not to try to do so by themselves. They should seek advice and assistance. It is important that an enterprise's work study staff take an active part in the course, but they **must know their subject and be able to teach it.**

38

NATIONAL COLLEGE
LIBRARY
OF INDUSTRIAL RELATIONS

If a course for management is to be run, however, the work study man must try as hard as he can to persuade the man at the top to attend and, if possible, to open the proceedings. Not only will this show everyone that he has the support of the top management, but departmental and other managers will make efforts to attend if they think their "boss" is going to be there.

3. Work study and the supervisor

The work study man's most difficult problem may often be the attitude of the foremen and supervisors. They must be won over if he is to obtain good results from his work; indeed, their hostility may prevent him from doing any effective work at all. The foremen and their assistants represent the management to the worker on the floor of the shop, and just as departmental managers will take their attitudes from the top manager, so the workers will take theirs from their supervisors. If it is evident that the foreman thinks that "this work study stuff is nonsense", the workers will not respect the specialist and will make no efforts to carry out his suggestions, which, in any case, have to come to them through their foreman.

Before the work study man starts his work, the whole purpose of work study and the procedures involved must have been very carefully explained to the foreman, so that he understands exactly what is being done and why. Unless this is done, the foreman is likely to be difficult, if not actually obstructive, for many reasons. Among these reasons are the following:

(1) He is the person most deeply affected by work study. The work for which he may have been responsible for years is being challenged; if, through the application of work study methods, the efficiency of the operations for which he is responsible is greatly improved, he may feel that his prestige in the eyes of his superiors and of the workers will be lessened.

(2) In most firms where specialists have not been used, the whole running of a certain operation—planning of the programmes of work, development of job methods, making up of time sheets, setting of piece rates, hiring and firing of labour—may have been done by the foreman. The mere fact that some of his responsibilities have been taken away from him is likely to make him feel that his status has been reduced. No one likes to think he has "lost face".

(3) If disputes arise or the workers are upset, he is the first person who will be called upon to clear matters up, and it is difficult for him to do so fairly if he does not understand the problem.

The sources from which foremen and supervisors are recruited differ widely in different parts of the world. In some countries the foreman is often selected on a basis of seniority from among the best skilled men in the company. This means that he is often middle-aged and may be set in his ways. Because most foremen have practised their occupation or skills for many years, they find it difficult to believe that they have anything to learn from someone who has not spent a very long time in the same occupation.

The foreman may therefore resent the introduction of a work study man into his department unless he has had some training to prepare him for it. Since

39

foremen are nearer to the practical side of the job than the management, and so are more intimately connected with work study, the work study course that they should take should be longer and more detailed than that given to the management. Foremen should know enough to be able to help in the selection of jobs to be studied and to understand the factors involved, should disputes arise over methods or time standards. This means that they should be acquainted with the principal techniques of method study and work measurement and the particular problems and situations in which they should be applied. Generally speaking, courses for foremen should be full-time and of not less than one week's duration. The trainees should be given opportunities of making one or two simple method studies and of measuring the time of an operation. The value to the work study man of a foreman who understands and is enthusiastic about what he is trying to do **cannot be overemphasised.** He is a powerful ally.

The work study man will only retain the friendship and respect of the foreman if he shows from the beginning that he is not trying to usurp his place. The following rules **must** be observed:

(1) The work study man must **never** give a direct order to a worker. All instructions must be given through the foreman. The only exception to this is in matters connected with methods improvements where the worker has been ordered **by the foreman** to carry out the instructions of the work study man.

(2) Workers asking questions calling for decisions outside the technical field of work study should **always** be referred to their foreman.

(3) The work study man should **never** allow himself to express opinions to a worker which may be interpreted as critical of the foreman (however much he may feel like it!). If the worker later says to the foreman: " . . . but Mr._____ said . . .", there will be trouble!

(4) The work study man must **not** allow the workers to "play him off" against the foreman or to use him to get decisions altered which they consider harsh.

(5) The work study man should seek the foreman's advice in the selection of jobs to be studied and in all technical matters connected with the process (even if he knows a great deal about the process). Remember, the foreman has to make it work from day to day.

(6) At the start of every investigation the work study man should be introduced to the workers concerned **by the foreman.** The work study man should never try to start on his own.

This list of "Do's" and "Don't's" may look frightening but is mainly common sense and good manners. The workers in any shop can only have **one** boss —their foreman—and everything must be done to uphold his authority. Of course, once the work study man and the foreman have worked together and understand one another, there can be some relaxation; but that is a matter of judgement, and any suggestion for relaxation should come from the foreman.

A great deal of space has been given to the relationship between the work study man and the foreman because it is the most difficult of all the relationships, and it must be good. One of the best methods of ensuring that this is so is to provide both parties with the proper training.

4. Work study and the worker

When the first conscious attempts at work study were made at the turn of the century, little was known about the way people behaved at work. As a result, workers often resisted or were hostile to work study. During the past 40 years, however, a great deal of research has been carried out to discover more about the way people behave—the aim being not only to explain that behaviour but, if possible, also to predict how people will react to a new situation. For a work study specialist this is an important consideration, since through his interventions he is invariably and continuously creating new situations.

Behavioural scientists believe that individuals are motivated to act in a certain way by a desire to satisfy certain needs. One of the widely accepted notions about needs was developed by Abraham Maslow, who postulated that there are certain essential needs for every individual and that these needs arrange themselves in a hierarchical pattern. Maslow argues that it is only when one need becomes largely satisfied that the next need in the hierarchy will start to exert its motivating influence.

At the bottom of the hierarchy are **physiological needs.** These are the basic needs that must be met to sustain life itself. Satisfying his physiological needs will be the primary concern of any person, and until he has done so he will not be concerned with any other issues. However, once a worker feels reasonably sure of fulfilling his physiological needs, he will seek to satisfy the next need in the hierarchy, that of **security.** Security is taken to mean a feeling of protection against physical and psychological harm, as well as security of employment. For a worker who has already satisfied both his physiological and his security needs, the next motivating factor is that of **affiliation,** that is wanting to belong to a group or an organisation and to associate with others. Next on the hierarchical scale is the **need to be recognised,** and this is followed by the need for **fulfilment** (sometimes called "self-actualisation"). This last need expresses the desire of a person or a worker to be given an opportunity to show his particular talents.

Maslow's hierarchy of needs

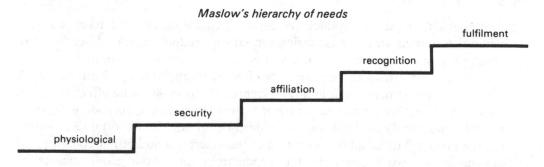

In practice, most people satisfy some of these needs in part and are left with some that are unsatisfied. In developing countries people are probably preoccupied more with satisfying needs at the lower end of the hierarchy, and their behaviour would appear to reflect this fact. In developed countries, on the other hand, where physiological and security needs are normally largely met, people would seem to be motivated more by needs at the upper end of the hierarchy.

41

One of the interesting results of the research carried out in this area, and which should be of concern to us here, is the discovery that, in order to satisfy affiliation needs, workers associate with each other to form various types of informal groups. Thus a worker is usually a member of a task group, that is a group composed of workers performing a common task with him. He may also be a member of various other groups, such as a friendship group composed of fellow workers with whom he has something in common or with whom he would like to associate.

This means that in every organisation we have a formal and an informal structure. The formal structure is defined by the management in terms of authority relationships. Similarly, there also exists an informal organisation composed of a great number of informal groups which have their own goals and activities and which bear the sentiments of their members. Each group, it was found, expects its members to conform to a certain standard of behaviour, since otherwise the group cannot achieve its goal, whether this be accomplishing a task or providing a means for friendly interaction. It was found, for example, that a task group tends to establish among its members a certain quota for production which may or may not be in line with what a foreman or a manager wants. In a typical situation, a worker will produce more or less according to this informally accepted quota. Those who are very high or very low producers, and who thus deviate substantially from that norm, will be subjected to pressure from the group to conform to the norm.

Disregarding or ignoring such basic and elementary notions of behaviour has often created resentment and outright hostility. It is now easy to understand that a work study man who makes a unilateral decision to eliminate an operation, resulting in the loss of a job for a worker or a number of workers, is in fact undermining the basic need for security; a negative reaction can therefore be expected. Similarly, the imposition of an output quota on a worker or a group of workers without prior consultation or winning their co-operation can yield resentment and breed resistance.

How, then, should a work study man act? The following are some useful hints:

(1) The problem of raising productivity should be approached in a balanced way, without too great an emphasis being placed on productivity of labour. In most enterprises in developing countries, and even in industrialised countries, great increases in productivity can generally be effected through the application of work study to improve plant utilisation and operation, to make more effective use of space and to secure greater economy of materials before the question of increasing the productivity of the labour force need be raised. The importance of studying the productivity of all the resources of the enterprise and of not confining the application of work study to the productivity of labour alone cannot be overemphasised. It is only natural that workers should resent efforts being made to improve their efficiency while they can see glaring inefficiency on the part of the management. What is the use of halving the time a worker takes to do a certain job or of imposing a production output on him by well applied work study if he is held back by a lack of materials or by frequent machine breakdowns resulting from bad planning by his superiors?

(2) It is important that the work study man be open and frank as to the purpose of his study. Nothing breeds suspicion like attempts to hide what is being done; nothing

dispels it like frankness, whether in answering questions or in showing information obtained from studies. Work study, honestly applied, has nothing to hide.

(3) Workers' representatives should be kept fully informed of what is being studied, and why. They should receive induction training in work study so that they can understand properly what is being attempted. Similarly, involving the workers in the development of an improved method of operation can win them over to the new method and can sometimes produce unexpected results. Thus, by asking workers the right questions and by inviting them to come forward with explanations or proposals, several work study specialists have been rewarded by clues or ideas that had never occurred to them. After all, a worker has an intimate knowledge of his own job and of details that can escape a work study man. One tried and tested practice is to invite the workers in a section to be studied to nominate one of their number to join the work study specialist and, together with the foreman, to form a team that can review the work to be done, discuss the results achieved and agree on steps for implementation.

(4) Although asking for a worker's suggestions and ideas implicitly serves to satisfy his need for recognition, this can be achieved in a more direct way by giving proper credit where it is due. In many instances a foreman, a worker or a staff specialist contributes useful ideas that assist the work study man to develop an improved method of work. This should be acknowledged readily, and the work study man should resist the temptation of accumulating all the glory for himself.

(5) It is important that the work study man should remember that his objective is not merely to increase productivity but also to improve job satisfaction, and that he should devote enough attention to this latter issue by looking for ways to minimise fatigue and to make the job more interesting and more satisfying. In recent years several enterprises have developed new concepts and ideas to organise work to this end and to attempt to meet the workers' need for fulfilment. These are treated briefly in the last chapter of this book.

5. The work study man

We have talked a great deal in the preceding sections about what is required from the work study man, suggesting by our requirements a human who is almost too good to be true. The ideal man for the job is likely to be found very rarely, and if he is he will quickly leave the ranks of work study men to rise to greater heights. Nevertheless, there are certain qualifications and qualities which are essential for success.

EDUCATION

The very minimum standard of education for anyone who is to take charge of work study application in an enterprise is a good secondary education with matriculation or the equivalent school-leaving examination. It is unlikely that anyone who has not had such an education will be able to benefit fully from a full work study training course, although there may be a few exceptions. However, if a work study man is also to be involved in studying other production management problems, a university degree in engineering or management or the equivalent becomes an important asset.

PRACTICAL EXPERIENCE

It is desirable that candidates for posts as work study specialists should have had practical experience in the industries in which they will be working. This experience should include a period of actual work at one or more of the processes of the industry. This will enable them to understand what it means to do a day's work under the conditions in which the ordinary workers with whom they will be dealing have to work. Practical experience will also command respect from foremen and workers, and an engineering background enables a man to adapt himself to most other industries.

PERSONAL QUALITIES

Anyone who is going to undertake improvements in methods should have an inventive turn of mind, be capable of devising simple mechanisms and devices which can often save a great deal of time and effort, and be able to gain the co-operation of the engineers and technicians in developing them. The type of man who is good at this is not always so good at human relations, and in some large companies the methods department is separated from the work measurement department, although both are under the same chief.

The following are essential qualities:

☐ **Sincerity and honesty**

The work study man must be sincere and he must be honest; only if he is will he gain the confidence and respect of those with whom he has to deal.

☐ **Enthusiasm**

He must be really keen on his job, believe in the importance of what he is doing and be able to transmit his enthusiasm to the people around him.

☐ **Interest in and sympathy with people**

He must be able to get along with people at all levels. To get along with people it is necessary to be interested in them, to be able to see their points of view and to understand the motives behind their behaviour.

☐ **Tact**

Tact in dealing with people comes from understanding people and not wishing to hurt their feelings by unkind or thoughtless words, even when these may be justified. Without tact no work study man is going to get very far.

☐ **Good appearance**

He must be neat and tidy and look efficient. This will inspire confidence in him among the people with whom he has to work.

□   **Self-confidence**

This can only come with good training and experience of applying work study successfully. The work study man must be able to stand up to top management, foremen, trade union officials or workers in defence of his opinions and findings, and do so in such a way that he will win respect and not give offence.

The personal qualities, particularly the ability to deal with people, can all be further developed with the right training. Far too often this aspect of the training of work study men is neglected, the assumption being that, if the right man is selected in the first place, that is all that needs to be done. In most work study courses more time should be given to the human side of applying work study.

It will be seen from these requirements that the results of work study, however "scientifically" arrived at, must be applied with "art", just like any other management technique. In fact, the qualities which go to make a good work study man are the same qualities as go to make a good manager. Work study is an excellent training for young men destined for higher management. People with these qualities are not easy to find, but the careful selection of men for training as work study specialists will repay itself in the results obtained, in terms both of increased productivity and of improved human relations in the factory.

Having described the background against which work study is to be applied, we can now turn to the question of applying it, starting with method study. Before we do so, however, some attention must be given to some general factors which have considerable bearing on its effect, namely the conditions under which the work is done in the area, factory or workshop concerned.

Chapter 6
Working conditions and the working environment

1. General considerations

It has taken a long time for the full extent of the interdependence between working conditions and productivity to be properly recognised. The first move in this direction came when people began to realise that occupational accidents had economic as well as physical consequences, although at first only their direct costs (medical care, compensation) were perceived. Subsequently, attention was paid to occupational diseases as well; and as a final step it was realised that the indirect costs of occupational accidents (working time lost by the injured person, the witnesses and the accident investigators, production stoppages, material damage, work delays, possible legal and other costs, reduced output when the injured person is replaced and subsequently when he returns to work, and so on) are usually far higher—as much as four times higher in some cases—than the direct costs.

The reduction in productivity and the increase in production rejects and manufacturing waste that result from fatigue due to excessively long working hours and bad working conditions—in particular, lighting and ventilation—have shown that the human body, in spite of its immense capacity for adaptation, is far more productive when working under optimal conditions. Indeed, in certain developing countries it has been found that productivity can be improved merely by improving the conditions under which people work.

Generally speaking, occupational safety and health and ergonomics have not been given sufficient consideration in modern management techniques, in spite of the modern tendency to consider an industrial undertaking as a total system or a combination of subsystems.

These problems have been seen in a different light since public opinion and, in particular, the trade unions became aware of them. It has been possible to detect in the stresses imposed by modern industrial technology the source of those forms of dissatisfaction which occur, in particular, amongst workers employed on the most elementary type of repetitive and monotonous jobs which are lacking in any interest whatsoever.

Thus, not only may a hazardous working environment be a direct cause of occupational accidents and diseases, but the worker's dissatisfaction with working conditions which are not in line with his current cultural and social level may also be at the root of a decline in production quality and quantity, excessive labour turnover and increased absenteeism. Obviously, the consequences of such a situation will vary according to the socio-cultural environment. What, in the industrialised countries, is nowadays called the "social cost of labour" has sometimes been aggravated by combative attitudes (deliberate waste, threats of violence, conflicts) whereas this kind of reaction has not been encountered elsewhere. Nevertheless, wherever there is a demand for labour, it would be foolish to believe that firms whose working conditions have not developed in line with technical progress and economic growth can count on a stable workforce and achieve profitable levels of productivity.

In the developing countries the widespread lack of statistical data on industrial injuries and on absenteeism makes a detailed study of working conditions impossible; moreover, for workers in these countries working conditions may be only a secondary consideration, to be placed after the employment itself and the wages that accompany it. However, if one wishes to avoid, in the short term, the wastage of human and material resources—which is all the more serious in a developing country—and, in the long term, socio-political tension, great attention must be devoted to working conditions, and it must be recognised that nowadays the undertaking has an important social role to play in addition to its technical and economic function.

2. Occupational safety and health organisation

The most effective method of obtaining good results in accident prevention is to establish good safety organisation within the enterprise. The organisational structure need not be formalised, nor need it require the employment of specialists; its essential features should be a precise delegation of responsibilities within a structure which can ensure sustained action and a joint effort by employers and workers to "raise the quality of the working environment, in all its technical, organisational and psychological aspects, to a satisfactorily high standard".[1] This implies the introduction of an effective occupational safety and health education and training programme and the provision of the necessary first-aid and medical services.

3. Safety criteria

Studies of occupational hazards in modern industry have revealed the extremely complex nature of the possible causes of occupational accidents or diseases.

OCCUPATIONAL ACCIDENTS

The causes of occupational accidents are never simple, even in an apparently commonplace accident; consequently, the number and variety of accident classifications are great. Statistics show that the most common causes of accidents are not the most dangerous machines (circular saws, spindle moulding machines, power presses, for example) nor the most dangerous substances (explosives or volatile flammable liquids), but rather quite ordinary actions like stumbling, falling, the faulty

---

[1] Council of Europe, Committee of Ministers: *Resolution 76(1) on safety services in firms*, 20 Jan. 1976.

Figure 8. *The four basic methods of controlling occupational hazards classified by decreasing order of effectiveness*

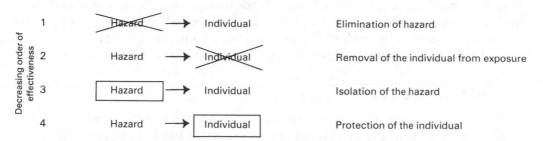

Source: Adapted from E. Gniza: "Zur Theorie der Wege der Unfallverhütung", in *Arbeitsökonomik und Arbeitsschutz* (Berlin), Vol. 1, 1957, No. 1.

handling of goods or use of hand tools, or being struck by a falling object.[1] Similarly, those who have accidents most frequently are not the disabled but, on the contrary, those who are the best equipped from the physical and psycho-sensorial point of view, i.e. young workers.

Technical progress has created new health hazards whilst at the same time greatly reducing the severity of conventional hazards and significantly improving the standards of machinery guarding (nevertheless, accidents do still happen even on the most carefully guarded machines). In addition, since in many countries commuting accidents have now been brought under the heading of occupational accidents, the demarcation line between occupational and non-occupational hazards has become less distinct and the role of the human factor and the importance of the circumstances attending an accident have become increasingly clear. An accident is often the result of a combination of technical, physiological and psychological factors: it depends on both the machine, the environment (lighting, noise, vibration, vaporising substances, oxygen deficiency), posture and work-induced fatigue; but it is also conditioned by commuting circumstances and other activities outside the plant, ill-temper, feelings of frustration, youthful exuberance and other specific physical or mental states. In the developing countries there are, in addition, malnutrition, endemic diseases, lack of adaptation to industrial work and the immense changes that industry has brought to the worker's individual and family life and customs. It is therefore not surprising that, nowadays, increasing attention is being paid to the accident hazards inherent in human behaviour, be it in the factory or elsewhere, and that the problems of safeguarding the worker's health and welfare are now being examined from a global viewpoint which admits of no fragmentation for purely administrative reasons.

The first precaution to take in order to avoid accidents is the elimination of potential causes, both technical and human. The ways of doing this are too numerous and varied to be listed extensively here. However, to mention but a few, there are the observance of technical rules and standards, careful supervision and maintenance, safety training for all workers, and the establishment of good working relationships.

The main technical safety criteria are listed in decreasing order of effectiveness in the diagram developed by Gniza (see figure 8).

---

[1] ILO: *Accident prevention: A workers' education manual* (Geneva, 8th imp., 1976).

Some 30 per cent of all accidents occur in manual handling; work study can contribute to reducing the incidence of these accidents quite simply by reducing the number of handling operations and the distance that goods have to be transported. A significant percentage of other accidents could be prevented by eliminating dangerous operations through prior work study, process analysis and flow charts process and, in general, by a critical examination of work organisation with a view to accident prevention.

OCCUPATIONAL DISEASES

The situation relating to the causes of occupational diseases and ways of preventing them is equally complex. Technical progress has been so rapid that it has often created new and totally unrecognised hazards which have resulted in occupational diseases even before the disease was recognised as such. Yet this same technical progress has provided extremely effective tools for the early detection of signs or symptoms of occupationally induced morbidity, and even exposure tests for evaluating a hazard before it has any biological effect. The study and monitoring of the working environment have, in this way, assumed a fundamental importance in the prevention of occupational diseases.

The traditional approach which made a sharp distinction between occupational and non-occupational diseases on the basis of insurance criteria has gradually lost favour in face of a much more realistic understanding of the severity of the hazards to which the individual is exposed outside the plant—not only home and traffic accidents (which have a much higher incidence than occupational accidents) but also noise, air pollution in residential areas, the nervous tension of daily life, and so on. Moreover, the effects of exposure to occupational hazards are much more severe in persons who are suffering from pre-existent disease, and who, in the most developed countries, are increasingly finding their way into the industrial environment. Thus industrial hygiene has developed at an extraordinary pace and the true task of the occupational physician has taken on a new significance. Many of the conditions to which workers are subject may be of psycho-neural or psycho-somatic origin—a field in which any distinction between the occupational and non-occupational causes of disease is illusory. The task of the plant medical officer therefore extends to protecting the individual from mental and nervous stresses that are often of unidentifiable primary origin.

Industrial hygiene measures are similar to those that have already been mentioned for accident prevention. One important point needs to be made, however. Industrial hygiene has been a subject of study for a much shorter period than occupational safety. It is a discipline which involves both medical and technical knowledge, and this may explain why it is still neglected even today by both occupational health and occupational safety services. This is the risk run by any interdisciplinary activity, and ergonomics is no exception to this rule. It is therefore essential that the management of an enterprise comes to grips with the problem and adopts the most suitable approaches for its solution; such approaches are not, however, of universal application since they have to be matched to the individual circumstances of the enterprise and its workers.

A number of basic general criteria in industrial hygiene can nevertheless be put forward. First of all, as has been found in the field of mechnical safety, in industrial hygiene too the most effective means of prevention is that which occurs at the design stage—be it of a building, plant or work process—since any subsequent improvement or modification may perhaps be too late to protect the worker's health and will certainly be more expensive. Dangerous operations (for example, those resulting in environmental pollution or producing noise or vibration) and harmful substances which may contaminate the atmosphere at the workplace should be replaced by harmless or less harmful operations or substances. Where it is impossible to provide group safety equipment, use should be made of supplementary work organisation measures which, in certain cases, may include a reduction of the duration of exposure to risk. Where group technical measures and administrative measures do not reduce exposure to acceptable levels, workers must be provided with suitable personal protective equipment. However, other than in exceptional cases or for special types of work, reliance should not be placed on personal protective equipment as the basic means of safety. This is not only for physiological reasons but also a matter of principle, since the worker may, for a wide range of reasons, fail to make use of this equipment.

4. Fire prevention and protection

The prevention of fire and, in certain cases, explosion and the appropriate protective measures should receive particular attention, especially in hot and dry countries and above all in certain industries where a fire may lead to widespread material damage and, should it occur during working hours, to injury and even death.

The first principle of prevention is to design and construct buildings with adequate fire resistance in relation to the hazards that are encountered. The second principle is to give adequate training to the workers and enforce fire prevention regulations such as bans on smoking and the prohibition of the use of sources of ignition in high-risk areas. It is essential to ensure that, wherever a fire risk may occur, there is an adequate number of serviceable fire extinguishers which, in themselves, should not constitute a supplementary hazard (for example, of poisoning or explosion); that alarm systems function correctly and that the warning they emit is audible throughout the enterprise; and finally, that emergency exits are kept clear. In particularly high-risk plants such as are found in the textile industry, sprinklers or similar automatic fire-fighting apparatus should be installed. It is also important that the management and foremen should be fully acquainted with their role in the event of a fire and that the workers themselves should know what they should do; panic at the outbreak of a fire, especially in a multi-storey buiding, may cause more loss of life than the fire itself. Where there is a significant fire hazard, fire protection will entail—

☐   a trained fire-fighting team which carries out regular fire-fighting exercises;

☐   a system of periodic inspection which may include full-time inspectors;

☐   suitable liaison with the fire brigade;

☐   in large enterprises and with due regard to the costs involved, periodic fire alarm and evacuation exercises.

51

5. Working premises

It would be inappropriate to deal here with the technical details of plant location and construction, but certain basic principles need to be appreciated and applied if the management is subsequently to obtain viable results. This point should be borne in mind by the work study specialist, especially when plant installation is being studied.

Neighbourhood and environmental protection are nowadays of such importance and so closely connected with the prevention of pollution and the suppression of noise and vibration, even inside the plant, that every enterprise is virtually obliged to make an **over-all** study of these problems when considering plant location and installation. An over-all study is in fact the most economic one in view of the complex requirements that have to be met. Moreover, in many countries it is compulsory to submit to the competent authority—which may be spread over several ministries—any plans for a new industrial building in order at least to ensure that all existing standards are adhered to.

As far as the layout of the workplace is concerned, emphasis should be placed on the principle of isolating any operation which is hazardous or constitutes a nuisance. Wherever possible, work premises should be above ground level and equipped with windows having a surface area of not less than 17 per cent of the floor area. Minimum ceiling height should not be less than 3 metres and each worker should have at least 10 cubic metres of air (or more where temperatures or the level of atmospheric pollution are high). For the purposes of accident prevention, it is important to ensure that each worker has an adequate minimum free-floor area which should not be less than 2 square metres per person.

Walls and ceilings should have a finish which prevents the accumulation of dirt, avoids moisture absorption and, where necessary, reduces noise transmission; floor coverings (table 2) should be of the non-slip, non-dust-forming and easy-to-clean type and should, where necessary, have good electrical and thermal insulation properties.

Traffic aisles should be sufficiently wide to allow, if necessary, the simultaneous movement of vehicles and workers at peak hours (meal times, closing times) and rapid evacuation in the event of an emergency. When discussing fire protection, we emphasised that emergency exits should always be kept clear; to this end, fire exits should not be used for any other purpose. The national regulations of certain countries specify that no workplace should be more than 35 metres from the nearest emergency exit or fire escape.

6. Cleanliness and good housekeeping

Building work premises in accordance with safety and hygiene regulations is not enough, however, if the plant or workshop is not kept clean and tidy. Good housekeeping, which when used with reference to a factory or workplace is a general term embracing tidiness and general state of repair, not only contributes to accident prevention but also is a factor in productivity. If aisles and gangways are allowed to

Table 2. Properties of various industrial floor surfaces[1]

Properties	Type of surface								
	Concrete	Ceramic tiles	Plastics (2-component compounds)	Plastics (sheet or strip)	Xylolite	Wood blocks	Parquet	Poured asphalt	Rolled bituminous surfaces
Abrasion resistance	Very good	Very good	Very good[3]	Medium to good	Poor	Good	Medium to good	Good	Good
Compression resistance	Very good	Very good	Very good[3]	Medium	Medium	Good	Medium to good	Medium	Good
Impact resistance	Medium	Medium	Dependent on type	Good	Good	Very good	Good to very good	Good	Good to very good
Thermal insulation (contact)	Bad	Bad	Bad[3]	Bad to medium	Medium	Very good	Very good	Medium	Medium
Shrinkage, stretching	Dependent on type	None	Poor	Poor	Dependent on moisture content	Dependent on moisture content	Dependent on moisture content	None	None
Acid resistance	Bad	Very good[2]	Good	Usually good	Bad	Good	Good	Poor[4]	Medium to bad
Alkali resistance	Good	Very good	Poor to very good depending on type	Usually good	Bad	Medium to good	Medium to good	Good	Good
Water resistance	Good	Very good	Good	Good	Bad	Bad	Bad	Very good	Good
Oil and fuel resistance	Unsuitable unless specially treated	Very good[2]	Good	Medium to good	Unsuitable	Good	Good	Unsuitable	Good
Solvent resistance	Good	Very good	Certain types resistant	Good	Unsuitable	Good	Good	Bad	Medium
Dust formation	Yes	No	No	No	Yes	Yes	No	No	No
Ease of cleaning	Satisfactory	Good	Very good	Good	Satisfactory	Relatively bad	Satisfactory to good	Good	Medium to good
Fire resistance	Very good	Very good	Bad	Medium	Good	Bad	Bad	Medium	Quite good
Dielectric properties	Bad	Good	Good	Good	Depends on atmospheric humidity	Good (if dry)	Good (if dry)	Good	Quite good
Friction sparking	Yes	Yes	No	No	No	No	No	No	Yes

[1] Determined by the Swiss Federal Materials Testing Laboratory and Research Institute (Laboratoire fédéral d'essai des matériaux et Institut de recherches), Dübendorf, August 1969.   [2] Except perhaps the joints.   [3] In these cases in particular, the characteristics depend on the filler employed.   [4] The "acid-resistant" type is unaffected by non-oxidising inorganic acids.

Source: Office fédéral de l'industrie, des arts et métiers et du travail (Suisse): Hygiène et prévention des accidents dans les entreprises industrielles, ordonnance 3 relative à la loi sur le travail (Berne, 1975).

become cluttered with stacks of materials and other obstructions, time will be lost by workers having to clear their way for the transport of raw materials or finished products; it may take hours to find a batch of semi-finished products lost in the general disorder. Finally, stacks of raw materials or semi-finished products, as well as tools and equipment that may have been abandoned for some considerable time, tie up capital and take up space which could be used for productive purposes. Tools, jigs, fixtures and other equipment should not be left lying around the workshop but should be returned to store or stowed on shelves or racks or in bins located at suitable points. Gangways should be marked on the ground with white or yellow lines at least 5 cm wide and objects should not be allowed to project into them. Depot and storage areas should be marked in a similar manner and goods should be carefully stacked.

Cleanliness is no less important than good housekeeping, in particular as regards the protection of workers against infection, infestation, accidents and occupational diseases. Where necessary, measures should be taken to exterminate rodents, insects and other vermin which may be the vectors of epidemic diseases. Indeed, problems such as this should be prevented by the careful daily cleaning of workshops, gangways, staircases and any other areas where waste or deposits may attract animals. Waste bins should be leak-free; they should be easy to clean, and they should be kept clean.

Residues which may be the source of dangerous emissions of vapour, gases or dust (such as toxic liquids, refractories, asbestos and lead oxide) should be collected in a suitable way: dust should be removed by vacuum cleaners or wet methods and chemicals should be neutralised or diluted. Deposits of certain toxic substances can be more readily identified if the floor, walls and, where necessary, the work benches are painted in a colour which contrasts with that of the substance in question.

Working clothes must be kept clean in order to reduce the skin-absorption hazard of certain toxic substances (analine and its derivatives, benzene, its homologues and derivatives, organo-phosphorus compounds, tetraethyl lead and other organic metal compounds, carbon tetrachloride and other solvents, nicotine, and so on) and the problem of skin sensitisation and chronic or acute irritation. Prolonged contact of the skin with certain substances (especially mineral oils and aromatic hydrocarbons) may produce chronic dermatitis, sometimes followed by the development of cancer. Workers exposed to toxic substances should have twin-compartment clothing lockers to keep their working clothes separate from their other clothes, so as to prevent the danger of their family being exposed to the industrial toxic substance. Similarly, it is advisable to provide a centralised laundry service for working clothes in plants using highly toxic substances.

Workers employed on dirty jobs or exposed to dangerous or toxic substances should have wash-rooms with a tap for every three or four workers and a shower for every three workers (and never less than one for every eight workers) to ensure that workers do not give up taking a shower because they have to wait too long.

An important factor for the worker's health is the provision of sufficient and, where possible, cooled drinking water in the factory. This water should be approved by the health authority and its purity should be tested periodically. Where possible, the water should be on tap.

7. Lighting

It is estimated that 80 per cent of the information required in doing a job is perceived visually. Good visibility of the equipment, the product and the data involved in the work process is an essential factor in accelerating production, reducing the number of defective products, reducing waste and preventing visual fatigue and headaches amongst the workers. It may also be added that both inadequate visibility and glare are frequently a cause of accidents.

Visibility depends on a number of factors: the size of the workpiece, its distance from the eyes, the persistance of the image, the lighting intensity, the colour of the workpiece and contrasts of colour and lighting levels with the background. All these factors should be studied in the case of precision work, work in a dangerous environment or where there are other reasons for dissatisfaction or complaint. Lighting is often the most important factor and the one which is most easy to correct.

Above all, the lighting should be adapted to the type of work: however, the level of illumination should be increased not only in relation to the degree of precision or miniaturisation of the work (table 3) but also in relation to the worker's age, since older people require a higher level of illumination than young persons if they are to recognise detail and maintain a sufficiently rapid visual reaction; moreover, older persons are highly susceptible to glare since their recovery time is longer. It is not sufficient to provide for an optimal lighting level when the workplace layout plans are being drawn up, since, after installation, lighting intensity rapidly falls by 10 to 25 per cent and then more slowly until it is only 50 per cent or less of the original level. This is because of the accumulation of dust and the wear of the lighting elements. Lighting intensity at the work surface should be checked periodically and all lighting surfaces

Table 3.   Recommended minimum values of illumination for various classes of visual task

Class of visual task	Minimum illumination of task (lux)[1]	Typical examples
Casual seeing	20	To permit safe movement (e.g. in corridors with little traffic)
	100	Boilerhouse (coal and ash handling); dead storage of rough, bulky materials; locker rooms
Ordinary rough tasks	150	Rough, intermittent bench and machine work; rough inspection and counting of stock parts; assembly of heavy machinery
Moderately critical tasks	300	Medium bench and machine work, assembly and inspections. Ordinary office work such as reading, writing, filing
Critical tasks	700	Fine bench and machine work, assembly and inspection; extra-fine painting, spraying; sewing dark-coloured goods
Very critical tasks	1500	Assembly and inspection of delicate mechanisms; tool- and die-making; gauge inspection; fine grinding work
Exceptionally difficult or important tasks	3000 or more	Fine watchmaking and repairing

[1] These figures refer to the mean value of illumination obtained during the life of the installation and averaged over the work plane or specific task area (i.e. the so-called "service value of illumination").

Source: ILO, International Occupational Safety and Health Information Centre (CIS): *Artificial lighting in factory and office,* CIS Information sheet no. 11 (Geneva, 1965).

Table 4. Recommended maximum lighting intensity ratios

Points involved	Ratio
Between the work and the immediate environment	5 to 1
Between the work and distant surfaces	20 to 1
Between the light source or the sky and adjacent surfaces	40 to 1
All points in the worker's immediate vicinity	80 to 1

should be kept clean. In general, the light should be uniformly diffused (figures 9, 10 and 11); slight shadows help to distinguish objects, but shadows that are too pronounced should be avoided. Excessive contrasts in lighting levels between the worker's task and the general surroundings should also be avoided. Table 4 shows the maximum intensity ratios that should be observed in order to prevent the development of visual fatigue and health disorders such as conjunctivitis and headaches.

Natural lighting should be used wherever possible, through windows which should have an area equal to at least one-sixth of the floor area. However, since the intensity of natural lighting is extremely variable (even where the inflow can be modified by the use of shutters, blinds or shades), since its level falls rapidly as the distance from the windows increases, and since it is likely that reflected sunlight will cause glare, artificial lighting must be provided to ensure suitable conditions of visibility in all seasons, at all times and in all weather conditions. Fluorescent lighting offers considerable potential for rational use, provided that glare is avoided (figure 12), since it has particularly good colour-rendering properties and its annual cost (including depreciation and installation costs) falls, in relation to incandescent lighting, as the number of hours of use increases (figure 13). Thus the number of hours an installation is likely to be used per year should influence the type of lighting chosen.

USE OF COLOURS

Experience shows that the careful choice of interior colour schemes makes a valuable contribution to good lighting (figure 14). The colours used at the workplace have psychological effects which should not be overlooked, and when the time comes to repaint workshops and offices it costs very little, if anything, more to select pleasing rather than drab colours; the workers will see in this a clear sign that the management is making an effort to make working conditions more pleasant.

The colours of machinery and equipment are supplementary safety factors and their importance has been recognised by the manufacturers of machine tools and electrical equipment, as a result of the work of the International Organization for Standardization.

8. Noise and vibration[1]

NOISE

High levels of mechanisation, increased machine speeds, the density of machinery at the workplace and the lack, until recently, of detailed knowledge of the

[1] For further information on this subject, see ILO: *Protection of workers against noise and vibration in the working environment* (Geneva, 1977).

Figure 9. Mounting of general lighting units

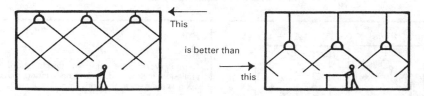

General lighting units should preferably be mounted as high as possible

Source: ILO, CIS: *Artificial lighting . . .,* op. cit.

Figure 10. Need for general lighting

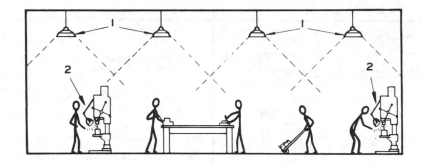

Some general lighting is always needed even when tasks are locally lit. (1) Uniform general lighting (2) Local supplementary lighting.

Source: ILO, CIS: *Artificial lighting . . .,* op. cit.

Figure 11. Maximum recommended spacing for industrial type units

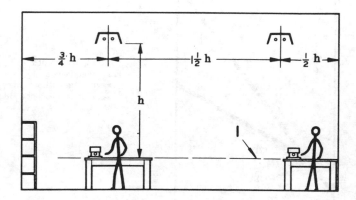

Measurements are to the centre point of the unit in all cases, and are expressed as a multiple of the mounting height *h* above the work plane (I). The ¾ *h* figure applies when there is a gangway next to the wall, whilst the ½ *h* figure is used when people work close to the wall. For louvred units, maximum spacing between fittings should be reduced to 1¼ *h*.

Source: ILO, CIS: *Artificial lighting . . .,* op. cit.

57

Figure 12.   Factors influencing the degree of glare produced by a given diffusing fitting (or a bare fluorescent lamp unit)

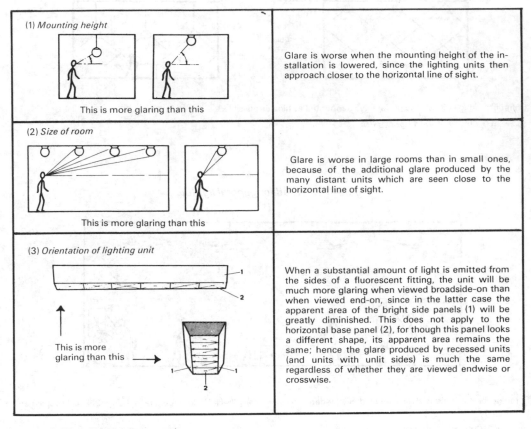

(1) *Mounting height* This is more glaring than this	Glare is worse when the mounting height of the installation is lowered, since the lighting units then approach closer to the horizontal line of sight.
(2) *Size of room* This is more glaring than this	Glare is worse in large rooms than in small ones, because of the additional glare produced by the many distant units which are seen close to the horizontal line of sight.
(3) *Orientation of lighting unit* This is more glaring than this →	When a substantial amount of light is emitted from the sides of a fluorescent fitting, the unit will be much more glaring when viewed broadside-on than when viewed end-on, since in the latter case the apparent area of the bright side panels (1) will be greatly diminished. This does not apply to the horizontal base panel (2), for though this panel looks a different shape, its apparent area remains the same; hence the glare produced by recessed units (and units with unlit sides) is much the same regardless of whether they are viewed endwise or crosswise.

Source: ILO, CIS: *Artificial lighting . . .,* op. cit.

Figure 13.   Relative cost of incandescent and fluorescent lighting

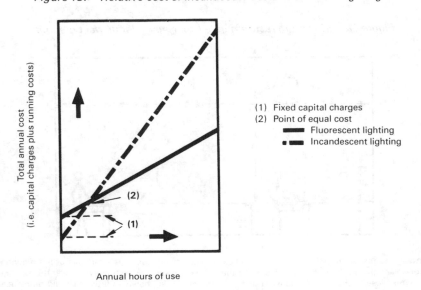

(1) Fixed capital charges
(2) Point of equal cost
▬▬▬   Fluorescent lighting
▪▬▪▬   Incandescent lighting

Total annual cost (i.e. capital charges plus running costs)

Annual hours of use

Source: ILO, CIS: *Artificial lighting . . .,* op. cit.

Figure 14.   Recommended ranges of reflection factor for main interior surfaces

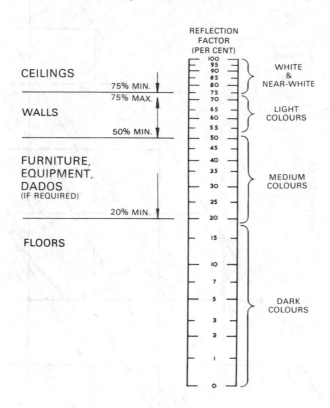

Source: ILO, CIS: *Artificial lighting . . .,* op. cit.

hazards and nuisance factor of noise have resulted, in many plants, in workers being exposed to noise levels which are nowadays considered excessive. Noise is the cause of various problems. It impedes sound communication (figure 15), first, by the acoustical masking effect which every sound has on other sounds of the same frequency or immediately higher frequencies and which reduces the intelligibility of speech that is not more than 10 dB louder than the background noise; and second, by temporarily raising the acoustic threshold in the event of exposure to a noise exceeding 78-80 dB (figure 16). It may cause sensori-motor, neuro-vegetative and metabolic disorders; it has been named as a cause of industrial fatigue, irritation, reduced productivity and occupational accidents. Prolonged exposure to noise above certain levels causes permanent damage to hearing and results in occupational deafness.

It is considered that exposure to continuous noise levels of 90 dB(A) or above is dangerous to hearing; but the figure of 85 dB(A) is already a warning level which should not be exceeded. Special care should be taken in the case of impulse noises, i.e. noises of very short duration at a level of at least 3 dB above the background noise and separated by intervals of at least one second, which the more rudimentary type of measuring instrument may not be able to detect. However, not all acoustic frequencies have the same effects on hearing: the most dangerous frequencies are those around 4,000 Hz (and higher in the case of impulse noise). Each time the sound level increases by 6 dB, the sound pressure doubles and the acoustic energy is

59

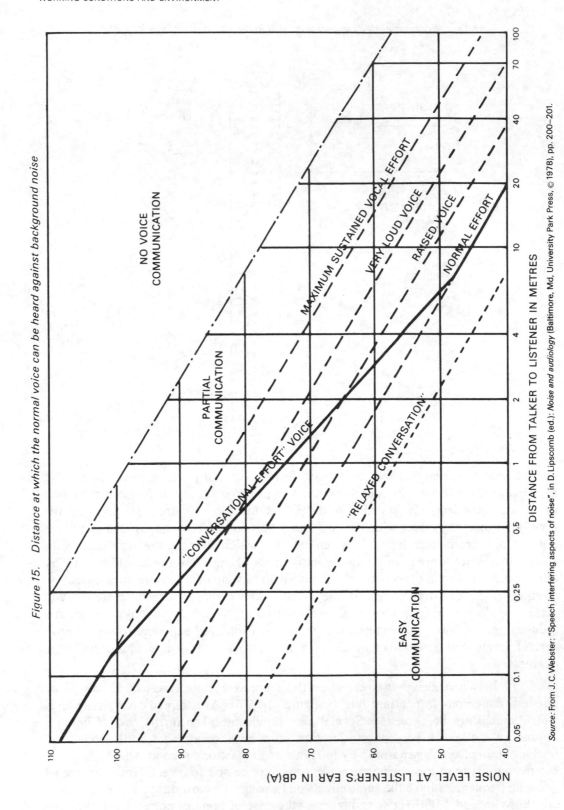

Figure 15. Distance at which the normal voice can be heard against background noise

Source: From J.C. Webster: "Speech interfering aspects of noise", in D. Lipscomb (ed.): Noise and audiology (Baltimore, Md, University Park Press, © 1978), pp. 200–201.

Figure 16.   *Temporary hearing threshold shift in dB as a function of duration of exposure to wide-band noise*

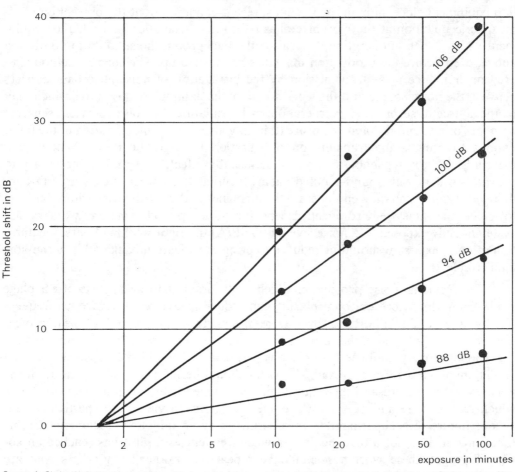

Source: A. Glorig, W. D. Ward and J. Nixon: "Damage risk criteria and noise-included hearing loss", in *Archives of Otolaryngology* (Chicago III.), Vol. 74, 1961, p. 413. Copyright 1961, American Medical Association.

quadrupled; thus it is considered that, for an increase of 3 to 5 dB in the sound level, the duration of exposure must be halved if the biological effect is to remain unchanged. Nobody should be exposed to levels of over 115 dB without hearing protection.

Anyone who has done intellectual work, or work requiring intense concentration, in a noisy environment such as a weaving mill or a workshop full of automatic machines—even where the noise level does not reach levels which may cause occupational deafness—will know just how fatiguing noise can be. Intermittent noise from rams used for digging the foundations for heavy machines, riveting hammers, pile-drivers or large mechanical presses is particularly disturbing. Numerous investigations have shown that a reduction in the background noise is accompanied by a marked decrease in the number of errors and a significant improvement in production.

The most effective method of noise control is to reduce the noise at source by, for example, replacing noisy machines or equipment by less noisy ones; this means (as is always the case with preventive action) that these measures must be borne in mind at the design stage of a production process, the construction of a building or the purchase of equipment (tables 5 and 6). Particular attention should be given to ventilation equipment since, in many workshops, recent concern about the prevention of atmospheric pollution at the workplace has led to the installation of ventilation equipment which, when in operation, has raised the background noise to 85 to 90 dB and above, even before the production machines are started up. The second method is to prevent or reduce noise transmission by the installation of noise-absorbant barriers between the noise source and the worker and by the damping of structures which may be the source of secondary reverberation, or by isolating the noise source in separate premises or a sound-proofed enclosure (this may also require modification of the foundations to prevent the transmission of vibration through the floor). Where such measures are not applicable or are not sufficiently effective, it may be necessary to provide workers with sound-proofed cabins (ventilated or, where necessary, air-conditioned) from which they can operate the machines and do their work without having to enter the noisy environment except for short periods. Where workers are systematically exposed to a noise level of 90 dB(A) for eight working hours, the duration of noise exposure should be reduced to bring the situation back within acceptable limits (table 7).

Personal noise protection, which in its simplest form consists of ear-plugs made from glass fibre or foam plastic, can reduce exposure to hazardous frequencies by at least 15 to 20 dB; however, workers sometimes object to this type of protection. In fact, personal noise protection should be considered as no more than a provisional remedy until the workplace is permanently modified or whenever special conditions make its use necessary. Workers should be informed of the nature of the noise exposure hazard and the requisite protective measures, including work methods which reduce noise and noisy work to specific hours. In view of the particularly insidious nature of occupational deafness (which may go unnoticed for a considerable time since it does not affect the human-voice frequencies until it has reached an advanced stage), these warnings should be repeated periodically. Workers who are systematically exposed to noise levels above the danger level should receive a periodic audiometric examination.

VIBRATION

Although only a limited number of workers are exposed to vibrations which constitute a health hazard, the necessary protective measures should not be neglected. The most effective protection is afforded by technical and organisational methods which, if applied to the extent required, can prevent health impairment.

9. Climatic conditions

If productivity is to be maintained, climatic conditions at the workplace must not place an extra burden on the worker; this is also a factor in safeguarding the worker's health and comfort. Members of the first ILO productivity mission to India reported that in some of the factories and mills they visited nothing or virtually nothing had been done to mitigate the effects of heat, so that the workers had to go into the open air to recover from the "unbearable working conditions". As a result a great deal of time was lost.

Table 5.   Calculation of noise level obtained by adding a new background noise source
to a pre-existing noise

Difference in dB between the two noise levels	Increase in dB of the higher noise level
0	3
1	2.8
2	2.1
3	1.8
4	1.5
5	1.2
6	1.0
7	0.8
8	0.6
9	0.5
10	0.4

Table 6.   Calculation of noise level obtained by removing a source of noise
from the background noise

Difference in dB between the two noise levels	Reduction in dB of the higher noise level
1	7.0
2	4.4
3	3.0
4	2.2
5	1.8
6	1.3
7	1.0
8	0.8
9	0.6
10	0.5

Table 7.   Duration of continuous noise exposure which should not be exceeded to ensure
the prevention of occupational deafness amongst the majority of workers

Daily duration of noise in hours	Noise level in dB(A) (measured "slow")
16	80
8	85
4	90
2	95
1	100
1/2	105
1/4	110
1/8	115

Source: American Conference of Governmental Industrial Hygienists (ACGIH): *Threshold limit values for chemical substances and physical agents in the workroom environment adopted by the ACGIH for 1977* (Cincinnati, Ohio).

Figure 17.   Limits of heat exposure

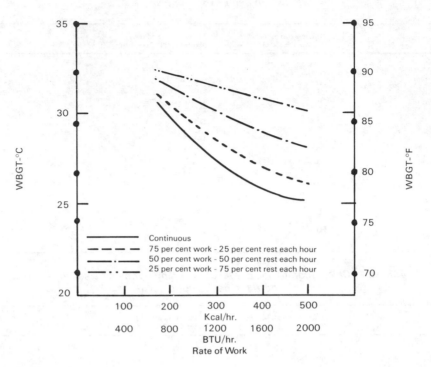

Source: ACGIH, op. cit.

.The human body's job here is to keep the central nervous system and the internal organs at a constant temperature. It maintains the necessary thermal balance by continuous heat exchange with the environment. The extent of this exchange depends, on the one hand, on air temperature, ventilation, humidity and radiant heat and, on the other, on body metabolism. During physical activity, metabolic values may be up to ten times as much as those encountered at rest. Under normal climatic conditions, in order to avoid over-heating (which sooner or later proves fatal) the heat that the body is continually producing must be dissipated in larger quantities when work is being done and in still larger quantities again if it is absorbing heat from a high-temperature environment.

In all cases it is essential to consider thermal burden in relation to the energy expenditure required by the work, since the body has to deal with a combination of these stress factors. The more burdensome the climatic conditions, the longer the work breaks should be (figure 17).

HOT WORK

In a hot working environment the only way, or almost the only way, in which the body can dissipate heat is by sweat vaporisation. This vaporisation is more intense, and consequently more effective and refreshing, where it is made easier by adequate ventilation; it is less effective when the relative humidity of the air is high. Thus the working conditions that are most difficult to bear are those encountered in deep mines, in spinning and weaving mills in hot countries, in sugar refineries and, in general, in all work entailing exposure to hot, humid conditions, especially in tropical countries. However, highly unfavourable working conditions may also be found in a desert-type, dry climate when radiant heat and a high air temperature are combined, in iron and steel works, in foundries, around surface treatment furnaces and in glass works, hot rolling mills and forges.

In view of the difficulty of evaluating conditions—which are determined by four parameters (air temperature, ventilation, humidity, radiant heat) which are all independently variable—several indices of thermal stress have been adopted, the most common being the wet bulb globe temperature (WBGT) index. Prevention may take various forms, for example, technical and work organisation measures which, if they are applied at the right level, can prevent any deleterious health effects.

COLD WORK

Work in low temperatures is more common now than it was, but practitioners in occupational medicine are still less familiar with it than with work in high temperatures. Workers in refrigerated premises should be well protected from the cold by suitable clothing and footwear, and exposure to low temperatures should alternate with periods at normal temperatures; moreover, workers should be protected from dehydration by frequently taking hot drinks. In the case of workers in non-heated premises, modern technology may provide means of localised heat, such as infra-red heaters directed at the workers, which can prolong the exposure time without affecting the worker's health or producing too marked a fall in output. For work in the open, national regulations usually require the installation of sheds or other means of protection against the weather.

WET WORK

As has already been mentioned, high levels of humidity are poorly tolerated at high temperatures, in particular when there is a significant workload. It is considered that the temperature as indicated by the wet-bulb thermometer at the workplace should not exceed 70°F (21°C). It is extremely difficult to keep within this limit in hot countries, in circumstances where (as in the textile industry) the process requires a high level of atmospheric humidity or (as in laundries, canning plants and various chemical plants) produces large quantities of steam. In the first case it is necessary to reduce the temperature by ventilation; in the second, to remove the steam by exhaust ventilation.

Excessive humidity is also poorly tolerated in combination with low temperatures; the relative humidity should be kept within a range of 40 to 70 per cent. Excessively dry air can be a cause of respiratory tract diseases; consequently, this should be avoided in winter in over-heated premises.

TEMPERATURE AT THE WORKPLACE

In view of the complexity of the physical factors affecting a worker's appreciation of the climatic environment, and the role of energy expenditure and personal factors such as nutrition, personal habits, age, sex and clothing, it would be a hopeless task to attempt to ensure the thermal comfort of all workers (i.e. a situation in which they require neither cooler nor warmer air). Experience shows that, among

65

the workers in a given shop, some would prefer more ventilation and some less, some tend to feel cold whilst others feel at ease. It may often be found that the main objective reason for these differences in a single shop is that the jobs being done by certain workers demand greater physical effort than those being done by others. The following air temperatures have been recommended for various types of work:

	°F	°C
Sedentary work	68-72	20-22
Light physical work in a seated position	66-68	19-20
Light work in a standing position (e.g. on machine-tools)	63-65	17-18
Moderate work in a standing position (e.g. assembly)	61-63	16-17
Heavy work in a standing position (e.g. drilling)	57-61	14-16

Working premises should be laid out and the work stations arranged in such a way as to ensure the greatest uniformity of energy expenditure amongst the persons working in a given area, in order to provide optimum climatic conditions for the majority of workers, with allowance being made for the effect of thermal comfort on output, especially in the case of intellectual work.

VENTILATION

The cubic volume of working premises can never be large enough to make ventilation unnecessary, since ventilation is the dynamic parameter that complements the concept of air space: for a given number of workers, the smaller the work premises the more intense should be the ventilation.

Ventilation must not be confused with air circulation: the first replaces contaminated air by fresh air, whereas the second merely moves the air without renewing it. Where the air temperature and humidity are high, merely to circulate the air is not only ineffective but, beyond certain limits, increases heat absorption by convection; nevertheless, there still exist hot workplaces fitted with fans which simply stir the air without renewing it.

Workplace ventilation—

☐   disperses the heat generated by machines and men at work (the mechanical efficiency is such that usually only 20 per cent of the energy employed is converted into work whereas 80 per cent is released as heat); consequently, where machines or workers are grouped together, ventilation should be intensified;

☐   dilutes atmospheric contamination; it is easy to calculate the ventilation intensity required, on the basis of the quantity of substances being released into the air and the maximum concentration that should be observed;

☐   maintains the feeling of air freshness.

In all, adequate ventilation should be looked upon as an important factor in maintaining the worker's health and productivity.

Except for confined spaces, all working premises have some minimum ventilation; however, to ensure the necessary air flow (which should not be lower than 50 cubic metres of air per hour per worker), air usually needs to be changed between four and eight times per hour in offices or for sedentary workers and between eight and 12 times per hour in workshops; the air flow may be as high as 15 to 30 air changes or more for public premises and where there are high levels of atmospheric pollution or humidity.

The air speed used for workplace ventilation should be adapted to the air temperature and the energy expenditure: for sedentary work, it should not exceed 0.2 metre per second but for a hot environment the optimum speed is between 0.5 and 1 metre per second. For arduous work it may be even higher. Certain types of hot work can be made tolerable by directing a stream of cold air at the workers. Ventilation, correctly used, is one of the most important technical means of making tolerable certain types of extremely arduous working conditions such as are encountered in deep mines and tropical countries, i.e. anywhere where there is a combination of high atmospheric temperature and relative humidity.

Natural ventilation, obtained by opening windows or wall or roof air-vents, can produce significant air flows but can usually be used only in relatively mild climates. The effectiveness of this type of ventilation depends largely on external conditions that usually vary considerably. When ventilation is most needed, natural ventilation is often at its least effective; moreover, it is relatively difficult to regulate. In addition, for natural ventilation to be effective, the outlet vents must be correctly located and of sufficient size, especially in hot countries where ventilation apertures are, only too often, too small.

Where natural ventilation is inadequate, artificial ventilation has to be used. A choice may be made between a blown-air system or an exhaust-air system, or a combination of both systems. Blown-air ventilation or blown-and-exhaust-air combinations allow better regulation of air movement. The majority of blown-air ventilation systems are used both to heat and to ventilate premises; when the temperature is high, they can also be used for cooling. However, in the long term, the air inflow deposits dust at the workplace and a layer of dirt on free surfaces and electric light bulbs; in the presence of flammable or explosive vapours, it is a source of danger. Wherever there are large emissions of gas, vapours, mists, fumes or dust, it is preferable to instal exhaust ventilation, which promotes the convection of heated air and avoids the dispersion of pollutants into neighbouring premises.

Where general ventilation is inadequate, local exhaust ventilation is required, by means of exhaust hoods or other devices which can be designed to meet the requirements of each case. The specific gravity of the pollutant in relation to that of air should be ascertained, in order to decide whether the exhaust ventilation should be downwards or upwards. The substance exhausted is never pure but is mixed with air in varying ratios, and it is the specific gravity of this mixture that should be considered; what is essential is to ensure that the exhausted air does not pass through the worker's breathing zone. Exhaust ventilation installations should be made from corrosion-resistant and non-combustible materials in view of the corrosive action of certain pollutants and the fire or explosion hazard of various organic or metallic dusts, solvent vapours and other volatile substances; the additional cost of the installation will always be lower than that of any possible accidents and the repeated replacement of ducting.

67

WORKING CONDITIONS AND ENVIRONMENT

10. Exposure tests

The protection of the worker's health against toxic substances should combine control of the working environment by the exposure limit method and medical supervision, including exposure tests. Such tests exist for a number of occupational hazards (lead, benzene, toluene, mercury, carbon disulphide, carbon monoxide, various organo-phosphorus insecticides, cadmium, etc.) and make it possible to monitor the degree of exposure of a worker even where no clinical signs or symptoms are detectable by conventional medical examinations, specialised though these may be. They are of great preventive value; unfortunately, however, in the majority of cases they require relatively complex equipment and trained and experienced personnel, neither of which are easily found in a developing country. In these countries and in small enterprises in general, the most effective and least expensive means of protection should be selected. Monitoring the environment makes it possible to protect the majority of workers without, however, guaranteeing 100 per cent protection of every exposed person; in addition, monitoring is relatively inexpensive. Medical supervision is more effective for a population which is exposed not only to occupational hazards but also to endemic, infectious and parasitic diseases and to malnutrition, as is often the case in developing countries. However, in conditions such as these, the specific control of occupational hazards is neglected, first, because it is terribly time-consuming for the physician, and second, because of lack of resources and knowledge.

In more developed countries medical check-ups and exposure tests may be resisted if they are not imposed by law or incorporated in collective bargaining agreements. These tests are still relatively expensive at present and involve a certain loss of working time and careful organisation. Where the competent authority is prepared to make exceptions to the rule regarding very frequent compulsory periodical medical examinations on condition that exposure tests give satisfactory results, these tests may be very economical since they are always less expensive than a medical examination and are of much greater specific effectiveness. Although medical examinations will still continue, they will be carried out less frequently.

Finally, no matter what method or combination of methods is finally selected, it is unthinkable to protect the worker's health against occupational hazards without the worker's own comments being taken into account. These are of specific value in cases of exposure to irritant or sensitising substances.

11. Personal protective equipment

For certain severe occupational hazards, neither technical prevention nor administrative arrangements can ensure an adequate degree of protection. It is therefore necessary to institute a third level of defence, i.e. personal protective equipment. This type of equipment is justified in emergency situations such as a severe accident, a leak or a fire, or under exceptional circumstances such as those attending work in confined spaces. In other cases the provision and maintenance of this equipment may be expensive and some workers may resist its use. It is therefore advisable for representatives of the management and the workers to examine the matter jointly beforehand and to seek the opinion of the safety and health committee, where one exists.

Where there is no other effective means of protection, the enterprise must provide a sufficient quantity of suitable personal protective equipment, instruct the workers in its correct use and ensure that it is worn. The choice of equipment should be made with the assistance of specialists, since advice is required both on the equipment's effectiveness and on its ergonomic characteristics, i.e. its adaptation to the worker's physical and functional characteristics.

12. Ergonomics

The effects of health and safety on productivity cannot be properly discussed without touching on the concept of ergonomics. This term covers a field which in recent years has expanded to an extraordinary degree and whose boundaries are far from clear. Ergonomic measures may, however, be defined as those that go beyond the mere protection of the worker's physical integrity and aim at ensuring his well-being through the attainment of optimal working conditions and by the most suitable use of his physical characteristics and physiological and psychological capabilities. Productivity is therefore not the primary objective of ergonomics but is usually one of the end products. The task is to develop the most comfortable conditions for the worker as regards lighting, climate and noise level, to reduce the physical workload (in particular in hot environments), to improve working postures and reduce the effort of certain movements, to facilitate psycho-sensorial functions in reading instrument displays, to make the handling of machine levers and controls easier, to make better use of spontaneous and stereotyped reflexes, to avoid unnecessary information recall efforts, and so on.

Many ergonomic measures are of a kind that should be introduced at the design stage of a building, appliance or machine, or when equipment is being installed, since subsequent modifications are generally less effective and much more expensive. A machine user should incorporate the application of specific ergonomic standards in the clauses of his contract with the machine manufacturer. The contract should cover safety colours, warning lights and controls that have already been standardised by the International Organization for Standardization and the International Electrotechnical Commission, in particular display panels and dials (figures 18 and 19). In addition, attention should be given not only to items affecting production but also to critical maintenance features.

It would be wrong to consider ergonomics as merely a collection of sophisticated actions reserved for the latest technology; improvements are often possible in manual handling also. In general, for work requiring frequent lifting, it is advisable to use a well trained worker. The correct technique is to bend the knees, holding the back straight so that the lifting is done by the powerful thigh muscles rather than by the weaker back muscles (figure 20). The instruction of manual-handling workers in kinetic techniques and systematic training is essential for the prevention of low-back pain and injuries to the lumbar spine which are among the most frequent causes of absenteeism, especially amongst older workers.

In medium-sized and large enterprises a well tried technique for introducing an ergonomic programme is to set up one or more interdisciplinary teams comprising

69

Figure 18. Ergonomic display design

A. TYPES OF DISPLAY

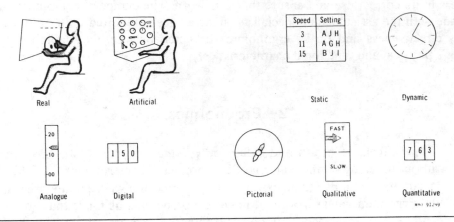

B. SCALE PATTERNS

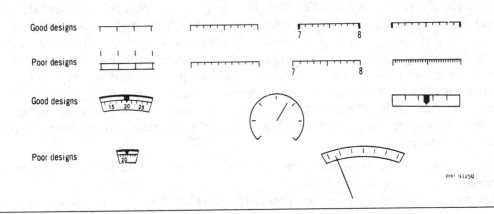

C. DIAL PATTERNS

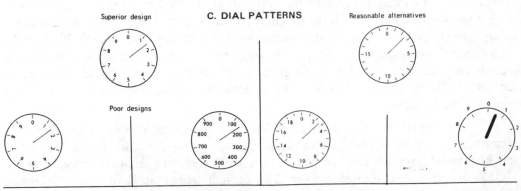

D. DISPLAY STEREOTYPES

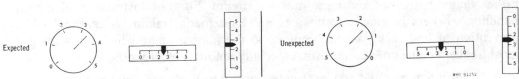

Source: W. T. Singleton: *Introduction to ergonomics* (Geneva, World Health Organization, 1972), pp. 79-80.

Figure 19. Ergonomic design of controls

A. TYPES OF CONTROL

		Use	Special design requirements
Button		In arrays for rapid selection between alternatives	To avoid slipping finger and accidental activation
Toggle		For definite, rarely used action involving only choice of two (normally on/off)	To avoid excessive finger pressure or nail damage
Selector		For more than two and less than ten choices	To avoid excessive wrist action make total movement less than 180°. Do not use simple circular shape
Knob		For continuous variables	Size depends mainly on resistance to motion. Use circular shape with serrated edge
Crank		When rotation through more than 360° is needed	Grip handle should turn freely on shaft
Lever		For higher forces or very definite activity	Identification of neutral or zero
Wheel		For precise activity involving large angles or rotation	Identification of particular positions Avoid slipping

B. CRITERIA FOR CONTROL POSITIONS

ANATOMICAL			
Which limb ?	Which joint ?	When used	
		Force	Precision
Hand	Shoulder	High	Low
	Elbow	Medium	Medium
	Wrist/finger	Low	High
Foot	Ankle	High	Low
	Thigh/knee	Maximum	Minimum

PSYCHOLOGICAL	
Identification	Position
	Size
	Shape
	Colour
	Legend
Selectivity	Position in sequence
	Relative importance
	Frequency of use

C. IDENTIFICATION OF CONTROLS

METHOD		WHEN USED
	EXAMPLE	
POSITION		Best placed near to controlled function (mechanical device or dial) provided access is reasonable and high speed is not essential.
SIZE		Important in relation to high frequency of use (e.g.,space bar on typewriter) or in relation to operating force. Size should be increased with required force.
SHAPE		Useful when controls must be operated without visual attention.
COLOUR		Useful only as secondary cue or as warning unless there are many controls together. Even so number of colours used should not be more than five.
LEGEND	MAIN STAND-BY	Useful secondary cue. Should not be obscured when control is operated.

D. CONTROL STEREOTYPES

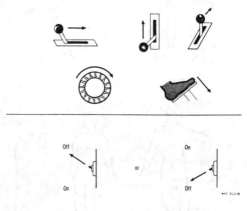

Arrows indicate direction of movement expected to produce an increase.

Standard position of switch indicating "on" or "off" differs from one country to another.

Source: W. T. Singleton, op. cit., pp. 69-70.

Figure 20.   Optimal use of physical effort

A. ASPECTS OF WEIGHT DISTRIBUTION

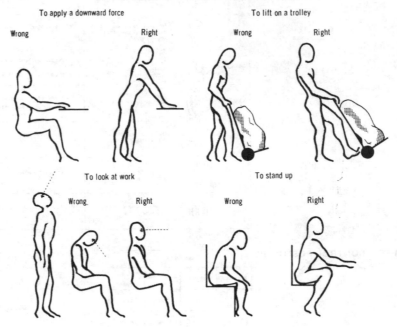

B. LIFTING AND CARRYING

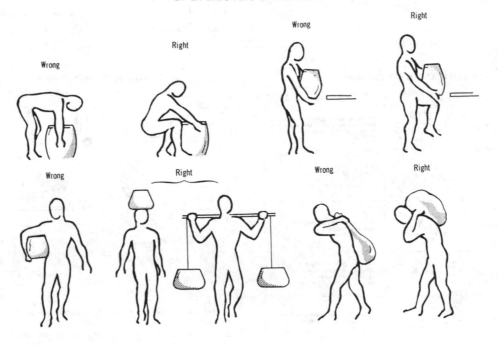

Source: W. T. Singleton, op. cit., p. 25.

work study specialists, a safety specialist, the works medical officer, a representative of the personnel department and representatives of the workers in the shops in question.

13. Arrangement of working time[1]

HOURS OF WORK

In most countries working hours are nowadays regulated by law and are negotiated through collective bargaining procedures. In some countries about 40 hours per week are worked, although elsewhere (for example, in certain enterprises in Sweden and the United States) the figure has been reduced to 36 hours and further reductions are under consideration. In other countries, such as Switzerland, the figure still exceeds 40 hours, reaching 48 hours in many of the smaller enterprises. Overtime poses a problem in that some workers, with an eye to economic gain, tend to accept this kind of work readily. In the long run this can adversely affect both the quality and the quantity of the work produced. Limits should be set and applied regarding the amount of overtime that may be worked during a given period. Similarly, workers below 18 years of age and expectant mothers should not be allowed to work overtime.

BREAKS

Only some 30 years ago, the need for rest breaks during the working day was recognised by few industries. Although recent technological progress has, generally speaking, reduced the arduousness of various types of physical work, it has often increased the psycho-physical workload by accelerating the work tempo and eliminating work preparation time. These changes have made it necessary to introduce breaks during the working day in order to dissipate fatigue and restore the worker's physical and nervous energy. During these breaks a person doing hard physical work should be able to stop work, sit down and if possible lie down; a person doing intellectual work should be able to move around and even do some light gymnastics. Interruptions for meals or resulting from accidents should not be counted as breaks.

THE CONTINUOUS WORKING DAY

The continuous working day, in which there is only a short break for a light meal at midday, represents a compromise between established eating and social habits and the new requirements created by industrialisation. Where the continuous working day is introduced, the workers' leisure time is increased and the number of commuting journeys is reduced. Consequently, fatigue is reduced too and there are fewer accidents; from the employers' point of view, productivity is increased as a result of the introduction of a continuous working schedule and the satisfaction of a union demand. Even where the continuous working day has met with resistance (this is particularly

---

[1] This subject is dealt with in greater detail in the following ILO publications: *Hours of work in industrialised countries,* by A. A. Evans (Geneva, 1975); *Flexible working hours,* by H. Allenspach (Geneva, 1975); *Shift work: Economic advantages and social costs,* by M. Maurice (Geneva, 1975); *Adapting working hours to modern needs,* by D. Marić (Geneva, 1977); *Management of working time in industrialised countries* (Geneva, 1978).

likely from older workers), the system has been encouraged because it is in the interests both of the enterprise itself and of the majority of the workers.

STAGGERING OF WORK SCHEDULES

Systems of staggered hours of work are now being adopted in the most industrialised countries. Workers are usually content with systems of this kind since they tend to reduce the amount of peak-hour road and rail traffic and allow workers to shop and to make use of public services during the week, without requesting special permission from their employer. Moreover, the system has the advantage that it increases social intercourse and contacts. It is difficult to introduce and organise staggered hours, however, for workers engaged on continuous or line production. Before such a system is adopted, all interested parties, in particular the representatives of the workers, should meet together and carefully study all its implications.

FLEXIBLE WORKING HOURS

A major innovation in the arrangement of working time was carried through when variable or flexible patterns of work were successfully adopted in certain European countries. This system, of which there are several forms with varying degrees of flexibility, allows the worker to choose the times at which he wishes to start and finish his working day, provided that he observes a "core" period of compulsory attendance and puts in a certain number of working hours each day, month, or even longer working period. It is difficult to apply a system of flexible working hours for shift work or semi-shift work or where production is organised in a number of very fragmented operations. However, it lends itself particularly well to jobs in the tertiary sector, where workers have been highly satisfied with the system because it allows them to choose their hours of work to fit in with their life style or individual or group work tempo. Where such a system can be introduced without provoking too much friction between the various categories of worker or too much resistance from certain people in the industrial hierarchy who are often hostile to any innovation, the enterprise can put the flexible working hours system to good use in solving certain problems of manpower and management and also in facilitating the employment of married women.

SHIFT WORK

Shift work is common in several industries, particularly for certain operations such as oil refining, continuous steel production, and so on. Shift work may take one of three forms:

(a) two shifts of eight hours each (indicated as 2×8) with an interruption of work at the end of the day and of the week;

(b) three shifts of eight hours each (or 3×8) with an interruption for the week-end; or

(c) fully continuous operations with no stoppages and including work on Sundays and public holidays. Such a system needs more than three shifts (4×8 or 5×8).

Shift workers may either work the same shift or alternating shifts. Shift work can have an effect on the health of workers, particularly in the case of fully continuous operations where alternating shift work may cause some workers to develop nervous, digestive or circulatory problems. Permanent and occasional night-shift workers should therefore be given periodic medical examinations. In order to alleviate other drawbacks of shift work, for instance those concerning the family and social life of the workers concerned, compensatory measures should be applied to the greatest extent possible. These include better distribution of work among the various shifts, reduction of working time, additional rest periods, limitation of the time spent on shift work and better canteen, transport and housing facilities.

Part two
Method study

Chapter 7
Introduction to method study and the selection of jobs

1. Definition and objects of method study

Method study has already been defined in Chapter 4, but the definition is worth repeating at this point.

> **Method study is the systematic recording and critical examination of existing and proposed ways of doing work, as a means of developing and applying easier and more effective methods and reducing costs**

The term "method study" is being increasingly used in place of "motion study", although the latter was intended by its inventor, Frank B. Gilbreth, to cover almost exactly the same field. *Industrial engineering terminology,* published by the American Society of Mechanical Engineers, gives separate definitions for "method study" and "motion study", the latter being confined to hand and eye movements at the workplace. However, "motion study" is sometimes used in textbooks with the same meaning as "method study".

The objects of method study are—

☐ The improvement of processes and procedures.

☐ The improvement of factory, shop and workplace layout and of the design of plant and equipment.

☐ Economy in human effort and the reduction of unnecessary fatigue.

☐ Improvement in the use of materials, machines and manpower.

☐ The development of a better physical working environment.

There are a number of method study techniques suitable for tackling problems on all scales from the layout of complete factories to the smallest movements of workers on repetitive work. In every case, however, the method of procedure is basically the same and must be carefully followed.

79

2. Basic procedure

When any problem is examined there should be a definite and ordered sequence of analysis. Such a sequence may be summarised as follows:

1. *DEFINE* the problem.
2. *OBTAIN* all the facts relevant to the problem.
3. *EXAMINE* the facts critically but impartially.
4. *CONSIDER* the courses open and decide which to follow.
5. *ACT* on the decision.
6. *FOLLOW UP* the development.

We have already discussed the basic procedure for the whole of work study, which embraces the procedures of both method study and work measurement. Let us now examine the basic procedure for method study, selecting the proper steps. They are as follows:

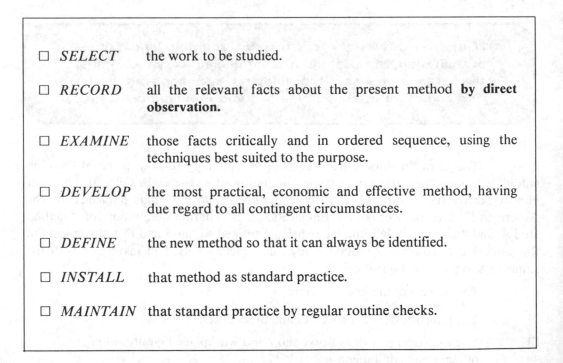

☐ *SELECT*   the work to be studied.

☐ *RECORD*   all the relevant facts about the present method **by direct observation.**

☐ *EXAMINE*   those facts critically and in ordered sequence, using the techniques best suited to the purpose.

☐ *DEVELOP*   the most practical, economic and effective method, having due regard to all contingent circumstances.

☐ *DEFINE*   the new method so that it can always be identified.

☐ *INSTALL*   that method as standard practice.

☐ *MAINTAIN*   that standard practice by regular routine checks.

These are the seven essential stages in the application of method study: none can be excluded. Strict adherence to their sequence, as well as to their content, is essential for the success of an investigation. They are shown diagrammatically on the chart in figure 21.

Do not be deceived by the simplicity of the basic procedure into thinking that method study is easy and therefore unimportant. On the contrary, method study may on occasion be very complex, but for purposes of description it has been reduced to these few simple steps.

Figure 21.   Method study

(Reproduction and adapted by permission of Imperial Chemical Industries Ltd, London)

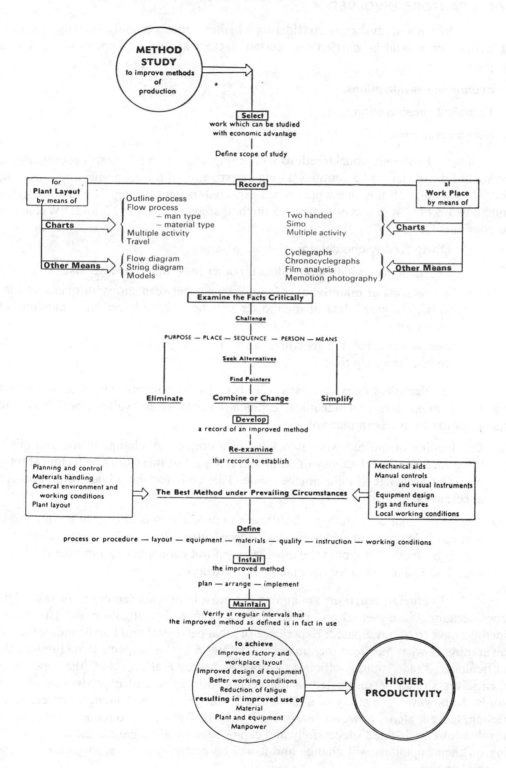

3. Selecting the work to be studied

SOME FACTORS INVOLVED

When a studyman is considering whether a method study investigation of a particular job should be carried out, certain factors should be kept in mind. These are—

1. **Economic considerations.**

2. **Technical considerations.**

3. **Human reactions.**

1. **Economic considerations** will be important at all stages. It is obviously a waste of time to start or to continue a long investigation if the economic importance of the job is small, or if it is one which is not expected to run for long. The first questions must always be: "Will it pay to begin a method study of this job?", and: "Will it pay to continue this study?"

Obvious early choices are—

"bottlenecks" which are holding up other production operations;

movements of material over long distances between shops, or operations involving a great deal of manpower or where there is repeated handling of material;

operations involving repetitive work using a great deal of labour and liable to run for a long time.

2. **Technical considerations** will normally be obvious. The most important point is to make sure that adequate technical knowledge is available with which to carry out the study. Examples are—

(a) The loading of unfired ware into kilns in a pottery. A change in method might bring increased productivity of plant and labour, but there may be technical reasons why a change should not be made. This calls for the advice of a specialist in ceramics.

(b) A machine tool constituting a bottleneck in production is known to be running at a speed below that at which the high-speed cutting tools will operate effectively. Can it be speeded up, or is the machine itself not robust enough to take the faster cut? This is a problem for the machine-tool expert.

3. **Human reactions** are among the most important factors to be taken into consideration, since mental and emotional reactions to investigation and changes of method have to be anticipated. Experience of local personnel and local conditions, and awareness of what has been mentioned in Chapter 6 in this respect, should reduce the difficulties. Trade union officials, workers' representatives and the operatives themselves should be instructed in the general principles and objectives of method study. If, however, the study of a particular job appears to be leading to unrest or ill-feeling, **leave it alone,** however promising it may be from the economic point of view. If other jobs are tackled successfully and can be seen by all to benefit the people working on them, opinions will change and it will be possible, in time, to go back to the original choice.

THE FIELD OF CHOICE

The range of jobs which may be tackled by method study in any factory or other place where materials are moved or manual work is carried on (including routine office work) is usually very wide. Table 8 gives the general field of choice, starting from the most comprehensive investigation covering, possibly, the whole operation of the plant and working down to the study of the movements of the individual worker. Beside each type of job are listed the recording techniques with which it may be tackled. It should be pointed out that, in the course of a single investigation, two or more of these techniques may be used. These techniques will be described in subsequent chapters.

When selecting a job for method study it will be found helpful to have a standardised list of points to be covered. This prevents factors from being overlooked and enables the suitability of different jobs to be easily compared. A sample list[1] is given below which is fairly full, but lists should be adapted to individual needs.

1. *Product and operation.*
2. *Person who proposes investigation.*
3. *Reason for proposal.*
4. *Suggested limits of investigation.*
5. *Particulars of the job.*

 (a) How much is[2] (many are) produced or handled per week?

 (b) What percentage (roughly) is this of the total produced or handled in the shop or plant?

 (c) How long will the job continue?

 (d) Will more or less be required in future?

 (e) How many operatives are employed on the job—
 (i) directly?
 (ii) indirectly?

 (f) How many operatives are there in each grade and on each rate of pay?

 (g) What is the average output per operative (per team) per day?

 (h) What is the daily output compared with the output over a shorter period? (e.g. an hour)

 (i) How is payment made? (team work, piecework, premium bonus, time rate, etc.)

 (j) What is the daily output—
 (i) of the best operative?
 (ii) of the worst operative?

 (k) When were production standards set?

 (l) Has the job any especially unpleasant or injurious features? Is it unpopular (a) with workers? (b) with supervisors?

---

[1] This list has been adapted from one given in Anne G. Shaw: *The purpose and practice of motion study* (Buxton (United Kingdom), Columbine Press, 2nd ed., 1960).

[2] For bulk materials measured in tons, pounds, feet, kilograms, metres, etc.

Table 8. Typical industrial problems and appropriate method study techniques

Type of job	Examples	Recording technique
Complete sequence of manufacture	Manufacture of an electric motor from raw material to dispatch. Transformation of thread into cloth from preparation to inspection. Receipt, packing and dispatch of fruit.	Outline process chart Flow process chart Flow diagram
Factory layout: movement of materials	Movements of a diesel engine cylinder head through all machining operations. Movements of grain between milling operations.	Outline process chart Flow process chart—material type Flow diagram Travel chart Models
Factory layout: movement of workers	Labourers servicing spinning machinery with bobbins. Cooks preparing meals in a restaurant kitchen.	Flow process chart—man type String diagram Travel chart
Handling of materials	Putting materials into and taking them out of stores. Loading lorries with finished products.	Flow process chart—material type Flow diagram String diagram
Workplace layout	Light assembly work on a bench. Typesetting by hand.	Flow process chart—man type Two-handed process chart Multiple activity chart Simo chart Cyclegraph Chronocyclegraph
Gang work or automatic machine operation	Assembly line. Operator looking after semi-automatic lathe.	Multiple activity chart Flow process chart—equipment type
Movements of operatives at work	Females operatives on short-cycle repetition work. Operations demanding great manual dexterity.	Films Film analysis Simo chart Memotion photography Micromotion analysis

6. *Equipment.*

   (a) What is the approximate cost of plant and equipment?

   (b) What is the present machine utilisation index?[1]

7. *Layout.*

   (a) Is the existing space allowed for the job enough?

   (b) Is extra space available?

   (c) Does the space already occupied need reducing?

8. *Product.*

   (a) Are the frequent design changes causing modifications?

   (b) Can the product be altered for easier manufacture?

   (c) What quality is demanded?

   (d) When and how is the product inspected?

[1] Machine utilisation index = the ratio of Machine Running Time to Machine Available Time.

9. *What savings or increase in productivity may be expected from a method improvement?*

   (a) Through reduction in the work content of the product or process.

   (b) Through better machine utilisation.

   (c) Through better use of labour.

(Figures may be given in money, man-hours or machine-hours or as a percentage).

     Item 4 deserves some comment. It is important to set clearly defined limits to the scope of the investigation. Method study investigations so often reveal scope for even greater savings that there is a strong temptation to go beyond the immediate objective. This should be resisted, and any jobs shown up as offering scope for big improvements through method study should be noted and tackled separately.

     Such a list will prevent the work study man from going first for a small bench job which will entail a detailed study of the worker's movements and yield a saving of a few seconds per operation, unless the job is one that is being done by a large number of operatives, so that the total saving will significantly affect the operating costs of the factory. It is no use playing around with split seconds and inches of movement when a great waste of time and effort is taking place as a result of bad shop layout and the handling of heavy materials.

     Finally, remember the adage: "Do not use a spoon when a steam shovel is needed."

     Subject to the considerations listed above, tackle first the job most likely to have the greatest over-all effect on the productivity of the enterprise as a whole.

Chapter 8
Record, examine, develop

1. Recording the facts

The next step in the basic procedure, after selecting the work to be studied, is to **record all** the facts relating to the existing method. The success of the whole procedure depends on the accuracy with which the facts are recorded, because they will provide the basis of both the critical examination and the development of the improved method. It is therefore essential that the record be clear and concise.

The usual way of recording facts is to write them down. Unfortunately, this method is not suited to the recording of the complicated processes which are so common in modern industry. This is particularly so when an exact record is required of every minute detail of a process or operation. To describe exactly everything that is done in even a very simple job which takes perhaps only a few minutes to perform would probably result in several pages of closely written script, which would require careful study before anyone reading it could be quite sure that he had grasped all the detail.

To overcome this difficulty other techniques or "tools" of recording have been developed, so that detailed information may be recorded precisely and at the same time in standard form, in order that it may be readily understood by all method study men, in whatever factory or country they may be working.

The most commonly used of these recording techniques are **charts** and **diagrams.** There are several different types of standard chart available, each with its own special purposes. They will be described in turn later in this chapter and in subsequent chapters. For the present it will be sufficient to note that the charts available fall into two groups—

(a) those which are used to record a process **sequence,** i.e. a series of events or happenings **in the order in which they occur,** but which do not depict the events to scale; and

(b) those which record events, also in sequence, but **on a time scale,** so that the interaction of related events may be more easily studied.

The names of the various charts were listed in table 8 in the last chapter against the types of job for which they are most suitable. They are shown again in table 9, which lists them in the two groups given above, and also lists the types of **diagram** commonly used.

87

Table 9.   The most commonly used method study charts and diagrams

A. *CHARTS* indicating process SEQUENCE
Outline Process Chart
Flow Process Chart—Man Type
Flow Process Chart—Material Type
Flow Process Chart—Equipment Type
Two-Handed Process Chart

B. *CHARTS* using a TIME SCALE
Multiple Activity Chart
Simo Chart

C. *DIAGRAMS* indicating movement
Flow Diagram
String Diagram
Cyclegraph
Chronocyclegraph
Travel Chart

Diagrams are used to indicate movement more clearly than charts can do. They usually do not show all the information recorded on charts, which they supplement rather than replace. Among the diagrams is one which has come to be known as the Travel Chart, but despite its name it is classed as a diagram.

PROCESS CHART SYMBOLS

The recording of the facts about a job or operation on a process chart is made much easier by the use of a set of five standard[1] symbols, which together serve to represent all the different types of activity or event likely to be encountered in any factory or office. They thus serve as a very convenient, widely understood type of shorthand, saving a lot of writing and helping to show clearly just what is happening in the sequence being recorded.

The two principal activities in a process are **operation** and **inspection.** These are represented by the following symbols:

⭕ *OPERATION*

> **Indicates the main steps in a process, method or procedure. Usually the part, material or product concerned is modified or changed during the operation**

---

[1] The symbols used throughout this book are those recommended by the American Society of Mechanical Engineers and adopted in the B.S. *Glossary,* op. cit. There is another set of symbols still in fairly common use, an abbreviated form of the set originated by F. B. and L. M. Gilbreth. It is recommended that the ASME symbols should be adopted in preference to those of Gilbreth.

It will be seen that the symbol for an operation is also used when charting a procedure, as for instance a clerical routine. An operation is said to take place when information is given or received, or when planning or calculating takes place.

INSPECTION

Indicates an inspection for quality and/or check for quantity

The distinction between these two activities is quite clear—

An **operation** always takes the material, component or service a stage further towards completion, whether by changing its shape (as in the case of a machined part) or its chemical composition (during a chemical process) or by adding or subtracting material (as in the case of an assembly). An operation may equally well be a preparation for any activity which brings the completion of the product nearer.

An **inspection** does not take the material any nearer to becoming a completed product. It merely verifies that an operation has been carried out correctly as to quality and/or quantity. Were it not for human shortcomings, most inspections could be done away with.

Often a more detailed picture will be required than can be obtained by the use of these two symbols alone. In order to achieve this, three more symbols are used—

TRANSPORT

Indicates the movement of workers, materials or equipment from place to place

A **transport** thus occurs when an object is moved from one place to another, except when such movements are part of an operation or are caused by the operative at the work station during an operation or an inspection. This symbol is used throughout this book whenever material is handled on or off trucks, benches, storage bins, etc.

TEMPORARY STORAGE OR DELAY

Indicates a delay in the sequence of events: for example, work waiting between consecutive operations, or any object laid aside temporarily without record until required

89

Examples are work stacked on the floor of a shop between operations, cases awaiting unpacking, parts waiting to be put into storage bins or a letter waiting to be signed.

 PERMANENT STORAGE

Indicates a controlled storage in which material is received into or issued from a stores under some form of authorisation; or an item is retained for reference purposes

A permanent **storage** thus occurs when an object is kept and protected against unauthorised removal.

The difference between a "permanent storage" and a "temporary storage or delay" is that a requisition, chit or other form of formal authorisation is generally required to get an article out of permanent storage but not out of temporary storage.

In this book, for the sake of simplicity, **temporary storage or delay** will be referred to in brief as "delay", and **permanent storage** as just "storage".

Combined Activities. When it is desired to show activities performed at the same time or by the same operative at the same work station, the symbols for those activities are combined, e.g. the circle within the square represents a combined operation and inspection.

THE OUTLINE PROCESS CHART

It is often valuable to obtain a "bird's-eye" view of a whole process or activity before embarking on a detailed study. This can be obtained by using an **outline process chart.**

An outline process chart is a process chart giving an over-all picture by recording in sequence only the main operations and inspections

In an outline process chart, only the principal operations carried out and the inspections made to ensure their effectiveness are recorded, irrespective of who does them and where they are performed. In preparing such a chart, only the symbols for "operation" and "inspection" are necessary.

In addition to the information given by the symbols and their sequence, a brief note of the nature of each operation or inspection is made beside the symbol, and the time allowed for it (where known) is also added.

An example of an outline process chart is given in figure 23. In order that the reader may obtain a firm grasp of the principles involved, the assembly represented on this chart is shown in a sketch (figure 22) and the operations charted are given in some detail below.

EXAMPLE OF AN OUTLINE PROCESS CHART: ASSEMBLING A SWITCH ROTOR[1]

The assembly drawing (figure 22) shows the rotor for a slow make-and-break switch.

Figure 22. Switch rotor assembly

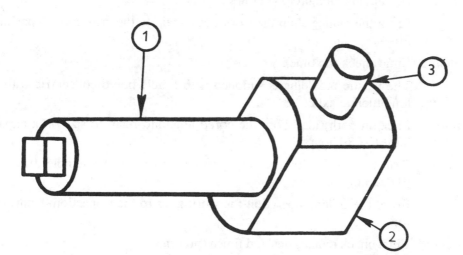

It consists of a spindle (1); a plastic moulding (2); a stop pin (3).

In making an outline process chart it is usually convenient to start with a vertical line down the right-hand side of the page to show the operations and inspections undergone by the principal unit or component of the assembly (or compound in chemical processes)—in this case the spindle. The time allowed per piece in hours is shown to the left of each operation. No specific time is allowed for inspections as the inspectors are on time work.

The brief descriptions of the operations and inspections which would normally be shown alongside the symbols have been omitted so as not to clutter the figure.

The operations and inspections carried out on the spindle which is made from 10 mm diameter steel rod are as follows:

Operation 1 Face, turn, undercut and part off on a capstan lathe (0.025 hours).

Operation 2 Face opposite end on the same machine (0.010 hours).

After this operation the work is sent to the inspection department for—

---

[1] This example is adapted from W. Rodgers: *Methods engineering chart and glossary* (Nottingham (United Kingdom), School of Management Studies Ltd.).

Inspection 1 Inspect for dimensions and finish (no time fixed). From the inspection department the work is sent to the milling section.

Operation 3 Straddle-mill four flats on end on a horizontal miller (0.070 hours).

The work is now sent to the burring bench.

Operation 4 Remove burrs at the burring bench (0.020 hours).

The work is returned to the inspection department for—

Inspection 2 Final inspection of machining (no time).

From the inspection department the work goes to the plating shop for—

Operation 5 Degreasing (0.0015 hours).

Operation 6 Cadmium plating (0.008 hours).

From the plating shop the work goes again to the inspection department for—

Inspection 3 Final check (no time).

The plastic moulding is supplied with a hole bored concentric with the longitudinal axis.

Operation 7 Face on both sides, bore the cored hole and ream to size on a capstan lathe (0.080 hours).

Operation 8 Drill cross-hole (for the stop pin) and burr on two-spindle drill press (0.022 hours).

From the drilling operation the work goes to the inspection department for—

Inspection 4 Final check dimensions and finish (no time).

It is then passed to the finished-part stores to await withdrawal for assembly.

It will be seen from the chart that the operations and inspections on the moulding are on a vertical line next to that of the spindle. This is because the moulding is the first component to be assembled to the spindle. The stop-pin line is set further to the left, and if there were other components they would be set out from right to left in the order in which they were to be assembled to the main item.

Note especially the method of numbering the operations and inspections.

It will be seen that both operations and inspections start from 1. The numbering is continuous from one component to another, starting from the right, to the point where the second component joins the first. The sequence of numbers is then transferred to the next component on the left and continues through its assembly to the first component until the next assembly point, when it is transferred to the component about to be assembled. Figure 23 makes this clear. The assembly of any component to the main component or assembly is shown by a horizontal line from the vertical operation line of the minor component to the proper place in the sequence of operations on the main line. (Sub-assemblies can, of course, be made up of any number of components before being assembled to the principal one; in that case the

Figure 23.   Outline process chart: switch rotor assembly

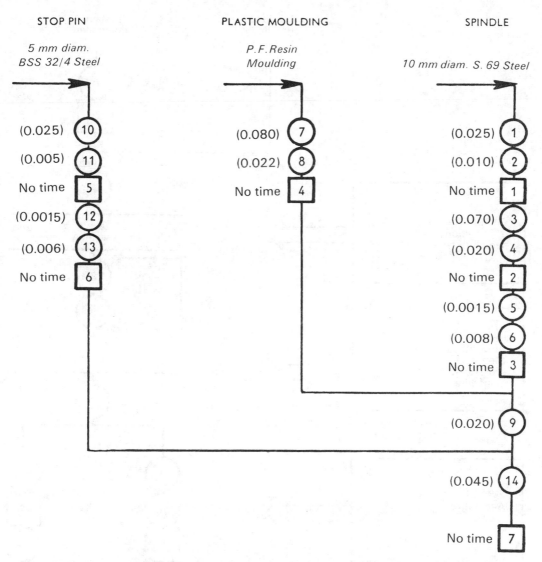

horizontal joins the appropriate vertical line which appears to the right of it.) The assembly of the moulding to the spindle, followed by the operation symbol and number, is clearly shown in the figure.

Operation 9   Assemble the moulding to the small end of the spindle and drill the stop-pin hole right through (0.020 hours).

Once this has been done the assembly is ready for the insertion of the stop pin (made from 5 mm diameter steel rod), which has been made as follows:

Operation 10   Turn 2 mm diameter shank, chamfer end and part off, on a capstan lathe (0.025 hours).

Operation 11   Remove the "pip" on a linisher (0.005 hours).

The work is then taken to the inspection department.

93

Figure 24. *Some charting conventions*

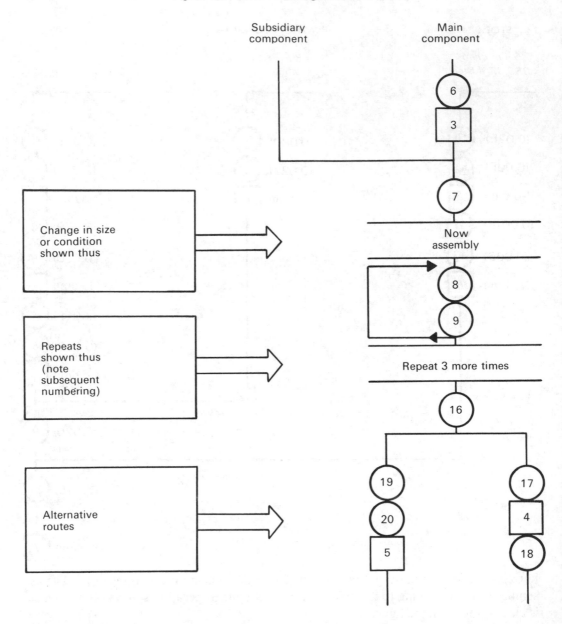

Inspection 5   Inspect for dimensions and finish (no time).

                    After inspection the work goes to the plating shop for—

Operation 12 Degreasing (0.0015 hours).

Operation 13 Cadmium plating (0.006 hours).

                    The work now goes back to the inspection department for—

Inspection 6   Final check (no time).

                    It then passes to the finished-part stores and is withdrawn for—

Operation 14 Stop pin is fitted to assembly and lightly riveted to retain it in position (0.045 hours).

Inspection 7 The completed assembly is finally inspected (no time).

It is then returned to the finished-parts store.

In practice, the outline process chart would bear against each symbol, beside and to the right of it, an abbreviated description of what is done during the operation or inspection. These entries have been left out of figure 23 so that the main sequence of charting may be seen more clearly.

Figure 24 shows some of the conventions used when drawing outline process charts. In this instance the subsidiary component joins the main part after inspection 3, and is assembled to it during operation 7. The assembly undergoes two more operations, numbers 8 and 9, each of which is performed four times in all, as is shown by the "repeat" entry. Note that the next operation after these repeats bears the number 16, not 10.

As was explained earlier in this chapter, the outline process chart is intended to provide a first "bird's-eye" view of the activities involved, for the purpose of eliminating unnecessary ones or combining those that could be done together. It is usually necessary to go into detail greater than the outline process chart provides. In the following pages the flow process chart will be described and its use as a tool of methods improvement illustrated.

FLOW PROCESS CHARTS

Once the general picture of a process has been established, it is possible to go into greater detail. The first stage is to construct a **flow process chart.**

A flow process chart is a process chart setting out the sequence of the flow of a product or a procedure by recording all events under review using the appropriate process chart symbols.

Flow process chart —*man type:* **A flow process chart which records what the worker does.**

Flow process chart —*material type:* **A flow process chart which records how material is handled or treated.**

Flow process chart —*equipment type:* **A flow process chart which records how the equipment is used.**

95

A flow process chart is prepared in a manner similar to that in which the outline process chart is made, but using, in addition to the symbols for "operation" and "inspection", those for "transport", "delay" and "storage".

Whichever type of flow process chart is being constructed, the same symbols are always used and the charting procedure is very similar. (It is customary to use the active voice of verbs for entries on man type charts, and the passive voice on material type and equipment type charts. This convention is more fully explained in Chapter 10, section 3). In fact, it is usual to have only one printed form of chart for all three types, the heading bearing the words "Man/Material/Equipment Type", the two words not required being deleted.

Because of its greater detail, the flow process chart does not usually cover as many operations per sheet as may appear on a single outline process chart. It is usual to make a separate chart for each major component of an assembly, so that the amount of handling, delays and storages of each may be independently studied. This means that the flow process chart is usually a single line.

An example of a material type flow process chart constructed to study what happened when a bus engine was stripped, degreased and cleaned for inspection is given in figure 25. This is an actual case recorded at the workshop of a transport authority in a developing country. After discussing the principles of flow process charting and the means of using them in the next few pages, we shall go on to consider this example in detail. Man type charts are discussed in Chapter 10.

When flow process charts are being made regularly, it is convenient to use printed or stencilled sheets similar to that shown in figure 26. (In charts of this kind the five symbols are usually repeated down the whole length of the appropriate columns. This has not been done in the charts presented in this book, which have been simplified to improve clarity). This also ensures that the studyman does not omit any essential information. In figure 26 the operation just described on the chart in figure 25 is set down again.

Before we go on to discuss the uses of the flow process chart as a means of examining critically the job concerned with a view to developing an improved method, there are some points which must always be remembered in the preparation of process charts. These are important because process charts are the most useful tool in the field of method improvement; whatever techniques may be used later, the making of a process chart is always the first step.

(1) Charting is used for recording because it gives a complete picture of what is being done and helps the mind to understand the facts and their relationship to one another.

(2) The details which appear on a chart must be obtained from **direct observation.** Once they have been recorded on the chart, the mind is freed from the task of carrying them, but they remain available for reference and for explaining the situation to others. Charts must not be based on memory but must be prepared **as the work is observed** (except when a chart is prepared to illustrate a proposed new method).

(3) A high standard of neatness and accuracy should be maintained in preparing fair copies of charts constructed from direct observation. The charts will be used in

Figure 25. *Flow process chart: engine stripping, cleaning and degreasing*

CHART No. *1*   SHEET No. *1*   OF *1*   METHOD: *Original*

PRODUCT: *Bus Engines*   OPERATIVE (S):

                                LOCATION: *Degreasing shop*

PROCESS: *Stripping, degreasing and*   CHARTED BY:

           cleaning used engines   APPROVED BY: DATE:

DISTANCE (m)	SYMBOL	ACTIVITY	TYPE OF ACTIVITY
	▽	In old-engine stores	
	1 ⇨	Picked up engine by crane (electric)	Non-productive
24	2 ⇨	Transported to next crane	,,
	3 ⇨	Unloaded to floor	,,
	4 ⇨	Picked up by second crane (electric)	,,
30	5 ⇨	Transported to stripping bay	,,
	6 ⇨	Unloaded to floor	,,
	①	Engine stripped	Productive
	②	Main components cleaned and laid out	,,
	☐1	Components inspected for wear; inspection report written	Non-productive
3	7 ⇨	Parts carried to degreasing basket	,,
	8 ⇨	Loaded for degreasing by hand-operated crane	,,
1.5	9 ⇨	Transported to degreaser	,,
	10 ⇨	Unloaded into degreaser	,,
	③	Degreased	Productive
	11 ⇨	Lifted out of degreaser by crane	Non-productive
6	12 ⇨	Transported away from degreaser	,,
	13 ⇨	Unloaded to ground	,,
	▽1	To cool	,,
12	14 ⇨	Transported to cleaning benches	,,
	④	All parts completely cleaned	Productive
9	15 ⇨	All cleaned parts placed in one box	Non-productive
	▽2	Awaiting transport	,,
	16 ⇨	All parts except cylinder block and heads loaded on trolley	,,
76	17 ⇨	Transported to engine inspection section	,,
	18 ⇨	Parts unloaded and arranged on inspection table	,,
	19 ⇨	Cylinder block and head loaded on trolley	,,
76	20 ⇨	Transported to engine inspection section	,,
	21 ⇨	Unloaded on ground	,,
237.5	▽3	Stored temporarily awaiting inspection	,,

(Adapted from an original)

Figure 26. Flow process chart—material type: engine stripping, cleaning and degreasing (original method)

FLOW PROCESS CHART				~~MAN~~/MATERIAL/~~EQUIPMENT~~ TYPE			
CHART No. *1*	SHEET No. *1*	OF *1*		S U M M A R Y			
Subject charted: *Used bus engines*			ACTIVITY	PRESENT	PROPOSED	SAVING
			OPERATION ○	*4*		
			TRANSPORT ⇨	*21*		
ACTIVITY: *Stripping, cleaning and degreasing* *prior to inspection*			DELAY D	*3*		
			INSPECTION □	*1*		
			STORAGE ▽	*1*		
METHOD: PRESENT/~~PROPOSED~~			DISTANCE (m)	*237.5*		
LOCATION: *Degreasing Shop*			TIME *(man-min)*	—	—	—

OPERATIVE(S):	CLOCK Nos. *1234*	*571*	COST
			  LABOUR
			  MATERIAL
				—
				—
				—		

CHARTED BY: APPROVED'BY:		DATE:	TOTAL	—	—	—

DESCRIPTION	QTY.	DIST-ANCE (m)	TIME (min)	○	⇨	D	□	▽	REMARKS
Stored in old-engine store									
Engine picked up									*Electric crane*
Transported to next crane		24							" "
Unloaded to floor									
Picked up									" "
Transported to stripping bay		30							" "
Unloaded to floor									
Engine stripped									
Main components cleaned and laid out									
Components inspected for wear; *inspection report written*									
Parts carried to degreasing basket		3							
Loaded for degreasing									
Transported to degreaser		1.5							*Hand crane*
Unloaded into degreaser									
Degreased									
Lifted out of degreaser									" "
Transported away from degreaser		6							" "
Unloaded to ground									
To cool									
Transported to cleaning benches		12							*By hand*
All parts cleaned completely									
All cleaned parts placed in one box		9							*By hand*
Awaiting transport									
All parts except cylinder block and heads *loaded on trolley*									
Transported to engine inspection section		76							*Trolley*
Parts unloaded and arranged on inspection *table*									
Cylinder block and head loaded on trolley									
Transported to engine inspection section		76							*Trolley*
Unloaded to ground									
Stored temporarily awaiting inspection									
TOTAL		237.5		4	21	3	1	1	

(Adapted from the original)

explaining proposals for standardising work or improving methods. An untidy chart will always make a bad impression and may lead to errors.

(4) To maintain their value for future reference and to provide as complete information as possible, all charts should carry a heading giving the following information (see figure 26):

(a) The name of the product, material or equipment charted, with drawing numbers or code numbers.

(b) The job or process being carried out, clearly stating the starting point and the end point, and whether the method is the present or proposed one.

(c) The location in which the operation is taking place (department, factory, site, etc.).

(d) The chart reference number, sheet number and the total number of sheets.

(e) The observer's name and, if desired, that of the person approving the chart.

(f) The date of the study.

(g) A key to the symbols used. This is necessary for the benefit of anyone who may study the chart later and who may have been accustomed to using different symbols. It is convenient to show these as part of a table summarising the activities in the present and proposed methods (see figure 26).

(h) A summary of distance, time and, if desired, cost of labour and material, for comparison of old and new methods.

(5) Before leaving the chart, check the following points:

(a) Have the facts been correctly recorded?

(b) Have any over-simplifying assumptions been made (e.g. is the investigation so incomplete as to be inaccurate)?

(c) Have all the factors contributing to the process been recorded?

So far we have been concerned only with the record stage. We must now consider the steps necessary to **examine critically** the data recorded.

2. Examine critically: the questioning technique

> **The questioning technique is the means by which the critical examination is conducted, each activity being subjected in turn to a systematic and progressive series of questions**

The five sets of activities recorded on the flow process chart fall naturally into two main categories, namely—

☐ those in which something is actually happening to the material or workpiece under consideration, i.e. it is being worked upon, moved or examined; and

☐ those in which it is not being touched, being either in storage or at a standstill owing to a delay.

99

Activities in the first category may be subdivided into three groups:

- ☐ **"MAKE READY" activities** required to prepare the material or workpiece and set it in position ready to be worked on. In the example in figure 25 these are represented by the loading and transporting of the engine to the degreasing shop, transporting it to the cleaning benches, etc.

- ☐ **"DO" operations** in which a change is made in the shape, chemical composition or physical condition of the product. In the case of the example these are the dismantling, cleaning and degreasing operations.

- ☐ **"PUT AWAY" activities** during which the work is moved aside from the machine or workplace. The "put away" activities of one operation may be the "make ready" activities of the next—as, for example, transport between operations from the degreaser to the cleaning benches. Putting parts into storage, putting letters into an "Out" tray and inspecting finished parts are other examples.

It will be seen that, while "make ready" and "put away" activities may be represented by "transport" and "inspection" symbols, "do" operations can only be represented by "operation" symbols.

The aim is obviously to have as high a proportion of "do" operations as possible, since these are the only ones which carry the product forward in its progress from raw material to completion. ("Do" operations in non-manufacturing industries are those operations which actually carry out the activity for which the organisation exists, for example the act of selling in a shop or the act of typing in an office.) These are "productive" activities; all others, however necessary, may be considered as "non-productive" (see figure 25). The first activities to be challenged must therefore be those which are obviously "non-productive", including storages and delays which represent tied-up capital that could be used to further the business.

THE PRIMARY QUESTIONS

The questioning sequence used follows a well established pattern which examines—

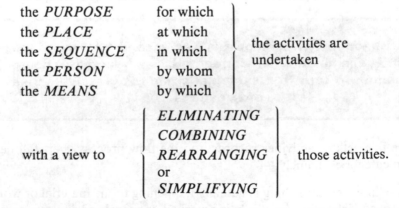

the *PURPOSE*	for which	
the *PLACE*	at which	
the *SEQUENCE*	in which	the activities are undertaken
the *PERSON*	by whom	
the *MEANS*	by which	

with a view to *ELIMINATING* *COMBINING* *REARRANGING* or *SIMPLIFYING* those activities.

In the first stage of the questioning technique, the Purpose, Place, Sequence, Person, Means of every activity recorded is systematically queried, and a reason for each reply is sought.

The primary questions therefore are—

PURPOSE:	**What** is actually done?[1] **Why** is the activity necessary at all?	*ELIMINATE* unnecessary parts of the job.
PLACE:	**Where** is it being done? **Why** is it done at that particular place?	*COMBINE* wherever possible or *REARRANGE* the sequence of operations for more effective results.
SEQUENCE:	**When** is it done? **Why** is it done at that particular time?	
PERSON:	**Who** is doing it? **Why** is it done by that particular person?	
MEANS:	**How** is it being done? **Why** is it being done in that particular way?	*SIMPLIFY* the operation.

THE SECONDARY QUESTIONS

> The secondary questions cover the second stage of the questioning technique, during which the answers to the primary questions are subjected to further query to determine whether possible alternatives of place, sequence, persons and/or means are practicable and preferable as a means of improvement upon the existing method

Thus, during this second stage of questioning (having asked already, about every activity recorded, what is done and why is it done), the method study man goes on to inquire: What else might be done? And, hence: What should be done? In the same way, the answers already obtained on place, sequence, person and means are subjected to further inquiry.

Combining the two primary questions with the two secondary questions under each of the headings "purpose, place", etc., yields the following list, which sets out the questioning technique in full:

PURPOSE:	**What** is done?
	Why is it done?
	What **else** might be done?
	What **should** be done?

---

[1] Many investigators use the question: What is actually achieved?

PLACE:	**Where** is it done?
	Why is it done **there**?
	Where **else** might it be done?
	Where **should** it be done?
SEQUENCE:	**When** is it done?
	Why is it done **then**?
	When **might** it be done?
	When **should** it be done?
PERSON:	**Who** does it?
	Why does **that** person do it?
	Who **else** might do it?
	Who **should** do it?
MEANS:	**How** is it done?
	Why is it done **that** way?
	How **else** might it be done?
	How **should** it be done?

These questions, in the above sequence, must be asked systematically every time a method study is undertaken. They are the basis of successful method study.

EXAMPLE: ENGINE STRIPPING, CLEANING AND DEGREASING

Let us now consider how the method study men who prepared the flow process chart in figure 25 set about examining the record of facts which they had obtained in order to develop a improved method. Before doing so, we shall transfer the same record to a standard flow process chart form (figure 26) with the necessary information on the operation, location, etc., duly filled in.

This form, like all the forms in this book, is designed so that it can be prepared on a standard typewriter. The arrangement of the symbols in the columns is to enable those used most to be closest together.

To help the reader to visualise the operation, a flow diagram showing the layout of the degreasing shop and the path taken by the engine in its journey from the old-engine stores to the engine-inspection section is given in figure 27. It is evident from this that the engine and its parts follow an unnecessarily complicated path.

Examination of the flow process chart shows a very high proportion of "non-productive" activities. There are in fact only four operations and one inspection, while there are 21 transports and three delays. Out of 29 activities, excluding the original storage, only five can be considered as "productive".

Detailed examination of the chart leads to a number of questions. For example, it will be seen that an engine being transported from the old-engine stores has to change cranes in the middle of its journey. Let us apply the questioning technique to these first transports:

Q. **What** is done?

A. The engine is carried part of the way through the stores by one electric crane, is placed on the ground and is then picked up by another which transports it to the stripping bay.

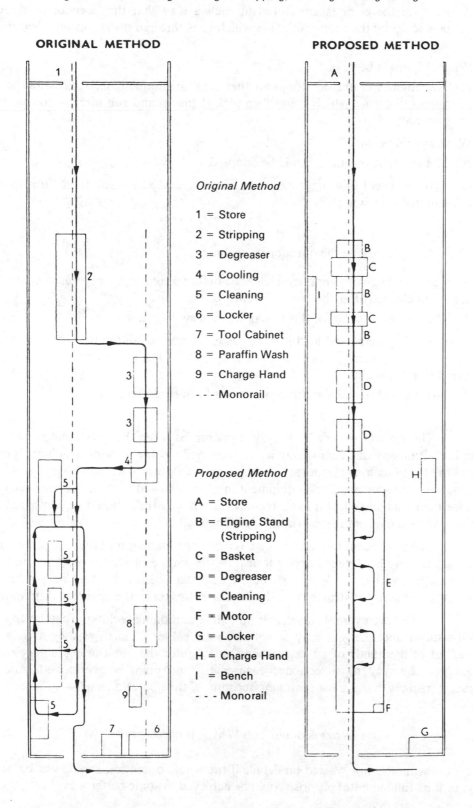

Figure 27. Flow diagram: engine stripping, cleaning and degreasing

Q. **Why** is this done?

A. Because the engines are stored in such a way that they cannot be directly picked up by the monorail crane which runs through the stores and degreasing shop.

Q. What **else** might be done?

A. The engines could be stored so that they are immediately accessible to the monorail crane, which could then pick them up and run directly to the stripping bay.

Q. What **should** be done?

A. The above suggestion should be adopted.

In the event this suggestion was adopted, and as a result three "transports" were eliminated (see figure 28).

Let us continue the questioning technique.

Q. **Why** are the engine components cleaned **before** going to be degreased since they are again cleaned after the grease is removed?

A. The original reason for this practice has been forgotten.

Q. **Why** are they inspected at this stage, when it must be difficult to make a proper inspection of greasy parts and when they will be inspected again in the engine-inspection section?

A. The original reason for this practice has been forgotten.

This answer is very frequently encountered when the questioning technique is applied. On many occasions, activities are carried out for reasons which are important at the time (such as temporary arrangements to get a new shop going quickly in the absence of proper plant and equipment) and are allowed to continue long after the need for them has passed. If no satisfactory reason why they should be continued can be given, such activities must be ruthlessly eliminated.

The next questions which arise refer to the loading into the degreaser. Here it appears to have been necessary to transport the parts 3 metres in order to put them into the degreaser basket. **Why** cannot the degreaser basket be kept near at hand? Cannot the parts be put straight into the degreaser basket as the engine is dismantled?

The above example illustrates how the questioning technique can be applied. The questions and answers may sometimes look rather childish as they are set out above, but in the hands of an experienced investigator the questioning is very rapid. Sticking to the very rigid sequence ensures that no point is overlooked. And, of course, starting with the most searching scrutiny of the operation itself—

What is done? and **Why** is it necessary?

ensures that time is not wasted on details if the whole operation should not be necessary, or if its fundamental purpose could be achieved in some better way.

Figure 28. Flow process chart — material type: engine stripping, cleaning and degreasing (improved method)

FLOW PROCESS CHART				MAN/MATERIAL/EQUIPMENT TYPE				
CHART No. *2* SHEET No. *1* OF *1*				S U M M M A R Y				
Subject charted:				ACTIVITY		PRESENT	PROPOSED	SAVING
Used bus engines				OPERATION ○		4	3	1
				TRANSPORT ⇨		21	15	6
ACTIVITY:				DELAY D		3	2	1
Stripping, degreasing and cleaning prior to inspection				INSPECTION □		1	–	1
				STORAGE ▽		1	1	1
METHOD: PRESENT/PROPOSED				DISTANCE (m)		237.5	150.0	87.5
LOCATION: *Degreasing shop*				TIME *(man-min)*		—	—	—
OPERATIVE(S): CLOCK Nos. *1234*			*571*	COST				
				LABOUR				
CHARTED BY:				MATERIAL				
APPROVED BY: DATE:				TOTAL		—	—	—

DESCRIPTION	QTY.	DIST-ANCE (m)	TIME (min)	SYMBOL ○	⇨	D	□	▽	REMARKS
Stored in old-engine store		—	—						
Engine picked up									*Electric*
Transported to stripping bay		55							*hoist on mono-*
Unloaded on to engine stand									*rail*
Engine stripped									
Transported to degreaser basket		1							*By hand*
Loaded into basket									*Hoist*
Transported to degreaser		1.5							"
Unloaded into degreaser									"
Degreased									
Unloaded from degreaser									"
Transported from degreaser		4.5							"
Unloaded to ground									
Allowed to cool									
Transported to cleaning benches		6							"
All parts cleaned									
All parts collected in special trays		6							
Awaiting transport									
Trays and cylinder block loaded on trolley									
Transported to engine inspection section		76							*Trolley*
Trays slid on to inspection benches and blocks on to platform									
TOTAL		150		3	15	2	—	1	

3. Develop the improved method

There is an old saying that to ask the right question is to be half-way towards finding the right answer. This is especially true in method study. From the very brief example of the use of the questioning sequence given above, it will be seen that once the questions have been asked most of them almost answer themselves. Once the questions—

☐   **What** should be done?

☐   **Where** should it be done?

☐   **When** should it be done?

☐   **Who** should do it?

☐   **How** should it be done?

have been answered, it is the job of the method study man to put his findings into practice.

The first step in doing so is to make a record of the proposed method on a flow process chart, so that it can be compared with the original method and can be checked to make sure that no point has been overlooked. This will also enable a record to be made in the "summary" of the total numbers of activities taking place under both methods, the savings in distance and time which may be expected to accrue from the change and the possible savings in money which will result. The improved method for the example discussed is shown charted in figure 28.

It will be seen from the summary that there have been considerable reductions in the number of "non-productive" activities. The number of "operations" has been reduced from four to three by the elimination of the unnecessary cleaning, and the inspection carried out directly after it has also been eliminated. "Transports" have been reduced from 21 to 15 and the distances involved have also been cut from 237.5 to 150 metres—a saving of over 37 per cent in the travel of each engine. In order not to complicate this example, times of the various activities have not been given; but a study of the two flow process charts will make it evident that a very great saving in the time of operation per engine has been achieved.

No further example of a flow process chart is given in this chapter because flow process charts will be used later in the book in association with other techniques.

Chapter 9
The flow and handling of materials

1. Plant layout

Invariably, in conducting a method study, it becomes desirable at some stage to look critically at the movement of men and materials through the plant or work area and to examine the plant layout. This is so because in many factories either the initial layout was not well thought out or, as the enterprise expanded or changed some of its products or processes, extra machines, equipment or offices were added wherever space could be found. In other cases temporary arrangements may have been made to cope with an emergency situation, such as the sudden increase in demand for a certain product; but then these arrangements remain on a permanent basis even if the situation that provoked them subsequently changes. The net result is that material and workers often have to make long, roundabout journeys in the course of the manufacturing process; this leads to a loss of time and energy without anything being added to the value of the product. Improving plant layout is, therefore, part of the job of the work study specialist.

> **Plant layout is the arrangement of the desired machinery and equipment of a plant, established or contemplated, in the way which will permit the easiest flow of materials, at the lowest cost and with the minimum of handling, in processing the product from the receipt of raw materials to the dispatch of the finished product** [1]

2. Some notes on plant layout

There are four major types of layout, although in practice a combination of two or more may be found in the same plant. These are shown in figure 29 and are as follows:

---

[1] Based on a definition given by R. W. Mallick and A. T. Gaudreau in *Plant layout and practice* (New York, John Wiley, 1966).

Figure 29. Types of layout

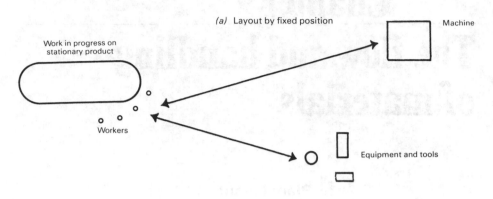

(a) Layout by fixed position

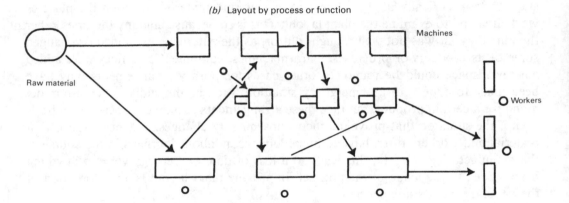

(b) Layout by process or function

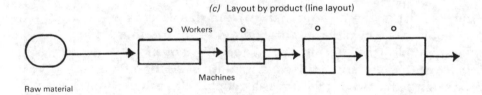

(c) Layout by product (line layout)

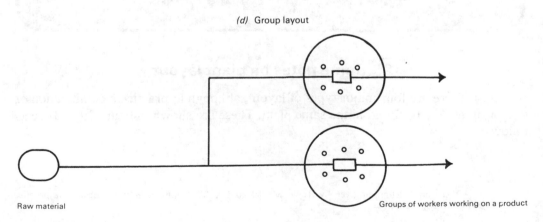

(d) Group layout

(1) Layout by **fixed** position. This arrangement is used when the material to be processed does not travel round the plant but stays in one place: all the necessary equipment and machinery is brought to it instead. This is the case when the product is bulky and heavy and when only a few units are made at a time. Typical examples are shipbuilding and the manufacture of diesel engines or large motors or aircraft construction.

(2) Layout by **process** or **function.** Here all operations of the same nature are grouped together: for example, in the garment industries all the cutting of material is carried out in one area, all the sewing or stitching in another area, all the finishing in a third area, and so on. This layout is usually chosen where a great many products which share the same machinery are being made and where any one product has only a relatively low volume of output. Examples are textile spinning and weaving, maintenance workshops and the garment industries.

(3) Layout by **product,** or **line** layout, sometimes popularly referred to as "mass production". In this layout all the necessary machinery and equipment needed to make a given product is set out in the same area and in the sequence of the manufacturing process. This layout is mainly used where there is a high demand for one or several products that are more or less standardised. Typical examples are soft drinks bottling, car assembly and some canning operations.

(4) Layout making possible **group production methods,** or **group** layout. Recently, in an effort to increase job satisfaction, several enterprises have arranged their operations in a new way, with a group of workers working together on a given product or on a part of a product and having at hand all the machinery and equipment needed to complete their work. In such cases the workers distribute the work among themselves and usually interchange jobs. Further details of this method of production are given in Chapter 24.

With these various kinds of layout in mind, we may now analyse the flow of materials in the plant. In some situations, rapid changes in output may be realised by switching from one type of layout to another. This is particularly true when a shift is made from a layout by function to a line layout for one or more products of which the output has been increased significantly.

In most cases, however, a careful analysis of the flow is called for before any decision is taken to change a given layout, since this is usually a costly process, and the management has to be convinced that real savings will result before sanctioning the change.

3. Developing a layout

The following steps are taken when a layout for a plant or a work area is designed:

(1) The equipment and machinery needed for processing is determined by the type of product or products.

(2) The number of units of each machine and item of equipment needed to manufacture each product is determined by the volume of expected sales (based on sales forecasts).

(3) The space requirements for machinery are determined by calculating the dimensions of each machine and multiplying by the number of machines needed.

(4) Provision is made for the space needed for materials (both for raw materials and for the storage of finished products), for goods-in-process and for material-handling equipment.

(5) Provision is made for additional space for auxiliary services (washrooms, offices, cafeteria, etc.).

(6) The total space requirement for the plant is determined by adding the space needed for machinery to the space needed for storage and for auxiliary services.

(7) The different departments with their respective areas are so arranged that the most economical flow of work is achieved.

(8) The plan of the building is largely determined by the positioning of working areas, storage areas and auxiliary services.

(9) The size and design of the site is determined by allocating additional space for parking, receiving and shipping and landscaping.

However, a work study man is rarely called upon to make a complete design of a plant, starting from the very basic steps described above. This is more the task of the industrial engineer or the production management specialist. It is more common for the work study man to be faced with a problem of modifying an already existing layout. In this case, the major issue becomes that of determining the best possible flow of work, and several diagrams can be helpful here (see figure 30).[1] The use of any of these diagrams depends on whether the flow is being studied for one product or process or for a number of products and processes performed simultaneously.

DEVELOPING THE FLOW FOR ONE PRODUCT OR PROCESS

To develop a flow for only one product or process, it is customary to use the flow process chart described in the previous chapter, supplementing it with a **flow diagram.** The flow process chart is useful in recording travel distances and the time taken for the various operations. Its value lies in its use as an analytical tool to question the existing method. The flow diagram, on the other hand, is a plan (drawn substantially to scale) of the factory or the work area, correctly indicating the positions of machines and working positions. As a result of on-the-spot observation, the paths of movement of the product or its components are traced, sometimes using the process chart symbols to denote the activities carried out at the various points. For example, from a simple flow diagram drawn in a workshop to represent the movements of the material used in the assembly and welding of legs to frames for the seats of motor buses, it was clear at a glance that there was far too much travelling of material between workplaces. In this particular case, and after the studyman had examined the flow diagrams and flow process charts of these activities, the distance travelled was reduced from 575 to 194 metres.

---

[1] Readers who wish to go into more detail in the area of plant layout are referred to Richard Muther: *Practical plant layout* (New York and London, McGraw-Hill, 1956) and H. B. Maynard (ed.): *Industrial engineering handbook* (New York and London, McGraw-Hill, 3rd ed., 1971).

Figure 30.   Examples of various types of flow between work stations,
including flow in a multi-storey building

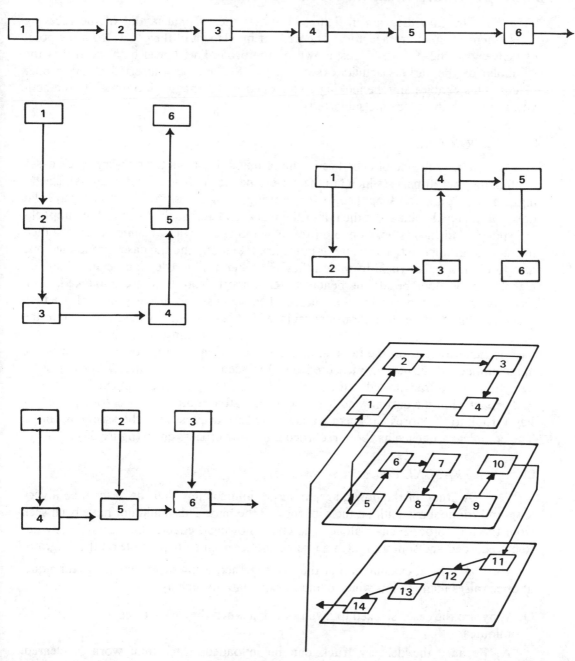

The flow diagram can also be used for the study of movement on several floors of a multi-storey building, as can be seen from the example given in figure 30. Ordinary flow diagrams of each floor can, of course, be made as well.

EXAMPLE OF THE USE OF A FLOW DIAGRAM WITH A FLOW PROCESS CHART: RECEIVING AND INSPECTING AIRCRAFT PARTS[1]

The flow diagram in figure 31 shows the original layout of the receiving department of an aircraft factory. The path of movement of the goods from the point of delivery to the storage bins is shown by the broad line. It will be noticed that the symbols for the various activities (see Chapter 8) have been inserted at the proper places. This enables anyone looking at the diagram to imagine more readily the activities to which the goods are subjected.

☐ *RECORD*

The sequence of activities is one of unloading from the delivery truck cases containing aircraft parts (which are themselves packed individually in cartons), checking, inspecting and marking them before putting them into store. These cases are slid down an inclined plane from the tail of the truck, slid across the floor to the "unpacking space" and there stacked one on top of another to await opening. They are then unstacked and opened. The delivery notes are taken out and the cases are loaded one at a time on a hand truck, by which they are taken to the reception bench. They are placed on the floor beside the bench. After a short delay they are unpacked; each piece is taken out of its carton and checked against the delivery note. It is then replaced in its carton; the cartons are replaced in the case and the case is moved to the other side of the receiving bench to await transport to the inspection bench. Here the case is again placed on the floor until the inspectors are ready for it. The parts are again unpacked, inspected, measured and replaced as before. After a further short delay the case is transported to the marking bench. The parts are unpacked, numbered and repacked in the cartons and the case, which after another delay is transported by hand truck to the stores and there placed in bins to await issue to the assembly shops. The complete sequence has been recorded on a flow process chart (figure 32).

☐ *EXAMINE critically*

A study of the flow diagram shows immediately that the cases take a very long and roundabout path on their journey to the bins. This could not have been seen from the flow process chart alone. The chart, however, enables the various activities to be recorded and summarised in a manner not conveniently possible on the diagram.

A critical examination of the two together, using the questioning technique, at once raises many points which demand explanation, such as:

Q. Why are the cases stacked to await opening when they have to be unstacked in 10 minutes?

A. Because the delivery truck can be unloaded faster than work is cleared.

Q. What else could be done?

A. The work could be cleared faster.

---

[1] This example has been taken, with some adaptation, from *Simplification du travail* (the French version of a handbook produced by the North American Aviation Company Inc., Texas Division) (Paris, Editions Hommes et Techniques, 2nd ed., 1950).

Figure 31.   Flow diagram: inspecting and marking incoming parts (original method)

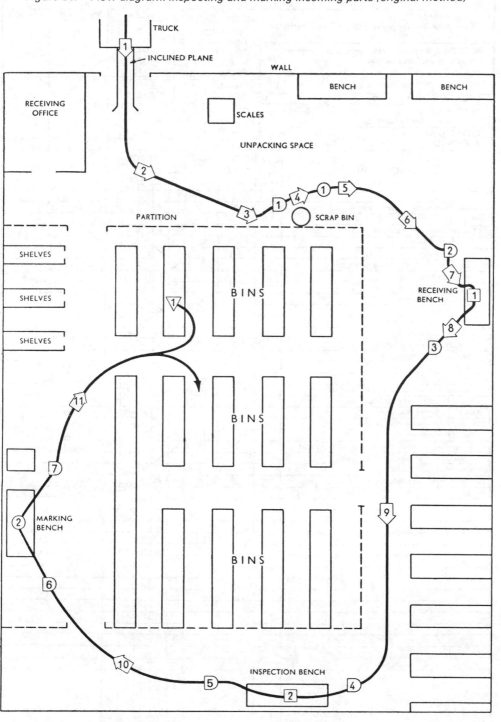

Figure 32.   Flow process chart: inspecting and marking incoming parts (original method)

FLOW PROCESS CHART				MAN/MATERIAL/EQUIPMENT TYPE			
CHART No. 3 SHEET No. 1 OF 1				S U M M A R Y			
Subject charted:				ACTIVITY	PRESENT	PROPOSED	SAVING
Case of BX 487 Tee-pieces (10 per case in cartons)				OPERATION ○	2		
				TRANSPORT ⇨	11		
ACTIVITY: Receive, check, inspect and number				DELAY D	7		
tee-pieces and store in case				INSPECTION □	2		
				STORAGE ▽	1		
METHOD: PRESENT/PROPOSED				DISTANCE (m)	56.2		
LOCATION: Receiving Dept.				TIME (man-h.)	1.96		
OPERATIVE(S): CLOCK No.				COST			
See Remarks column				LABOUR	$10.19		
CHARTED BY: DATE:				MATERIAL	—		
APPROVED BY: DATE:				TOTAL	$10.19		

DESCRIPTION	QTY. 1 case	DIST-ANCE (m)	TIME (min)	○	⇨	D	□	▽	REMARKS
Lifted from truck: placed on inclined plane		1.2							2 labourers
Slid on inclined plane		6	10						2 ,,
Slid to storage and stacked		6							2 ,,
Await unpacking		—	30						
Case unstacked		—							
Lid removed: delivery note taken out		—	5						2 ,,
Placed on hand truck		1							
Trucked to reception bench		9	5						2 ,,
Await discharge from truck		—	10						
Case placed on bench		1	2						2 ,,
Cartons taken from case: opened: checked									
replaced contents		—	15						Storekeeper
Case loaded on hand truck		1	2						2 labourers
Delay awaiting transport		—	5						
Trucked to inspection bench		16.5	10						1 labourer
Await inspection		—	10						Case on truck
Tee-pieces removed from case and cartons:		1	20						Inspector
inspected to drawing: replaced									
Await transport labourer		—	5						Case on truck
Trucked to numbering bench		9	5						1 labourer
Await numbering		—	15						Case on truck
Tee-pieces withdrawn from case and cartons:		—	15						Stores labourer
numbered on bench and replaced									
Await transport labourer		—	5						Case on truck
Transported to distribution point		4.5	5						1 labourer
Stored									
TOTAL		56.2	174	2	11	7	2	1	

Q. Why are the reception, inspection and marking points so far apart?

   A. Because they happen to have been put there.

Q. Where else could they be?

   A. They could be all together.

Q. Where should they be?

   A. Together at the present reception point.

Q. Why does the case have to go all round the building to reach the stores?

   A. Because the door of the stores is located at the opposite end from the delivery point.

No doubt the reader who examines the flow diagram and the flow process chart carefully will find many other questions to ask. There is evidently much room for improvement. This is a real-life example of what happens when a series of activities is started without being properly planned. Examples with as much waste of time and effort can be found in factories all over the world.

☐   *DEVELOP the improved method*

The solution arrived at by the work study men in this factory can be seen in figures 33 and 34. It is clear that among the questions they asked were those suggested above, because it will be seen that the case is now slid down the inclined plane from the delivery truck and put straight on a hand truck. It is transported straight to the "Unpacking space", where it is opened while still on the truck and the delivery note is taken out. It is then transported to the reception bench, where, after a short delay, it is unpacked and the parts are put on the bench. The parts are counted and checked against the delivery note. The inspection and numbering benches have now been placed beside the reception bench so that the parts can be passed from hand to hand for inspection, measuring and then numbering. They are finally replaced in their cartons and repacked in the case, which is still on the truck.

It is evident that the investigators were led to ask the same question as we asked, namely: "Why does the case have to go all round the building to reach the stores?" Having received no satisfactory answer, they decided to make a new doorway into the stores opposite the benches, so that the cases could be taken in by the shortest route.

It will be seen from the summary on the flow process chart (figure 34) that the "inspections" have been reduced from two to one, the "transports" from eleven to six and the "delays" (or temporary storages) from seven to two. The distance travelled has been reduced from 56.2 to 32.2 metres.

The number of man-hours involved has been calculated by multiplying the time taken for each item of activity by the number of workers involved, e.g. "trucked to reception bench" = 5 minutes × 2 labourers = 10 man-minutes. Delays are not included as they are caused by operatives being otherwise occupied. In the improved method the inspector and stores labourer are considered to be working simultaneously on inspecting and numbering respectively, and the 20 minutes therefore becomes 40 man-minutes. Labour cost is reckoned at an average of US$ 5.20 per hour for all labour. The cost of making a new doorway is not included, since it will be spread over many other products as well.

Figure 33.   Flow diagram: inspecting and marking incoming parts (improved method)

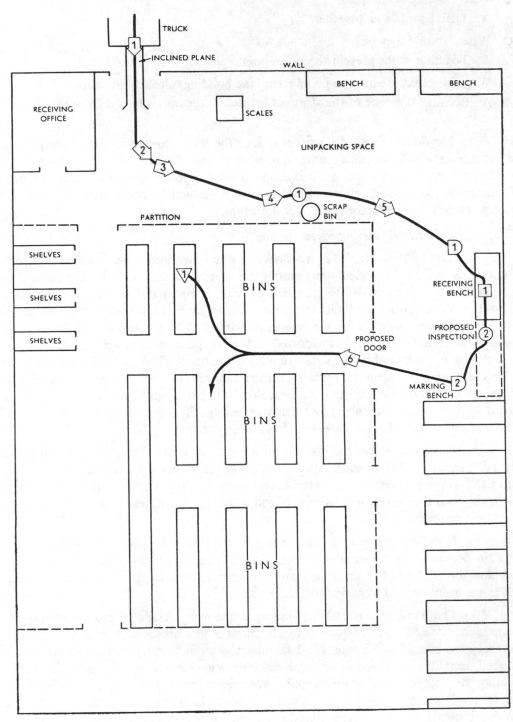

Figure 34. Flow process chart: inspecting and marking incoming parts (improved method)

FLOW PROCESS CHART				MAN/MATERIAL/EQUIPMENT TYPE				
CHART No. 4 SHEET No. 1 OF 1				S U M M A R Y				
Subject charted:				ACTIVITY		PRESENT	PROPOSED	SAVING
Case of BX 487 tee-pieces (10 per case in cartons)				OPERATION ◯		2	2	—
				TRANSPORT ⇨		11	6	5
ACTIVITY: Receive, check, inspect and number				DELAY D		7	2	5
tee-pieces: store in case				INSPECTION □		2	1	1
				STORAGE ▽		1	1	—
METHOD: PRESENT/PROPOSED				DISTANCE (m)		56.2	32.2	24
LOCATION: Receiving Dept.				TIME (man-h.)		1.96	1.16	0.80
OPERATIVE(S) CLOCK No.				COST per case				
See Remarks column				LABOUR		$10.19	$6.03	$4.16
CHARTED BY: DATE:				MATERIAL		—	—	—
APPROVED BY: DATE:				TOTAL		$10.19	$6.03	$4.16

DESCRIPTION	QTY. 1 case	DIST-ANCE (m)	TIME (min)	◯	⇨	D	□	▽	REMARKS
Crate lifted from truck: placed on inclined plane		1.2							2 labourers
Slid on inclined plane		6	5						2 ,,
Placed on hand truck		1							2 ,,
Trucked to unpacking space		6	5						1 labourer
Lid taken off case		—	5						1 ,,
Trucked to receiving bench		9	5						1 ,,
Await unloading		—	5						
Cartons taken from case: opened and tee-pieces placed on bench: counted and inspected to drawing		—	20						Inspector
Numbered and replaced in case									Stores labourer
Await transport labourer		—	5						
Trucked to distribution point		9	5						1 labourer
Stored		—	—						
TOTAL		32.2	55	2	6	2	1	1	

117

DEVELOPING THE FLOW FOR A NUMBER OF PRODUCTS OR PROCESSES

If several products are being made or several processes are being carried out at the same time, another type of chart is used to determine the ideal placing of the machinery or operations. This is the **cross chart.**

As can be seen from figure 35, the cross chart is drawn up by listing the various operations (or machinery) through which the different products pass at the various stages of production, on both the horizontal and vertical dimensions of the chart. The example in figure 35 illustrates the use of the cross chart for a company making decorated metal products. In this case, the company is producing 70 products, each of which passes through some of the operations indicated.

To complete this chart, take one product at a time and enter its sequence of manufacturing in the appropriate square on the chart. If a product moves from "Form" to "Normalise", a stroke is made in the square "Form/Normalise". If it subsequently moves from "Normalise" to "Plate", a stroke is entered in the corresponding square, and so on until the whole sequence of operations for that particular product is entered. The same process is then repeated for each of the other 70 products. The completed cross chart will appear as in figure 35.

The next step is to decide which operations should be placed adjacent to each other. From the chart it is clear that 27 products out of 70 (i.e. 39 per cent of the products) pass directly from "Form" to "Pack and ship". These two operations should therefore be adjacent. Similarly, all 22 products that were subjected to plating passed from "Plate" to "Coat" and from "Coat" to "Polish". Hence, these three operations should follow each other in sequence. By following the same line of reasoning it is possible to reach the preferred sequence of operations.

A variation on this technique is to complete the cross chart by taking a sample of the most frequently produced items. If the plant is producing over 100 different items, it may become cumbersome to follow the method indicated above. However, investigation may reveal that, say, 15 or 20 items account for possibly 80 per cent of the production volume. The sequence of operations of these items would then be entered on the cross chart, and the flow determined in the same way as that described above.

VISUALISING THE LAYOUT

Once the dimensions and the relative position of machinery, storage facilities and auxiliary services have been determined, it is advisable to make a visual presentation of the proposed layout before proceeding with the actual rearrangement of the workplace, which may be a costly operation. This can be done by the use of "templates", or pieces of cardboard cut out to scale. Different coloured cards may be used to indicate different items of equipment, such as machines, storage racks, benches or material-handling equipment. When positioning these templates, make sure that gangways are wide enough to allow the free movement of material-handling equipment and goods-in-process.

Alternatively, scale models may be used to provide a three-dimensional display of the layout. Various types of model for many well-known items of machinery and equipment are readily available on the market and are particularly useful for training purposes.

Figure 35. Developing the flow for a number of products, using the cross chart

To → / From ↓	Form	Normalise	Machine	Burr/trim	Paint	Plate	Coat	Polish	Wrap	Pack and ship	Total
Form		14	8	6	14				1	27	70
Normalise			4		17	1					18
Machine				3	2	2				1	8
Burr/trim					11			1	3	2	10
Paint				1		19		13	2		46
Plate							22				22
Coat								22			22
Polish					2				33	1	36
Wrap										39	39
Pack and ship											0
Total	0	18	8	10	46	22	22	36	39	70	

Source: Taken from Richard Muther: "Plant layout", in H. B. Maynard: *Industrial engineering handbook* (New York and London, McGraw-Hill, 3rd ed. 1971), and used by kind permission of the McGraw-Hill Book Company.

4. The handling of materials

A good deal of time and effort is often expended in moving material from one place to another in the course of processing. This handling is costly and adds nothing to the value of the product. In essence, therefore, there should ideally be **no handling** at all. Unfortunately this is not possible. A more realistic aim would be to move material by the most appropriate methods and equipment at the lowest possible cost and with regard to safety. This aim may be met by—

☐   eliminating or reducing handling;

☐   improving the efficiency of handling;

☐   making the correct choice of material-handling equipment.

ELIMINATING OR REDUCING HANDLING

There is often ample scope for eliminating or reducing handling. In practice, it becomes obvious that there is a need to improve an existing situation when certain symptoms are observed, e.g. too much loading and unloading, repeated manual handling of heavy weights, material travelling considerable distances, non-uniform flow of work with congestion in certain areas, frequent damage or breakage resulting from handling, and so on. These are some of the most frequent phenomena that invite the intervention of the work study specialist. The approach to be followed here is similar to the traditional method study approach, using outline and flow process charts and flow diagrams and asking the same questions as to "where, when, who, how" and, above all, "why" this handling is done.

However, such a study may frequently have to be preceded by or carried out in conjunction with a study of the layout of the working area, in order to reduce movement to a minimum.

IMPROVING THE EFFICIENCY OF HANDLING

The observance of certain precepts can improve the efficiency of handling. These precepts are—

(1) Increase the size or number of units being handled at any one time. If necessary, review product design and packaging to see if you can achieve this result more readily.

(2) Increase the speed of handling if this is possible and economical.

(3) Let gravity work for you as much as possible.

(4) Have enough containers, pallets, platforms, boxes, etc., available in order to make transportation easier.

(5) Give preference in most cases to material-handling equipment that lends itself to a variety of uses and applications.

(6) Try to ensure that materials move in straight lines as much as possible, and ensure that gangways are kept clear.

MAKING THE CORRECT CHOICE OF HANDLING EQUIPMENT

The work study man should be aware of the different kinds and types of material-handling equipment. Although there are literally hundreds of various types, these may be classified in four major categories.

☐ *CONVEYORS*

Conveyors are useful for moving material between two fixed work stations, either continuously or intermittently. They are mainly used for continuous or mass production operations—indeed, they are suitable for most operations where the flow is more or less steady. Conveyors may be of various types, with either rollers, wheels or belts to help to move the material along: these may be power-driven or may roll freely. The decision to provide conveyors must be taken with care, since they are usually costly to install; moreover, they are less flexible and, where two or more converge, it is necessary to co-ordinate the speeds at which the two conveyors move.

☐ *INDUSTRIAL TRUCKS*

Industrial trucks are more flexible in use than conveyors since they can move between various points and are not permanently fixed in one place. They are therefore most suitable for intermittent production and for handling various sizes and shapes of material. There are many types of truck—petrol-driven, electric, hand-powered, and so on. Their greatest advantage lies in the wide range of attachments available; these increase the trucks' ability to handle various types and shapes of material.

☐ *CRANES AND HOISTS*

The major advantage of cranes and hoists is that they can move heavy material through overhead space. However, they can usually serve only a limited area. Here again, there are several types of crane and hoist, and within each type there are various loading capacities. Cranes and hoists may be used both for intermittent and for continuous production.

☐ *CONTAINERS*

These are either "dead" containers (e.g. cartons, barrels, skids, pallets) which hold the material to be transported but do not move themselves, or "live" containers (e.g. wagons, wheelbarrows). Handling equipment of this kind can both contain and move the material, and is usually operated manually.

Figure 36 shows some types of material-handling equipment.

The choice of material-handling equipment is not easy. In several cases the same material may be handled by various items of equipment (see figure 37). Nor does the great diversity of equipment available make the problem any easier. In several cases, however, the nature of the material to be handled does narrow the choice.

Among the most important factors to be taken into consideration when choosing material-handling equipment are the following:

121

Figure 36.   Different types of material-handling equipment

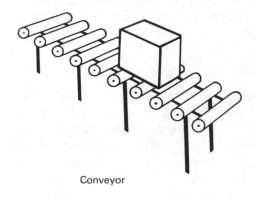

Conveyor

Fork-lift industrial truck

Crane

Hoist

CONTAINERS

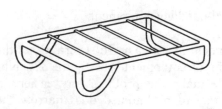

Skid ("dead" container)

Trolley for ceramics or pastries
("live" container)

Figure 37.   Different possibilities of handling the same object

(1) **Properties of the material.** Whether it is solid, liquid or gas, and in what size, shape and weight it is to be moved, are important considerations and can already lead to a preliminary elimination from the range of available equipment under review. Similarly, if a material is fragile, corrosive or toxic this will imply that certain handling methods and containers will be preferable to others.

(2) **Layout and characteristics of the building.** Another restricting factor is the availability of space for handling. Low-level ceilings may preclude the use of hoists or cranes, and the presence of supporting columns in awkward places can limit the size of the material-handling equipment. If the building is multi-storeyed, chutes, or ramps for industrial trucks, may be used. Finally, the layout itself will indicate the type of production operation (continuous, intermittent, fixed position or group) and can already indicate some items of equipment that will be more suitable than others.

(3) **Production flow.** If the flow is fairly constant between two fixed positions that are not likely to change, fixed equipment such as conveyors or chutes can be successfully used. If, on the other hand, the flow is not constant and the direction changes occasionally from one point to another because several products are being produced simultaneously, moving equipment such as trucks would be preferable.

(4) **Cost considerations.** This is one of the most important considerations. The above factors can help to narrow the range of suitable equipment. Costing can help in taking a final decision. Several cost elements need to be taken into consideration when comparisons are made between various items of equipment that are all capable of handling the same load. There is the initial cost of the equipment, from which one can derive the investment cost in terms of interest payment (i.e. if the company has to borrow money to buy the equipment) or opportunity costs (i.e. if the company possesses the funds and does not have to borrow, but the purchase of the equipment would deprive it of an opportunity to invest the funds at a certain rate of return). From the cost of the equipment one can also calculate the depreciation charges per year, to which will be added other charges such as insurance, taxes and additional overheads. Apart from these fixed charges, there are also operating costs, such as the cost of operating personnel, power, maintenance and supervision. By calculating and comparing the total cost for each of the items of equipment under consideration, a more rational decision can be reached on the most appropriate choice.

Chapter 10
Movement of workers in the working area

1. Factory layout and the movements of workers and material

There are many types of activity in which workers move at irregular intervals between a number of points in the working area, with or without material. This situation occurs very often in industry and commerce and even in the home. In manufacturing concerns it occurs when—

bulk material is being fed to or removed from a continuous process, and is stored around the process;

an operative is looking after two or more machines;

labourers are delivering materials to or removing work from a series of machines or workplaces.

Outside manufacturing operations, examples of its occurrence are—

in stores and shops where a variety of materials are being removed from or put away into racks or bins;

in restaurant and canteen kitchens during the preparation of meals;

in control laboratories where routine tests are carried out at frequent intervals.

2. The string diagram

One technique for recording and examining this form of activity is the **string diagram.** It is one of the simplest of the techniques of method study and one of the most useful.

> **The string diagram is a scale plan or model on which a thread is used to trace and measure the path of workers, material or equipment during a specified sequence of events**

The string diagram (see figure 38) is thus a special form of flow diagram, in which a string or thread is used to measure distance. Because of this it is necessary that the string diagram be drawn correctly to scale, whereas the ordinary flow

Figure 38.   A string diagram

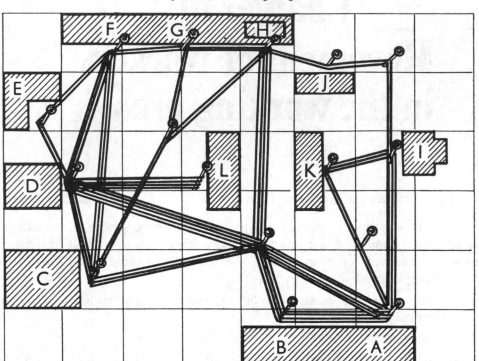

diagram will probably be drawn only approximately to scale, with pertinent distances marked on it so that scaling off is unnecessary. The string diagram is started in exactly the same way as all other method studies: by recording all the relevant facts from direct observation. Like the flow diagram, it will most often be used to supplement a flow process chart, the two together giving the clearest possible picture of what is actually being done. As always, the flow process chart will be examined critically in order to make sure that all unnecessary activities are eliminated before a new method is developed.

A string diagram can be used to plot the movements of materials, and this is sometimes done, especially when a work study man wants to find out easily just how far the materials travel. We could have constructed a string diagram for each of the examples in the last chapter, but this was not necessary. The simple flow diagram showed all that was needed, and was quicker to prepare for the circumstances illustrated. The string diagram is most often used, however, for plotting the movements of workers, and it is this application which is considered in the examples given in the present chapter.

The work study man proceeds to follow the worker in whom he is interested as he moves from point to point in doing his job. (If the working area is a fairly small one and he can see the whole of it from one point, he can watch the worker without moving.) The studyman notes methodically each point to which the worker moves and, if the journeys are fairly long, the times of arrival and departure. It will save a good deal of writing if the observer codes the various machines, stores and other points of call by numbers, letters or other means.

Figure 39.   Simple movement study sheet

MOVEMENT STUDY SHEET

CHART No. 1 SHEET No. 1 OF 2   OPERATIVE(S):

OPERATION: Transport biscuit tiles

from inspection to storage bins and   CHARTED BY:

unload into bins   DATE:

LOCATION: Biscuit warehouse   CROSS-REFERENCE: String diagrams

1 and 2

1 TIME DEP.	2 TIME ARR.	3 TIME ELAPSED	4 MOVE TO	5 NOTES
			Inspection bench (I)	
			to Bin 4	
			I 13	
			I 5	
			I 32	
			I 18	

The form of study sheet required is very simple. A sample of the headings required is given in figure 39. Continuation sheets need only give columns 1, 2, 3, 4 and 5.

The recording of movements will continue for as long as the work study man thinks is necessary to obtain a representative picture of the worker's movements, which may be a few hours, a day, or even longer. The studyman must be sure that he has noted **all** the journeys made by the worker and has seen them made enough times to be sure of their relative frequency. Insufficient study may produce a misleading picture, since the work study man may only have watched the worker during a part of the complete cycle of activities when he was using only a few of his various paths of movement. Later in the cycle he may not use these at all but use others a great deal. Once the studyman is satisfied that he has a true picture—which should be checked with the worker concerned to make sure that there is nothing else which is usually done that has not been observed—the string diagram may be constructed.

A scale plan of the working area similar to that required for a flow diagram must be made (the same plan may be used so long as it has been accurately drawn).

127

Machines, benches, stores and all points at which calls are made should be drawn in to scale, together with such doorways, pillars and partitions as are likely to affect paths of movements. The completed plan should be attached to a softwood or composition board, and pins driven into it firmly at every stopping point, the heads being allowed to stand well clear of the surface (by about 1 cm). Pins should also be driven in at all the turning points on the route.

A measured length of thread is then taken and tied round the pin at the starting point of the movements (the inspection bench (I) in figure 38). It is then led around the pins at the other points of call in the order noted on the study sheet until all the movements have been dealt with.

The result is an over-all picture of the paths of movement of the operative, those which are most frequently traversed being covered with the greatest number of strings, the effect being as in figure 38.

It will be seen from the sketch that certain paths—in particular those between A and D, A and H, and D and L—are traversed more frequently than the others. Since most of these points are at a fair distance from one another, the diagram suggests that critical examination is called for, with a view to moving the work points which they represent closer together.

It will be remembered that the thread used was measured before the studyman started to make the diagram. By measuring the length remaining and subtracting this from the total length, the length used can be found. This will represent, to scale, the distance covered by the worker. If two or more workers are studied over the same working area, different coloured threads may be used to distinguish between them.

The **examination** of the diagram and the **development** of the new layout can now proceed on the same lines as with a flow diagram, with templates being used and the pins and templates being moved around until an arrangement is found by which the same operations can be performed with a minimum movement between them. This can be ascertained by leading the thread around the pins in their new positions, starting from the same point and following the same sequence. When the thread has been led around all the points covered by the study, the length left over can again be measured. The difference in length between this and the thread left over from the original study will represent the reduction in distance travelled as a result of the improved layout. The process may have to be repeated several times until the best possible layout (i.e. the layout with which the minimum length of thread is used) is achieved.

The string diagram is a useful aid in explaining proposed changes to management, supervisors and workers. If two diagrams are made, one showing the original layout and one the improved layout, the contrast is often so vivid—particularly if brightly coloured thread is used—that the change will not be difficult to "sell". Workers especially are interested in seeing the results of such studies and discovering how far they have to walk. The idea of reducing one's personal effort appeals to almost everyone!

The following example shows this technique as applied to the movements of labourers storing tiles after inspection.

EXAMPLE OF A STRING DIAGRAM: STORING TILES AFTER INSPECTION

☐ *RECORD*

In the operation studied in this example, "biscuit" tiles (i.e. tiles after first firing and before glazing) are unloaded from kiln trucks on to the bench, where they are inspected. After inspection they are placed on platforms according to size and type. The loaded platforms are taken on hand-lift trucks to the concrete bins where the tiles are stored until required for glazing. The original layout of the store is shown in figure 40.

It was decided to make a study using a string diagram to find out whether the arrangement, which appeared to be a logical one, was in fact the one involving the least transport. Studies were made of a representative number of kiln truck loads. This was because the types of tile on each truck varied somewhat, although 10 cm × 10 cm and 15 cm × 15 cm plain tiles formed by far the largest part of each load.

A form of the type shown in figure 39 above was used for recording the information. Only a portion is shown, since the nature of the record is obvious. (The bin numbers are those shown in figure 40.)

It will be seen that, in this case, times were not recorded. It is more useful to record times when long distances are involved (such as in trucking between departments of a factory).

The string diagram was then drawn up in the manner shown (figure 40). The width of the shaded bands represents the number of threads between any given points and hence the relative amount of movement between them.

☐ *EXAMINE critically*

A study of the diagram shows at once that the most frequent movement is up the 10 cm × 10 cm and 15 cm × 15 cm rows of bins. The bin into which any particular load of tiles is unloaded depends on which are full or empty (tiles are constantly being withdrawn for glazing). Travel in the case of the 10 cm × 10 cm and 15 cm × 15 cm tiles may therefore be anywhere up or down the rows concerned.

It is equally obvious that the "special feature" tiles (used for decorative purposes in comparatively small numbers) are handled only rarely, and are generally placed by the inspectors on one truck and delivered to several bins at once. Deliveries of tiles other than those mentioned are fairly evenly distributed.

☐ *DEVELOP the new layout*

The first step in developing the new layout is to locate the bins containing the most handled tiles as near as possible to the inspection bench and those containing "special feature" tiles as far away as possible. This certainly spoils the tidy sequence and may, for a time, make tiles a little more difficult to find; however, the bins, which have concrete partitions between them about 1 metre high, can carry cards with the contents marked on them. The cards can be seen from a distance, and the arrangement will soon be memorised by the workers. After a number of arrangements had been tried out, the one shown in figure 41 proved to be the most economical of transport time. The distances covered were reduced from 520 to 340 metres, a saving of 35 per cent.

Figure 40.   String diagram: storing tiles (original method)

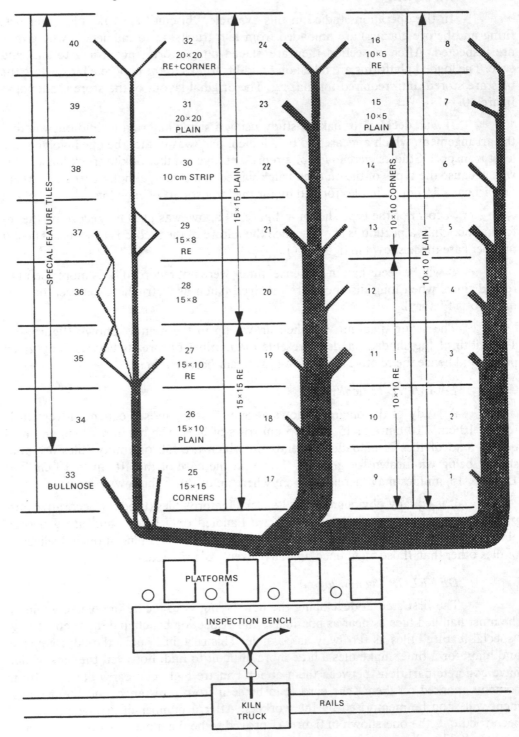

Figure 41. String diagram: storing tiles (improved method)

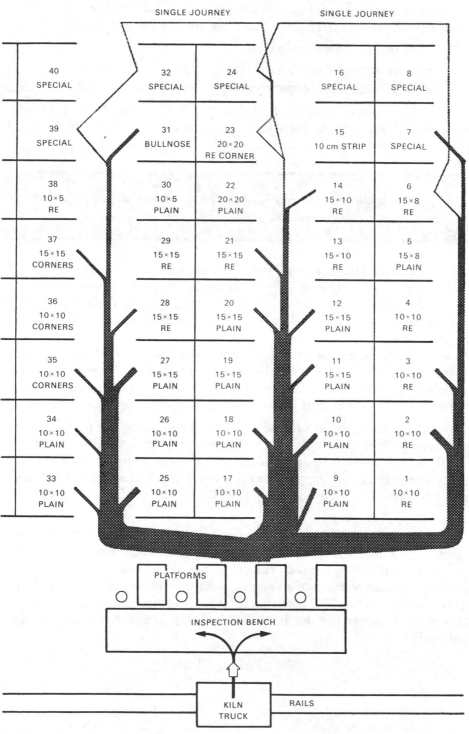

3. The man type flow process chart

In table 9 in Chapter 8 five different types of process chart were listed. The outline process chart was described in Chapter 8, and the two-handed process chart will be dealt with in Chapter 11. The other three are flow process charts:

Flow process chart—man type

Flow process chart—material type

Flow process chart—equipment type

Several examples of material type flow process charts have already been given (figures 26 and 28 in Chapter 8; figures 32 and 34 in Chapter 9). We shall now deal with man type flow process charts.

> **A man type flow process chart is a flow process chart which records what the worker does**

The same techniques as have been used to follow materials through the operations and movements which they undergo can be used to record the movements of a man. Man type flow process charts are frequently used in the study of jobs which are not highly repetitive or standardised. Service and maintenance work, laboratory procedure and much of the work of supervisors and executives can be recorded on charts of this type. Since the charts follow one individual or a group performing the same activities in sequence, the standard flow process chart forms can be used. It is usually essential to attach to the man type flow process chart a sketch showing the path of movement of the worker while he is carrying out the operation charted.

The charting procedure used in compiling a man type flow process chart is almost exactly the same as that used on material type flow process charts. There is one slight difference however—a useful charting convention which helps to distinguish man type charts from the other two flow process charts, and which will be found quite natural in practice.

The definition of the man type chart given above states that it records what the worker **does.** The definitions of the other two flow process charts, however, state that they record (material type) how material is **handled** or **treated,** and (equipment type) how the equipment **is used.** The definitions thus reflect the charting practice, which is to use mainly the **active voice** on man type charts, and mainly the **passive voice** on the other two. The convention, which has been followed on all the flow process charts illustrated in this book, will be clear from the following examples of typical entries:

Flow Process Charts

Man type	Material type
Drills casting	Casting drilled
Carries to bench	Carried to bench
Picks up bolt	(bolt) Picked up
Inspects for finish	Finish inspected

An example of a man type flow process chart applied to hospital activities is given below.

EXAMPLE OF A MAN TYPE FLOW PROCESS CHART: SERVING DINNERS IN A HOSPITAL WARD

☐ *RECORD*

Figure 42 shows the layout of a hospital ward containing 17 beds. When dinners were served by the original method, the nurse in charge of the ward fetched a large tray bearing the first course, together with the plates for the patients, from the kitchen. The food was usually contained in three dishes, two of which held vegetables and the third the main dish. The nurse placed the tray on the table marked "Serving Table" in the diagram. She set the large dishes out on the table, served one plate with meat and vegetables and carried it to bed 1. She returned to the serving table and repeated the operation for the remaining 16 beds. The paths which she followed are shown by the **full** lines in the diagram. When she had served all the patients with the first course, she returned to the kitchen with the tray and the empty dishes, collected the dishes and plates for the second course and returned to the ward. She then repeated the complete operation, replacing the plates emptied by the patients with plates containing their portions of the second course and returning the used plates to the serving table, where she stacked them. Finally she made a tour of the ward, collecting up the empty plates from the second course, and carried everything on the tray back to the kitchen. (To avoid confusion on the diagram, the final collection of empty plates is not shown. In both the original and the improved method the distance covered and the time taken are the same, since it is possible for her to carry several plates at a time and move from bed to bed.) The operation has been recorded in part on the flow process chart in figure 43 but only enough has been shown to demonstrate to the reader the method of recording, which it will be seen is very similar to that used for material type flow process charts, bearing in mind that it is a person and not a product that is being followed. As an exercise the reader may wish to work out the serving cycles for himself on the basis provided by the diagram. The dimensions of the ward are given. It is, of course, possible to complete the man type flow process chart in much greater detail if desired.

☐ *EXAMINE critically*

A critical examination of the flow process chart in conjunction with the diagram suggests that there is considerable room for improvement. The first "Why?" which may come to mind is: "Why does the nurse serve and carry only one plate at a time? How many could she carry?" The answer is almost certainly: "At least two." If she carried two plates at a time, the distance she would have to walk would be almost halved. One of the first questions asked would almost certainly be: "Why is the serving table there, in the middle of the ward?" followed, after one or two other questions, by the key questions: "Why should it stand still? Why can it not move round? Why not a trolley?" This leads straight to the solution which was adopted.

☐ *DEVELOP the new method*

It will be seen from the **broken** line in the diagram (representing the revised path of movement of the nurse when provided with a trolley) and from the flow

133

Figure 42. Flow diagram: serving dinners in a hospital ward

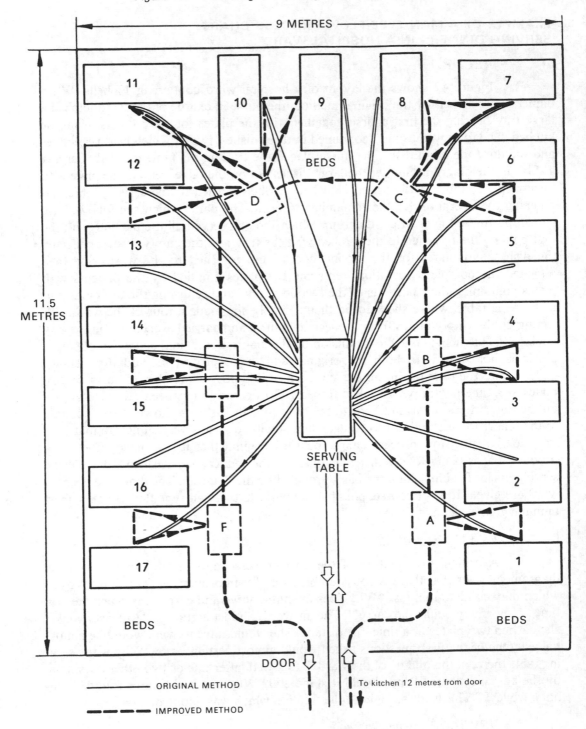

*Figure 43.   Flow process chart—man type: serving dinners
in a hospital ward*

FLOW PROCESS CHART				MAN/~~MATERIAL/EQUIPMENT~~ TYPE					
CHART No. 7 SHEET No. 1 OF 1				S U M M A R Y					
Subject charted: Hospital nurse				ACTIVITY		PRESENT	PROPOSED	SAVING	
				OPERATION ◯		34	18	16	
				TRANSPORT ⇨		60	72	(—12)	
ACTIVITY: Serve dinners to 17 patients				DELAY ◻		—	—	—	
				INSPECTION ◻		—	—	—	
				STORAGE ▽		—	—	—	
METHOD: PRESENT/PROPOSED				DISTANCE (m)		436	197	239	
LOCATION: Ward L				TIME (man-h)		39	28	11	
OPERATIVE(S): CLOCK No.				COST:		—	—	—	
				LABOUR		—	—	—	
CHARTED BY: DATE:				MATERIAL (Trolley)		—	$24	—	
APPROVED BY: DATE: —				TOTAL (Capital)			$24		

DESCRIPTION ORIGINAL METHOD	QTY. (plates)	DIST-ANCE (m)	TIME (min)	◯	⇨	◻	◻	▽	REMARKS
Transports first course and plates —									Awkward load
kitchen to serving table on tray	17	16	.50						
Places dishes and plates on table	17	—	.30						
Serves from three dishes to plate	—	—	.25						
Carries plate to bed 1 and return	1	7.3	.25						
Serves	—	—	.25						
Carries plate to bed 2 and return	1	6	.23						
Serves	—	—	.25						
(Continues until all 17 beds are served. See figure 42 for distances)									
Service completed, places dishes on tray									
and returns to kitchen	—	16	.50						
Total distance and time, first cycle		192	10.71	17	20	—	—	—	
REPEATS CYCLE FOR SECOND COURSE		192	10.71	17	20	—	—	—	
Collects empty second course plates		52	2.0	—	20	—	—	—	
TOTAL		436	23.42	34	60				
IMPROVED METHOD									
Transports first course and plates —									Serving
kitchen to position A — trolley	17	16	.50						trolley
Serves two plates	—	—	.40						
Carries two plates to bed 1; leaves one;		(1.5							
carries one plate from bed 1 to bed 2;	2	{0.6	.25						
returns to position A		1.5)							
Pushes trolley to position B	—	3.0	.12						
Serves two plates	—	—	.40						
Carries two plates to bed 3; leaves one;		1.5							
carries one plate from bed 3 to bed 4;	2	{0.6	.25						
returns to position B		1.5							
(Continues until all 17 beds are served. See figure 32 and note variation at bed 11)									
Returns to kitchen with trolley	—	16	.50						
Total distance and time, first cycle	—	72.5	7.49	9	26				
REPEATS CYCLE FOR SECOND COURSE	—	72.5	7.49	9	26				
Collects empty second course plates	—	52	2.00	—	20				
TOTAL	—	197	16.98	18	72				

process chart that the final solution involves the nurse in serving and carrying two plates at a time (which also saves a small amount of serving time).

The result, as will be seen from the process chart, is a reduction of over 54 per cent in the total distance walked in serving and clearing away the dinners (the saving is 65 per cent if the distance walked in removing the second-course plates, which is the same in both the old and the new methods, is excluded).

What is important here is not so much the reduction in cost, which is very small, as the fact that the nurse's fatigue, resulting from the considerable distance which she had to walk within the ward and while carrying the loaded tray to and from the kitchen, is lessened.

4. The multiple activity chart

We come now to the first of the charts listed in table 9 which use a time scale—the **multiple activity chart.** This is used when it is necessary to record on one chart the activities of one subject in relation to another.

> **A multiple activity chart is a chart on which the activities of more than one subject (worker, machine or item of equipment) are each recorded on a common time scale to show their inter-relationship**

By using separate vertical columns, or bars, to represent the activities of different operatives or machines against a common time scale, the chart shows very clearly periods of idleness on the part of any of the subjects during the process. A study of the chart often makes it possible to rearrange these activities so that such ineffective time is reduced.

The multiple activity chart is extremely useful in organising teams of operatives on mass-production work, and also on maintenance work when expensive plant cannot be allowed to remain idle longer than is absolutely necessary. It can also be used to determine the number of machines which an operative or operatives should be able to look after.

In making a chart, the activities of the different operatives or of the different operatives and machines are recorded in terms of working time and idle time. These times may be recorded by ordinary wristwatch or by stop-watch, according to the duration of the various periods of work and idleness (i.e. whether they are a matter of minutes or seconds). Extreme accuracy is not required, but timing must be accurate enough for the chart to be effective. The times are then plotted in their respective columns in the manner shown in figure 44.

136   The use of the multiple activity chart can best be shown by an example.

Figure 44.   Multiple activity chart: inspection of catalyst in a converter (original method)

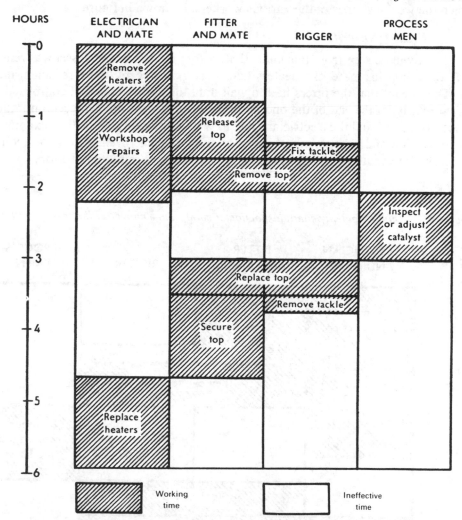

EXAMPLE OF A MULTIPLE ACTIVITY CHART APPLIED TO TEAM WORK: INSPECTION OF CATALYST IN A CONVERTER[1]

☐   *RECORD*

This is an application in the field of plant maintenance and is useful in showing that method study is not confined to repetition or production operations.

During the "running-in" period of a new catalytic converter in an organic chemical plant, it was necessary to make frequent checks on the condition of the catalyst. In order that the converter should not be out of service for any longer than was strictly necessary during these inspections, the job was studied.

In the original method the removal of the top of the vessel was not started until the heaters had been removed, and the replacement of the heaters was not started

---

[1] Adapted from an example in *Method study,* a handbook issued by Imperial Chemical Industries Ltd. Work Study Department.

until the top had been completely fixed. The original operation, with the relationships between the working times of the various workers, is shown in figure 44.

☐   *EXAMINE critically*

It will be seen from this chart that, before the top of the vessel was removed by the fitter and his mate, the heaters had to be removed by the electrician and his mate. This meant that the fitters had to wait until the electricians had completed their work. Similarly, at the end of the operation the heaters were not replaced until the top had been replaced, and the electricians had to wait in their turn. A critical examination of the operation and questioning of the existing procedure revealed that in fact it was not necessary to wait for the heaters to be removed before removing the top.

Figure 45.   *Multiple activity chart: inspection of catalyst in a converter (improved method)*

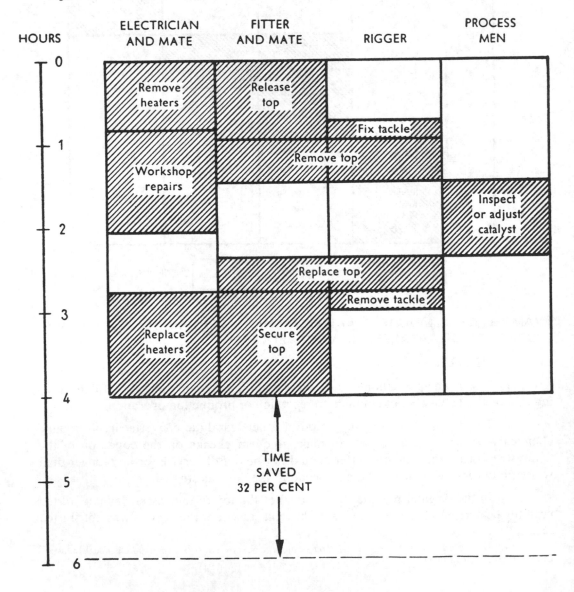

☐ *DEVELOP the new method*

Once this had been determined, it was possible to arrange for the top to be unfastened while the heaters were being removed and for the heaters to be replaced while the top was being secured in place. The result appears on the chart in figure 45.

It will be seen that the idle time of the electrician and fitter and their respective mates has been substantially reduced, although that of the rigger remains the same. Obviously the rigger and the process men will be otherwise occupied before and after performing their sections of the job and are not, in fact, idle while the heaters and cover are being removed or replaced. The saving effected by this simple change was 32 per cent of the total time of the operation.

The simple form of multiple activity chart shown here can be constructed on any piece of paper having lines or squares which can be used to form a time scale. It is more usual, however, to use printed or duplicated forms, similar in general layout to the standard flow process charts, and to draw vertical bars to represent the activities charted. Figures 46, 47 and 50 show multiple activity charts drawn on printed forms.

The multiple activity chart can also be used to present a picture of the operations performed simultaneously by a man and one or more machines. The chart may be drawn in the manner shown in figure 46, with the vertical activity bars close to each other down the middle of the sheet. In this way the beginning and end, and hence the duration, of every period of activity of either man or machine are clearly seen in relation to one another. By a study of these activities it is possible to determine whether better use can be made of the operative's time or of the machine time. In particular, it offers a means of determining whether a man minding a machine, whose time is only partly occupied, can manage to service another machine, or whether the increase in ineffective time of the two machines will offset any gain to be obtained from employing the man's time more fully. This is an important question in those countries where manpower is more readily available than machines and other capital equipment.

EXAMPLE OF A MULTIPLE ACTIVITY CHART RECORDING MAN AND MACHINE: FINISH MILL CASTING ON A VERTICAL MILLER

☐ *RECORD*

Figure 46 represents a common form of man-and-machine multiple activity chart recording the operation of a vertical milling machine finish-milling one face of a cast iron casting parallel to the opposite face, which is used for locating it in the fixture. This is a very simple example, typical of the sort of operation carried out every day in an engineering shop.

The heading of the chart records the usual standard information, with one or two additions. The graduated scale on the edge of the chart can be made to represent any scale of time required; in this case one large division equals 0.2 of a minute. The making of the chart and noting of the operations are self-evident and should not require further explanation.

139

Figure 46. Multiple activity chart—man and machine: finish mill casting (original method)

MULTIPLE ACTIVITY CHART						
CHART No. *8*	SHEET No. *1*		OF *1*	S U M M A R Y		
PRODUCT:					PRESENT	PROPOSED	SAVING
B. 239 Casting				CYCLE TIME	(min)		
		DRAWING No. *B. 239/1*		Man	*2.0*		
PROCESS:				Machine	*2.0*		
Finish mill second face				WORKING			
				Man	*1.2*		
				Machine	*0.8*		
MACHINE(S):		SPEED	FEED	IDLE			
Cincinnati No. 4		*80*	*15*	Man	*0.8*		
vertical miller		*r.p.m.*	*in./min*	Machine	*1.2*		
				UTILISATION			
OPERATIVE:		CLOCK No. *1234*		Man	*60%*		
CHARTED BY:		DATE:		Machine	*40%*		

TIME (min)	MAN	MACHINE	TIME (min)
0.2	Removes finished casting / Cleans with compressed air		0.2
0.4	Gauges depth on surface plate		0.4
0.6	Breaks sharp edge with file / Cleans with compressed air	Idle	0.6
0.8	Places in box / Obtains new casting		0.8
1.0	Cleans machine with compressed air		1.0
1.2	Locates casting in fixture: / starts machine and auto feed		1.2
1.4			1.4
1.6	Idle	Working / Finish mill second face	1.6
1.8			1.8
2.0			2.0
2.2			2.2
2.4			2.4
2.6			2.6
2.8			2.8
3.0			3.0
3.2			3.2
3.4			3.4
3.6			3.6
3.8			3.8

Figure 47.   Multiple activity chart—man and machine: finish mill casting (improved method)

MULTIPLE ACTIVITY CHART					
CHART No. *9* SHEET No. *1* OF *1*			S U M M A R Y		
PRODUCT				PRESENT	PROPOSED	SAVING
B 239 Casting		CYCLE TIME	(min)		
DRAWING No. *B.239/1*		Man	*2.0*	*1.36*	*0.64*
PROCESS		Machine	*2.0*	*1.36*	*0.64*
Finish mill second face		WORKING			
		Man	*1.2*	*1.12*	*0.08*
		Machine	*0.8*	*0.8*	—
MACHINE(S) SPEED FEED		IDLE			
Cincinnati No. 4 vertical miller *80* *15*		Man	*0.8*	*0.24*	*0.56*
r.p.m. *in./min*		Machine	*1.2*	*0.56*	*0.64*
		UTILISATION			*Gain*
OPERATIVE: CLOCK No. *1234*		Man	*60%*	*83%*	*23%*
CHARTED BY: DATE:		Machine	*40%*	*59%*	*19%*

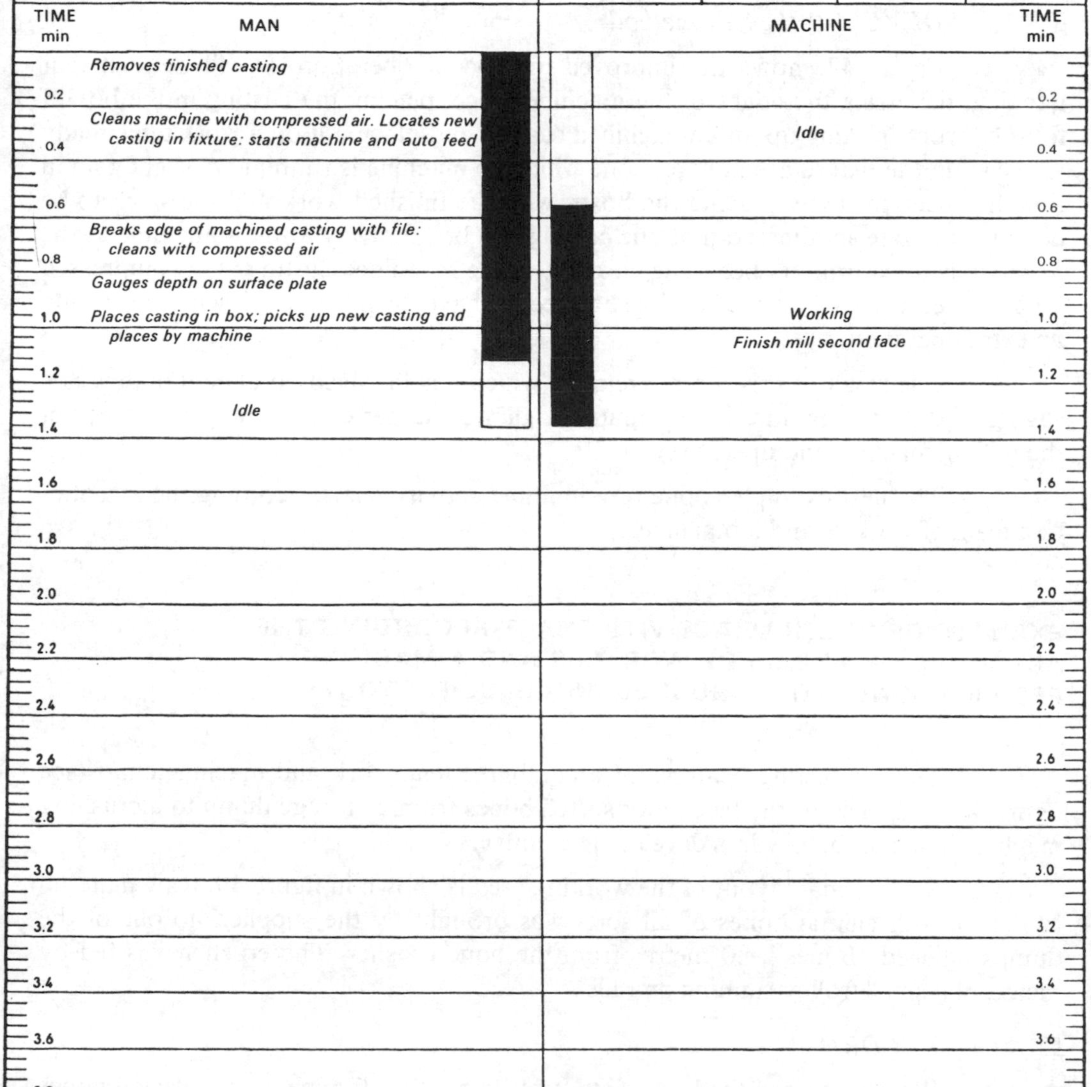

TIME min	MAN	MACHINE	TIME min
0.2	Removes finished casting		0.2
0.4	Cleans machine with compressed air. Locates new casting in fixture: starts machine and auto feed	Idle	0.4
0.6			0.6
0.8	Breaks edge of machined casting with file: cleans with compressed air		0.8
1.0	Gauges depth on surface plate. Places casting in box; picks up new casting and places by machine	Working. Finish mill second face	1.0
1.2			1.2
1.4	Idle		1.4
1.6			1.6
1.8			1.8
2.0			2.0
2.2			2.2
2.4			2.4
2.6			2.6
2.8			2.8
3.0			3.0
3.2			3.2
3.4			3.4
3.6			3.6
3.8			3.8

141

☐   *EXAMINE critically*

It will be seen from figure 46, which represents the method by which the operative was doing the job before the study was made, that the machine remains idle during nearly three-quarters of the operation cycle. This is due to the fact that the operative is carrying out all his activities with the machine stopped, but remains idle while the machine is running on an automatic feed.

Examination of the chart shows that the work carried out by the operative can be divided into two parts: that which must be done with the machine stopped, such as removing and locating the workpiece, and that which can be done while the machine is running, such as gauging. It is obviously an advantage to do as much as possible while the machine is running as this will reduce the over-all operation cycle time.

☐   *DEVELOP the new method*

Figure 47 shows the improved method of operation. It will be seen that gauging, deburring the edges of the machined face, placing the casting in the box of finished work, picking up an unmachined casting and placing it on a work table ready to locate in the fixture are now all done while the machine is running. A slight gain in time has been made by placing the boxes with the finished work and the work to be done next to one another, so that one casting can be put away at the same time as the new one is lifted from its box. The cleaning of the machined casting with compressed air has been deferred until after the sharp edges have been broken down, thus saving an extra operation.

The result of this rearrangement, which has involved no capital outlay, is a saving of 0.64 of a minute on 2 minutes, a gain of 32 per cent in the productivity of the milling machine and operative.

The next example is one of a multiple activity chart recording the activities of a team of workers and a machine.

EXAMPLE OF MULTIPLE ACTIVITY CHART RECORDING THE ACTIVITIES OF A TEAM OF WORKERS AND A MACHINE: FEEDING BONES TO A CRUSHER IN A GLUE FACTORY

This interesting example of a combined teamwork and machine chart (see figure 48) is applied to the feeding of sorted bones from a storage dump to a crushing machine in a glue factory in a developing country.

The original layout of the working area is shown in figure 49. Raw material in the form of animal bones of all sorts was brought by the suppliers to one of the dumps labelled "Bones", 80 metres from the bone crusher. The crusher was fed by means of a small trolley running on rails.

☐   *RECORD*

Workers sorted the bones into "soft" and "hard" types. The selected bones were carried to a heap, ready for loading by two workers into the trolley. The loading was done by hand. These two workers were idle during the time that the trolley was

Figure 48. Combined team work and machine multiple activity chart: crushing bones (original method)

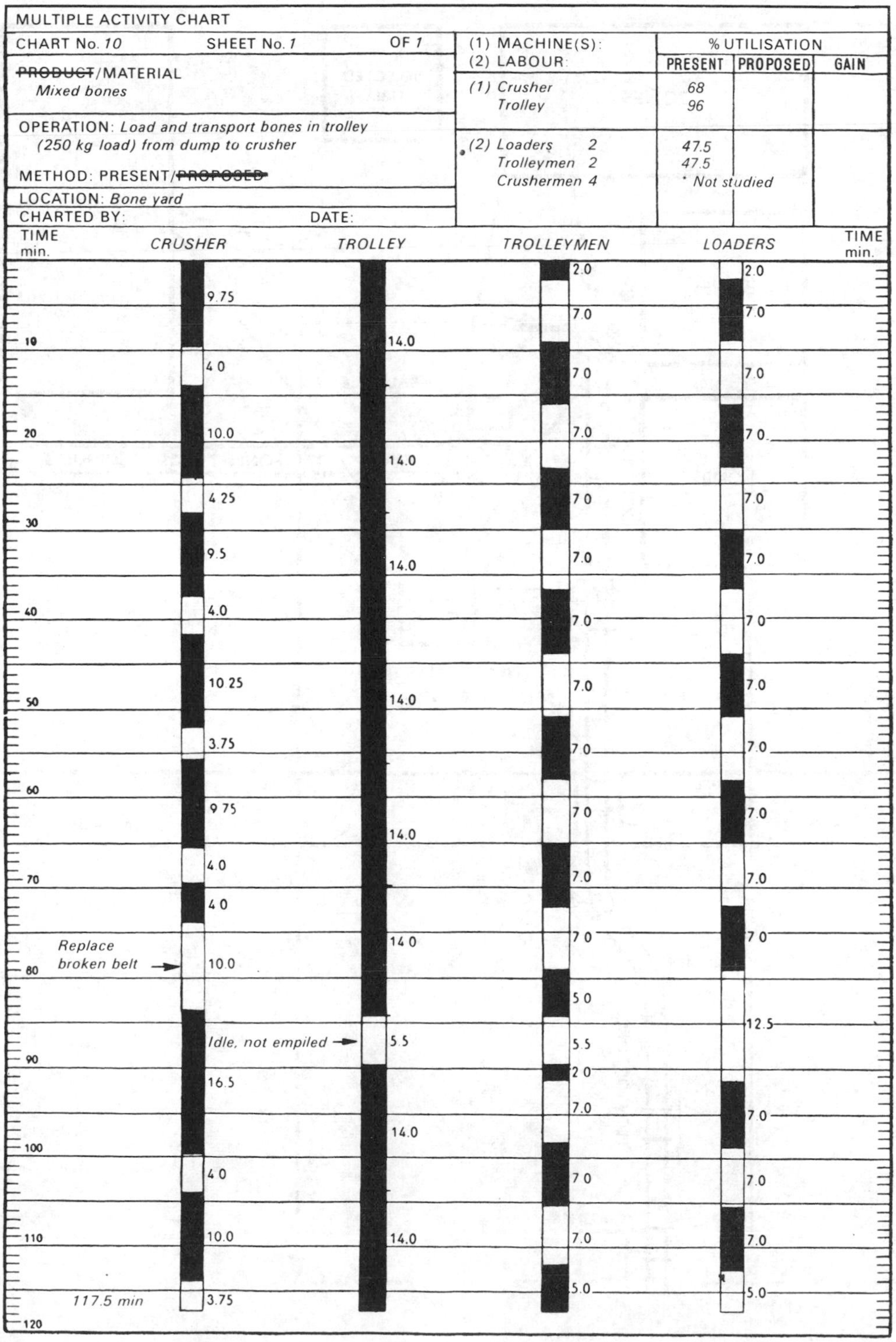

MULTIPLE ACTIVITY CHART

CHART No. *10*	SHEET No. *1*	OF *1*

PRODUCT/MATERIAL
  Mixed bones

OPERATION: *Load and transport bones in trolley
  (250 kg load) from dump to crusher*

METHOD: PRESENT/PROPOSED

LOCATION: *Bone yard*

CHARTED BY: DATE:

(1) MACHINE(S):				
(2) LABOUR:	% UTILISATION			
		PRESENT	PROPOSED	GAIN
(1) Crusher		68		
Trolley		96		
(2) Loaders 2		47.5		
Trolleymen 2		47.5		
Crushermen 4		* Not studied		

TIME min.	CRUSHER	TROLLEY	TROLLEYMEN	LOADERS	TIME min.

CRUSHER: 9.75, 4.0, 10.0, 4.25, 9.5, 4.0, 10.25, 3.75, 9.75, 4.0, 4.0, Replace broken belt → 10.0, Idle, not empiled → 16.5, 4.0, 10.0, 117.5 min 3.75

TROLLEY: 14.0, 14.0, 14.0, 14.0, 14.0, 5.5, 14.0, 14.0

TROLLEYMEN: 2.0, 7.0, 7.0, 7.0, 7.0, 7.0, 7.0, 7.0, 7.0, 7.0, 7.0, 7.0, 5.0, 5.5, 2.0, 7.0, 7.0, 7.0, 5.0

LOADERS: 2.0, 7.0, 7.0, 7.0, 7.0, 7.0, 7.0, 7.0, 7.0, 7.0, 7.0, 12.5, 7.0, 7.0, 7.0, 5.0

Figure 49.   Crushing bones: layout of working area

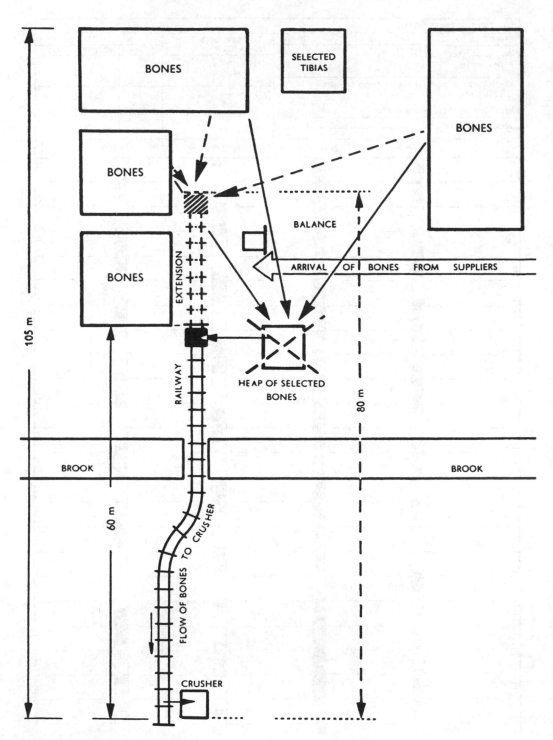

being pushed to the crusher, emptied into it and brought back. Two other workers pushed the trolley; they were idle while it was being loaded.

The following figures relate to the activities of the loaders, the trolley and the crushing machine during eight cycles, which lasted 117.5 minutes.

Trolley loading time	7 min (2 men)
Trolley to crusher, empty and return	7 min (2 men)
Trolley load	250 kg
Weight transported in 117.5 minutes	$8 \times 250 = 2,000$ kg
Crusher waiting time	37.75 min

A chart (figure 48) has been made relating the activities of the crusher, trolley, trolleymen and loaders. From this it will be seen that 10 minutes of the crusher waiting time was taken up in replacing a broken belt; however, after the belt was repaired, the crusher ran continuously for 16.5 minutes instead of the usual 10, because a fresh trolley load was ready for it. If a normal 4 minutes of idleness is allowed, the net idleness due to the broken belt becomes only 6 minutes.

☐   *EXAMINE critically*

A critical examination of the chart shows at once that the crusher was normally idle for 31.75 out of 111.5 minutes (37.75 out of 117.5 minutes if the 6 minutes breakdown time is included), or 28.5 per cent of the possible working time. Each of the two groups of men (loaders and trolleymen) was idle for 50 per cent of its available time. The first question that might arise in the mind of someone studying the diagram and chart is: "Why cannot the trolleymen load the trolley?"

The answer to this question is that, if they did so, they would get no rest and would have to work continuously just to keep the crusher going for the same percentage of its time as at present. There would be a saving of manpower but no improvement in the productivity of the plant. In any case, no one can work for three or four hours on end without some rest, especially when engaged on heavy work like loading and pushing the trolley, where the allowance would normally be 25 per cent or possibly more of the total time allowed for the job (for the treatment of relaxation allowances see Chapter 18). If the two trolleymen took their relaxation allowances, the productivity of the crusher would be still lower.

A study of the diagram of the working area and of the information given above shows that the workers sorting the bones at the dumps labelled "Bones" have to carry the sorted bones from the points where they are working to the "Heap of selected bones", so that they can be loaded into the trolley. This raises the question: "Why cannot the bone sorters load the sorted bones straight into the trolley?"

The answer is that they could do so, if the rails were extended another 20 metres to the bone dumps.

This eliminates the loaders but still leaves the problem of the 4 minutes of idle time of the crusher, while it is waiting for the trolley to return with a load. There are more bone sorters than loaders and they can load the trolley more quickly; if each trolley load were reduced, it would take less time to load and would require less effort to push. In this way it might be possible to keep up with the cycle of the crusher. The load was therefore reduced to 175 kilograms. Waiting time was eliminated.

☐   *DEVELOP the improved method*

The line of crosses in figure 49 shows the extension of the rails to the bone dumps. The loaders who were eliminated were transferred to other work in the factory. This was probably made possible by the fact that, as will be seen, the crusher output rose substantially as a result of the change of method.

Figure 50 is the multiple activity chart showing the improved method. It will be seen from this that the percentage running time of the crusher has considerably improved.

Performance figures are now—

Trolley loading time	1 min
Trolley to crusher, empty and return . .	6 min
Trolley load	175 kg
Weight transported in 115.5 minutes . .	$15 \times 175 = 2,625$ kg
Crusher waiting time	6 min

The crusher waiting time will be seen from the chart to include 3 minutes for clearing hard bones—an abnormal occurrence. If this time is excluded to enable the original and improved performances to be compared, the over-all time during which the crusher is available for action is 112.5 minutes. The increase in output from the crusher over almost identical periods is 625 kilograms; the increase in productivity of the crusher is 29.5 per cent.

Two labourers out of eight have been released for other work; the labour productivity has therefore increased by

$$\left(\frac{2625 \times 8}{2000 \times 6} - 1 \right) \times 100 = 75 \text{ per cent.}$$

The space formerly occupied by the "Heap of selected bones" is now available for other uses.

This example is a dramatic illustration of the manner in which the productivity of land, plant and labour can be increased by method study properly and systematically applied, at a cost of only 20 metres of light railway track.

5. The travel chart

The string diagram is a very neat and effective way of recording for critical examination the movement of workers or materials about the shop, especially when readily understood "before" and "after" models are needed to help in presenting the merits of a proposed change. String diagrams do take rather a long time to construct, however, and when a great many movements along complex paths are involved the diagram may end up looking like a forbidding maze of criss-crossing lines. When the movement patterns are complex, the **travel chart** is a quicker and more manageable recording technique.

Figure 50.   Combined team work and machine multiple activity chart: crushing bones (improved method)

MULTIPLE ACTIVITY CHART

CHART No. 11	SHEET No. 1	OF 1

MATERIAL: Mixed bones

OPERATION: Load and transport bones in trolley (175 kg. load) from dump to crusher

METHOD: ~~PRESENT~~/PROPOSED

LOCATION: Bone yard

CHARTED BY: DATE:

(1) MACHINE(S):
(2) LABOUR:

	% UTILISATION		
	PRESENT	PROPOSED	GAIN
(1) Crusher	68	93	25
Trolley	96	95	—1
(2) Loaders 2	47.5	Transferred	
Trolleymen 2	47.5	81	33.5
•Crushermen 4	• Not studied		

N. B. Loading now done by sorters

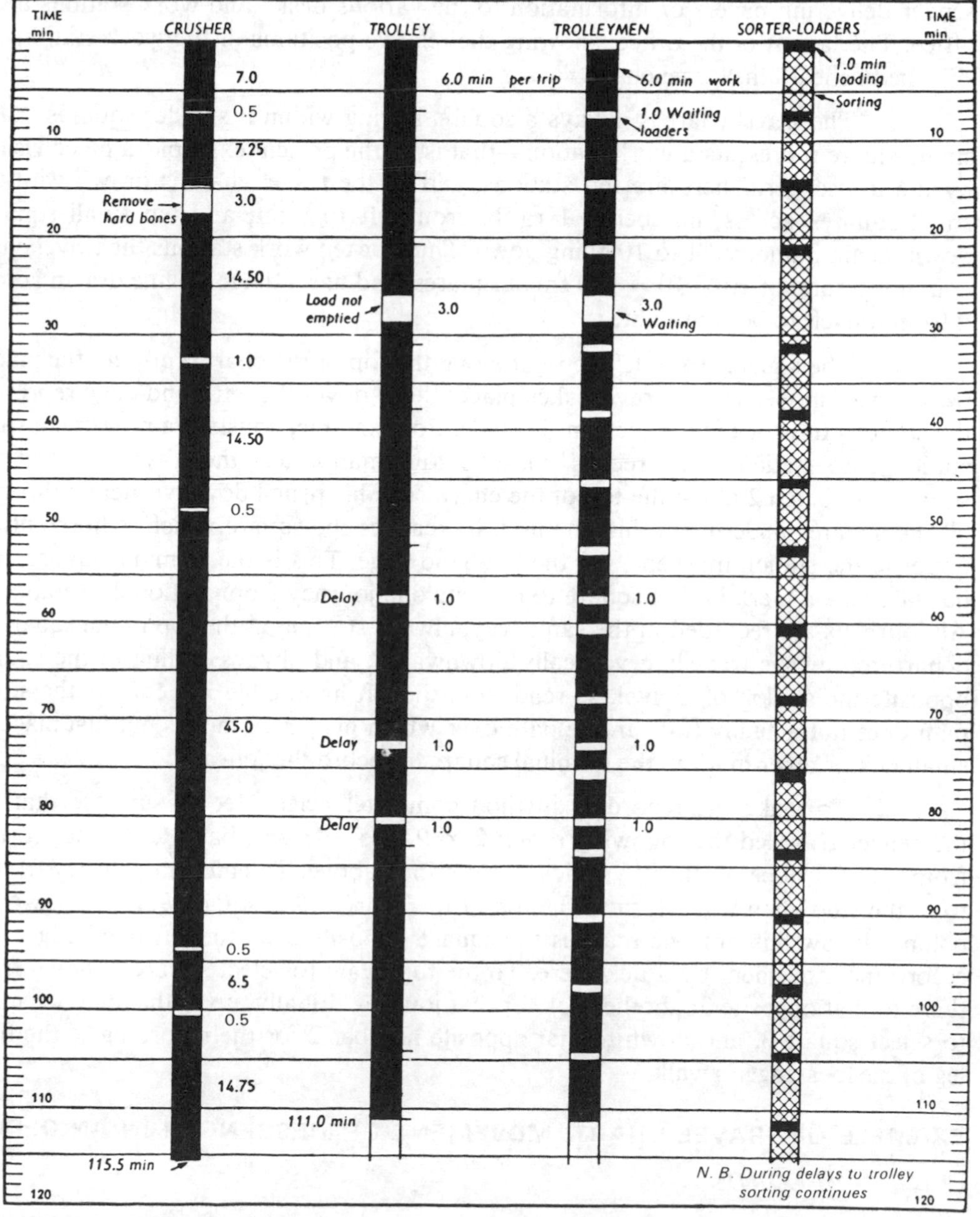

Chart columns (TIME min): CRUSHER, TROLLEY, TROLLEYMEN, SORTER-LOADERS

CRUSHER: 7.0; 0.5; 7.25; Remove hard bones 3.0; 14.50; 1.0; 14.50; 0.5; 45.0; 0.5; 6.5; 0.5; 14.75 — 115.5 min

TROLLEY: 6.0 min per trip; Load not emptied 3.0; Delay 1.0; Delay 1.0; Delay 1.0; 111.0 min

TROLLEYMEN: 6.0 min work; 1.0 Waiting loaders; 3.0 Waiting; 1.0; 1.0; 1.0

SORTER-LOADERS: 1.0 min loading; Sorting

N. B. During delays to trolley sorting continues

147

> **A travel chart is a tabular record for presenting quantitative data about the movements of workers, materials or equipment between any number of places over any given period of time**

Figure 51 shows a typical travel chart. It records the movements of a messenger delivering papers or information to the various desks and work stations in an office. The layout of the office, showing the relative positions of the work stations, is sketched beneath the travel chart.

The travel chart is always a square, having within it smaller squares. Each small square represents a work station—that is, in the present example, a place visited by the messenger. There are ten stations, and so the travel chart is drawn with ten small squares across, numbered 1 to 10 from left to right, and ten small squares down, again numbered 1 to 10 going down. Thus for ten work stations the travel chart contains a total of $10 \times 10 = 100$ small squares, and has a diagonal line drawn across it from top left to bottom right.

The squares from left to right along the top of the chart represent the places **from where** movement or travel takes place: those down the left-hand edge represent the stations **to which** the movement is made. For example, consider a movement from station 2 to station 9. To record this, the studyman enters the travel chart at the square numbered 2 along the top of the chart, runs his pencil down vertically through all the squares underneath this one until he reaches the square which is horizontally opposite the station marked 9 on the left-hand edge. This is the terminal square, and he will make a mark in that square to indicate one journey from station 2 to station 9. All journeys are recorded in the same way, always starting at the top in the square of departure, always travelling vertically downwards, and always ending in the square opposite the station of arrival, as read from the left-hand edge. Of course, the study man does not actually trace in the path over which his pencil moves but just places a small tick or other mark in the terminal square to record the journey.

To make the recording method completely clear, let us suppose that the messenger travelled the following route: 2 to 9 to 5 to 3 and back to 2. The journey from 2 to 9 will be marked by a tick as described above. To enter the journey from 9 to 5, the studyman will return to the top of the chart, select square 9, move down the column below this until he reaches the square opposite 5 on the left-hand edge, and record the movement by a tick there. To the top again to select square 5, down from there to that opposite 3; another tick for that journey. Finally, up to the top once more to select square 3, and down to that opposite number 2 for the recording of the final leg of the messenger's walk.

EXAMPLE OF TRAVEL CHART: MOVEMENT OF MESSENGER IN AN OFFICE

☐　　*RECORD*

The first stage of the recording process, that is when the method study man observes the movement of the messenger actually in the office, can be carried out very

Figure 51.   Travel chart: movements of messenger in office

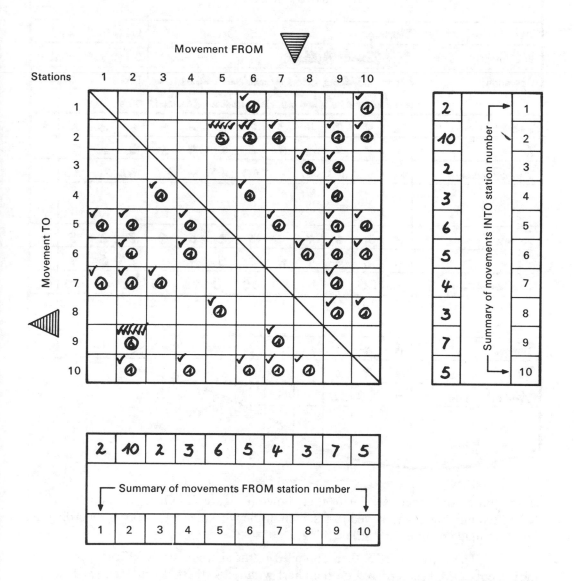

Layout sketch
of office
showing location
of stations

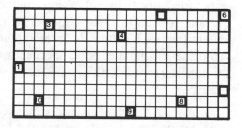

Figure 52. Simple study sheet

STUDY SHEET													
Department: *Mixing*							Section /			Study No. 147			
Equipment: *Lift Truck: Pallets*										Sheet: / of 2			
Operation: *Move 25-litre cans of material to mixing*										Taken by: CBA			
machines and then to inspection (Station 6)										Date:			
From	2	9	7	4	3	9	6	1	9	6	3	2	9
To	9	7	4	3	9	6	1	9	6	3	2	9	7
No. of cans	10	–	20	10	–	30	10	–	30	10	–	30	–
From	7	1	6	4	9	8	2	5	9	7	2	5	9
To	1	6	4	9	8	2	5	9	7	2	5	9	6
No. of cans	10	20	–	30	40	20	30	40	10	20	10	30	40
From	6	1	9										
To	1	9	6										
No. of cans	–	30	30										

simply on a study sheet similar to that shown in figure 52. Once the stations visited have been numbered and keyed to a sketch of the workplace, the entries recording the journeys made require very little writing.

The travel chart is then compiled in the method study office. After all the movements have been entered on the chart with ticks, the ticks in each small square are added up, the total being entered in the square itself. The movements are then summarised, in two ways. Down the right-hand side of the chart, the number of movements **into** each station is entered against the square representing the station, as read from the left-hand edge. Underneath the chart, the number of movements **from** each station is recorded, this time under the relevant squares as read off the top of the chart.

In the chart in figure 51 there were two movements **into** station 1, as can be seen by running an eye across the line of squares against station 1 on the left-hand edge. Similarly, in the next horizontal line of squares, that opposite station 2, there are altogether 10 movements shown, **into** station 2. For the movements **from** stations, the totalling is carried out vertically: it will be seen that there were 10 movements *from* station 2, as shown in the column of squares under station 2 at the top of the chart. With very little practice, the chart and its summaries can be compiled extremely quickly – much quicker than it takes to describe what is done.

In figure 51 the summary of movements **into** each station shows the same number of movements as those recorded at the bottom as being made **from** that station, indicating that the messenger ended his travels at the same station as he started out from when the study commenced. If he had finished somewhere else (or if the study had been broken off when he was somewhere else), there would have been one station where there was one more movement in than the number of movements out, and this would be where the study finished.

☐   *EXAMINE critically*

An examination of the chart shows that ten journeys have been made into station 2, seven into station 9, and six into station 5. These are the busiest stations. A scrutiny of the body of the chart helps to confirm this: there were six journeys from station 2 to station 9, and five from station 5 to station 2. The busiest route is 5–2–9. This suggests that it would be better to locate these stations next to each other. It might then be possible for the clerk at station 5 to place finished work directly into the in-tray at station 2, and the clerk there to pass his work on to station 9, thus relieving the messenger of a good deal of his travelling.

EXAMPLE OF A TRAVEL CHART: MATERIAL HANDLING

An example of a travel chart compiled as part of a material-handling study is shown in figure 53. In the shop in which the study was made, eight mixing machines were used to mix materials in different proportions, the final mixtures being taken to an inspection bench (station 6). The mixes were transported in 25-litre cans, which were placed on pallets and moved by a low lift truck.

☐   *RECORD*

Movements were recorded on the shop floor on a study sheet of the type shown in figure 52. The entries show not only the journeys made but also the number of cans carried on each trip. In the travel chart shown in figure 53, there are nine stations, the eight mixing machines and the inspection bench. The travel chart was made exactly as in the previous example, except that in this instance the number of cans delivered was also entered in the destination squares, beside the ticks for the journeys, and both journeys and cans delivered have been summarised. It will be seen that, for instance, two journeys were made from station 5 to station 9, one with a load of 40 cans and the other with 30.

☐   *EXAMINE critically*

Not much can be learned from the study sheet, except that seven of the 29 trips made were run without any load, and that the size of load varied from 10 to 40 cans. The travel chart, however, shows at once that stations 6 and 9 are busy ones. Five trips were made to station 6, with a total of 150 cans being delivered. (Station 6 was the inspection bench.) Four of these trips were from station 9, bringing in a total of 130 cans. The largest number of trips, and the greatest quantity of cans, was from

151

Figure 53.   Travel chart: materials

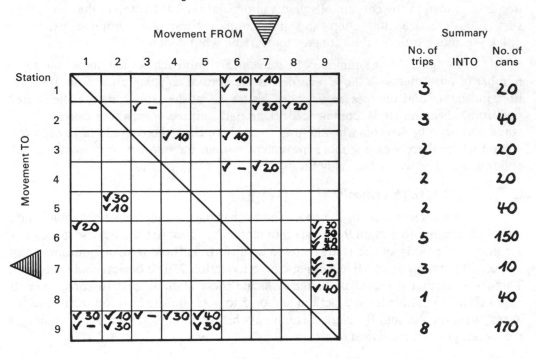

station 9 to the inspection bench, suggesting that this route might be laid out so that it would be as short as possible. It might be possible to install a roller conveyor between these points, thus relieving the lift truck of a great deal of work.

Eight trips were made into station 9, to deliver 170 cans. The cans came from stations 1, 2, 4 and 5, one trip without load being made from station 3. Stations 1, 2, 4 and 5 appear to feed station 9, which sends its work on to the inspection bench (longer study might be necessary to confirm this). If so, there would be a case for modifying the layout of the shop in order to bring these stations closer together, when roller conveyors might allow gravity to do most of the transporting between them. In this example there is no sketch of the shop layout or table of distances between stations, both of which are essential complements to a travel chart.

It is interesting to note that four trips were made from station 2, but only three into the station; and that only four were made from station 6, although five were made into it. This is because the study started at station 2 and finished at the inspection bench.

Chapter 11
Methods and movements at the workplace

1. General considerations

In this book we have gradually moved from the wide field of the productivity of industry as a whole to considering in a general way how the productivity of men and machines can be improved through the use of work study. Still moving from the broader to the more detailed approach, we have also examined procedures of a general nature for improving the effectiveness with which complete sequences of operations are performed and with which material flows through the working area. Turning from material to men, we have discussed methods of studying the movements of men around the working area and the relationships between men and machines or of men working together in groups. We have done so following the principle that the broad method of operation must be put right before we attempt improvements in detail.

The time has now come to look at one man working at a workplace, bench or table and to apply to him the principles which have been laid down and the procedures shown in the examples given.

In considering the movements of men and materials on the larger scale, we have been concerned with the better utilisation of existing plant and machinery (and, where possible, materials) through the elimination of unnecessary idle time, the more effective operation of processes and the better utilisation of the services of labour through the elimination of unnecessary and time-consuming movement within the working area of factory, department or yard.

As our example (Chapter 10) of the trolleymen's need for relaxation shows, the factor of fatigue affects the solution of problems even when we are dealing with areas larger than the individual workplace. But when we come to study the operative at the workplace, the way in which he applies his effort and the amount of fatigue resulting from his manner of working become primary factors affecting his productivity.

Before embarking on a detailed study of an operative doing a job at a single workplace, it is important to make certain that the job is in fact necessary and is being done as it should be done. The questioning technique must be applied as regards—

☐   *PURPOSE*

to ensure that the job is necessary;

☐ *PLACE*

to ensure that it is being done where it should be done;

☐ *SEQUENCE*

to ensure that it is in its right place in the sequence of operations;

☐ *PERSON*

to ensure that it is being done by the right person.

Once these have been verified and it is certain that the job cannot be eliminated or combined with another operation, it is possible to go on to determine the

☐ *MEANS*

by which the job is being done

and to simplify them as much as is economically justified.

Later in this chapter we shall consider the recording techniques adopted to set out the detailed movements of an operative at his workplace in ways which facilitate critical examination and the development of improved methods, in particular the **two-handed process chart.** Before doing this, however, it is appropriate to discuss the principles of motion economy and a number of other matters which influence the design of the workplace itself, so as to make it as convenient as possible for the worker to perform his task.

2. The principles of motion economy[1]

There are a number of "principles" concerning the economy of movements which have been developed as a result of experience and which form a good basis for the development of improved methods at the workplace. They were first used by Frank Gilbreth, the founder of motion study, and have been amplified by other workers, notably Professor Barnes.[2] They may be grouped under three headings—

A. **Use of the human body**

B. **Arrangement of the workplace**

C. **Design of tools and equipment**

They are useful in shop and office alike and, although they cannot always be applied, they do form a very good basis for improving the efficiency and reducing the fatigue of manual work. The ideas expounded by Professor Barnes are described here in a somewhat simplified fashion.

A. **Use of the human body**

When possible—

---

[1] In the B.S. *Glossary,* op. cit., the term "characteristics of easy movement" is preferred, rather than "principles of motion economy". The earlier term has been retained here, however, as being more descriptive of the rest of this section of the chapter.

[2] See Ralph M. Barnes: *Motion and time study: Design and measurement of work* (New York and London, John Wiley, 6th ed., 1969), Chapters 17-19.

1. The two hands should begin and complete their movements at the same time.

2. The two hands should not be idle at the same time except during periods of rest.

3. Motions of the arms should be symmetrical and in opposite directions and should be made simultaneously.

4. Hand and body motions should be made at the lowest classification at which it is possible to do the work satisfactorily (see section 3 below).

5. Momentum should be employed to help the worker, but should be reduced to a minimum whenever it has to be overcome by muscular effort.

6. Continuous curved movements are to be preferred to straight-line motions involving sudden and sharp changes in direction.

7. "Ballistic" (i.e. free-swinging) movements are faster, easier and more accurate than restricted or controlled movements.

8. Rhythm is essential to the smooth and automatic performance of a repetitive operation. The work should be arranged to permit easy and natural rhythm whenever possible.

9. Work should be arranged so that eye movements are confined to a comfortable area, without the need for frequent changes of focus.

B. Arrangement of the workplace

1. Definite and fixed stations should be provided for all tools and materials to permit habit formation.

2. Tools and materials should be pre-positioned to reduce searching.

3. Gravity feed, bins and containers should be used to deliver the materials as close to the point of use as possible.

4. Tools, materials and controls should be located within the maximum working area (see figure 54) and as near to the worker as possible.

5. Materials and tools should be arranged to permit the best sequence of motions.

6. "Drop deliveries" or ejectors should be used wherever possible, so that the operative does not have to use his hands to dispose of the finished work.

7. Provision should be made for adequate lighting, and a chair of the type and height to permit good posture should be provided. The height of the workplace and seat should be arranged to allow alternate standing and sitting.

8. The colour of the workplace should contrast with that of the work and thus reduce eye fatigue.

C. Design of tools and equipment

1. The hands should be relieved of all work of "holding" the workpiece where this can be done by a jig, fixture or foot-operated device.

2. Two or more tools should be combined wherever possible.

3. Where each finger performs some specific movement, as in typewriting, the load should be distributed in accordance with the inherent capacities of the fingers.

155

Figure 54.   Normal and maximum working areas

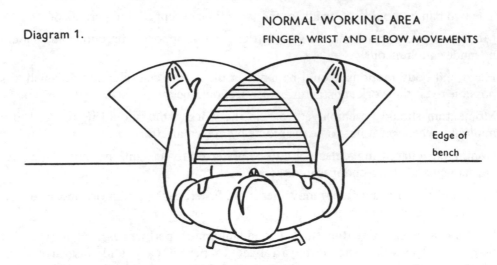

Diagram 1.

NORMAL WORKING AREA
FINGER, WRIST AND ELBOW MOVEMENTS

Edge of
bench

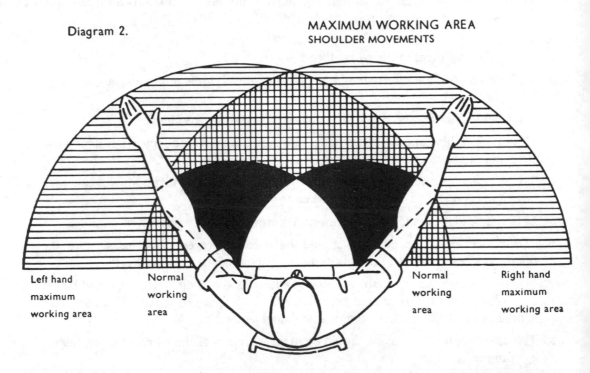

Diagram 2.

MAXIMUM WORKING AREA
SHOULDER MOVEMENTS

Left hand maximum working area

Normal working area

Normal working area

Right hand maximum working area

4. Handles such as those on cranks and large screwdrivers should be so designed that as much of the surface of the hand as possible can come into contact with the handle. This is especially necessary when considerable force has to be used on the handle.

5. Levers, crossbars and handwheels should be so placed that the operative can use them with the least change in body position and the greatest "mechanical advantage".

These "principles", which reflect those discussed in Chapter 6, can be made the basis of a summary "questionnaire" which will help, when laying out a workplace, to ensure that nothing is overlooked.

Figure 54 shows the normal working area and the storage area on the workbench for the average operative. As far as possible, materials should not be stored in the area directly in front of him, as stretching forwards involves the use of the back muscles, thereby causing fatigue. This has been demonstrated by physiological research.

3. Classification of movements

The fourth "rule" of motion economy in the use of the human body calls for movements to be of the lowest classification possible. This classification is built up on the pivots around which the body members must move, as shown in table 10.

Table 10.   Classification of movements

Class	Pivot	Body member(s) moved
1	Knuckle	Finger
2	Wrist	Hand and fingers
3	Elbow	Forearm, hand and fingers
4	Shoulder	Upper arm, forearm, hand and fingers
5	Trunk	Torso, upper arm, forearm, hand and fingers

It is obvious that each movement above Class 1 will involve movements of all classes below it. Thus the saving in effort resulting from using the lowest class possible is obvious. If, in laying out the workplace, everything needed is placed within easy reach, this will minimise the class of movement which the work itself requires from the operative.

4. Further notes on workplace layout

A few general notes on laying out the workplace may be useful.

1. If similar work is being done by each hand, there should be a separate supply of materials or parts for each hand.

2. If the eyes are used to select material, as far as possible the material should be kept in an area where the eyes can locate it without there being any need to turn the head.

3. The nature and the shape of the material influence its position in the layout.

4. Hand tools should be picked up with the least possible disturbance to the rhythm and symmetry of movements. As far as possible the operator should be able to pick up or put down a tool as the hand moves from one part of the work to the next, without making a special journey. Natural movements are curved, not straight; tools should be placed on the arc of movements, but clear of the path of movement of any material which has to be slid along the surface of the bench.

5. Tools should be easy to pick up and replace; as far as possible they should have an automatic return, or the location of the next piece of material to be moved should allow the tool to be returned as the hand travels to pick it up.

6. Finished work should be—

   (a) dropped down a hole or a chute;

   (b) dropped through a chute when the hand is starting the first motion of the next cycle;

   (c) put in a container placed so that hand movements are kept to a minimum;

   (d) if the operation is an intermediate one, placed in a container in such a way that the next operative can pick it up easily.

7. Always look into the possibility of using pedals or knee-operated levers for locking or indexing devices on fixtures or devices for disposing of finished work.

AN EXAMPLE OF A WORKPLACE LAYOUT

Let us now look at a typical workplace with the principles of motion economy and the notes in the previous section in mind.

Figure 55 shows a typical example of the layout of a workplace for the assembly of small electrical equipment (in this case electric meters). Certain points will be noticed at once:

(1) A fixture has been provided for holding the workpiece (here the chassis of the meter), leaving both the operative's hands free for assembly work. The use of one hand purely for holding the part being worked on should **always** be avoided, except for operations so short that a fixture would not be justified.

(2) The power screwdriver and box spanner are suspended in front of the operative so that she has to make only a very short and easy movement to grasp them and bring them to the work. They are, however, clear of the surface of the table and of the work. The hammer and hand screwdriver for use with the left hand are within easy reach, so that the operative can pick them up without searching, although picking up the screwdriver might involve a little fumbling. They are in line with the trays of parts but below them, and so do not get in the way.

(3) All the small parts are close to the operative, well within the "maximum working area". Each part has a definite location, and the trays are designed with "scoop" fronts for easy withdrawal, parts being drawn forward with the tips of the fingers and grasped as they come over the rounded edge. They are arranged for symmetrical movements of the arms, so that parts which are assembled simultaneously are picked up from trays in the same relative position to the operative, on either side of her. It will be noted that the trays come almost in front of the operative, but this is not very important in this case as the length of reach is not excessive and will not involve much play of the shoulder and back muscles.

(4) The operative has taken a small number of the formed wire parts normally kept in a tray to her left front and placed them conveniently in front of and to the side of the workpiece, in order to make a shorter reach.

(5) The backrest of the operative's chair is an interesting and ingenious improvisation. Special chairs with this type of backrest were not produced locally.

Figure 55.   *Assembling an electric meter*

5. Notes on the design of jigs, tools and fixtures

A jig holds parts in an exact position and guides the tool that works on them

A fixture is a less accurate device for holding parts which would otherwise have to be held in one hand while the other worked on them

The designer's object in providing jigs and fixtures is primarily accuracy in machining or assembly. Often, opening and closing them or positioning the workpiece calls for more movements on the part of the operative than are strictly necessary. For

159

example, a spanner may have to be used to tighten a nut when a wing nut would be more suitable; or the top of the jig may have to be lifted off when the part might be slid in.

Co-operation between the work study man and the jig and tool designers, in industries where they are employed (principally the engineering industry), should start in the early stages of designing, and tool designers should be among the first people to take appreciation courses in method study. Some points worth noting are—

(1) Clamps should be as simple to operate as possible and should not have to be screwed unless this is essential for accuracy of positioning. If two clamps are required, they should be designed for use by the right and left hands at the same time.

(2) The design of the jig should be such that both hands can load parts into it with a minimum of obstruction. There should be no obstruction between the point of entry and the point from which the material is obtained.

(3) The action of unclamping a jig should at the same time eject the part, so that additional movements are not required to take the part out of the jig.

(4) Where possible on small assembly work, fixtures for a part which does not require both hands to work on it at once should be made to take two parts, with sufficient space between them to allow both hands to work easily.

(5) In some cases jigs are made to take several small parts. It will save loading time if several parts can be clamped in position as quickly as one.

(6) The work study man should not ignore machine jigs and fixtures such as milling jigs. A great deal of time and power is often wasted on milling machines owing to the fact that parts are milled one at a time, when it may be quite feasible to mill two or more at once.

(7) If spring-loaded disappearing pins are used to position components, attention should be paid to their strength of construction. Unless the design is robust, such devices tend to function well for a while but then have to be repaired or redesigned.

(8) In introducing a component into a jig it is important to ensure that the operative should be able to see what he is doing at all stages; this should be checked before any design is accepted.

6. Machine controls and displays of dials

Until recently, machinery and plant of all kinds was designed with very little thought being given to the convenience of the operative. In short cycle work especially, the manipulation of the controls (changing speeds on a capstan lathe, for example) often involves awkward movements. There is not much that the user can do about the controls of a machine after he has bought it; but he **can** draw the attention of the makers to inconvenient controls so that they can make improvements in later models. There is some evidence that machinery makers generally are beginning to be more conscious of this problem, but a great deal remains to be done. In the few companies that make their own machinery or plant, the work study department should be called in at the earliest possible stage of the design process, to give assistance and advice.

Physiologists and psychologists have given some thought to the arrangement of dials with a view to minimising the fatigue to people who have to watch them. The arrangement of the control panels for chemical processes and similar types of process is often made at the works installing them, and the work study man should be consulted when this is done.

There is a good deal of published literature on the subject, and this can be consulted in order to arrive at an easily readable "display" or arrangement of dials or visual indicators.

The growing awareness of the importance of arranging machine controls and workplaces so that they are convenient for the people who have to do the work has led in recent years to the development of a new field of scientific study which is concerned entirely with such matters. This is **ergonomics:**[1] the study of the relationship between a worker and the environment in which he works, particularly the application of anatomical, physiological and psychological knowledge to the problems arising therefrom. Ergonomists have carried out many experiments to decide on matters such as the best layout for machine controls, the best dimensions for seats and worktops, the most convenient pedal pressures, and so on. It may be expected that their findings will gradually be incorporated in the designs of new machines and equipment over the next few years, and will eventually form the basis of standard practice.

7. The two-handed process chart

The study of the work of an operative at the bench starts, as does method study over the wider field, with a process chart. In this case the chart used is the fifth of the charts indicating process sequence (table 9), the one known as the **two-handed process chart.**

> **The two-handed process chart is a process chart in which the activities of a worker's hands (or limbs) are recorded in their relationship to one another**

The two-handed process chart is a specialised form of process chart because it shows the two hands (and sometimes the feet) of the operative moving or static in relation to one another, usually in relation to a time scale. One advantage of incorporating a time scale in the chart form is that the symbols for what the two hands are doing at any given moment are brought opposite each other.

---

[1] See Chapter 6.

The two-handed process chart is generally used for repetitive operations, when one complete cycle of the work is to be recorded. Recording is carried out in more detail than is normal on flow process charts. What may be shown as a single operation on a flow process chart may be broken down into a number of elemental activities which together make up the operation. The two-handed process chart generally employs the same symbols as the other process charts; however, because of the greater detail covered, the symbols are accorded slightly different meanings—

○   *OPERATION* is used for the activities of grasp, position, use, release, etc. of a tool, component or material.

⇨   *TRANSPORT* is used to represent the movement of the hand (or limb) to or from the work, or a tool, or material.

◻   *DELAY*   is used to denote time during which the hand or limb being charted is idle (although the others may be in use).

▽   *HOLD* ("Storage")   The term **storage** is not used in connection with the two-handed process chart. Instead, the symbol is redesignated as **hold** and is used to represent the activity of holding the work, a tool or material—that is, when the hand being charted is holding something.

The symbol for **inspection** is not much used because the hand movements when an operative is inspecting an article (holding it and examining it visually or gauging it) may be classified as "operations" on the two-handed chart. It may, however, sometimes be useful to employ the "inspection" symbol to draw attention to the examination of a piece.[1]

The very act of making the chart enables the work study man to gain an intimate knowledge of the details of the job, and the chart itself enables him to study each element of the job by itself and in relation to other elements. From this study ideas for improvements are developed. These ideas should be written down in chart form when they occur, just as in all other process charting. It may be that different ways of simplifying the work can be found; if they are all charted, they can be compared easily. The best method is generally that which requires the fewest movements.

The two-handed process chart can be applied to a great variety of assembly, machining and clerical jobs. In assembly operations, tight fits and awkward positioning present certain problems. In the assembly of small parts with close fits, "positioning before assembly" may be the longest element in the cycle. In such cases "positioning" should be shown as a separate movement ("Operation") apart from the actual movement of assembly (e.g. fitting a screwdriver in the head of a small screw). Attention can thus be focused on it and, if it is shown against a time scale, its relative importance can be assessed. Major savings can be made if the number of such positionings can be reduced, as for example by slightly countersinking the mouth of a hole and putting a chamfer on the end of the shaft fitting in it, or by using a screwdriver with a self-centring bit.

---

[1] Some authorities feel that the standard process-chart symbols are not entirely suitable for recording hand and body movements and have adopted variants, such as—

O: Operation.   H: Hold.
TL: Transport Loaded.   R: Rest.
TE: Transport Empty.

NOTES ON COMPILING TWO-HANDED PROCESS CHARTS

The chart form should include—

Spaces at the top for the usual information.

Adequate space for a sketch of the layout of the workplace (corresponding to the flow diagram used in association with the flow process chart), or sketch of jigs, etc.

Spaces for the movements of right and left hands.

Space for a summary of movements and analysis of idle time.

Examples are given in the following pages.

Some points on compiling charts are worth mentioning—

1. Study the operation cycle a few times before starting to record.

2. Chart **one** hand at a time.

3. Do not record more than a few symbols at a time.

4. The action of picking up or grasping a fresh part at the beginning of a cycle of work is a good point at which to start the record. Start with the hand that handles the part first or the hand that does the most work. The exact point of starting is not really important, as the complete cycle will eventually come round to it again, but the point chosen must be definite. Add in the second column the kinds of work done by the other hand.

5. Only record actions on the same level **when they occur at the same moment.**

6. Actions which occur **in sequence** must be recorded on the chart at different horizontal levels. Check the chart for the time relation of the hands.

7. Care must be taken to list **everything** the operative does and to avoid combining operations and transports or positionings, unless they actually occur at the same time.

EXAMPLE OF A TWO-HANDED PROCESS CHART: CUTTING GLASS TUBES

This very simple example describes how a two-handed process chart was constructed for cutting off short lengths of glass tube with the aid of a jig. This is illustrated on the form; the operations involved are self-explanatory (figure 56).

☐   *RECORD*

In the original method the tube was pressed to the stop at the end of the jig, marked with the file and then eased back for notching. It was then taken out of the jig for breaking. The chart goes into great detail in recording the movements of the hands, because in short cycle work of this kind fractions of seconds, when added together, may represent a large proportion of the total time needed for the job.

☐   *EXAMINE critically*

An examination of the details of the original method, using the questioning technique, at once raises certain points. (It is not considered necessary to go through

163

Figure 56.   *Two-handed process chart: cutting glass tubes (original method)*

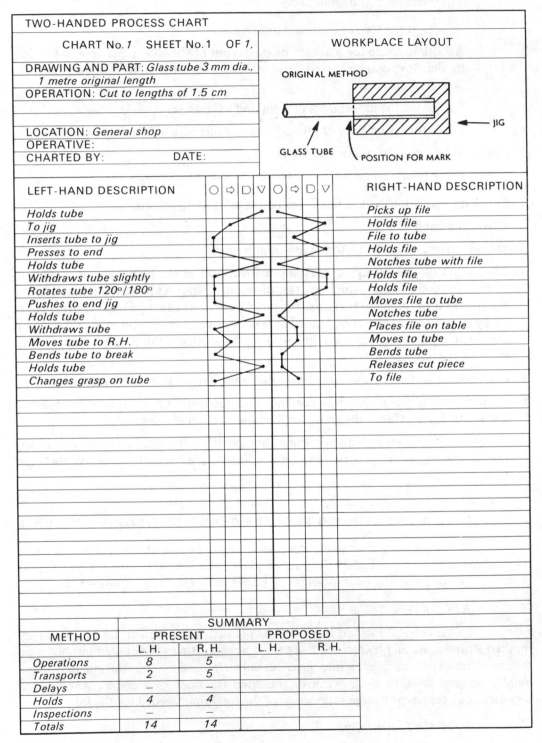

METHOD	PRESENT		PROPOSED	
	L.H.	R.H.	L.H.	R.H.
Operations	8	5		
Transports	2	5		
Delays	–	–		
Holds	4	4		
Inspections	–	–		
Totals	14	14		

164

the questions in sequence at this stage in the book: it is assumed that the reader will always do so.)

1. Why is it necessary to hold the tube in the jig?

2. Why cannot the tube be notched while it is being rotated instead of the right hand having to wait?

3. Why does the tube have to be taken out of the jig to break it?

4. Why pick up and put down the file at the end of each cycle? Can it not be held?

A study of the sketch will make the answers to the first three questions plain.

1. The tube will always have to be held because the length supported by the jig is short compared with the total length of the tube.

2. There is no reason why the tube cannot be rotated and notched at the same time.

3. The tube has to be taken out of the jig to be broken because, if the tube were broken by bending against the face of the jig, the short end would then have to be picked out—an awkward operation if very little were sticking out. If a jig were so designed that the short end would fall out when broken, it would not then be necessary to withdraw the tube.

The answer to the fourth question is also obvious.

4. Both hands are needed to break the tube using the old method. This might not be necessary if a new jig could be devised.

☐   *DEVELOP the new method*

Once these questions have been asked and answered, it is fairly easy to find a satisfactory solution to the problem. Figure 57 shows one possible solution. It will be seen that, in redesigning the jig, the studyman has arranged it in such a way that the notch is cut on the right-hand side of the supporting pieces, so that the short end will break away when given a sharp tap and it will no longer be necessary to withdraw the tube and use both hands to break off the end. The number of operations and movements has been reduced from 28 to six, as a result of which an increase in productivity of 133 per cent was expected. In fact this was exceeded, because the job is now more satisfactory following the elimination of irritating work such as "position tube in jig". The new method can be carried out without looking closely at the work, so that workers can be trained more easily and become less fatigued.

8. Reorganisation of a workplace by means of a two-handed process chart

ASSEMBLY OF POWER MOTOR STARTING WINDING TO CORE[1]

Figure 58 shows the workplace before reorganisation. Some thought has evidently been given to the operation, since a fixture has been provided for holding the

---

[1] This example from industrial practice was provided by the General Electric Company Ltd, Witton (United Kingdom), through whose courtesy the photographs and process charts have been made available. The process charts are reproduced in their original form. It will be seen that they differ somewhat from the newer practice recommended in this book, but careful examination will make them perfectly clear to the reader.

Figure 57.   *Two-handed process chart: cutting glass tubes (improved method)*

TWO-HANDED PROCESS CHART		
CHART No. *2* SHEET No. *1* OF *1*		WORKPLACE LAYOUT

DRAWING AND PART: *Glass tube 3 mm dia.,*
   1 metre original length
OPERATION: *Cut to lengths of 1.5 cm*

LOCATION: *General shop*
OPERATIVE:
CHARTED BY: DATE:

IMPROVED METHOD

GLASS TUBE   POSITION FOR NOTCH   JIG   STOP

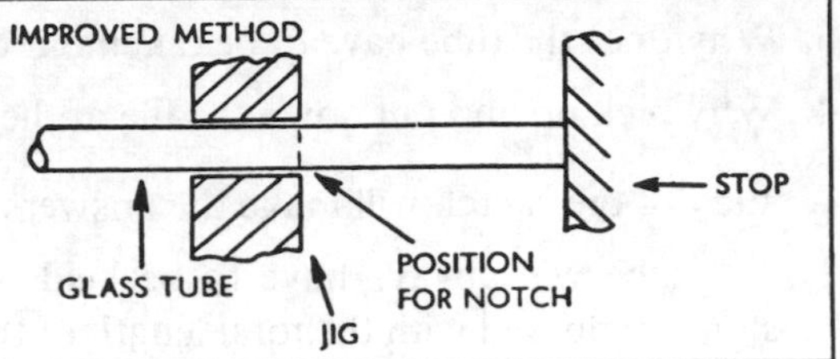

LEFT-HAND DESCRIPTION	○	⇨	D	▽	○	⇨	D	▽	RIGHT-HAND DESCRIPTION
Pushes tube to stop									Holds file
Rotates tube									Notches with file
Holds tube									Taps with file:
									end drops to box

SUMMARY

METHOD	PRESENT		PROPOSED	
	L. H.	R. H.	L. H.	R. H.
Operations	8	5	2	2
Transports	2	5	–	–
Delays	–	–	–	–
Holds	4	4	1	1
Inspections	–	–	–	–
Totals	14	14	3	3

166

assembly. Apart from this, the organisation of the workplace appears to have been left to the worker. The various tools and the ring gauge are placed quite conveniently at her right hand, although a study of the "Before" process chart shows that she always has to pick up the tamping tools with her right hand and pass them to her left. This occurs seven times in the course of one assembly. The handles of the tools are awkward to grasp since they lie flat on the bench. Lengths of systoflex tubing are upright in a tin in front of the fixture (a long reach for the worker). The prepared coils (not visible in this figure but seen in a tray in figure 59) are stated in the process chart to be placed on the shelf in front of the worker (another long reach).

Figure 61 shows the two-handed process charts before and after the alteration in method and re-laying out the workplace, in the original form in which they were drawn at the time. The process charts are accompanied (figure 60) by right- and left-handed activity charts (not described in this book) which show the relative activity of the individual hands. From these it will be seen that under the original method the left hand is idle during a considerable part of the cycle: the right hand performs nearly twice as many operations. Reference to the "Before" process chart shows that the left hand is used very largely either to hold components or to assist the right hand.

The "After" activity chart shows that the activities of the two hands are more nearly balanced. The number of operations performed by the right hand has been reduced to 143, although the number of delays has increased from nine to 16. This, however, is more than compensated by the reduction in both the number and the duration of the delays of the left hand, whose operations have been reduced to 129. It will be seen also in figure 61 that transport by hand (H) has been eliminated by the use of a conveyor (C).

The "After" process chart shows that the left hand is now much more usefully employed. There is only one "hold" for each hand; although the left hand is still used to some extent to assist the right, it is also used to carry out a number of operations of its own.

The process chart, although it gives details of the change in method, does not give any indication of the changes in the workplace layout. These may be seen in figure 59.

The workplace has been laid out according to the principles of motion economy and the working areas shown in figure 54. The workpiece and all the components and tools are well within the maximum working area. The fixture is the same, but it has been placed nearer the edge of the bench, where it is more convenient to the worker. The systoflex, wedges and other components are conveniently located in standard trays; the coils (a larger item) are in the large tray within easy reach of the worker's left hand. Special note should be taken of the positioning of the tools. These are located for the use of the appropriate hand with the handles in a position that is easy to grasp: even the scissors are tucked between the trays with their handles upwards. The ring gauge, which in figure 58 is to be seen lying flat on the bench (a difficult position from which to pick it up), is now upright in a specially shaped tin on the right-hand side of the bench where it is very simple to grasp: the operative need not look up from her work.

Figure 59 repays careful study. The compactness of the workplace encourages the operative to keep things in their proper places: a large amount of bench

167

Figure 58. *Example of workplace layout (original method)*

Figure 59. *Example of workplace layout (improved method)*

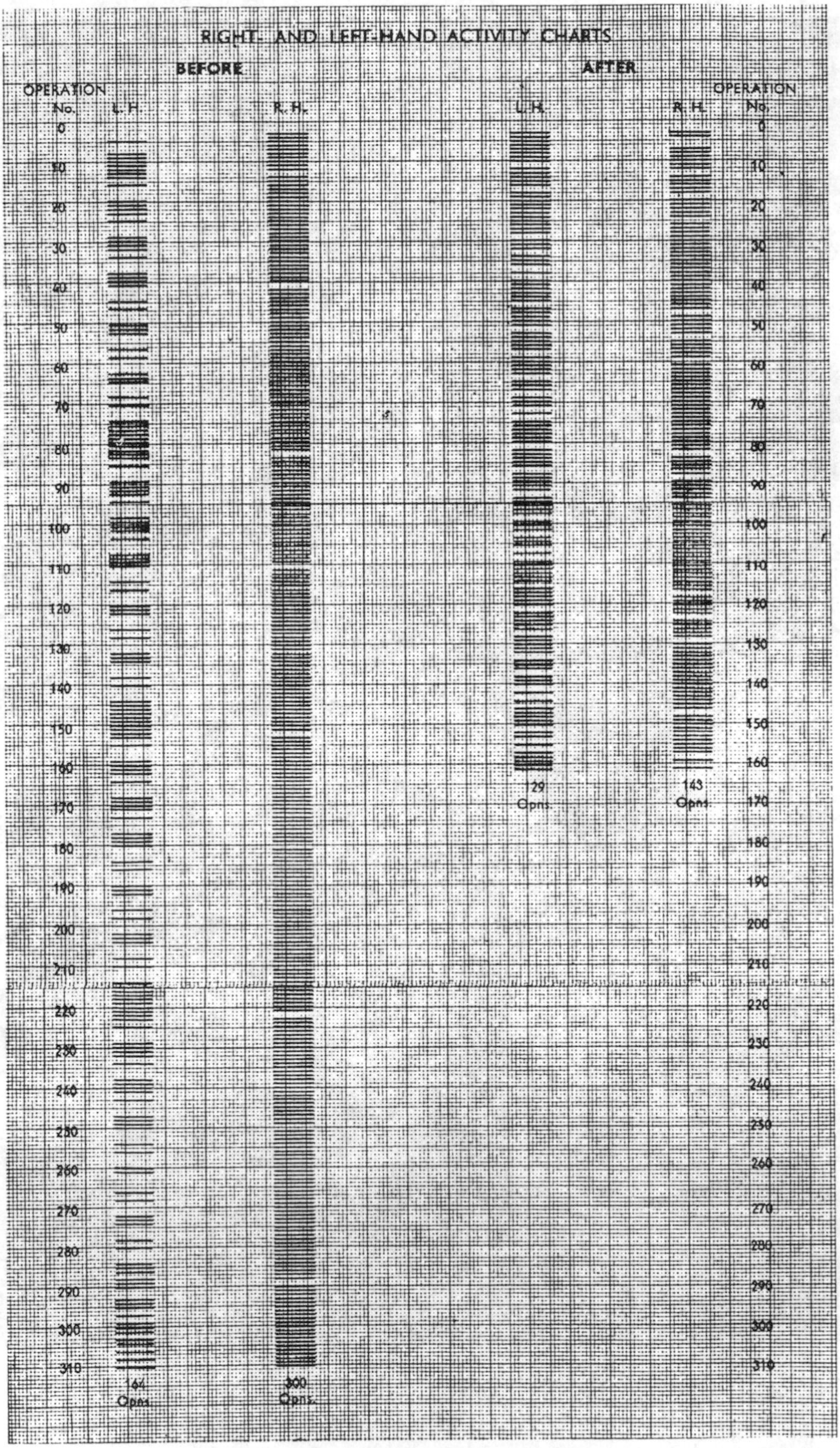

Figure 60. Right- and left-handed activity charts: assembly of power motor starting winding to core

space is an invitation to scatter tools and components on it. As regards economy of factory space, this new layout will pay for itself in two ways: first by making it possible to establish more workplaces in a given area; and second, by providing greater output from a given workplace. The operative will also find the work much less tiring because she no longer has to stretch and search.

9. Micromotion study

In certain types of operation, and particularly those with very short cycles which are repeated thousands of times (such as the packing of sweets into boxes or food cans into cartons), it is worth while going into much greater detail to determine

Table 11.   Therbligs

Symbol	Name	Abbreviation	Colour
	Search	Sh	Black
	Find	F	Grey
	Select	St	Light Grey
	Grasp	G	Red
	Hold	H	Gold ochre
	Transport Load	TL	Green
	Position	P	Blue
	Assemble	A	Violet
	Use	U	Purple
	Disassemble	DA	Light violet
	Inspect	I	Burnt ochre
	Pre-position	PP	Pale blue
	Release load	RL	Carmine red
	Transport Empty	TE	Olive green
	Rest for over-coming fatigue	R	Orange
	Unavoidable delay	UD	Yellow
	Avoidable delay	AD	Lemon yellow
	Plan	Pn	Brown

171

where movements and effort can be saved and to develop the best possible pattern of movement, thus enabling the operative to perform the operation repeatedly with a minimum of effort and fatigue. The techniques used for this purpose frequently make use of filming, and are known collectively as **micromotion study.**

The micromotion group of techniques is based on the idea of dividing human activity into divisions of movements or groups of movements (known as **therbligs**) according to the purpose for which they are made.

The divisions were devised by Frank B. Gilbreth, the founder of motion study; the word "therblig" is an anagram of his name. Gilbreth differentiated 17 fundamental hand or hand and eye motions, to which an eighteenth has subsequently been added. The therbligs cover movements or reasons for the absence of movement. Each therblig has a specific colour, symbol and letter for recording purposes. These are shown in table 11.

Therbligs refer primarily to motions of the human body at the workplace and to the mental activities associated with them. They permit a much more precise and detailed description of the work than any other method so far described in this book. On the other hand, considerable practice is required before they can be used for analysis with any degree of assurance.

It is not felt necessary in an introductory book of this kind to go deeply into these techniques, because so much can be done to improve productivity by using the simpler ones already described, before it becomes necessary to use such refinements. They are used much less than the simpler techniques, even in the highly industrialised countries, and then mainly in connection with mass-production operations, and they are more preached about than practised. They are, however, techniques for the expert, and in any case it would be imprudent for the trainee or comparatively inexperienced work study man to waste his time trying to save split seconds when there are sure to be plenty of jobs where productivity can be doubled and even trebled by using the more general methods.

10. The simo chart

Only one recording technique of micromotion study will be described here, namely the **simultaneous motion cycle chart,** known as the **simo chart** for short.

> **A simo chart is a chart, often based on film analysis, used to record simultaneously on a common time scale the therbligs or groups of therbligs performed by different parts of the body of one or more workers**

The simo chart is the micromotion form of the man type flow process chart. Because simo charts are used primarily for operations of short duration, often performed with extreme rapidity, it is generally necessary to compile them from films

Figure 62. A simo chart[1]

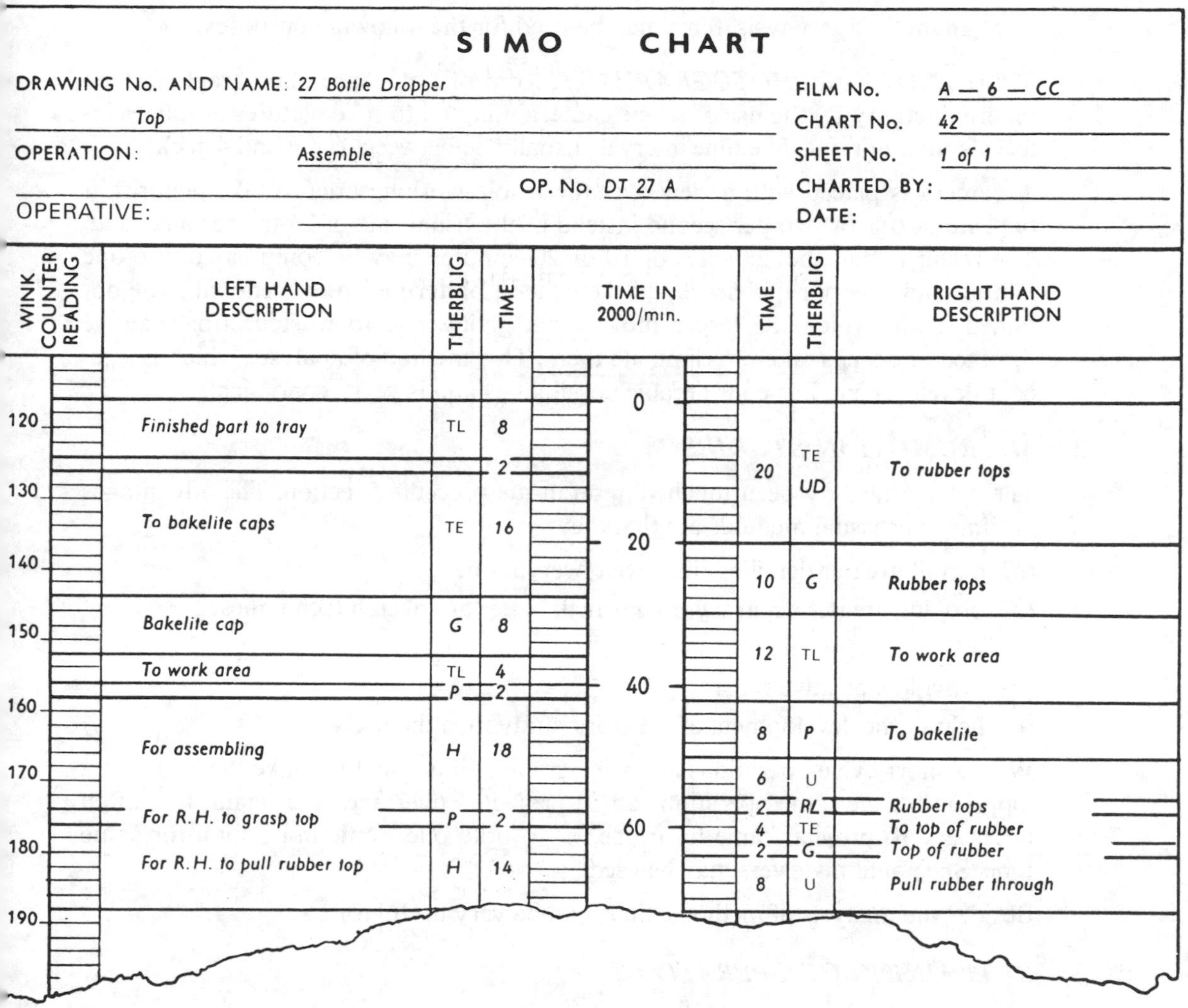

SIMO CHART

DRAWING No. AND NAME: *27 Bottle Dropper* FILM No. *A — 6 — CC*

 Top CHART No. *42*

OPERATION: *Assemble* SHEET No. *1 of 1*

 OP. No. *DT 27 A* CHARTED BY:

OPERATIVE: DATE:

WINK COUNTER READING		LEFT HAND DESCRIPTION	THERBLIG	TIME	TIME IN 2000/min.	TIME	THERBLIG	RIGHT HAND DESCRIPTION
120		Finished part to tray	TL	8	0			
				2		20	TE UD	To rubber tops
130		To bakelite caps	TE	16				
140					20	10	G	Rubber tops
150		Bakelite cap	G	8		12	TL	To work area
		To work area	TL	4				
			P	2	40			
160						8	P	To bakelite
		For assembling	H	18				
170						6	U	
		For R.H. to grasp top	P	2		2	RL	Rubber tops
					60	4	TE	To top of rubber
180						2	G	Top of rubber
		For R.H. to pull rubber top	H	14		8	U	Pull rubber through
190								

made of the operation which can be stopped at any point or projected in slow motion. It will be seen from the chart illustrated in figure 62 that the movements are recorded against time measured in "winks" (1 wink = 1/2000 minute). These are recorded by a "wink counter" placed in such a position that it can be seen rotating during the filming.

Motions are classified for each hand according to the list given in section 3 of this chapter. Some simo charts are drawn up listing the fingers used, wrist, lower and upper arms. The hatching in the various columns represents the therblig colours associated with the movements; the letters refer to the therblig symbols.

We shall not discuss the simo chart in any greater depth. The reader is advised not to try out micromotion study in practice without expert supervision.

---

[1] Adapted from Marvin E. Mundel: *Motion and time study: Principles and practice* (Englewood Cliffs, NJ, and Hemel Hempstead, UK, Prentice-Hall, 4th ed., 1970).

11. The use of films in methods analysis

In methods analysis, films may be used for the following purposes:

1. *MEMOMOTION PHOTOGRAPHY* (A form of time-lapse photography which records activity by the use of a ciné camera adapted to take pictures at longer intervals than normal. The time intervals usually lie between ½ sec and 4 sec).

A camera is placed with a view over the whole working area to take pictures at the rate of one or two per second instead of the usual rate of 24 frames a second. The result is that the activities of 10 or 20 minutes may be compressed into one minute and a very rapid survey of the general pattern of movements may be obtained, from which the larger movements giving rise to wasted effort can be detected and steps taken to eliminate them. This method of analysis, which is a recent development, has considerable possibilities and is very economical.

2. *MICROMOTION STUDIES*

These have already been touched upon in the preceding section. The advantages of films over visual methods are that they—

(a) permit greater detailing than eye observation;

(b) provide greater accuracy than pencil, paper and watch techniques;

(c) are more convenient;

(d) provide a positive record;

(e) help in the development of the work study men themselves.

Where short cycle operations are being studied, it is usual to make the film into a loop so that the same operation can be projected over and over again. It is often necessary to project frame by frame, or to hold one frame in position for some time. Special film viewers may be used.

Besides the analysis of methods, films can be very useful for

3. *RETRAINING OF OPERATIVES*

Both for this purpose and for analysis it may be necessary to have slow motion pictures of the process (produced by photographing at high speed); considerable use can be made of loops for this purpose.

12. Other recording techniques

Here we shall describe very briefly one or two other techniques of recording and analysis which have so far only been mentioned, and which will not be dealt with further in this introductory book.

Table 9 in Chapter 8 listed five diagrams indicating movement which are commonly used in method study. Three of these, the flow diagram, the string diagram and the travel chart, have already been described, with examples, in earlier chapters. The other two are the cyclegraph and the chronocyclegraph.

The **cyclegraph** is a record of a path of movement, usually traced by a continuous source of light on a photograph, preferably stereoscopic. The path of movement of a hand, for instance, may be recorded on a photograph in this way if the worker is asked to wear a ring carrying a small light which will make the trace on the photograph. Alternatively, such a light may be attached to a worker's helmet if the purpose is to obtain a record of the path over which he moves during the performance of a task.

The **chronocyclegraph** is a special form of cyclegraph in which the light source is suitably interrupted so that the path appears as a series of pear-shaped dots, the pointed end indicating the direction of movement and the spacing indicating the speed of movement.

In comparison with the other recording techniques outlined in this book, the cyclegraph and chronocyclegraph are of limited application, but there are occasions on which photographic traces of this sort can be useful.

13. The development of improved methods

In each of the examples of the different method study techniques given so far, our discussion has covered the three stages of *RECORD, EXAMINE* and *DEVELOP,* but has been focused primarily on the first two, the development stage being discussed only as far as was necessary to draw attention to the improvements made in method as a result of using the particular diagram or form being demonstrated.

It will now be appropriate to study a little more closely the manner in which improved methods can be developed.

One of the rewards of method study is the large saving which can often be made from quite small changes and inexpensive devices, such as chutes or suitable jigs.

An example of this is a small spring-loaded table, very cheaply made in plywood, for removing the tiles from an automatic tile-making machine. The spring was so calibrated that, each time a tile was pushed on to it by the machine, it was compressed until the top of the tile dropped to the level of the machine platform so that the table was ready to receive the next tile. This enabled the girl operating the machine to concentrate on loading the finished tiles on to a rack ready for firing while the new stack was piling up. When about a dozen tiles were in place, she was able to lift them off the table, which immediately sprang up to the level of the machine plat-form ready to receive the first tile of the next stack. This very simple device enabled the second operative formerly employed on this operation to be released for other work, an important feature in an area where skilled tile-pressers were difficult to ob-tain.

In many manufacturing plants the work study man may have to go beyond the study of the movements of materials and workers if he is going to make the most effective contribution to increased productivity. He must be prepared to discuss with the designers the possibility of using alternative materials which would make the product easier and quicker to manufacture. Even if he is not an expert in design—and, indeed, he cannot be expected to be—drawing attention to the possibilities of an alter-native may put ideas into the minds of the designers themselves which they had previously overlooked. After all, like everyone else, they are human and often hard-worked, and there is a strong temptation to specify a given material for a given product or component simply because it has always been used in the past.

Apart from the elimination of obviously wasteful movements—which can be done from the flow diagram or process chart—the development of improved methods calls for skill and ingenuity. It is likely to be more successful if the work study man is also well acquainted with the industry with which he is concerned. In any but the simplest manual operations, he will have to consult with the technical or supervisory staff and, even if he does know the right answer, it is better that he should do so, since a method which they have taken part in developing is likely to be accepted more readily than one which is introduced as someone else's idea. The same is true of the operatives. Let everyone put forward his ideas—two heads are better than one!

The fact that really successful methods improvement is a combined operation is being increasingly recognised. Many organisations, large and small, have set up groups for the improvement of manufacturing and operating methods. These groups may be permanent or set up for some particular job such as the re-laying out of a shop or factory, or the organisation of work. Such groups often decide on the division and allocation of work as well as other related functions such as the control of quality.

In the United Kingdom Joseph Lucas Ltd, manufacturers of electrical equipment and motor car accessories, have developed similar groups at various levels which consider every aspect of manufacturing efficiency from designing the product for more economic production onwards through all the processes and methods.

14. The methods laboratory

There is great value in having a small room or shop where the work study men can develop and try out new methods. It need not be elaborate or expensive; many devices can be tried out in wood before they are manufactured in metal. If the scale of the work study activities justifies it, one or two good all-round craftsmen can be seconded to this laboratory with some simple tools, such as a drill press and sheet-metal equipment, together with a good operative from the production shops who will try out the different "gadgets" in collaboration with the work study staff until the best method has been found. Having such a place saves interfering with the production shops or the plant engineer's department when things are wanted in a hurry, and the work study staff feel much freer to try out revolutionary ideas. New methods can be demonstrated to the management, foremen and operatives, who can be encouraged to try them out and make suggestions to be incorporated in the final version.

Do not let the work study shop become the place where everyone in the works comes when they "want a little job done quickly" or private repairs executed. There is a real danger of this, as more than one company has discovered.

On no account may the operative attached to the work study shop be used for the setting of time standards. It is quite acceptable to time him in order to compare the effectiveness of different methods, but time studies for standard setting must always be made in the shops under production conditions with regular operatives.

Chapter 12
Define, install, maintain

1. Obtaining approval for the improved method

Once a complete study of the job has been made, and the preferred new method developed, it is generally necessary to obtain the approval of the works management before proceeding to install it. The work study man should prepare a report giving details of the existing and proposed methods and should give his reasons for the changes suggested.

The report should show—

(1) Relative costs in material, labour and overheads of the two methods, and the savings expected.

(2) The cost of installing the new method, including the cost of any new equipment and of re-laying out shops or working areas, if this is required.

(3) Executive actions required to implement the new method.

Before it is finally submitted, the report should be discussed with the departmental supervision or management; if the costs of the change are small and all are agreed that it is a useful change, the work may proceed on the authority of the departmental manager or foreman.

If capital expenditure is involved, such as the purchase of material-handling equipment, or if complete agreement cannot be obtained from everyone concerned on the desirability of the change, the matter may have to be decided on by the management. In this case, it is almost certain that the work study man will be called upon to justify his estimates. If capital investment is involved to any extent, he will have to be able to convince doubting people, often non-technical, that it will really be justified. Great care must therefore be taken in preparing such estimates, since a failure to live up to them may damage both the work study man's own reputation and that of work study itself.

2. Defining the improved method

THE WRITTEN STANDARD PRACTICE

For all jobs other than those performed on standard machine tools or specialised machines where the process and methods are virtually controlled by the machine, it is desirable to prepare a written standard practice, also known as an "operative instruction sheet". This serves several purposes:

(1) It records the improved method for future reference, in as much detail as may be necessary.

(2) It can be used to explain the new method to the management, foremen and operatives. It also advises all concerned, including the works engineers, of any new equipment required or of changes needed in the layout of machines or workplaces.

(3) It is an aid to training or retraining operatives and can be used by them for reference until they are fully conversant with the new method.

(4) It forms the basis on which time studies may be taken for setting standards, although the element breakdown (see Chapter 16, section 6) will not necessarily be the same as the breakdown of motions.

The written standard practice outlines in simple terms the methods to be used by the operative. Therbligs and other method study symbols should not be used. Three sorts of information will normally be required—

(1) The tools and equipment to be used and the general operating conditions.

(2) A description of the method. The amount of detail required will depend on the nature of the job and the probable volume of production. For a job which will occupy several operatives for several months, the written standard practice may have to be very detailed, going into finger movements.

(3) A diagram of the workplace layout and, possibly, sketches of special tools, jigs or fixtures.

A very simple written standard practice for the operation studied in Chapter 11, section 7 (cutting glass tubes to length), is illustrated in figure 63. The same principle is followed in more complex cases. In some of these the description may run into several pages. The workplace layout and other diagrams may have to be put on a separate sheet. With the more widespread use in recent years of standardised printed sheets for process charts, it is becoming common practice to attach a fair copy of the appropriate process chart to the written standard practice, whenever the simple description entered thereon does not constitute a complete definition of the method.

3. Installing the improved method

The final stages in the basic procedure are perhaps the most difficult of all. It is at this point that active support is required from the management and trade unions alike. It is here that the personal qualities of the work study man, his ability to explain clearly and simply what he is trying to do and his gift for getting along with other people and winning their trust become of the greatest importance.

Installation can be divided into five stages, namely—

(1) Gaining acceptance of the change by the departmental supervision.

Figure 63.   Standard practice sheet

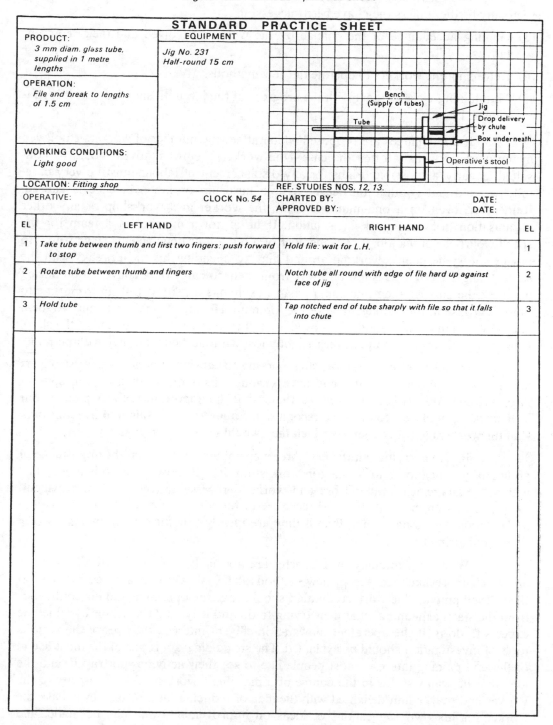

| STANDARD PRACTICE SHEET		
PRODUCT: 3 mm diam. glass tube, supplied in 1 metre lengths	**EQUIPMENT** Jig No. 231 Half-round 15 cm	
OPERATION: File and break to lengths of 1.5 cm		
WORKING CONDITIONS: Light good		
LOCATION: Fitting shop		**REF. STUDIES NOS.** 12, 13.
OPERATIVE:	**CLOCK No.** 54	**CHARTED BY:** DATE: **APPROVED BY:** DATE:

EL	LEFT HAND	RIGHT HAND	EL
1	Take tube between thumb and first two fingers: push forward to stop	Hold file: wait for L.H.	1
2	Rotate tube between thumb and fingers	Notch tube all round with edge of file hard up against face of jig	2
3	Hold tube	Tap notched end of tube sharply with file so that it falls into chute	3

(2) Gaining approval of the change by the management.

These two steps have already been discussed. There is little point in trying to go any further unless they have been successful.

(3) Gaining acceptance of the change by the workers involved and their representatives.

(4) Retraining the workers to operate the new methods.

(5) Maintaining close contact with the progress of the job until satisfied that it is running as intended.

If any changes are proposed which affect the number of workers employed in the operation—as is often the case—the workers' representatives should be consulted as early as possible. Plans for any displacement of labour must be very carefully worked out so that the least possible hardship or inconvenience is caused. Remember, even on a one-man operation, the worker in a workshop or any other organisation does not work in isolation. If he is not a member of a team for the specific purpose of his job, he is a member of a section or department; he gets used to having the same people working around him, to spending his meal breaks with the same "gang". Even if he is too far away from them to carry on a conversation during his work, he can see them; he can, perhaps, exchange a joke with them from time to time or grouse at the management or the foreman. He adjusts his personality to them and they to him. If he is suddenly moved, even if it is only to the other end of the shop, his social circle is broken up, he feels slightly lost without them and they without him.

In the case of a team or gang working together, the bonds are far stronger; and breaking up such a team may have serious effects on productivity, in spite of improved methods. It is only since the 1930s that the importance of group behaviour in a working area has come to be recognised. **Failure to take this into account may lead the workers to resist changes which they would otherwise accept.**

It is in carrying out the first three steps of installation that the importance of preliminary education and training in work study for all those likely to be concerned with it—management, supervisors and workers' representatives—becomes evident. People are much more likely to be receptive to the idea of change if they know and understand what is happening than if they are merely presented with the results of a sort of conjuring trick.

Where redundancy or a transfer are not likely to be involved, the workers are much more likely to accept new methods if they have been allowed to share in their development. The work study man should take the operative into his confidence from the start, explaining what he is trying to do and why, and the means by which he expects to do it. If the operative shows an intelligent interest, the uses of the various tools of investigation should be explained. The string diagram is one of the most useful of these in gaining interest: most people like to see their activities portrayed, and the idea that he walks so far in the course of a morning's work is often a surprise to the worker and makes him delighted with the idea of reducing his efforts. Always ask the worker for his own suggestions or ideas on improvements that can be made, and wherever they can be embodied, do so, **giving him the credit** for them (major suggestions may merit a monetary reward). Let him play as full a part as possible in the development of the new method, until he comes to feel it is mainly or partly his own.

It may not always be possible to obtain very active co-operation from un-skilled personnel, but even they usually have some views on how their jobs can be made easier—or less subject to interruption—which may give important leads to the work study man in reducing wasted time and effort.

Wholehearted co-operation at any level will only come as the result of confidence and trust. The work study man must convince the management that he knows what he is doing. He must have the respect of the supervisors and technicians, and they must realise that he is not there to displace them or show them up, but as a specialist at their disposal to help them. Finally, he must convince the workers that he is not going to harm them.

Where there is deep-rooted resistance to change, it may be necessary to decide whether the savings likely to be made by adopting the new method justify the time and trouble involved in putting the change through and retraining older operatives. It may be cheaper to concentrate on new trainees and let the older workers continue to work in the way they know.

In gaining the trust of the workers, the work study man will find that they will tend to turn to him for decisions rather than to the foreman (a danger already discussed). This situation must not be allowed to arise. The work study man must make certain from the first that everyone understands that he cannot give executive decisions and that the instructions concerning the introduction and application of the new methods must come from the foreman to the worker in the first instance. Only then can he proceed.

4. Training and retraining operatives

The extent to which the workers require retraining will depend entirely on the nature of the job. It will be greatest in the case of jobs involving a high degree of manual dexterity which have long been done by traditional methods. In such cases it may be necessary to resort to films to demonstrate the old and the new methods and the manner in which movements should be made. Each job will have to be treated on its merits.

In the training or retraining of operatives, the important thing is to develop the **habit** of doing the job in the correct way. Habit is a valuable aid to increased productivity as it reduces the need for conscious thought. Good habits can be formed just as easily as bad ones.

Beginners can be taught to follow a numbered sequence illustrated on a chart or they may be taught on the machine itself. Either way, they must be made to understand the reason for every movement. Still pictures together with instruction sheets have proved very successful. Film strips can also be used.

Films are particularly valuable when retraining. When old habits have to be broken, it may be found that the operative is quite unaware of what he is doing. A film in slow motion will enable him to see his exact movements and, once he knows, he can start to learn the new method. It is important that the new method should be really different from the old, otherwise the operative will tend to slip back into his old ways, especially if he is not young and has spent many years doing the job.

181

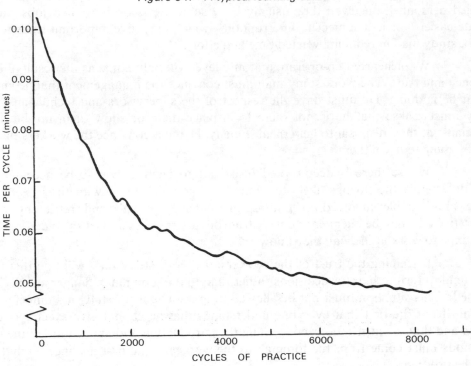

Figure 64. A typical learning curve

In learning a new series of movements, the operative gathers speed and reduces the time required to perform them very quickly at first. The rate of improvement soon begins to slow up, however, and it often requires long practice to achieve really high and consistent speed, although the adoption of modern accelerated training methods will considerably shorten the time needed. A typical "learning curve" is shown in figure 64.

Experiments have shown that in the first stages of learning, to obtain the best results, rests between periods of practice should be longer than the periods of practice themselves. This situation alters rapidly, however, and when the operative has begun to grasp the new method and to pick up speed, rest periods can be very much shorter.

As part of the process of installation it is essential to keep in close touch with the job, once it has been started, to ensure that the operative is developing speed and skill and that there are no unforeseen snags. This activity is often known as "nursing" the new method, and the term is an apt one. Only when the work study man is satisfied that the productivity of the job is at least at the level he estimated and that the operative has settled down to it can it be left—for a time.

5. Maintaining the new method

It is important that, when a method is installed, it should be **maintained** in its specified form, and that workers should not be allowed to slip back into old methods, or introduce elements not allowed for, unless there is very good reason for doing so.

To be maintained, a method must first be very clearly defined and specified. This is especially important where it is to be used for setting time standards for incentive or other purposes. Tools, layout and elements of movement must be specified beyond any risk of misinterpretation. The extent to which it is necessary to go into minute details will be determined by the job itself.

Action by the work study department is necessary to maintain the application of the new method because, human nature being what it is, workers and foremen or chargehands will tend to allow a drift away from the method laid down, if there is no check. Many disputes over time standards arise because the method being followed is not the one for which the time was specified; foreign elements have crept in. If the method is properly maintained, this cannot happen. If it is found that an improvement can be made in the method (and there are very few methods which cannot be improved in time, often by the operative himself), this should be officially incorporated, a new specification drawn up and new time standards set.

6. Conclusion

In this and the preceding chapters an attempt has been made to explain and illustrate some of the more common methods of improving productivity through the saving of wasted effort and time, and by reducing the work content of the process. Good method studies will do more than this, because they will draw attention to waste of material and waste of capital invested in equipment.

In the chapters which follow, we shall discuss work measurement. This is one of the principal tools of investigation by which sources of ineffective time can be disclosed. It is also the means of setting time standards on which planning and control of production, incentive schemes and labour cost control data can be based. All these are powerful tools for reducing ineffective time and for raising productivity.

Part three
Work measurement

Chapter 13
General remarks
on work measurement

1. Definition

In Chapter 4 it was said that work study consists of two complementary techniques—method study and work measurement. In that chapter both were defined, and before we go on to discuss work measurement it is worth while repeating the definition of that technique given there.

> **Work measurement is the application of techniques designed to establish the time for a qualified worker to carry out a specified job at a defined level of performance**

We shall have occasion to examine several features of this carefully thought-out definition in more detail in later chapters. For instance, the reader will have noted the references to "a qualified worker", and to "a defined level of performance". We need not concern ourselves with the exact meaning of these terms for the moment. It is worth noting, however, that the term "work measurement", which we have referred to hitherto as a technique, is really a term used to describe a family of techniques, any one of which can be used to measure work, rather than a single technique by itself. The principal techniques which are classed as work measurement techniques are listed in section 5 of this chapter.

2. The purpose of work measurement

In Chapter 2 we discussed the way in which the total time of manufacture of an article was increased by undesirable features of the product itself, by bad operation of the process and by ineffective time added in the course of production owing to shortcomings on the part of the management or to actions of the workers. All these factors tended to reduce the productivity of the enterprise.

In Chapter 3 we discussed the management techniques by which these factors could be eliminated or, at any rate, reduced. Method study has been shown to be one of the principal techniques by which the work involved in the product or the process could be decreased by the systematic investigation and critical examination of existing methods and processes and the development and installation of improved methods.

Reference to figures 4 and 5 (pp. 19 and 23) shows, however, that the reduction of the actual work involved in the product or the process to the minimum possible takes us only part of the way towards achieving maximum productivity from the resources of manpower and plant available. Even if the essential work is reduced to the minimum, there is quite likely to be a great deal of unnecessary time taken in the course of manufacture, due to the failure of the management to organise and control as efficiently as it might; and, beyond that, further time is likely to be wasted through the action or inaction of workers.

Method study is the principal technique for reducing the work involved, primarily by **eliminating unnecessary movement** on the part of material or operatives and by substituting good methods for poor ones. Work measurement is concerned with investigating, reducing and subsequently **eliminating ineffective time,** that is time during which no effective work is being performed, whatever the cause.

Work measurement, as the name suggests, provides the management with a means of measuring the time taken in the performance of an operation or series of operations in such a way that ineffective time is shown up and can be separated from effective time. In this way its existence, nature and extent become known where previously they were concealed within the total. One of the surprising things about factories where work measurement has never been employed is the amount of ineffective time whose very existence is unsuspected—or which is accepted as "the usual thing" and something inevitable that no one can do much about—that is built into the process. Once the existence of ineffective time has been revealed and the reasons for it tracked down, steps can usually be taken to reduce it.

Here work measurement has another role to play. Not only can it reveal the existence of ineffective time; it can also be used to set standard times for carrying out the work, so that, if any ineffective time does creep in later, it will immediately be shown up as an excess over the standard time and will thus be brought to the attention of the management.

Earlier it was mentioned that method study can reveal shortcomings of design, material and method of manufacture, and, as such, affects mainly technical people. Work measurement is more likely to show up the management itself and the behaviour of the workers. Because of this it is apt to meet with far greater resistance than method study. Nevertheless, if the efficient operation of the enterprise as a whole is being sought, the application of work measurement, properly carried out, is one of the best means of achieving it.

It is unfortunate that work measurement—and in particular time study, its principal technique—acquired a bad reputation in the past, especially in trade union circles. This was because in many early applications it was directed almost exclusively to reducing the ineffective time within the control of the operatives by setting standards of performance for them, while the ineffective time within the control of the management was virtually ignored. The causes of ineffective time over which the management has some control are much more numerous than those which lie within the direct control of the workers. Furthermore, experience has shown that, if causes of ineffective time such as hold-ups due to lack of raw materials or to plant breakdowns are allowed to go on without real efforts being made to eliminate them, operatives tend to get discouraged and slack, and "workers' ineffective time" increases. This is only to be expected: the attitude taken by the workers is, quite simply: "Well, if we are going to be stopped from doing our jobs by something which we can do nothing about and which it is the management's job to put right, why should we work harder? Let the management put its own house in order first." It is an argument that can hardly be countered.

Just as method study should precede work measurement in any reorganisation that takes place, so must the elimination of ineffective time due to management shortcomings precede any attack on the ineffective time within the control of the workers. Indeed, the mere fact of reducing the hold-ups and stoppages within the control of the management will tend to reduce the waste of time by the operatives, because they will find themselves faced with proper supplies of work and of material, and will have the general feeling that the management is "on its toes". This will in itself have a beneficial effect without the application of incentive schemes or of any form of coercion.

Work measurement may start a chain reaction throughout the organisation. How does this come about?

The first thing to realise is that breakdowns and stoppages taking effect at the shop floor level are generally only the end results of a series of management actions or failures to act.

Let us take an example of excessive idle time of an expensive machine, revealed by a study taken over several days. This piece of plant is very productive when operating but takes a long time to set up. It is found that a great deal of the idle time is due to the fact that the batches of work being put on this machine are very small, so that almost as much time is spent in resetting it to do new operations as is spent in actual production. The chain of reactions resulting from this discovery may be something like this:

☐ **The work study department**

 reports that work measurement reveals that the machine is idle for excessively long periods because of small orders coming from the planning office. This is substantially increasing the cost of manufacture. It suggests that the planning office should do some proper planning and either combine several orders for the same product into one large order or make more for stock.

☐ **The planning office**

 complains that it has to work on the instructions of the sales office, which never seems to sell enough of any one product to make up a decent-sized batch and cannot give any forecast of future orders so that more can be made for stock.

☐ **The sales office**

 says that it cannot possibly make forecasts or provide large orders of any one product as long as it remains the policy of top management to accept every variation that customers like to ask for. Already the catalogue is becoming too large: almost every job is now a "special".

189

☐   **The managing director**

when the effect of his marketing policy (or lack of it) on the production costs is brought to his attention, is surprised and says that he never thought of it like that; all he was trying to do was to prevent orders going to his competitors by being as obliging to his customers as possible.

One of the principal purposes of work study will have been served if the original investigation leads the managing director to think again about his marketing policy. Enthusiastic work study men may, however, find it well to pause a moment and think about the fact that such chains of reaction tend to make someone ask: "Who started this, anyway?" People do not like being "shown up". This is one of the situations in which a good deal of tact may have to be used. It is not the work study man's job to dictate marketing policy, but merely to bring to the attention of the management the effect of that policy on the company's costs and hence on its competitive position.

Thus it can be seen that the purposes of work measurement are to reveal the nature and extent of ineffective time, from whatever cause, so that action can be taken to eliminate it; and then to set standards of performance of such a kind that they will be attainable only if all avoidable ineffective time is eliminated and the work is performed by the best available method and by personnel suitable in training and ability to their tasks.

We can now go on to discuss in greater detail the uses and techniques of work measurement.

3. The uses of work measurement

Revealing existing causes of ineffective time through study, important though it is, is perhaps less important in the long term than the setting of sound time standards, since these will continue to apply as long as the work to which they refer continues to be done and will show up any ineffective time or additional work which may occur once they have been established.

In the process of setting standards it may be necessary to use work measurement—

(1) To compare the efficiency of alternative methods. Other conditions being equal, the method which takes the least time will be the best method.

(2) To balance the work of members of teams, in association with multiple activity charts, so that, as nearly as possible, each member has a task taking an equal time to perform (see Chapter 10, section 4).

(3) To determine, in association with man and machine multiple activity charts, the number of machines an operative can run (see Chapter 10, section 4).

The time standards, once set, may then be used—

(4) To provide information on which the planning and scheduling of production can be based, including the plant and labour requirements for carrying out the programme of work and the utilisation of available capacity.

(5) To provide information on which estimates for tenders, selling prices and delivery promises can be based.

(6) To set standards of machine utilisation and labour performance which can be used for any of the above purposes and as a basis for incentive schemes.

(7) To provide information for labour-cost control and to enable standard costs to be fixed and maintained.

It is thus clear that work measurement provides the basic information necessary for all the activities of organising and controlling the work of an enterprise in which the time element plays a part. Its uses in connection with these activities will be more clearly seen when we have shown how the standard time is obtained.

4. The basic procedure

In section 5 of Chapter 4 we described the basic steps of work study, embracing both method study and work measurement. The basic procedure of method study has been described separately in figure 21 (page 81) and in the text on page 80. We shall now isolate those steps which are necessary for the systematic carrying out of work measurement. These steps and the techniques necessary for achieving them are shown diagrammatically in figure 65. They are—

□	*SELECT*	the work to be studied.
□	*RECORD*	all the relevant data relating to the circumstances in which the work is being done, the methods and the elements of activity in them.
□	*EXAMINE*	the recorded data and the detailed breakdown **critically** to ensure that the most effective method and motions are being used and that unproductive and foreign elements are separated from productive elements.
□	*MEASURE*	the quantity of work involved in each element, in terms of *time,* using the appropriate work measurement technique.
□	*COMPILE*	the standard time for the operation, which in the case of stop-watch time study will include time allowances to cover relaxation, personal needs, etc.
□	*DEFINE*	precisely the series of activities and method of operation for which the time has been compiled and issue the time as standard for the activities and methods specified.

Figure 65.   Work measurement

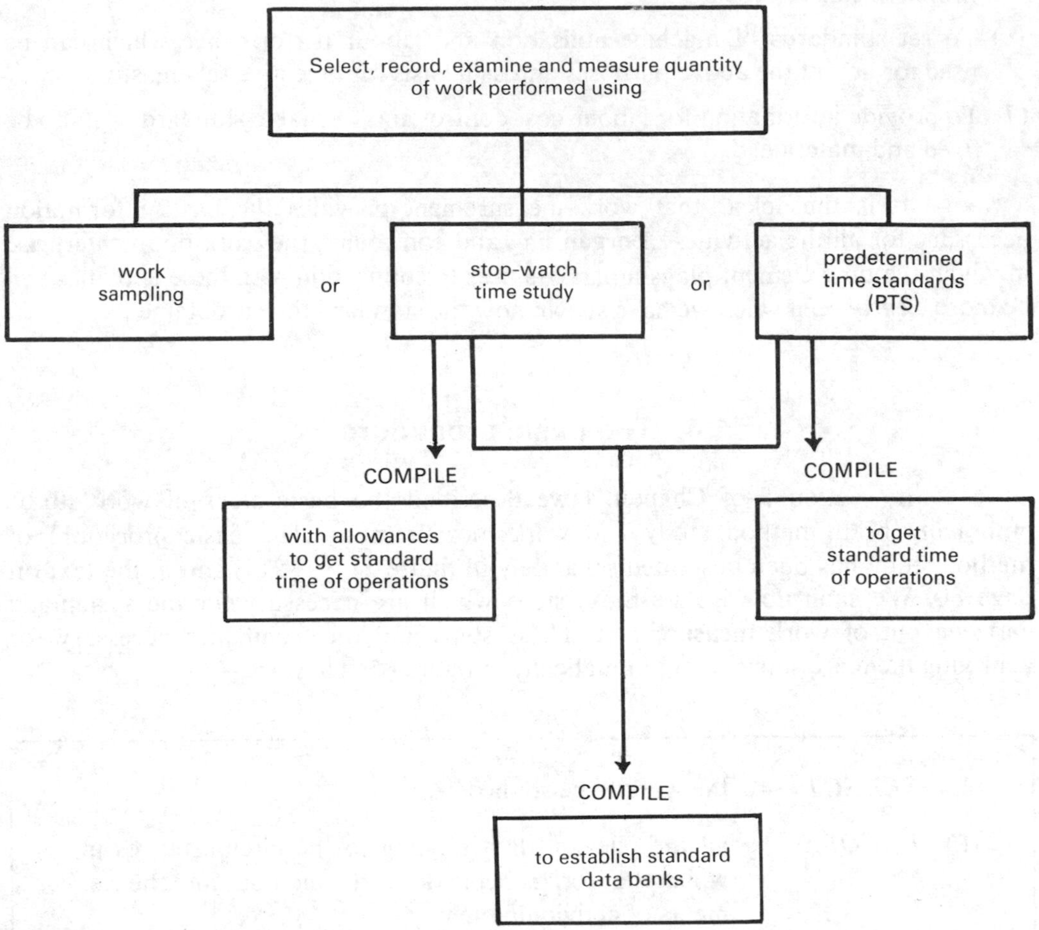

```
          ┌─────────────────────────────────────────┐
          │  Select, record, examine and measure     │
          │  quantity of work performed using         │
          └─────────────────────────────────────────┘
                            │
      ┌─────────────────────┼─────────────────────┐
      │                     │                     │
┌───────────┐        ┌───────────┐        ┌────────────────┐
│   work    │  or    │ stop-watch │  or   │ predetermined  │
│ sampling  │        │ time study │        │ time standards │
│           │        │            │        │     (PTS)      │
└───────────┘        └───────────┘        └────────────────┘
                      │        │                   │
                 COMPILE       │              COMPILE
              ┌───────────┐    │          ┌───────────┐
              │with allow-│    │          │  to get   │
              │ances to   │    │          │ standard  │
              │get standard│   │          │time of    │
              │time of    │    │          │operations │
              │operations │    │          └───────────┘
              └───────────┘    │
                               │
                           COMPILE
                        ┌───────────┐
                        │to establish│
                        │standard    │
                        │data banks  │
                        └───────────┘
```

It will be necessary to take the full range of steps listed above only if a time is to be published as a standard. When work measurement is being used only as a tool of investigation of ineffective time before or during a method study, or to compare the effectiveness of alternative methods, only the first four steps are likely to be needed.

5. The techniques of work measurement

The following are the principal techniques by which work measurement is carried out:

☐   work sampling;

☐   stop-watch time study;

☐   predetermined time standards (PTS);

☐   standard data.

In the next few chapters we shall describe each of these techniques in some detail.

Chapter 14
Work sampling

> **Work sampling is a method of finding the percentage occurrence of a certain activity by statistical sampling and random observations**

1. The need for work sampling

Work sampling (also known as "activity sampling", "ratio-delay study", "random observation method", "snap-reading method" and "observation ratio study") is, as the name implies, a sampling technique. Let us first see why such a technique is needed.

In order to obtain a complete and accurate picture of the productive time and idle time of the machines in a specific production area, it would be necessary to observe continuously all the machines in that area and to record when and why any of the machines were stopped. It would of course be quite impossible to do this unless a large number of workers spent the whole of their time on this task alone—an unrealistic proposition.

If it were possible to note at a glance the state of every machine in a factory at a given moment, however, it might be found that, say, 80 per cent of the machines were working and 20 per cent were stopped. If this action were repeated 20 or more times at different times of the day and if each time the proportion of machines working was always 80 per cent, it would be possible to say with some confidence that at any one time there were always 80 per cent of the machines working.

As it is not generally possible to do this either, the next best method has to be adopted: that of making tours of the factory at random intervals, noting which machines are working and which are stopped, and noting the cause of each stoppage. This is the basis of the **work sampling** technique. When the sample size is large enough and the observations made are indeed at random, there is quite a high probability that these observations will reflect the real situation, plus or minus a certain margin of error.

2. A few words about sampling

Unlike the costly and impractical method of continuous observation, sampling is mainly based on **probability.** Probability has been defined as "the extent to which an event is likely to occur". A simple and oft-mentioned example that illustrates the point is that of tossing a coin. When we toss a coin there are two possibilities: that it will come down "heads", or that it will come down "tails". The law of probability says that we are likely to have 50 heads and 50 tails in every 100 tosses of the coin. Note that we use the term "likely to have". In fact, we might have a score of 55-45, say, or 48-52, or some other ratio. But it has been proved that the law becomes increasingly accurate as the number of tosses increase. In other words, the greater the number of tosses, the more chance we have of arriving at a ratio of 50 heads to 50 tails. This suggests that the larger the size of the sample, the more accurate or representative it becomes with respect to the original "population", or group of items under consideration.

We can therefore visualise a scale where, at one end, we can have the complete accuracy achieved by continuous observation and, at the other end, very doubtful results derived from a few observations only. The size of the sample is therefore important, and we can express our confidence in whether or not the sample is representative by using a certain **confidence level.**

3. Establishing confidence levels

Let us go back to our previous example and toss five coins at a time, and then record the number of times we have heads and the number of times we have tails for each toss of these five coins. Let us then repeat this operation 100 times. The results could be presented as in table 12, or graphically as in figure 66.

Table 12.   Proportional distribution of "heads" and "tails" (100 tosses of five coins at a time)

Combination		Number of combinations
Heads (p)	Tails (q)	
5	0	3
4	1	17
3	2	30
2	3	30
1	4	17
0	5	3
		100

If we considerably increase the number of tosses and in each case toss a large number of coins at a time, we can obtain a smoother curve, such as that shown in figure 67.

This curve, called the **curve of normal distribution,** may also be depicted as in figure 68. Basically, this curve tells us that, in the majority of cases, the tendency is for the number of heads to equal the number of tails in any one series of tosses (when $p = q$ the number of tosses is a maximum). In few cases, however, is p markedly different from q due to mere chance.

194

Figure 66. Proportional distribution of "heads" and "tails" (100 tosses of five coins at a time)

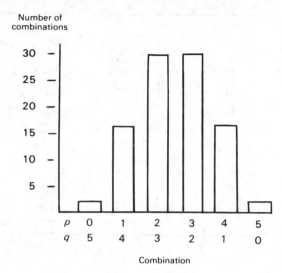

Curves of normal distribution may be of many shapes. They may be flatter, or more rounded. To describe these curves we use two attributes: $\overline{x}$, which is the average or measure of central dispersion; and σ, which is the deviation from the average, referred to as standard deviation. Since in this case we are dealing with a proportion, we use σp to denote the standard error of the proportion.

The area under the curve of normal distribution can be calculated. In figure 68 one σp on both sides of $\overline{x}$ gives an area of 68.27 per cent of the total area; two σp on both sides of $\overline{x}$ gives an area of 95.45 per cent and three σp on both sides of $\overline{x}$ gives an area of 99.73 per cent. We can put this in another way and say that, provided that we are not biased in our random sampling, 95.45 per cent of all our observations will fall within $\overline{x} \pm 2\ \sigma p$ and 99.73 per cent of all our observations will fall within $\overline{x} \pm 3\ \sigma p$.

Figure 67. Distribution curve showing probabilities of combinations when large samples are used

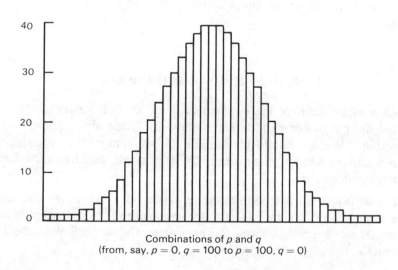

Combinations of p and q
(from, say, $p = 0$, $q = 100$ to $p = 100$, $q = 0$)

195

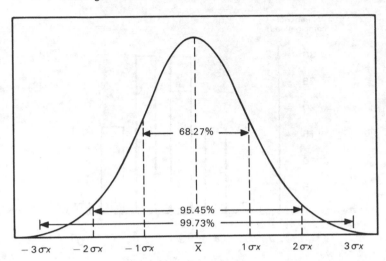

Figure 68. Curve of normal distribution

This is in fact the degree of confidence we have in our observations. To make things easier, however, we try to avoid using decimal percentages: it is more convenient to speak of a 95 per cent confidence level than of a 95.45 per cent confidence level. To achieve this we can change our calculations and obtain—

95   per cent confidence level or 95   per cent of the area under the curve $= 1.96 \; \sigma p$
99   per cent confidence level or 99   per cent of the area under the curve $= 2.58 \; \sigma p$
99.9 per cent confidence level or 99.9 per cent of the area under the curve $= 3.3 \;\; \sigma p$

In this case we can say that if we take a large sample **at random** we can be confident that in 95 per cent of the cases our observations will fall within $\pm 1.96 \; \sigma p$, and so on for the other values.

In work sampling the most commonly used level is the 95 per cent confidence level.

4. Determination of sample size

As well as defining the confidence level for our observations we have to decide on the margin of error that we can allow for these observations. We must be able to say that: "We are confident that for 95 per cent of the time this particular observation is correct within ± 5 per cent," or 10 per cent, or whatever other range of accuracy we may decide on.

Let us now return to our example about the productive time and the idle time of the machines in a factory. There are two methods of determining the sample size that would be appropriate for this example: the statistical method, and the nomogram method.

196

STATISTICAL METHOD

The formula used in this method is—

$$\sigma p = \sqrt{\frac{pq}{n}}$$

where

σp = standard error of proportion
p = percentage of idle time
q = percentage of working time
n = number of observations or sample size we wish to determine.

Before we can use this formula, however, we need to have at least an idea of the values of p and q. The first step is therefore to carry out a number of random observations in the working area. Let us assume that some 100 observations were carried out as a preliminary study and at random, and that these showed the machine to be idle in 25 per cent of the cases ($p = 25$) and to be working 75 per cent of the time ($q = 75$). We thus have approximate values for p and q; in order now to determine the value of n, we must find out the value of σp.

Let us choose a confidence level of 95 per cent with a 10 per cent margin of error (that is, we are confident that in 95 per cent of the cases our estimates will be $\pm$ 10 per cent of the real value).

At the 95 per cent confidence level

$$1.96 \, \sigma p = 10$$
$$\therefore \quad \sigma p = 5 \text{ (approx.)}.$$

We can now go back to our original equation to derive n:

$$\sigma p = \sqrt{\frac{pq}{n}}$$

$$\therefore \quad 5 = \sqrt{\frac{25 \times 75}{n}}$$

$$\therefore \quad n = 75 \text{ observations.}$$

If we reduce the margin of error to $\pm$ 5 per cent, we have

$$1.96 \, \sigma p = 5$$
$$\therefore \quad \sigma p = 2.5 \text{ (approx.)}$$

$$\therefore \quad 2.5 = \sqrt{\frac{25 \times 75}{n}}$$

$$\therefore \quad n = \frac{25 \times 75}{(2.5)^2}$$

$$= 300 \text{ observations.}$$

197

In other words, if we reduce the margin of error by half, the sample size will have to be quadrupled.

NOMOGRAM METHOD

An easier way to determine sample size is to read off the number of observations needed directly from a nomogram such as the one reproduced in figure 69. Taking our previous example, we draw a line from the "percentage occurrence" ordinate p (in this case 25-75) to intercept the "error (accuracy required)" ordinate (say, 5 per cent) and extend it until it meets the "number of observations" ordinate n, which it intercepts at 300 for the 95 per cent confidence level. This is a very quick way of determining sample size.

5. Making random observations

Our previous conclusions are valid provided that we can make the number of observations needed to attain the confidence level and accuracy required, and also provided that these observations are made **at random.**

To ensure that our observations are in fact made at random, we can use a random table such as the one in table 13. Various types of random table exist, and these can be used in different ways. In our case let us assume that we shall carry out our observations during a day shift of eight hours, from 7 a.m. to 3 p.m. An eight-hour day has 480 minutes. These may be divided into 48 ten-minute periods.

We can start by choosing any number at random from our table, for example by closing our eyes and placing a pencil point somewhere on the table. Let us assume that in this case we pick, by mere chance, the number 11 which is in the second block, fourth column, fourth row (see table 13). We now choose any number between 1 and 10. Assume that we choose the number 2; we now go down the column picking out every second reading and noting it down, as shown below (if we had chosen the number 3, we should pick out every third figure, and so on).

| 11 | 38 | 45 | 87 | 68 | 20 | 11 | 26 | 49 | 05 |

Looking at these numbers, we find that we have to discard 87, 68 and 49 because they are too high (since we have only 48 ten-minute periods, any number above 48 has to be discarded). Similarly, the second 11 will also have to be discarded since it is a number that has already been picked out. We therefore have to continue with our readings to replace the four numbers we have discarded. Using the same method, that is choosing every second number after the last one (05), we now have

| 14 | 15 | 47 | 22 |

These four numbers are within the desired range and have not appeared before. Our final selection may now be arranged numerically and the times of observation throughout the eight-hour day worked out. Thus our smallest number (05) represents the fifth ten-minute period after the work began at 7 a.m. Thus our first observation will be at 7.50 a.m., and so on (see table 14).

Table 13.   Table of random numbers

49 54 43 54 82	17 37 93 23 78	87 35 20 96 43	84 26 34 91 64
57 24 55 06 88	77 04 74 47 67	21 76 33 50 25	83 92 12 06 76
16 95 55 67 19	98 10 50 71 75	12 86 73 58 07	44 39 52 38 79
78 64 56 07 82	52 42 07 44 38	15 51 00 13 42	99 66 02 79 54
09 47 27 96 54	49 17 46 09 62	90 52 84 77 27	08 02 73 43 28
44 17 16 58 09	79 83 86 19 62	06 76 50 03 10	55 23 64 05 05
84 16 07 44 99	83 11 46 32 24	20 14 85 88 45	10 93 72 88 71
82 97 77 77 81	07 45 32 14 08	32 98 94 07 72	93 85 79 10 75
50 92 26 ⑪ 97	00 56 76 31 38	80 22 02 53 53	86 60 42 04 53
83 39 50 08 30	42 34 07 96 88	54 42 06 87 98	35 85 29 48 39
40 33 20 38 26	13 89 51 03 74	17 76 37 13 04	07 74 21 19 30
96 83 50 87 75	97 12 25 93 47	70 33 24 03 54	97 77 46 44 80
88 42 95 45 72	16 64 36 16 00	04 43 18 66 79	94 77 24 21 90
33 27 14 34 09	45 59 34 68 49	12 72 07 34 45	99 27 72 95 14
50 27 89 87 19	20 15 37 00 49	52 85 66 60 44	38 68 88 11 80
55 74 30 77 40	44 22 78 84 26	04 33 46 09 52	68 07 97 06 57
59 29 97 68 60	71 91 38 67 54	13 58 18 24 76	15 54 55 95 52
48 55 90 65 72	96 57 69 36 10	96 46 92 42 45	97 60 49 04 91
66 37 32 20 30	77 84 57 03 29	10 45 65 04 26	11 04 96 67 24
68 49 69 10 82	53 75 91 93 30	34 25 20 57 27	40 48 73 51 92
83 62 64 11 12	67 19 00 71 74	60 47 21 29 68	02 02 37 03 31
06 09 19 74 66	02 94 37 34 02	76 70 90 30 86	38 45 94 30 38
33 32 51 26 38	79 78 45 04 91	16 92 53 56 16	02 75 50 95 98
42 38 97 01 50	87 75 66 81 41	40 01 74 91 62	48 51 84 08 32
96 44 33 49 13	34 86 82 53 91	00 52 43 48 85	27 55 26 89 62
64 05 71 95 86	11 05 65 09 68	76 83 20 37 90	57 16 00 11 66
75 73 88 05 90	52 27 41 14 86	22 98 12 22 08	07 52 74 95 80
33 96 02 75 19	07 60 62 93 55	59 33 82 43 90	49 37 38 44 59
97 51 40 14 02	04 02 33 31 08	39 54 16 49 36	47 95 93 13 30
15 06 15 93 20	01 90 10 75 06	40 78 78 89 62	02 67 74 17 33
22 35 85 15 33	92 03 51 59 77	59 56 78 06 83	52 91 05 70 74
09 98 42 99 64	61 71 62 99 15	06 51 29 16 93	58 05 77 09 51
54 87 66 47 54	73 32 08 11 12	44 95 92 63 16	29 56 24 29 48
58 37 78 80 70	42 10 50 67 42	32 17 55 85 74	94 44 67 16 94
87 59 36 22 41	26 78 63 06 55	13 08 27 01 50	15 29 39 39 43
71 41 61 50 72	12 41 94 96 26	44 95 27 36 99	02 96 74 30 83
23 52 23 33 12	96 93 02 18 39	07 02 18 36 07	25 99 32 70 23
31 04 49 69 96	10 47 48 45 88	13 41 43 89 20	97 17 14 49 17
31 99 73 68 68	35 81 33 03 76	24 30 12 48 60	18 99 10 72 34
94 58 28 41 36	45 37 59 03 09	90 35 57 29 12	82 62 54 65 60

Figure 69.   Nomogram for determining number of observations

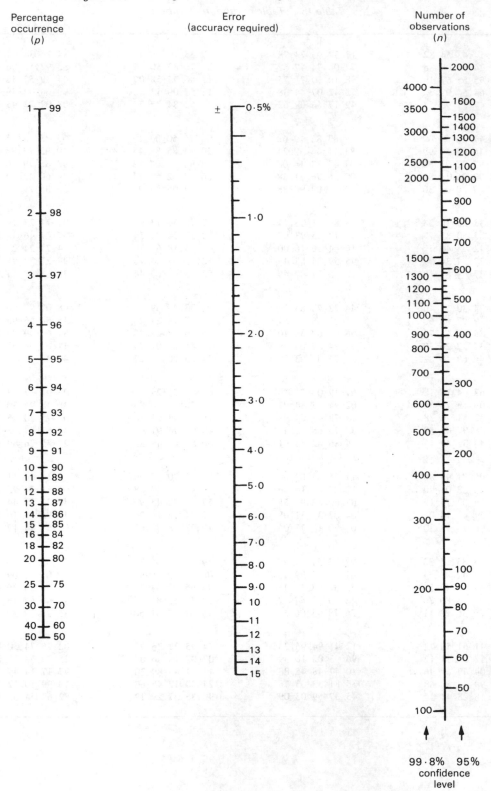

Table 14. *Determining the sequence of time for random observations*

Usable numbers as selected from the random table	Arranged in numerical order	Time of observation[1]
11	05	7.50 a.m.
38	11	8.50 a.m.
45	14	9.20 a.m.
20	15	9.30 a.m.
26	20	10.20 a.m.
05	22	10.40 a.m.
14	26	11.20 a.m.
15	38	1.20 a.m.
47	45	2.30 a.m.
22	47	2.50 a.m.

[1] Multiply each number by ten minutes and start from 7 a.m.

6. Conducting the study

DETERMINING THE SCOPE OF THE STUDY

Before making our actual observations, it is important that we decide on the **objective** of our work sampling. The simplest objective is that of determining whether a given machine is idle or working. In such a case, our observations aim at detecting one of two possibilities only:

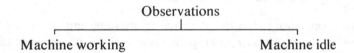

We can, however, extend this simple model to try and find out the cause of the stoppage of the machine:

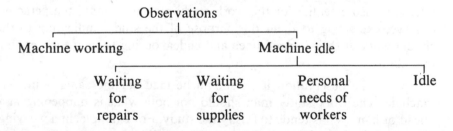

Again, we may be interested in determining the percentage of time spent on each activity while the machine is working:

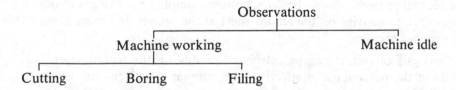

201

Or perhaps we may wish to get an idea of the percentage distribution of time when the machine is working and when it is idle, in which case we combine the last two models.

We may also be interested in the percentage time spent by a worker or groups of workers on a given element of work. If a certain job consists of ten different elements, by observing a worker at the defined points in time we can record on which element he is working and therefore arrive at a percentage distribution of the time he has been spending on each element.

The objectives to be reached by the study will therefore determine the design of the recording sheet used in work sampling, as can be seen from figures 70, 71 and 72.

MAKING THE OBSERVATIONS

So far we have taken the first five logical steps in conducting a work sampling study. To recapitulate, these consist of—

☐ Selecting the job to be studied and determining the objectives of the study.

☐ Making a preliminary observation to determine the approximate values of p and q.

☐ In terms of a chosen confidence level and accuracy range, determining n (the number of observations needed).

☐ Determining the frequency of observations, using random tables.

☐ Designing record sheets to meet the objectives of the study.

There is one more step to take: that of making and recording the observations and analysing the results. In making the observations, it is essential from the outset that the work study man is clear in his own mind about what he wants to achieve and why. He should avoid ambiguity when classifying activities. For example, if the engine of a fork-lift truck is running while the truck is waiting to be loaded or unloaded, he should decide beforehand whether this means that the truck is working or idle. It is also essential for the work study man to contact the persons he wishes to observe, explaining to them the purpose of the study, indicating to them that they should work at their normal pace and endeavouring to gain their confidence and co-operation.

The observation itself should be made at the same point relative to each machine. The work study man should not note what is happening at the machines ahead of him, as this tends to falsify the study. For example, in a weaving department, the observer may notice a loom that is stopped, just ahead of the one he is observing. The weaver may have it running again by the time he reaches it. If he were to note it as idle, he would be giving an untrue picture.

The recording itself, as can be seen, consists simply of making a stroke in front of the appropriate activity on the record sheet at the proper and predetermined time. No stop-watches are used.

The analysis of results can be calculated readily on the record sheet. It is possible to find out the percentage of effective time compared with that of delays, to

Figure 70.   Example of a simple work sampling record sheet

Date:	Observer:		Study No.:	
Number of observations: 75			Total	Percentage
Machine running	ЖІ ЖІ ЖІ ЖІ ЖІ ЖІ ЖІ ЖІ ЖІ ЖІ ЖІ ЖІ ІІ		62	82.7
Machine idle	ЖІ ЖІ ІІІ		13	17.3

Figure 71.   Work sampling record sheet showing machine utilisation and distribution of idle time

Date:		Observer:		Study No.:	
Number of observations: 75				Total	Percentage
Machine running		ЖІ ЖІ ЖІ ЖІ ЖІ ЖІ ЖІ ЖІ ЖІ ЖІ ЖІ ЖІ ІІ		62	82.7
Machine idle	Repairs	ІІ		2	2.7
	Supplies	ЖІ І		6	8.0
	Personal	І		1	1.3
	Idle	ІІІІ		4	5.3

Figure 72.   Work sampling record sheet showing distribution of time on ten elements of work performed by a group of four workers

	Elements of work									
	1	2	3	4	5	6	7	8	9	10
Worker No. 1										
Worker No. 2										
Worker No. 3										
Worker No. 4										

Date: Observer: Study No.:
Number of observations:

analyse the reasons for ineffective time and to ascertain the percentage time spent by a worker, groups of workers or a machine on a given work element. These, in themselves, provide useful information in a simple and reasonably quick way.

7. Using work sampling

Work sampling is widely used. It is a relatively simple technique that can be used advantageously in a wide variety of situations, such as manufacturing, servicing and office operations. It is, moreover, a relatively low-cost method and one that is less controversial than stop-watch time study. The information derived from work sampling can be used to compare the efficiency of two departments, to provide for a more equitable distribution of work in a group and, in general, to provide the management with an appreciation of the percentage of and reasons behind ineffective time. As a result, it may indicate where method study needs to be applied, material handling improved or better production planning methods introduced, as may be the case if work sampling shows that a considerable percentage of machine time is spent idle, waiting for supplies to arrive.

Chapter 15
Time study: The equipment

1. What is time study?

In Chapter 13 we listed the main techniques of work measurement. We shall now examine, in the next few chapters, one of the most important of these techniques, namely **time study.**

> Time study is a work measurement technique for recording the times and rates of working for the elements of a specified job carried out under specified conditions, and for analysing the data so as to obtain the time necessary for carrying out the job at a defined level of performance

2. Basic time study equipment

If time studies are to be made, certain items of equipment are essential. Basic time study equipment consists of—

☐ a stop-watch;

☐ a study board;

☐ time study forms.

The studyman will need this equipment with him whenever he makes a time study. In addition, in the study office there should be—

☐ a small calculator;

☐ a reliable clock, with a seconds hand;

☐ measuring instruments such as a tape measure, steel rule, micrometer, spring balance, and tachometer (revolution counter). Other measuring instruments may be useful, depending on the type of work being studied.

THE STOP-WATCH

Two types of watch are in general use for time study, namely the flyback and the non-flyback types. A third type—the split-hand stop-watch—is sometimes used.

205

These watches may be obtained with any one of three graduated scales—

(1) Recording one minute per revolution by intervals of one-fifth of a second, with a small hand recording 30 minutes.

(2) Recording one minute per revolution calibrated in 1/100ths of a minute, with a small hand recording 30 minutes (the decimal-minute watch).

(3) Recording 1/100th of an hour per revolution calibrated in 1/10,000ths of an hour; a small hand records up to one hour in 100 divisions (the decimal-hour watch).

It is also possible to obtain watches with the main scale in decimal minutes and an auxiliary scale outside it, usually in red, graduated in seconds and fifths of a second.

A flyback decimal-minute stop-watch—probably the type in most general use today—is shown in figure 73. The hand of the small dial makes 1/30th of a revolution for each revolution of the main hand, and thus makes a complete turn every 30 minutes.

In this type of watch the movement is started and stopped by a slide (A) at the side of the winding-knob (B). Pressure on the top of the winding-knob causes both the hands to fly back to zero without stopping the mechanism, from which point they immediately move forward again. If the slide is used, the hands can be stopped at any point on the dial and restarted without returning to zero as soon as the slide is released. This type of watch can be used for either "flyback" or "cumulative" timing (see Chapter 16, section 9).

Figure 73.   Decimal-minute stop-watch

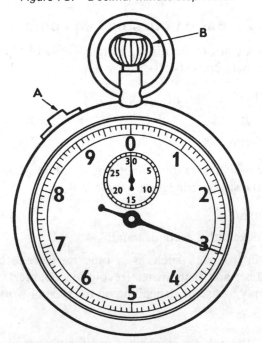

A = Slide for stopping and starting the movement.
B = Winding knob. Pressure on this knob returns both
       the hands to zero.

The non-flyback type is controlled by pressure on the top of the winding-knob. The first pressure starts the watch; the second pressure stops it; the third pressure returns the hands to zero. This watch is suitable only for cumulative timing.

In the split-hand type of watch, pressing a secondary knob causes one of the hands to stand still while the other continues to measure time. When the knob is pressed a second time, the stopped hand returns to the moving one and the two go on together. In this way, when a reading is taken a stopped hand is read instead of a moving one, giving greater accuracy of reading.

The split-hand watch is easier to read, but is heavier, more expensive and, because of its complexity, more troublesome to repair. With properly trained studymen, equally good results can be obtained with a simpler, lighter and less expensive watch. Unless there are special reasons for preferring one of the other types, the single-pressure, centre-sweep hand, flyback watch with the main dial graduated in 1/100ths of a minute and the smaller dial recording 30 minutes will be found most serviceable for time study. This is the type illustrated in figure 73.

Whatever type of watch is used, it should always be remembered that it is a delicate instrument which must be treated with care. Watches should be wound fully before each study, and should be allowed to run down overnight. At regular intervals they should be sent to a watchmaker for cleaning and routine overhaul.

THE STUDY BOARD

The study board is simply a flat board, usually of plywood or of suitable plastic sheet, on which to place the forms for recording time studies. It should be rigid and larger than the largest form likely to be used. It may have a fitting to hold the watch, so that the hands of the work study man are left relatively free and the watch is in a position to be read easily. For right-handed people the watch is normally placed at the top of the board on the right-hand side, so that the board may be rested on the left forearm with the bottom edge against the body and the forefinger or middle finger of the left hand used to press the winding knob when resetting the watch (see figure 74). Some work study men prefer to attach their watches with strong rubber bands or leather thongs around the two middle fingers of their left hands and to hold them at the top of the board in that way. It is largely a matter of individual preference, provided that the watch is securely held and can be easily read and manipulated. A strong spring clip should also be fitted to the board to hold the forms on which the study is recorded.

A study board which is either too short or too long for the studyman's arm soon becomes tiring to use. Most studymen prefer therefore to have their own individual boards made up to fit their own arm lengths, after they have had sufficient practice to know which size will be most comfortable.

3. Time study forms

Studies can be made on plain paper, but it is a nuisance having to rule up new sheets every time a study is made. It is more convenient to have printed forms of a standard size prepared, so that they can be filed neatly for reference, an essential

Figure 74.   Time study boards

(a) Study board for general purpose form

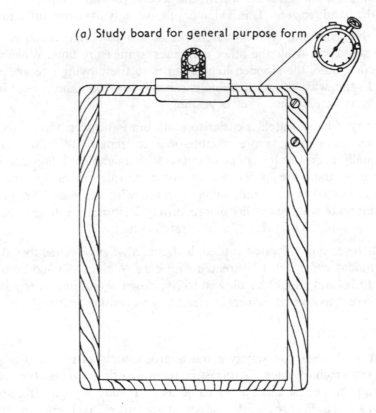

(b) Study board for short cycle form

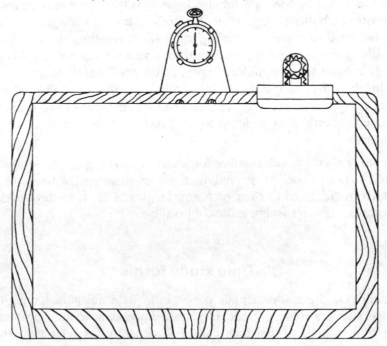

feature of well-conducted time study. Printed—or cyclostyled—forms also ensure that time studies are always made in a standard manner and that no essential data are omitted.

The number of different designs of time study forms is probably not far short of the number of work study departments in the world. Most experienced work study men have their own ideas on the ideal layout. The examples shown in this book represent designs which have been proved in practice to be satisfactory for general work.

The principal forms used in time study fall into two groups: those used at the point of observation while actually making the study, and which should therefore be of a size to fit conveniently on the study board; and those which are used after the study has been taken, in the study office.

FORMS USED ON THE STUDY BOARD

☐ **Time study top sheet:** the top and introductory sheet of a study, on which is recorded all the essential information about the study, the elements into which the operation being studied has been broken down, and the break points used. It may also record the first few cycles of the study itself. The example shown in figure 75 has spaces in the heading for all the information normally required about a study except the sketch of the workplace layout, which should either be drawn on the reverse of the sheet, if the layout is very simple, or should be drawn on a separate sheet (preferably of squared paper) and attached to the study.

☐ **Continuation sheet:** for further cycles of the study. An example is shown in figure 76, from which it will be seen that the form consists only of the columns and space for the study and sheet number. It is usual to print this ruling on both sides of the paper; on the reverse side the heading is not necessary.

These two forms are the ones most generally used. Together they are adequate for most general time study work. For the recording of short cycle repetitive operations, however, it is convenient to use a specially ruled form instead.

☐ **Short cycle study form.** Two examples of a short cycle form are illustrated. That in figure 77 shows a simple type of form which serves very well for most common short cycle work. The other, shown (front) in figure 78 and (reverse) in figure 79, is a more complicated form, adapted from one in general use in the United States; it may be more suitable if short cycle work is the rule rather than the exception.

The international standard A4 size of paper is a good one to use for these forms, as it is the biggest standard size which will fit conveniently on a study board. Foolscap is generally found to be a little too long.

FORMS USED IN THE STUDY OFFICE

☐ **Working sheet:** for analysing the readings obtained during the study and obtaining representative times for each element of the operation. One exam-

209

Figure 75.   General-purpose time study top sheet

TIME STUDY TOP SHEET

DEPARTMENT:		STUDY No.:
OPERATION:	M.S. No.:	SHEET No.: OF
		TIME OFF:
PLANT/MACHINE:	No.:	TIME ON:
		ELAPSED TIME:
TOOLS AND GAUGES:		OPERATIVE:
		CLOCK No.:
PRODUCT/PART:	No.:	STUDIED BY:
DWG. No.: MATERIAL		DATE:
QUALITY:		CHECKED:

N.B. Sketch the WORKPLACE LAYOUT/SET-UP/PART on the reverse, or on a separate sheet and attach

ELEMENT DESCRIPTION	R.	W.R.	S.T.	B.T.	ELEMENT DESCRIPTION	R.	W.R.	S.T.	B.T.

N.B.   R. = Rating.   W.R. = Watch Reading.   S.T. = Subtracted Time.   B.T. = Basic Time.

Figure 76. Continuation sheet for general-purpose time study (front)

STUDY No.:	TIME STUDY CONTINUATION SHEET				SHEET No.		OF	
ELEMENT DESCRIPTION	R.	W.R.	S.T.	B.T.	ELEMENT DESCRIPTION	R.	W.R.	S.T.	B.T.

N.B.   Reverse side similar, but without upper line of heading.

Figure 77. Simple type of short cycle study form

SHORT CYCLE STUDY FORM

DEPARTMENT:	SECTION:	STUDY No.
		SHEET No.: OF:
OPERATION:	M. S. No.:	TIME OFF:
		TIME ON:
PLANT/MACHINE:	No.	ELAPSED TIME:
TOOLS AND GAUGES:		OPERATIVE:
PRODUCT/PART:	No.	CLOCK No.:
DWG. No.	MATERIAL:	STUDIED BY:
QUALITY:	WORKING CONDITIONS:	DATE:
		CHECKED:

N.B.   Sketch the workplace overleaf.

El. No.	ELEMENT DESCRIPTION	Observed Time										Total O.T.	Average O.T.	R	B.T.
		1	2	3	4	5	6	7	8	9	10				

N.B.   R = Rating.   O.T. = Observed Time.   B.T. = Basic Time.

Figure 78. Short cycle study form (front)

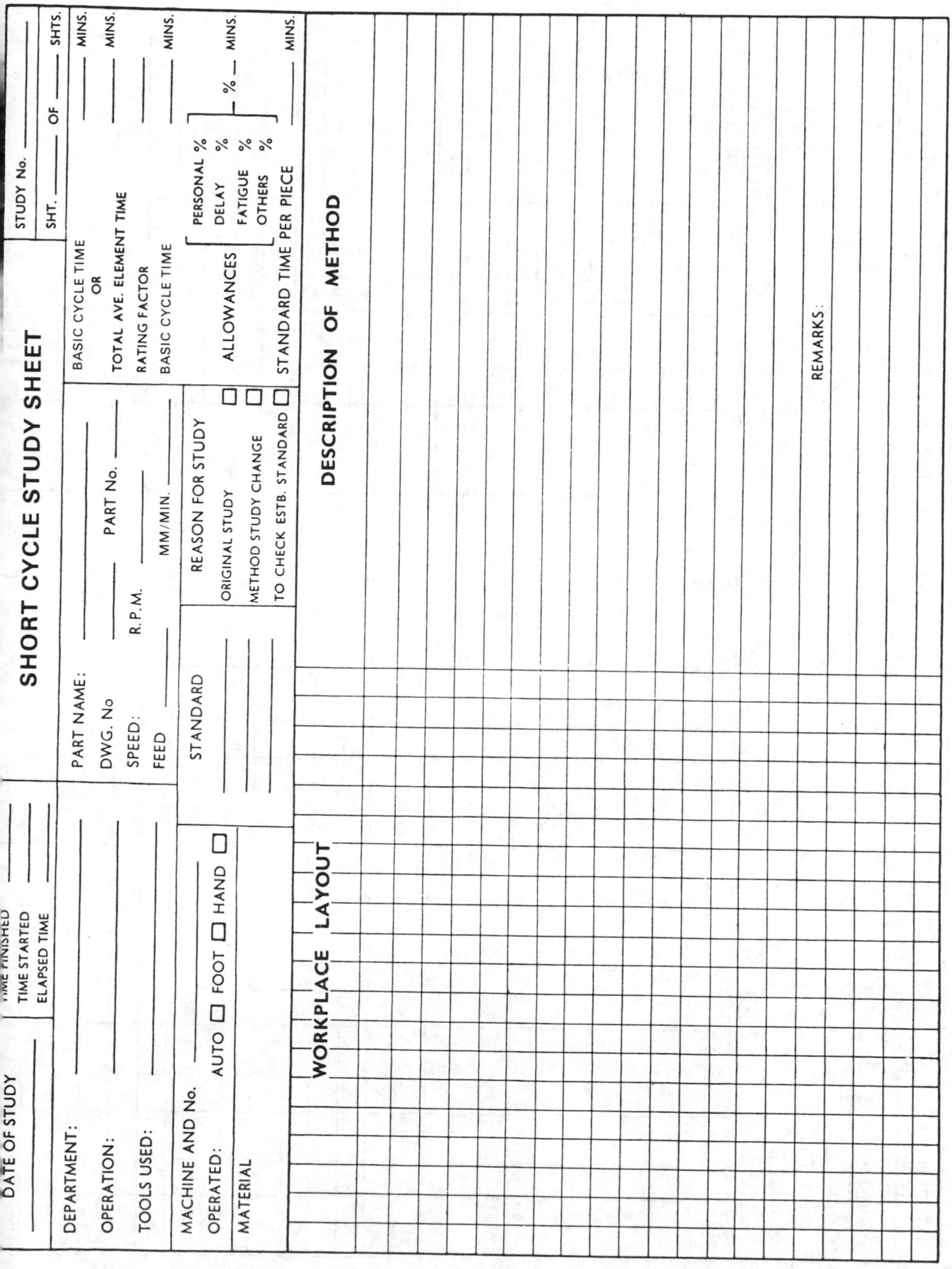

SHORT CYCLE STUDY SHEET

STUDY No. _____
SHT. _____ OF _____ SHTS.

DATE OF STUDY _____
TIME FINISHED _____
TIME STARTED _____
ELAPSED TIME _____

DEPARTMENT: _____
OPERATION: _____
TOOLS USED: _____

MACHINE AND No. _____
OPERATED: AUTO ☐ FOOT ☐ HAND ☐
MATERIAL _____

PART NAME: _____
DWG. No _____ PART No. _____
SPEED: _____ R.P.M.
FEED _____ MM/MIN.

STANDARD

REASON FOR STUDY
ORIGINAL STUDY ☐
METHOD STUDY CHANGE ☐
TO CHECK ESTB. STANDARD ☐

BASIC CYCLE TIME _____ MINS.
OR
TOTAL AVE. ELEMENT TIME _____ MINS.
RATING FACTOR _____
BASIC CYCLE TIME _____ MINS.

ALLOWANCES
PERSONAL %
DELAY %
FATIGUE %
OTHERS %
_____ % _____ MINS.

STANDARD TIME PER PIECE _____ MINS.

DESCRIPTION OF METHOD

REMARKS:

WORKPLACE LAYOUT

Figure 79.   Short cycle study form (back)

SHORT CYCLE STUDY SHEET

STUDY No.			
SHT.	OF	SHTS.	

NAME OF OPERATIVE

CLOCK No.

OBSERVED BY

APPROVED BY

FOREIGN ELEMENTS

SYMBOL	DESCRIPTION
A	
B	
C	
D	
E	
F	
G	
H	
I	
J	
K	
L	
M	
N	
O	
P	
Q	
R	
S	
T	

DATE OF STUDY

TIME FINISHED
TIME STARTED
ELAPSED TIME

ELEMENT No.

STANDING ☐
SITTING ☐
MOVING ABOUT ☐

ELEMENT No.	1	2	3	4	5	6	7	8	9	10
CYCLE No.										
1										
2										
3										
4										
5										
6										
7										
8										
9										
10										
11										
12										
13										
14										
15										
16										
17										
18										
19										
20										
TOTAL										
No. OF OBS.										
AVERAGE										
RATING %										
BASIC										

ple of a working sheet is shown in figure 100 in Chapter 20. As will be seen later, there are various ways in which the analysis may be made, each requiring a different ruling on the sheet. For this reason many studymen prefer to use simple lined sheets, of the same size as the study sheets, for making their analyses, clipping these to the study sheets when complete.

☐ **Study summary sheet:** to which the selected or derived times for all the elements are transferred, with the frequencies of the elements' occurrence. This sheet, as its name suggests, summarises neatly all the information which has been obtained during the course of the study. The heading includes all the details recorded about the operation at the top of the time study top sheet. The completed study summary sheet is clipped on top of all the other study sheets and is thus filed with them. The summary sheet should therefore be of the same size as that chosen for the study sheets. An example is shown in figure 80, from which it will be seen that the main body of the sheet has space for the ruling of additional columns, should these be needed for the particular study being summarised.

☐ **Analysis of studies sheet:** on which are recorded, from the study summary sheets, the results obtained in all the studies made on an operation. The analysis of studies sheet records the results of **all** the studies made of a particular operation, no matter when they were made or by whom. It is from the analysis of studies sheet that the basic times for the elements of the operation are finally compiled. The sheet is often much larger than the ordinary study forms. See figure 81, and figure 102 in Chapter 20.

☐ A specially ruled sheet for the compilation of **Relaxation Allowances** is also often used.

The use of all these forms, both those employed when actually making the study and those used afterwards to analyse and record it, will be described in detail in subsequent chapters.

4. Other equipment

As well as the stop-watch, other timing devices are used when very accurate measurement is required. They will not be discussed in detail in this book, as the stop-watch provides the accuracy necessary for the work that most readers are likely to undertake during the first few years of their application of work measurement techniques. Two of them may, however, be mentioned.

(1) The **motion picture camera** running at a constant speed, the film being projected at an equal constant speed.

(2) The **time study machine.** In this machine marks are made on a paper tape running at constant speed, by pressure of the fingers on two keys. Its only advantage over the stop-watch is that it leaves the work study man free to observe the operation continuously instead of having to look at and read the watch. It also enables very short elements to be timed. The tape has to be measured at the end of the study.

Figure 80. Study summary sheet

STUDY SUMMARY SHEET

DEPARTMENT:	SECTION:		STUDY No.:	
OPERATION:	M.S. No.:		SHEET No. OF:	
			DATE:	
PLANT/MACHINE:	No.:		TIME OFF:	
			TIME ON:	
			ELAPSED TIME:	
			CHECK TIME:	
TOOLS & GAUGES:			NET TIME:	
PRODUCT/PART:	No.:		OBS. TIME:	
DWG. No.:	MATERIAL:		UNACC. TIME:	
			U.T. AS %	
QUALITY:	WORKING CONDITIONS·		STUDIED BY:	
			CHECKED:	
OPERATIVE:	M/F CLOCK No.			

Sketch and Notes on back of Sheet 1

El. No.	ELEMENT DESCRIPTION	B.T.	F.	Obs.	

N.B. B.T. = Basic Time.   F. = Frequency of occurrence per cycle.   Obs. = No. of observations

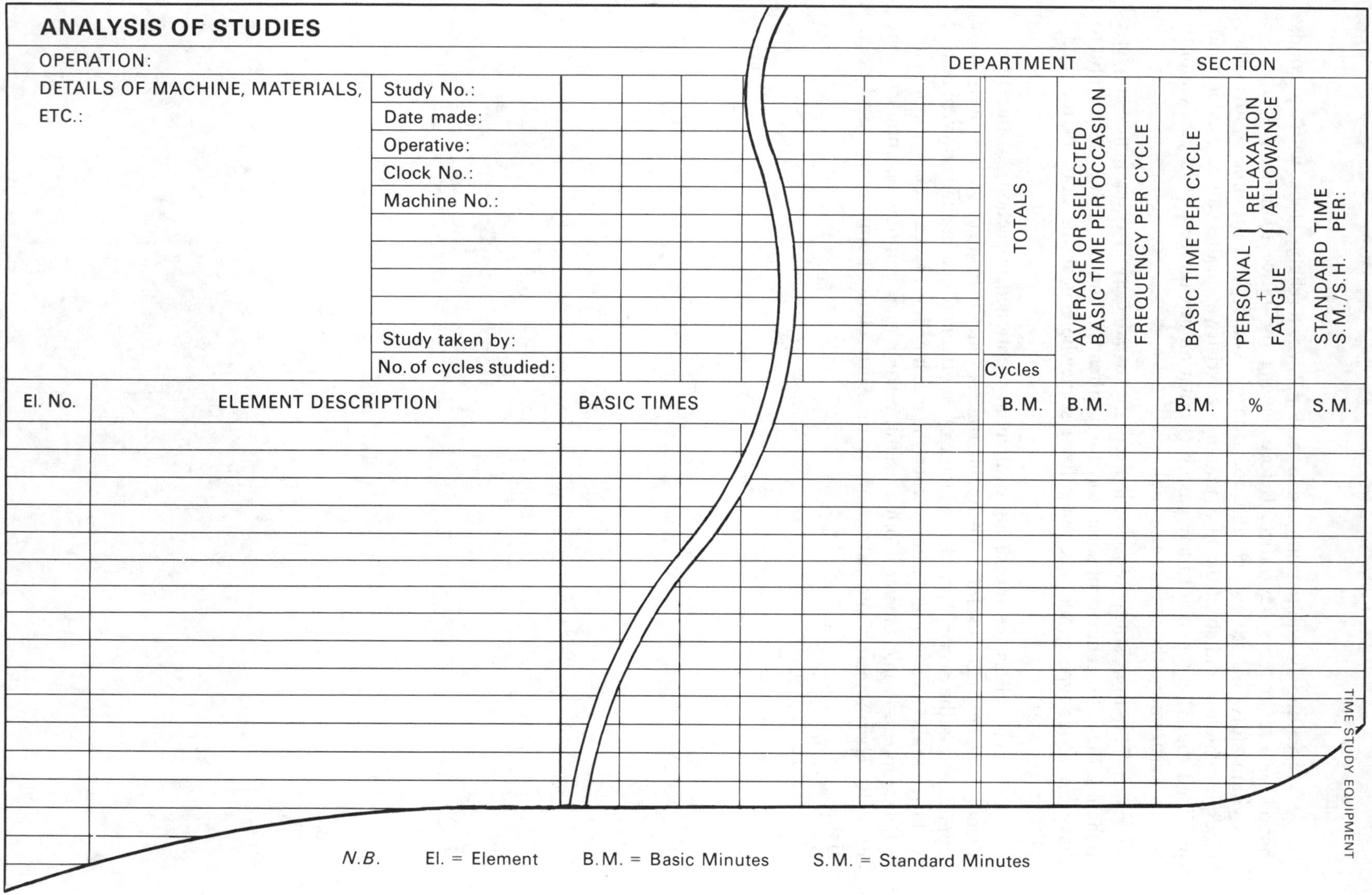

Figure 81. Analysis of studies sheet

ANALYSIS OF STUDIES

OPERATION:

DETAILS OF MACHINE, MATERIALS, ETC.:

DEPARTMENT

SECTION

Study No.:
Date made:
Operative:
Clock No.:
Machine No.:
Study taken by:
No. of cycles studied:

El. No.

ELEMENT DESCRIPTION

BASIC TIMES

TOTALS

Cycles

B.M.

AVERAGE OR SELECTED BASIC TIME PER OCCASION — B.M.

FREQUENCY PER CYCLE

BASIC TIME PER CYCLE — B.M.

RELAXATION ALLOWANCE { PERSONAL + FATIGUE } — %

STANDARD TIME S.M./S.H. PER: — S.M.

TIME STUDY EQUIPMENT

N.B.   El. = Element   B.M. = Basic Minutes   S.M. = Standard Minutes

217

Among the equipment listed in section 2 was a reliable clock, with a seconds hand, for use in the study office. Before leaving the office to make a study, the studyman starts his stop-watch and notes on his study sheet the time by the office clock at which he did so. If the studyman has a wrist-watch, this can be used instead, provided that it is reliable. In any case it is often an advantage for the studyman to have a wrist-watch, though not essential.

The time study office will need the usual clerical equipment—staplers, punches, files and cabinets of some sort to put them in, and so on. It is very useful to have an office-type pencil sharpener fixed somewhere near the door of the study office.

As well as the measuring equipment mentioned in section 2, other instruments may be found useful in particular trades. One instrument with a fairly wide application is the Servis Recorder, which can be attached to a machine or vehicle and will then make a record of the times when the machine it is placed on is in motion, and when stopped. A micrometer is often useful: reliable ones can now be obtained quite cheaply. Thermometers and instruments to measure relative humidity are often essential.

Chapter 16
Time study: Selecting and timing the job

1. Selecting the job

As in method study, the first step in time study is to **select** the job to be studied. Generally speaking, there are few occasions when a work study man can go into a factory or a department and select a job at random. There is nearly always a reason why a particular job requires attention. Some possible reasons are—

(1) The job in question is a new one, not previously carried out (new product, component, operation or set of activities).

(2) A change in material or method of working has been made and a new time standard is required.

(3) A complaint has been received from a worker or workers' representative about the time standard for an operation.

(4) A particular operation appears to be a "bottleneck" holding up subsequent operations and possibly (through accumulations of work in process behind it) previous operations.

(5) Standard times are required before an incentive scheme is introduced.

(6) A piece of equipment appears to be idle for an excessive time or its output is low, and it therefore becomes necessary to investigate the method of its use.

(7) The job needs studying as a preliminary to making a method study, or to compare the efficiency of two proposed methods.

(8) The cost of a particular job appears to be excessive.

If the purpose of the study is the setting of performance standards, it should not normally be undertaken until method study has been used to establish and define the most satisfactory way of doing the job. The reason for this is obvious: if the best method has not been discovered by systematic study, there is always the possibility that a much better way of doing it may be evolved, either by the worker himself or by technical staff—a way which may need considerably less work to achieve the results required. The amount and nature of the reduction in work may vary at different times, according to which worker happens to be doing the job and the method he chooses to employ. The quantity of work involved in the process or operation may actually increase, if an operative less skilled than the one originally timed does the job later on and uses a method more laborious than that on the basis of which the time was set.

Until the best method has been developed, defined and standardised, the amount of work which the job or process involves will not be stable. Planning of programmes will be thrown out, and, if the time standard is used for incentive purposes, the payment made to the operative may become uneconomic for the job. The worker may find the time unattainable, or, in the opposite case, may find that he can complete the work in a much shorter time than that set as the standard. If so, he will very probably restrict his output to the maximum which he thinks the management will tolerate without starting to make inquiries into the validity of the time standard which has been set. Although, in collective agreements introducing work study, it is customary to include a clause permitting the retiming of jobs when the work content is altered in either direction (and the management would, in theory, be justified in invoking this clause where a reduction in work content has been made, whether by worker or management), the retiming of jobs in such circumstances always tends to cause resentment, and if it is done frequently it will quickly shatter the confidence of the workers in both the competence of the work study staff and the honesty of the management. Therefore **make sure first that the method is right.** Remember, too, that any one time should refer only to **one specified method.**

There are problems in the selection of jobs to be studied which have nothing to do with the importance of the jobs to the enterprise or the abilities of the operatives. One difficult problem which may arise in factories where a piecework system is already in operation is that the existing piecework times on certain jobs, fixed by bargaining or estimation, may be so liberal that the workers have been earning high bonuses which cannot possibly be maintained if the jobs are properly reassessed. Attempts to alter the methods, which should automatically bring about a reassessment of the times allowed, may meet with such resistance that it is unwise to proceed with the studies. If this is the case, it is better, in an initial application, to tackle a number of jobs where it is evident that the earnings of the workers can be **increased** by the application of time study, even though these jobs may be less important to the performance of the shop as a whole. When the rest of the shop has been studied and confidence in the integrity of the work study man has been established, it may be possible to return to the "problem" jobs. It will almost certainly be necessary to negotiate on these problem jobs with the workers' representatives, and it may be necessary to compensate the workers concerned. It is nevertheless possible to carry through such negotiations successfully, if the purpose of the change is fully understood by all concerned.

2. The approach to the worker

The question of relationships between the work study man and the supervisors and workers in the enterprise was dealt with at some length in Chapter 5. The reason for mentioning it here is that what was said about work study in general applies with even more force to time study, especially with respect to the workers.

The purpose of a method study is usually obvious to everyone: it is to improve the method of doing the job, and everyone can see that it is a proper activity for the work study man to engage in. His efforts may even be welcomed by operatives, if he succeeds in relieving them of fatiguing or unpleasant work. The purpose of a time study is less obvious and, unless it is very carefully explained to everyone concerned, its object may be completely misunderstood or misrepresented, with consequent unrest and even strikes.

It is assumed that the work study man has already become a familiar figure in the shop while making method studies and that he is well known to the foreman and the workers' representatives. Nevertheless, if no time studies have previously been made there, he should first bring the workers' representatives and the supervisors together and explain in simple terms what he is going to do and why, and should invite them to handle the watch. All questions should be answered frankly. This is where the value of work study courses for workers' representatives and foremen shows itself.

If a choice of workers is available, it is good policy to ask the foreman and workers' representatives to suggest the one most suitable to be studied first, emphasising that he should be a competent, steady person. His rate of working should be average or slightly better than average. Some people are not temperamentally suited to being studied and cannot work normally while being watched. They should be avoided at all costs.

It is important, where the job is one likely to be done on a large scale (possibly by a large number of workers), to take studies on a number of **qualified** workers.

A distinction is made in time study practice between what are termed representative workers and qualified workers. A **representative** worker is one whose skill and performance is the average of the group under consideration. He is not necessarily a **qualified** worker. The concept of the qualified worker is an important one in time study. He is defined as follows:

> **A qualified worker is one who is accepted as having the necessary physical attributes, who possesses the required intelligence and education, and who has acquired the necessary skill and knowledge to carry out the work in hand to satisfactory standards of safety, quantity and quality**

There is a reason for this insistence on selecting qualified workers. In setting time standards, especially when they are to be used for incentives, the standard to be aimed at is one which can be attained by the qualified worker, and which can be maintained without causing him undue fatigue. Because workers work at different speeds, observed times have to be adjusted by factors to give such a standard. These factors are dependent on the judgement of the studyman. Experience has shown that accuracy of judgement is attainable only within a fairly narrow range of speeds close to that which is normal for a qualified worker. The study of slow or unskilled workers or of exceptionally fast workers will tend to result in the setting of time standards that are either unduly large (known as "loose" times), and hence uneconomic, or unduly short (known as "tight" times), in which case they are unfair to the worker and will probably be the subject of complaints later.

221

When the worker whose work is to be studied first has been selected, he should be approached in company with the foreman and the workers' representative. The purpose of the study and what is required should be carefully explained. The worker should be asked to work at his usual pace, taking whatever rest he is accustomed to take. He should be invited to explain any difficulties he may encounter. (This procedure becomes unnecessary as soon as work study is firmly established and its purpose well understood. It should, however, be carried out with new workers, and new members of the work study staff should be introduced to supervisors and workers when they start studies). It is important to impress on the supervisor that the worker is then to be **left alone.** Some workers are liable to become apprehensive if one of their direct supervisors is standing over them and watching them.

If a new method has been installed the worker must be allowed plenty of time to settle down before he is timed. The "learning curve" in figure 64 (page 182) shows that it takes quite a long time for an operative to become adapted and to reach his maximum steady speed. Depending on the duration and intricacy of the operation, it may be necessary to allow a job to run for days or even weeks before it is ready to be timed for the purpose of setting standards. In the same way, the work done by new operatives should never be used for timing until they have grown thoroughly accustomed to their jobs.

The position in which the studyman stands in relation to the operative is important. He should be so placed that he can see everything the operative does (especially the movements of his hands), without interfering with his movements or distracting his attention. The studyman should not stand directly in front of him, nor should he stand so close to him that he has the feeling of "having someone standing over him"—a frequent complaint made against time study. The studyman's exact position will be determined by the type of operation being studied, but the position generally recommended is to one side of the operative, slightly to the rear and about 2 metres away. In this position the operative can see him by turning his head a little, and they can speak if it is necessary to ask a question or explain some point in connection with the operation. The study board and watch should be held well up in line with the job, to make reading the watch and recording easy while maintaining continuous observation.

On no account should any attempt be made to time the operative without his knowledge, from a concealed position or with the watch in the pocket. It is dishonest and, in any case, someone is sure to see and the news will spread like wildfire. **Work study should have nothing to hide.**

It is equally important that the studyman should **stand up** while making his study. There is a tendency on the part of workers to regard themselves as having to do all the work while the studyman simply stands around and watches them. This will be increased if the latter settles himself into a comfortable position. He will quickly lose the workers' respect, which is his greatest asset. He should neither sit nor lean but should hold himself comfortably in a position which he can maintain, if necessary, over a long period. Time study demands intense concentration and alertness, especially when timing very short "elements" or "cycles" (defined later in this chapter), and it is generally agreed that this is better attained when standing.

Most operatives will quickly settle down to their normal working pace, but nervous workers, especially women, have a tendency to work unnaturally fast, which will cause them to fumble and make errors. If this happens, the studyman should stop the study and have a chat with the operative to put him at his ease, or even leave him to settle down for a bit.

More difficult to cope with is the "clever" worker who sets out to "put one across" the studyman. This is most likely to occur where it is known that the time standard to be set will be used as a basis for an incentive. The operative will go unnaturally slowly or insert unnecessary movements in the hope of getting a "looser" (longer) time. Some workers, usually the young ones, may do so out of devilment in order to match their wits against those of the studyman. It is hard to blame them, because many industrial jobs are dull enough in all conscience, and the battle adds a little spice to life! Nevertheless, from the studyman's point of view they are a nuisance.

On repetitive work it is generally easy to detect operatives who are deliberately working at a pace which is not natural to them because, if they are working naturally, there will be very little variation in the times of the different cycles once they have got going, whereas it is difficult for them to control their cycle times when they are not. When there are wide variations in successive cycle times, and when these are not due to variations in the material being worked on or to the tools or machine (in which case the studyman should report the variations to the proper authorities), the differing cycle times must be due to action on the operative's part. If this is the case, the studyman should discontinue the study and see the shop foreman. As a matter of practical diplomacy it may be wiser not to report the operative for attempting to "pull his leg", but to ask the foreman to come and look at the job as it does not seem to be running quite right. This is the sort of human situation that must be dealt with according to its merits if the studyman is not going to risk making himself unnecessarily unpopular, and is one of the reasons why the personal qualities of the studyman listed in Chapter 5 are so essential.

When technical considerations have a considerable influence on the job being studied, it may be much less easy to detect attempts to stretch the time of the job, unless the studyman himself is an expert is the process. This is especially so where craft skill is involved (as in some sheet-metal work, or turning and screw-cutting operations to fine tolerances and high finish on centre lathes), even where speeds and feeds have been specified by the process planning department. It is difficult to argue with a skilled craftsman if you are not one yourself! This is one of the reasons why it is so important to establish precisely the method and conditions of an operation before attempting to time it. A really good method study before the job is timed simplifies immensely the task of setting time standards.

In the foregoing paragraphs an effort has been made to suggest some of the practical problems the studyman will have to face in obtaining representative times; but there are many others which can be learned only in the hard school of experience, in the atmosphere of the workshop, among the men and women who work there. They cannot be translated into print. The human-hearted man will delight in them; the other sort should not become study men!

223

3. Steps in making a time study

When the work to be measured has been selected, the making of a time study usually consists of the following eight steps (see also figure 65):

(1) Obtaining and recording all the information available about the job, the operative and the surrounding conditions, which is likely to affect the carrying out of the work.

(2) Recording a complete description of the method, breaking down the operation into "elements".

(3) Examining the detailed breakdown to ensure that the most effective method and motions are being used, and determining the sample size.

(4) Measuring with a timing device (usually a stop-watch) and recording the time taken by the operative to perform each "element" of the operation.

(5) At the same time, assessing the effective speed of working of the operative relative to the observer's concept of the rate corresponding to standard rating.

(6) Extending the observed times to "basic times".

(7) Determining the allowances to be made over and above the basic time for the operation.

(8) Determining the "standard time" for the operation.

4. Obtaining and recording information

The following information (or those items which apply to the operation being studied) should be recorded from observation before starting the study proper. It is usual to do so on the time study top sheet. If the various headings are printed or stencilled, this helps to ensure that no vital piece of information is overlooked. The exact number of the items listed below which may have to be included when a time study form is designed will depend on the type of work carried out in the undertaking in which it is to be used. In non-manufacturing industries such as transport and catering, it should not be necessary to include space for the "product", etc. Factories where all the work is manual will require space for "tools" but not for "plant or machine".

Details of the workplace can be recorded more quickly and with greater accuracy when they are photographed with a simple instant-print-type camera with flash attachment (even the simplest cameras of this type are now equipped with automatic exposure control).

The filling-in of **all** the relevant information **from direct observation** is important in case the time study has to be referred to later; incomplete information may make a study practically useless a few months after it has been made. The forms shown in figures 75 to 79 are designed for manufacturing industry to show the maximum amount of information that is usually necessary.

The information to be obtained may be grouped as follows:

224

A. **Information to enable the study to be found and identified quickly when needed**

Study number.

Sheet number and number of sheets.

Name or initials of the studyman making the study.

Date of the study.

Name of the person approving the study (head of the work study department, production manager or other appropriate executive).

B. **Information to enable the product or part being processed to be identified accurately**

Name of product or part.

Drawing or specification number.

Part number (if different from drawing number).

Material.

Quality requirements.[1]

C. **Information to enable the process, method, plant or machine to be accurately identified**

Department or location where the operation is taking place.

Description of the operation or activity.

Method study or standard practice sheet numbers (where they exist).

Plant or machine (maker's name, type, size or capacity).

Tools, jigs, fixtures and gauges used.

Sketch of the workplace layout, machine set-up and/or part showing surfaces worked (on the reverse of the time study top sheet, or on a separate sheet attached to the study if necessary).

Machine speeds and feeds or other setting information governing the rate of production of the machine or process (e.g. temperature, pressure, flow, etc.). It is good practice to have the foreman initial the study form beside the record of information of this sort, as an endorsement of its correctness.

D. **Information to enable the operative to be identified**

Operative's name.

Clock number.[2]

---

[1] In the case of some engineering products, parts may be modified from time to time and the drawings reissued. It may therefore also be necessary to note the issue number.

For "Quality requirements" it may simply be sufficient to put a standard specification number or "Good finish". In engineering practice, tolerances and finish are generally specified on the drawing.

[2] In the case of new jobs or new operatives, it may be desirable to note the amount of experience the operative has had on the particular operation at the time of the study, so that the point that they have reached on the learning curve (see figure 64) may be assessed.

E.   **Duration of the study**

The start of the study ("Time on").

The finish of the study ("Time off").

Elapsed time.

F.   **Working conditions**

Temperature, humidity, adequacy of the lighting, etc., in supplement to the information recorded on the sketch of the workplace layout.

5. Checking the method

Before proceeding with the study, it is important to check the method being used by the operative. If the study is for the purpose of setting a time standard, a method study should already have been made and a written standard practice sheet completed. In this case it is simply a question of comparing what is actually being done with what is specified on the sheet. If the study is being made as the result of a complaint from a worker that he is unable to attain the output set by a previous study, his method must be very carefully compared with that used when the original study was made. It will often be found in such cases that the operative is not carrying out the work as originally specified: he may be using different tools, a different machine set-up or different speeds and feeds, temperatures, rates of flow or whatever the requirements of the process may be, or additional work may have crept in.

It may be that the cutting tools are worn, or have been sharpened to incorrect profiles. Times obtained when observing work carried out with worn tools or incorrect process conditions should not be used for the compilation of time standards.

In highly repetitive short cycle work, such as work on a conveyor band (light assembly, packing biscuits, sorting tiles), changes in method may be much more difficult to detect, since they may involve changes in the movements of the arms and hands of the operative ("motion patterns") which can be observed only with difficulty by the naked eye and require special apparatus to analyse.

Although it has been emphasised repeatedly in this book that a proper method study should be made before a time study is undertaken for the purpose of setting time standards, there are occasions when time standards may have to be set without a full-scale method study being conducted beforehand. This is most likely to occur with short-run jobs which are only done a few times a year in the shop concerned. In such cases the studyman should make a careful record of the method by which the job is being done, after putting right any obvious inefficiencies—in organisation, for instance, by providing containers for finished work in the proper positions or by checking machine speeds. This record becomes especially important as it will be the only record available, and changes in methods will be more likely to occur where operatives have not been instructed in one definite method.

226

6. Breaking the job into elements

Once the studyman has recorded all the information about the operation and the operative needed for proper identification in the future, and has satisfied himself that the method being used is the correct one or the best possible in the prevailing circumstances, he must start to break it down into **elements.**

> **An element is a distinct part of a specified job selected for convenience of observation, measurement and analysis**

> **A work cycle is the sequence of elements which are required to perform a job or yield a unit of production. The sequence may sometimes include occasional elements**

A work cycle starts at the beginning of the first element of the operation or activity and continues to the same point in a repetition of the operation or activity. That is the start of second cycle. This is illustrated in the fully worked-out example of a time study in Chapter 20.

A detailed breakdown into elements is necessary—

(1) To ensure that productive work (or effective time) is separated from unproductive activity (or ineffective time).

(2) To permit the rate of working to be assessed more accurately than would be possible if the assessment were made over a complete cycle. The operative may not work at the same pace throughout the cycle, and may tend to perform some elements more quickly than others.

(3) To enable the different types of element (see below) to be identified and distinguished, so that each may be accorded the treatment appropriate to its type.

(4) To enable elements involving a high degree of fatigue to be isolated and to make the allocation of fatigue allowances more accurate.

(5) To facilitate checking the method so that the subsequent omission or insertion of elements may be detected quickly. This may become necessary if at a future date the time standard for the job is queried.

(6) To enable a detailed work specification (see Chapter 23) to be produced.

(7) To enable time values for frequently recurring elements, such as the operation of machine controls or loading and unloading workpieces from fixtures, to be extracted and used in the compilation of standard data (see Chapter 22).

TYPES OF ELEMENT

Eight types of element are distinguished: repetitive, occasional, constant, variable, manual, machine, governing, and foreign elements. The definition of each, as given in the British Standards Institution's *Glossary of terms in work study,* op. cit., is listed below, together with examples—

☐ A **repetitive element** is an element which occurs in every work cycle of the job.

Examples: the element of picking up a part prior to an assembly operation; the element of locating a workpiece in a holding device; putting aside a finished component or assembly.

☐ An **occasional element** is an element which does not occur in every work cycle of the job, but which may occur at regular or irregular intervals.

Examples: adjusting the tension, or machine setting; receiving instructions from the foreman. The occasional element is useful **work** and a part of the job. It will be incorporated in the final standard time for the job.

☐ A **constant element** is an element for which the basic time remains constant whenever it is performed.

Examples: switch on machine; gauge diameter; screw on and tighten nut; insert a particular cutting tool into machine.

☐ A **variable element** is an element for which the basic time varies in relation to some characteristics of the product, equipment or process, e.g. dimensions, weight, quality, etc.

Examples: saw logs with handsaw (time varies with hardness and diameter); sweep floor (varies with area); push trolley of parts to next shop (varies with distance).

☐ A **manual element** is an element performed by a worker.

☐ A **machine element** is an element automatically performed by a power-driven machine (or process).

Examples: anneal tubes, fire tiles; form glass bottles; press car body shell to shape; most actual cutting elements on machine tools.

☐ A **governing element** is an element occupying a longer time than that of any other element which is being performed concurrently.

Examples: turn diameter on a lathe, while gauging from time to time; boil kettle of water, while setting out teapot and cups; develop photographic negative, while agitating the solution occasionally.

☐ A **foreign element** is an element observed during a study which, after analysis, is not found to be a necessary part of the job.

Examples: in furniture manufacture, sanding the edge of a board before planing has been completed; degreasing a part that has still to be machined further.

228

It will be clear from the definitions given above that a repetitive element may also be a constant element, or a variable one. Similarly, a constant element may also be repetitive or occasional; an occasional element may be constant or variable, and so on, for the categories are not mutually exclusive.

7. Deciding on the elements

There are some general rules concerning the way in which a job should be broken down into elements. They include the following:

☐ Elements should be easily identifiable, with definite beginnings and endings so that, once established, they can be repeatedly recognised. These beginnings and endings can often be recognised by a sound (e.g. the stopping of a machine, unlocking a catch of a jig, putting down a tool) or by a change of direction of hand or arm. They are known as the "break points" and should be clearly described on the study sheet. A break point is thus the instant at which one element in a work cycle ends and another begins.

☐ Elements should be as short as can be conveniently timed by a trained observer. Opinion differs on the smallest practical unit that can be timed with a stopwatch, but it is generally considered to be about 0.04 min (2.4 sec). For less highly trained observers it may be 0.07 to 0.10 min. Very short elements should, if possible, be next to longer elements for accurate timing and recording. Long manual elements should be rated about every 0.33 min (20 sec). (Rating is described and discussed in the next chapter.)

☐ As far as possible, elements—particularly manual ones—should be chosen so that they represent naturally unified and recognisably distinct segments of the operation. For example, consider the action of reaching for a wrench, moving it to the work and positioning it to tighten a nut. It is possible to identify the actions of reaching, grasping, moving to the workpiece, shifting the wrench in the hand to the position giving the best grip for turning it, and positioning. The worker will probably perform all these as one natural set of motions rather than as a series of independent acts. It is better to treat the group as a whole, defining the element as "get wrench" or "get and position wrench" and to time the whole set of motions which make up the group, than to select a break point at, say, the instant the fingers first touch the wrench, which would result in the natural group of motions being divided between two elements.

☐ Manual elements should be separated from machine elements. Machine time with automatic feeds or fixed speeds can be calculated and used as a check on the stop-watch data. Hand time is normally completely within the control of the operative. This separation is especially important if standard times are being compiled.

229

☐   Constant elements should be separated from variable elements.

☐   Elements which do not occur in every cycle (i.e. occasional and foreign elements) should be timed separately from those that do.

The necessity for a fine breakdown of elements depends largely on the type of manufacturing, the nature of the operation and the results desired. Assembly operations in the light electrical and radio industries, for example, generally have short cycle operations with very short elements.

The importance of the proper selection, definition and description of elements must again be emphasised. The amount of detail in the description will depend on a number of factors, for instance—

☐   Small batch jobs which occur infrequently require less detailed element descriptions than long-running, high-output lines.

☐   Movement from place to place generally requires less description than hand and arm movements.

Elements should be checked through a number of cycles and written down **before** timing begins.

Examples of element descriptions and of various types of element are shown in figures 95 and 97.

8. Sample size

Much of what we said in Chapter 14 on sampling, confidence levels and the application of random tables applies here also. In this case, however, we are not concerned with a proportion but with finding out the value of the representative average for each element. Our problem, therefore, is to determine the sample size or number of readings that must be made for each element, given a predetermined confidence level and accuracy margin.

Here again, we can apply a statistical method or a conventional method.

For the statistical method, we have first to take a number of preliminary readings (n'). We then apply the following equation[1] for the 95.45 confidence level and a margin of error of ± 5 per cent:

$$n = \left(\frac{40 \sqrt{n' \quad \Sigma x^2 - (\Sigma x)^2}}{\Sigma x} \right)^2$$

where

n = sample size we wish to determine
n' = number of readings taken in the preliminary study
Σ = sum of values
x = value of the readings.

---

[1] The explanation of the derivation of this formula falls outside the scope of this book. See Raymond Mayer: *Production and operations management* (New York and London, McGraw-Hill, 3rd ed., 1975), pp. 516-517.

An example will make the point clear. Let us suppose that we take five readings for a given element, and find that the value of the elapsed time in 1/100ths of a minute is 7, 6, 7, 7, 6. We can then calculate the squares and the sum of the squares of these numbers—

x	x^2
7	49
6	36
7	49
7	49
6	36
$\Sigma x = 33$	$\Sigma x^2 = 219$

$$n' = 5 \text{ readings.}$$

By substituting these values in the above formula, we obtain the value of n:

$$n = \left(\frac{40 \sqrt{5(219) - (33)^2}}{33} \right)^2 = 8.81 \text{ or 9 readings.}$$

Since the number of preliminary readings n' that we took is less than the required sample size of nine, the sample size must be increased. However, we cannot simply say that four more observations are needed. When we add the values obtained from these four additional observations, the values of x and x^2 will change, and this may affect the value of n. Consequently it may be found either that a still larger sample is required, or that the sample taken was in fact adequate or more than adequate.

If we choose a different confidence level and accuracy margin, the formula changes as well. Normally, however, we choose either the 95 or the 95.45 confidence level.

The statistical method of determining the sample size is valid to the extent that the assumptions made in deriving the formula are valid—in other words, that the observed variations in the readings are due to mere chance and are not made intentionally by the operative. The statistical method can be cumbersome, since a given work cycle is composed of several elements. As the sample size will vary with the readings for each element, we can arrive at different sample sizes for each element within a given cycle, unless of course the elements have more or less the same average. As a result, we may have to calculate the sample size, in the case of cumulative timing, by basing it on the element that will call for the largest sample size.

Some authors, and companies such as General Electric, have therefore adopted a conventional guide for the number of cycles to be timed, based on the total number of minutes per cycle (see table 15).

It is also important that the readings be continued over a number of cycles in order to ensure that occasional elements (such as handling boxes of finished parts, periodical cleaning of machines or sharpening of tools) can be observed several times.

In conducting the study the table of random numbers (see Chapter 14) may be used to determine the times at which the readings are to be taken.

Table 15.   Number of recommended cycles for time study

Minutes per cycle	To 0.10	To 0.25	To 0.50	To 0.75	To 1.0	To 2.0	To 5.0	To 10.0	To 20.0	To 40.0	Over 40
Number of cycles recommended	200	100	60	40	30	20	15	10	8	5	3

Source: A. E. Shaw: "Stop-watch time study", in H. B. Maynard (ed.): *Industrial engineering handbook,* op. cit. Reproduced by kind permission of the McGraw-Hill Book Company.

9. Timing each element: stop-watch procedure

When the elements have been selected and written down, timing can start.

There are two principal methods of timing with the stop-watch:

☐   Cumulative timing;

☐   Flyback timing.

In **cumulative** timing the watch runs continuously throughout the study. It is started at the beginning of the first element of the first cycle to be timed and is not stopped until the whole study is completed. At the end of each element the watch reading is recorded. The individual element times are obtained by successive subtractions after the study is completed. The purpose of this procedure is to ensure that all the time during which the job is observed is recorded in the study.

In **flyback** timing the hands of the stopwatch are returned to zero at the end of each element and are allowed to start immediately, the time for each element being obtained directly. The mechanism of the watch is never stopped and the hand immediately starts to record the time of the next element.

In all time studies it is usual to take an independent check of the over-all time of the study, using either a wrist-watch or the clock in the study office. This also serves the purpose of noting the time of day at which the study was taken, which may be important if a retiming is asked for. For example, the cycle time of an operative on a repetitive job may be shorter in the first hour or two of the morning, when he is fresh, than late in the afternoon, when he is tired.

In the case of flyback timing, the studyman walks to the clock; at an exact minute, preferably at the next major division such as the hour or one of the five-minute points, he sets his stop-watch running, noting the exact time in the "time on" space on the form. He returns to the workplace where he is going to carry out the time study with the watch running and allows it to do so continuously until he is ready to start timing. At the beginning of the first element of the first work cycle, he snaps back the hand, noting, as the first entry on the body of his study sheet, the time that has elapsed. At the end of the study, the hand is snapped back to zero on completion of the last element of the last cycle and thereafter allowed to run continuously until he can again reach the clock and note the time of finishing, when the watch is finally stopped. The final clock time is entered in the "time off" space on the form. The two times recorded before and after the study are known as "check times". The clock

232

reading at the beginning of the study is subtracted from the clock reading at the end of the study to give the "elapsed time", which is entered on the form.

The sum of the times of all the elements and other activities noted in the study plus ineffective time plus the check times is known as the "recorded time" and is also noted. It should in theory agree with the elapsed time, but in practice there is usually a small difference owing to the cumulative loss of very small fractions of time at the return of the hand to zero and, possibly, bad reading or missed elements. In certain firms it is the practice to discard any study in which the elapsed time differs from the recorded time by more than ± 2 per cent.

When the same practice is followed using cumulative timing, the elapsed time and recorded time should be identical since the stop-watch is only read and not snapped back.

Cumulative timing has the advantage that, even if an element is missed or some occasional activity not recorded, this will have no effect on the over-all time. It is strongly favoured by many trade unions, especially in the United States, since it is regarded by them as more accurate than flyback timing and gives no opportunity for altering times in favour of the management by omitting elements or other activities. Its disadvantage is, of course, the amount of subtraction which has to be done to arrive at individual element times, which greatly increases the time taken in working up the study afterwards.

Flyback timing is still widely used. In competent hands it is almost as accurate as cumulative timing. Mundel quotes some comparative tests of the two methods carried out by Lazarus at the Purdue University Motion and Time Study Laboratory with a number of experienced time study observers, in which the average error in reading the watch using the cumulative method was + 0.000097 min per reading and using the flyback method was − 0.00082 min per reading.[1] Errors of this order are not large enough to influence subsequent calculations. It should be noted, however, that these very small average errors were made by experienced observers. There is reason to suppose that people being trained in the use of the stop-watch attain a fair degree of accuracy more quickly when using the cumulative method than when using the flyback method.

The experience of ILO missions in training in and applying time study has in fact shown that, generally speaking, cumulative timing should be taught and used, for the following reasons:

(1) Experience suggests that trainees achieve reasonable accuracy in the use of the stop-watch more quickly if they use the cumulative method.

(2) It does not matter if element times are occasionally missed by inexperienced observers; the over-all time of the study will not be affected. Foreign elements and interruptions are automatically included since the watch is never stopped.

(3) In assessing the working pace of the operative ("rating"), it is less easy to fall into the temptation to adjust the rating to the time taken by the element than with the flyback method, since only watch readings and not actual times are recorded.

[1] L. P. Lazarus: "The nature of stop-watch time study errors", in *Advanced Management,* May 1950, pp. 15-16.

(4) Workers and their representatives are likely to have greater faith in the fairness of time studies as a basis for incentive plans if they can see that no time could have been omitted. The introduction of time study into an undertaking or an industry may be made easier.

In the flyback method, errors in reading the watch may be added to the slight delay which occurs when the hand is snapped back to zero. The percentage error becomes greater for short elements. Cumulative timing is therefore likely to be more accurate for short-element short-cycle work, while flyback timing can be more safely used in jobs with long elements and cycles, since the error becomes too small to matter. The question of the confidence of the workers is important as well.

There is a third method of timing which is employed for short-element short-cycle work, and which may indeed be the only way of getting accurate times with a stop-watch, for elements which are so very short that there is not enough time for the studyman to read his watch and make a recording on his study sheet. In this situation the method used is that known as **differential timing.** With differential timing, elements are timed in groups, first including and then excluding each small element, the time for each element being obtained subsequently by subtraction. For example, if the job consists of seven short elements, the studyman may time numbers 1 to 3, and 4 to 7 for the first few cycles, recording only these two readings per cycle. He would then time 1 to 4 and 5 to 7 for a few cycles; and so on. If differential timing is applied in this fashion, either the cumulative or the flyback method of watch manipulation may be used.

We have now discussed all the preliminaries to making a time study, from the selection of the job, through the recording of all relevant data, the breakdown of the job into elements and the examination of the methods employed, to the recording of the actual element times. In the next chapter we shall discuss the means of modifying these observed times to take into account variations in rates of working.

Chapter 17
Time study: Rating

In section 3 of the previous chapter, the making of a time study was broken down into eight steps or stages, the first four of which were discussed in that chapter. We now come to the fifth step, namely "assessing the effective speed of working of the operative relative to the observer's concept of the rate corresponding to standard rating".

The treatment of rating which follows has been selected because experience in the use of this book for training purposes by ILO management and productivity missions suggests that this approach to the subject is best suited to the conditions in most of the countries for which the book is primarily intended.

Rating and "allowances" (dealt with in the next chapter) are the two most controversial aspects of time study. Most time studies in industry are used to determine standard times for setting workloads and as a basis for incentive plans. The procedures employed have a bearing on the earnings of the workers as well as on the productivity and, possibly, the profits of the enterprise. Time study is not an exact science, although much research has been and continues to be undertaken to attempt to establish a scientific basis for it. Rating (the assessment of a worker's rate of working) and the allowances to be given for recovery from fatigue and other purposes are still, however, largely matters of judgement and therefore of bargaining between management and labour.

Various methods of assessing the rate of working, each of which has its good and bad points, have been developed. The procedures set out in this chapter represent sound current practice and, properly applied, should be acceptable to management and workers alike, particularly when used to determine standards for medium-batch production, which is the most common type in industry all over the world outside the United States and a few large or specialised undertakings elsewhere. They will certainly provide the reader with a sound basic system which will serve him well for most general applications, and one which can later be refined if the particular nature of certain special operations requires a modification of the system, so as to rate something other than effective speed.

1. The qualified worker

It has already been said that time studies should be made, as far as possible, on a number of qualified workers; and that very fast or very slow workers should be

235

avoided, at least while making the first few studies of an operation. What is a "qualified worker"?

Different jobs require different human abilities. For example, some demand mental alertness, concentration, visual acuity; others, physical strength; most, some acquired skill or special knowledge. Not all workers will have the abilities required to perform a particular job, though if the management makes use of sound selection procedures and job training programmes, it should normally be possible to arrange that most of the workers engaged on it have the attributes needed to fit them for the task. The definition of a qualified worker given in the previous chapter is repeated here—

> **A qualified worker is one who is accepted as having the necessary physical attributes, who possesses the required intelligence and education, and who has acquired the necessary skill and knowledge to carry out the work in hand to satisfactory standards of safety, quantity and quality**

The acquisition of skill is a complicated process. It has been observed[1] that among the attributes which differentiate the experienced worker from the inexperienced are the following. The experienced worker—

achieves smooth and consistent movements;

acquires rhythm;

responds more rapidly to signals;

anticipates difficulties and is more ready to overcome them;

carries out the task without giving the appearance of conscious attention, and is therefore more relaxed.

It may take a good deal of time for a worker to become fully skilled in the performance of a job. In one study (see figure 64) it was noted that it was only after some 8,000 cycles of practice that the times taken by workers began to approach a constant figure—which was itself half the time they took when they first essayed the operation. Thus time standards set on the basis of the rate of working of inexperienced workers could turn out to be quite badly wrong, if the job is one with a long learning period. Some jobs, of course, can be learned very quickly.

It would be ideal if the time study man could be sure that, whatever job he selected for study, he would find only properly qualified workers performing it. In practice this is too much to hope for. It may indeed be that none of the workers engaged on the task can really be said to be completely qualified to carry it out, though it may be possible to alter this in time, by training; or that, though some of the

---

[1] W. D. Seymour: *Industrial training for manual operations* (London, Pitman, 1966).

workers are qualified, these are so few in number that they cannot be considered to be average or representative of the group. A representative worker is defined as one whose skill and performance is the average of a group under consideration. He is not necessarily a qualified worker.

If the working group is made up wholly or mainly of qualified workers, there will be one—or perhaps several—of these qualified workers who can be considered as representative workers also. The concept of a standard time is, at root, that it is a time for a job or operation that should normally be attainable by the average qualified worker, working in his ordinary fashion, provided that he is sufficiently motivated to want to get on with the job. In theory, therefore, the time study man should be looking for the average qualified worker to study. In practice, this is not as easy as it might seem. It is worth looking more closely into what "average" might mean in this context.

2. The "average" worker

The truly average worker is no more than an idea. A completely average worker does not exist, any more than an "average family" or an "average man" exists. They are the inventions of statisticians. We are all individuals: no two of us are exactly alike. Nevertheless, among a large number of people from, for instance, the same country or area, variations in measurable characteristics such as height and weight tend to form a pattern which, when represented graphically, is called the "normal distribution curve". To take one characteristic, height: in many western European countries the average height for a man is about 5 ft. 8 in. (172 cm). If a crowd is a western European crowd, a large number of the men in it will be between 5 ft. 7 in. and 5 ft. 9 in. tall (170-175 cm). The number of men of heights greater or smaller than this will become fewer and fewer as those heights approach the extremes of tallness and shortness.

The case as regards the performance of operatives is exactly the same. This can be shown very conveniently in a diagram (figure 82). If 500 qualified workers in a given factory were to do the same operation by the same methods and under the same conditions, the whole operation being within the control of the worker himself, the times taken to perform the operation would be distributed in the manner shown in the figure. To simplify the figure, the times have been divided into groups at intervals of four seconds. It will be seen that the workers fall into the groups shown in table 16.

If the time groups are examined, it will be seen that 32.4 per cent of the times are less than 46 seconds and 34.8 per cent of the times are greater than 50 seconds. The largest single group of times (32.8 per cent) lies between 46 and 50 seconds. We should therefore be justified in saying that for this group of 500 workers the average time taken to perform this operation was between 46 and 50 seconds (say, 48 seconds). We could call 48 seconds the time taken by the average qualified worker to do this job under these conditions. The time might not hold good for any other factory. Factories which are well run, where working conditions and pay are good, tend to attract and keep the best workers, so that in a better run factory the average worker's time might be less (say, 44 seconds), while in a poorly run factory with less able workers it might be more (say, 52 seconds).

237

Figure 82.   Distribution of times taken by workers to perform a given job

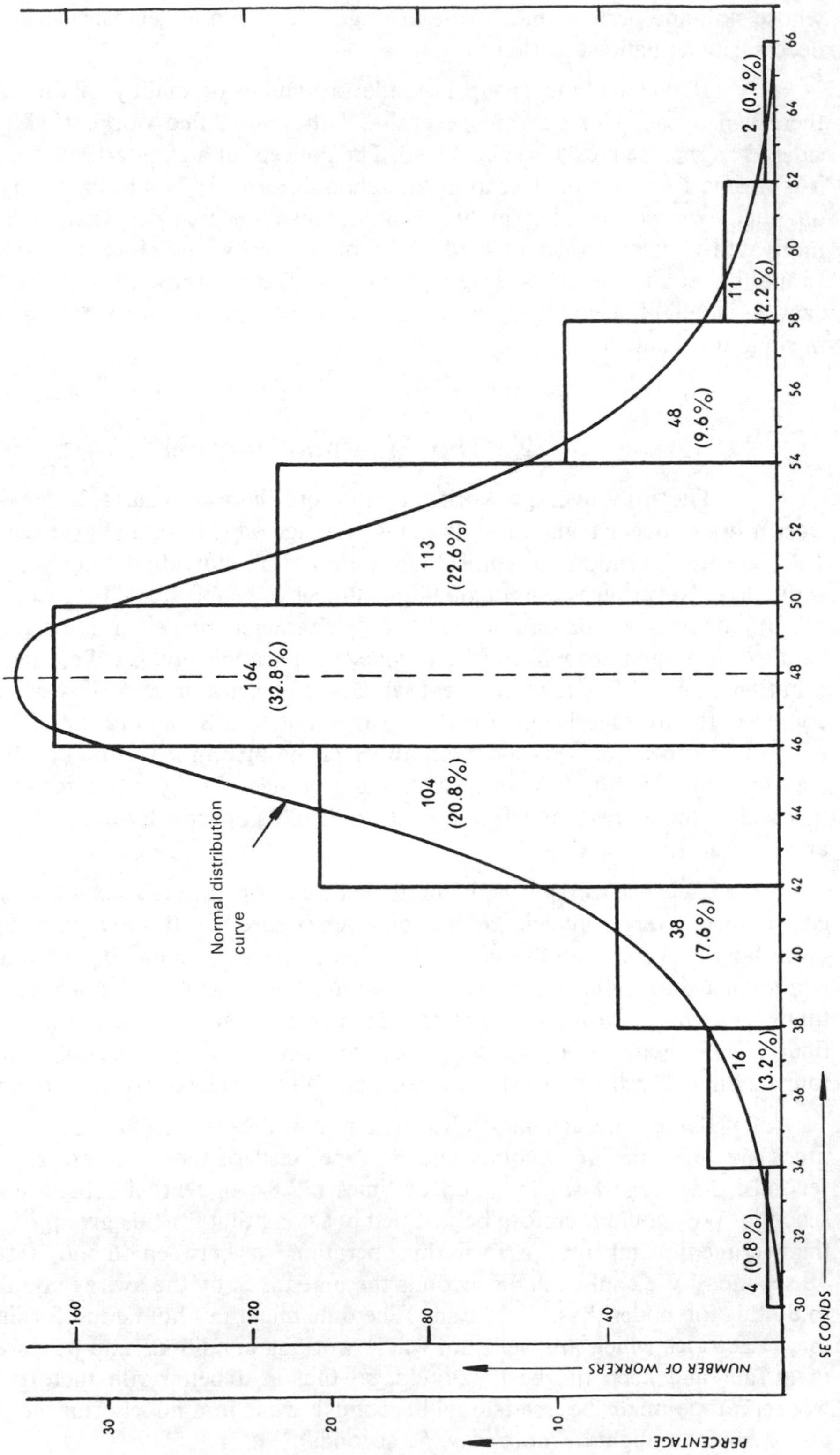

Table 16. *Specimen performance distribution*

Time group (sec)	Number of workers (out of 500)	Percentage of total workers	
30-34	4	0.8	
34-38	16	3.2	32.4
38-42	38	7.6	
42-46	104	20.8	
46-50	164	32.8	32.8
50-54	113	22.6	
54-58	48	9.6	34.8
58-62	11	2.2	
62-66	2	0.4	
	500	100.0	100.0

If a curve is drawn to fit this distribution it will be found to assume the shape of the curve in the figure. This is known as the "normal distribution curve". In general, the larger the sample the more the curve will tend to be symmetrical about the peak value, but this can be altered if special conditions are introduced. For example, if the slower workers were to be transferred to other work, the right-hand side of the curve of performances of the group would probably become foreshortened, for there would be fewer workers returning the very long times.

3. Standard rating and standard performance

In Chapter 13 it was said that the principal use of work measurement (and hence of time study) is to set time standards which can be used for a number of different purposes (including programme planning, estimating, and as a basis for incentives) for the various jobs carried out in the undertaking.[1] Obviously, if those time standards are to be of any value at all, their achievement must be within the capacity of the majority of workers in the enterprise. It would be no use setting standards so high that only the best could attain them, since programmes or estimates based on them would never be fulfilled. Equally, to set standards well within the achievement of the slowest workers would not be conducive to efficiency.

How does the work study man obtain such a fair time from time studies?

We have already said that, as far as possible, studies should be taken on qualified workers. If it were possible to obtain the times taken by 500 qualified operatives for a single operation and plot them in the manner shown in figure 82, a reliable average time would be obtained. Unfortunately, this is hardly ever possible. It is not always possible to time a job on an average qualified worker; moreover, even if it were, people do not work consistently from day to day or even from minute to minute. The work study man has to have some means of assessing the rate of working of the operative he is observing and of relating it to standard pace. This process is known as **rating.**

---

[1] For details of various well known types of incentive plans, see ILO: *Payment by results,* Studies and reports, New series, No. 27 (Geneva, 14th impr., 1977).

> **Rating is the assessment of the worker's rate of working relative to the observer's concept of the rate corresponding to standard pace[1]**

By definition, rating is a comparison of the rate of working observed by the work study man with a picture of some standard level which he is holding in his mind. This standard level is the average rate at which qualified workers will naturally work at a job, when using the correct method and when motivated to apply themselves to their work. This rate of working corresponds to what is termed the **standard rating,** and is denoted by 100 on the rating scale recommended to readers of this book (see section 7 below). If the standard pace is maintained and the appropriate relaxation is taken, a worker will achieve **standard performance** over the working day or shift.

> **Standard performance is the rate of output which qualified workers will naturally achieve without over-exertion as an average over the working day or shift, provided that they know and adhere to the specified method and provided that they are motivated to apply themselves to their work**
>
> **This performance is denoted as 100 on the standard rating and performance scales**

The rate of working most generally accepted in the United Kingdom and the United States as corresponding to the standard rating is equivalent to the speed of motion of the limbs of a man of average physique walking without a load in a straight line on level ground at a speed of 4 miles an hour (6.4 kilometres per hour). This is a brisk, business-like rate of walking, which a man of the right physique and well accustomed to walking might be expected to maintain, provided that he took appropriate rest pauses every so often. This pace has been selected, as a result of long experience, as providing a suitable benchmark to correspond to a rate of working which would enable the average qualified worker who is prepared to apply himself to his task to earn a fair bonus by working at that rate, without there being any risk of imposing on him any undue strain which would affect his health, even over a long period of time. (As a matter of interest, a man walking at 4 miles an hour (6.4 km/h) appears to be moving with some purpose or destination in mind: he is not sauntering, but on the other hand he is not hurrying. Men hurrying, to catch a train for instance,

---

[1] The definition given in the B.S. *Glossary,* op. cit., concludes with the words "standard rating", rather than "standard pace", as used here. It is considered that the word "pace" more exactly conveys the sense of a rate of working than "rating", which has connotations implying a factor, or ratio, which do not help clarity at this point in the explanation.

often walk at a considerably faster pace before breaking out into a trot or a run, but it is a pace which they would not wish to keep up for very long.)

It should be noted, however, that the "standard pace" applies to Europeans and North Americans working in temperate conditions; it may not be a proper pace to consider standard in other parts of the world. In general, however, given workers of proper physique, adequately nourished, fully trained and suitably motivated, there seems little evidence to suggest that different standards for rates of working are needed in different localities, though the periods of time over which workers may be expected to average the standard pace will vary very widely with the environmental conditions. At the very least, the standard rate as described above provides a theoretical datum line with which comparisons of performance in different parts of the world could be made in order to determine whether any adjustment may be necessary. Another accepted example of working at the standard rate is dealing a pack of 52 playing cards in 0.375 minutes.

Standard performance on the part of the average qualified worker (that is, one with sufficient intelligence and physique, adequately trained and experienced in the job he is doing) will probably show as such only over a period of several hours. Anyone doing manual work will generally carry out the motions directly concerned with his work at his own natural working rate, which may not be exactly the standard rate, since some men work faster than others. There will of course be different standard paces (or speeds of movement) for different activities, according to the complexity or arduousness of the element making up the activity (among other things), so that working at the standard rate will not always mean moving the hands or limbs at the same speed. And in any event, it is not uncommon for workers to work faster at some periods of the day than at others, so that the standard performance is rarely achieved as the result of working, without any deviation, at the standard rate throughout the working periods of the shift, but rather as the cumulative outcome of periods of work at varying paces.

When time standards are used as a basis for payment by results, many union-management agreements stipulate that the time standards should be such that a representative or average qualified worker on incentive pay can earn 20-35 per cent above his time rate by achieving the standard performance. If the worker has no target to aim at and no incentive to make him desire a higher output, he will (apart from any time he may waste consciously) tolerate the intrusion of small pieces of ineffective time, often seconds or fractions of seconds between and within elements of work. In this way he may easily reduce his performance over an hour or so to a level much below that of the standard performance. If, however, he is given enough incentive to make him want to increase his output, he will get rid of these small periods of ineffective time, and the gaps between his productive movements will narrow. This may also alter the pattern of his movements.[1] The effect of the elimination of these small periods of ineffective time under the influence of an incentive can be illustrated diagrammatically (see figure 83).

---

[1] Research carried out under the late Professor T. U. Matthew at the University of Birmingham (United Kingdom) tended to confirm this.

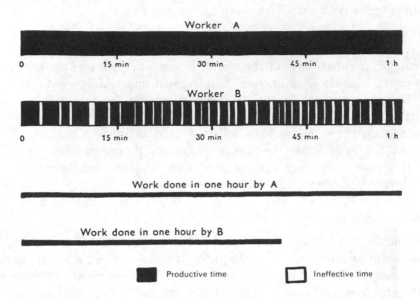

Figure 83.   Effect of ineffective time on performance

What happens may be seen in the case of a man working a lathe who has to gauge his workpiece from time to time. His gauge is laid on the tool locker beside him. If he has no particular reason to hurry, he may turn his whole body round every time he wishes to pick up the gauge, turn back to the lathe, gauge the workpiece and turn again to put the gauge down, each of these movements being carried out at his natural pace. As soon as he has reason to speed up his rate of working, instead of turning his whole body he will merely stretch out his arm, perhaps glancing round to check the position of the gauge on the locker, pick up the gauge, gauge the workpiece and replace the gauge on the locker with a movement of his arm, without bothering to look. In neither case would there be a deliberate stopping of work, but in the second some movements—ineffective from the point of view of furthering the operation—would have been eliminated.

The effect of putting a whole shop or factory (such as the 500 workers in figure 82) on an incentive is shown in figure 84.

Offering an incentive in the form of payment in proportion to output will not make the unskilled or slow worker as fast or as skilled as the skilled or naturally fast worker; but if everyone in the shop is put on a well designed incentive plan, other conditions remaining the same, the result will be that everyone will tend to work more consistently. The short periods of ineffective time discussed above will disappear, and everyone's average time for the job will be reduced. (This is an over-simplification but true enough for purposes of illustration.) The normal distribution curve shown in figure 82 will move to the **left** while retaining approximately the same shape. This is quite clearly shown in figure 84, where the peak of the curve (the average time) now comes at 36 seconds instead of 48—a reduction of 25 per cent.

It should be added that, although the standard rate of working is that at which the average qualified worker will naturally perform his movements when

242

Figure 84.   Effect of a payment-by-results incentive on the time taken to perform an operation

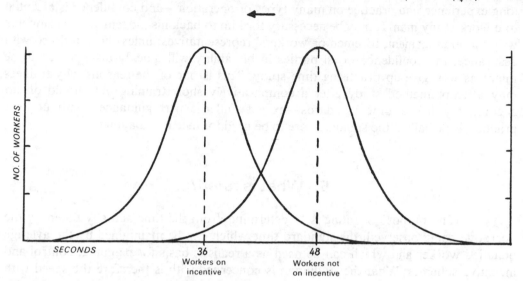

motivated to apply himself to his task, it is of course quite possible and indeed normal for him to exceed this rate of working if he wishes to do so, just as a man can walk faster than 4 miles an hour if he wants to. Men will be observed to be working, sometimes faster, sometimes slower than the standard rate, during short periods. Standard performance is achieved by working over the shift at paces which average the standard rate.

4. Comparing the observed rate of working with the standard

How is it possible accurately to compare the observed rate of working with the theoretical standard? By long practice.

Let us return once more to our man walking. Most people, if asked, would be able to judge the rate at which a man is walking. They would start by classifying rates of walking as slow, average or fast. With a little practice they would be able to say: "About 3 miles an hour, about 4 miles an hour, or about 5 miles an hour" (or of course the equivalent rates in kilometres if they are more used to kilometres). If, however, a reasonably intelligent person were to spend all his time watching men walking at different speeds, he would soon reach the point where he could say: "That man is walking at 2½ miles an hour and this one at 4¼ miles an hour", and he would be right, within close limits. In order to achieve such accuracy, however, he would need to have in his mind some particular rate with which to compare those which he sees.

That is exactly what the work study man does in rating; but, since the operations which he has to observe are far more complex than the simple one of walking without load, his training takes very much longer. Judgement of walking pace is only used for training work study men in the first stages; it bears very little resemblance to most of the jobs that have to be rated. It has been found better to use films or live demonstrations of industrial operations.

243

Confidence in the accuracy of one's rating can be acquired only through long experience and practice on many types of operation—and confidence is essential to a work study man. It may be necessary for him to back his judgement in arguments with the management, foremen or workers' representatives; unless he can do so with assurance, the confidence of all parties in his ability will quickly disappear, and he might as well give up practising time study. This is one of the reasons why trainees may attempt method study after a comparatively short training but should on no account try to set time standards—except under expert guidance—without long practice, especially if the standards are to be used for incentive payments.

5. What is rated?

The purpose of rating is to determine, from the time actually taken by the operative being observed, the standard time which can be maintained by the average qualified worker and which can be used as a realistic basis for planning, control and incentive schemes. What the studyman is concerned with is therefore the speed with which the operative carries out the work, in relation to the studyman's concept of a normal speed. In fact, speed of working as recorded by the time taken to carry out the elements of the operation is the only thing which can be measured with a stop-watch. Most authorities on time study agree on this point.

Speed of what? Certainly not merely speed for movement, because an unskilled operative may move extremely fast and yet take longer to perform an operation than a skilled operative who appears to be working quite slowly. The unskilled operative puts in a lot of unnecessary movements which the experienced operative has long since eliminated. The only thing that counts is the **effective speed** of the operation. Judgement of effective speed can only be acquired through experience and knowledge of the operations being observed. It is very easy for an inexperienced studyman either to be fooled by a large number of rapid movements into believing that an operative is working at a high rate or to underestimate the rate of working of the skilled operative whose apparently slow movements are very economical of motion.

A constant source of discussion in time study is the rating of **effort.** Should effort be rated, and if so, how? The problem arises as soon as it becomes necessary to study jobs other than very light work where little muscular effort is required. Effort is very difficult to rate. The result of exerting effort is usually only seen in the speed.

The amount of effort which has to be exerted and the difficulty encountered by the operative is a matter for the studyman to judge in the light of his experience with the type of job. For example, if an operative has to lift a heavy mould from the filling table, carry it across the shop and put it on the ground near the ladle, only experience will tell the observer whether the speed at which he is doing it is normal, above normal or sub-normal. Anyone who had never studied operations involving the carrying of heavy weights would have great difficulty in making an assessment the first time he saw such an operation.

Operations involving **mental activities** (judgement of finish, for example, in inspection of work) are most difficult to assess. Experience of the type of work is required before satisfactory assessments can be made. Inexperienced studymen can be

244

made to look very foolish in such cases, and moreover can be unjust to above-average and conscientious workers.

In any job the speed of accomplishment must be related to an idea of a normal speed for the same type of work. This is an important reason for doing a proper method study on a job before attempting to set a time standard. It enables the studyman to gain a clear understanding of the nature of the work and often enables him to eliminate excessive effort or judgement and so bring his rating process nearer to a simple assessment of speed.

In the next section some of the factors affecting the rate of working of the operative will be discussed.

6. Factors affecting the rate of working

Variations in actual times for a particular element may be due to factors outside or within the control of the worker. Those outside his control may be—

☐ Variations in the quality or other characteristics of the material used, although they may be within the prescribed tolerance limits.

☐ Changes in the operating efficiency of tools or equipment within their useful life.

☐ Minor and unavoidable changes in methods or conditions of operation.

☐ Variations in the mental attention necessary for the performance of certain of the elements.

☐ Changes in climatic and other surrounding conditions such as light, temperature, etc.

These can generally be accounted for by taking a sufficient number of studies to ensure that a representative sample of times is obtained.

Factors within his control may be—

☐ Acceptable variations in the quality of the product.

☐ Variations due to his ability.

☐ Variations due to his attitude of mind, especially his attitude to the organisation for which he works.

The factors within the worker's control can affect the times of similarly described elements of work by affecting—

☐ The pattern of his movements.

☐ His working pace.

☐ Both, in varying proportions.

The studyman must therefore have a clear idea of the pattern of movement which a qualified worker should follow, and of how this pattern may be varied to meet the range of conditions which that worker may encounter. Highly repetitive work

245

likely to run for long periods should have been studied in detail through the use of refined method study techniques, and the worker should have been suitably trained in the patterns of movement appropriate to each element.

The optimum pace at which the worker will work depends on—

☐   The physical effort demanded by the work.

☐   The care required on the part of the worker.

☐   His training and experience.

Greater physical effort will tend to slow up the pace. The ease with which the effort is made will also influence the pace. For example, an effort made in conditions where the operative cannot exert his strength in the most convenient way will be made much more slowly than one of the same magnitude in which he can exert his strength in a straightforward manner (for instance, pushing a car with one hand through the window on the steering wheel, as opposed to pushing it from behind). Care must be taken to distinguish between slowing up due to effort and slowing up due to fatigue.

When the element is one in which the worker is heavily loaded, so that he has to exert considerable physical effort throughout, it is unlikely that he will perform it at anything other than his natural best pace. In such circumstances rating may be superfluous: it may be sufficient to determine the average of the actual times taken during an adequate number of observations. This was very strikingly shown during an ILO study of manual earth-moving operations carried out in India. The workers— men, women and youths—carried loads of earth up to 84 lb (38 kg) in weight on their heads, in wicker baskets. A man with 84 lb on his head does not dawdle. He is anxious to get to the end of his walk and get rid of the load, and so performs the task at the best rate that he can naturally achieve. In doing so he shortens his stride, taking very short paces very quickly so that it looks almost as though he is going to break out into a trot at any moment. In point of fact, the stop-watch showed that the time taken for the loaded walk was a good deal longer than that needed for the apparently more leisurely return unloaded, so that the studyman without experience of the effort involved in the operation could very easily be led into making false ratings. In fact, for the loaded walk ratings were not necessary, except when contingencies occurred. Similar heavily loaded elements occur in factories, as in carrying sacks, picking them up, or throwing them down on to stacks. These operations are most likely to be carried out at the best natural pace which the worker can manage.

An increased need for care in carrying out an element will reduce the pace. An example is placing a peg with parallel sides in a hole, which requires more care than if the peg is tapered.

Fumbling and hesitation on the part of the worker are factors which the studyman must learn to recognise and cope with. A worker's natural skill and dexterity combined with training and experience will reduce the introduction of minor method variations (fumbling), and also the foreign element "consider" (hesitation). Very slight deviations from the standard method can be taken into account by assigning a lower rating, but fumbling and hesitation usually signal a need for further training.

246

The studyman should be careful not to rate too highly when—

☐ The worker is worried or looks hurried.

☐ The worker is obviously being over-careful.

☐ The job looks difficult to the studyman.

☐ The studyman himself is working very fast, as when recording a short-element study.

Conversely, there is a danger of rating too low when—

☐ The worker makes the job look easy.

☐ The worker is using smooth, rhythmic movements.

☐ The worker does not pause to think when the studyman expects him to do so.

☐ The worker is performing heavy manual work.

☐ The studyman himself is tired.

The studyman must take such factors into account. Rating is very much easier if a good method study has been made first, in which the activities calling for special skill or effort have been reduced to a minimum. The more the method has been simplified, the less the element of skill to be assessed and the more rating becomes a matter of simply judging pace.

7. Scales of rating

In order that a comparison between the observed rate of working and the standard rate may be made effectively, it is necessary to have a numerical scale against which to make the assessment. The rating can then be used as a factor by which the observed time can be multiplied to give the basic time, which is the time it would take the qualified worker, motivated to apply himself, to carry out the element at standard rating.

There are several scales of rating in use, the most common of which are those designated the 100-133 scale, the 60-80, the 75-100, and the British Standard scale used in this book (essentially a restatement of the 75-100 scale) which is the 0-100 scale.

Table 17 shows examples of various rates of working on the scales mentioned.

In the 100-133, 60-80 and 75-100 scales, the lower figure in each instance was defined as the rate of working of an operative on time rates of pay; and the higher, in each case one-third higher, corresponded to the rate of working we have called the standard rate, that of a qualified worker who is suitably motivated to apply himself to his work, as for instance by an incentive scheme. The underlying assumption was that workers on incentive perform, on average, about one-third more effectively than those who are not. This assumption has been well substantiated by practical experience over many years, but it is largely irrelevant in the construction of a rating scale. All the scales are linear. There is therefore no need to denote an

Table 17.   Examples of various rates of working on the principal rating scales

Scales				Description	Comparable walking speed[1]	
60-80	75-100	100-133	0-100 Standard		(mi/h)	(km/h)
0	0	0	0	No activity.		
40	50	67	**50**	Very slow; clumsy, fumbling movements; operative appears half asleep, with no interest in the job.	2	3.2
60	75	100	**75**	Steady, deliberate, unhurried performance, as of a worker not on piecework but under proper supervision; looks slow, but time is not being intentionally wasted while under observation.	3	4.8
80	100	133	**100 (Standard Rating)**	Brisk, business-like performance, as of an average qualified worker on piecework; necessary standard of quality and accuracy achieved with confidence.	4	6.4
100	125	167	**125**	Very fast; operative exhibits a high degree of assurance, dexterity and co-ordination of movement, well above that of an average trained worker.	5	8.0
120	150	200	**150**	Exceptionally fast; requires intense effort and concentration, and is unlikely to be kept up for long periods; a "virtuoso" performance achieved only by a few outstanding workers.	6	9.6

[1] Assuming an operative of average height and physique, unladen, walking in a straight line on a smooth level surface without obstructions.
Source: Freely adapted from a table issued by the Engineering and Allied Employers (West of England) Association, Department of Work Study.

intermediate point between zero and the figure chosen to represent the standard rating as we have defined it. Whichever scale is used, the final time standards derived should be equivalent, for the work itself does not change even though different scales are used to assess the rate at which it is being carried out.

The newer 0-100 scale has, however, certain important advantages which have led to its adoption as the British Standard. It is commended to readers of this book and is used in all the examples which follow. In the 0-100 scale, 0 represents zero activity and 100 the normal rate of working of the motivated qualified worker—that is, the standard rate.

8. How the rating factor is used

The figure 100 represents standard performance. If the studyman decides that the operation he is observing is being performed with less effective speed than his concept of standard, he will use a factor of less than 100, say 90 or 75 or whatever he considers represents a proper assessment. If, on the other hand, he decides that the effective rate of working is above standard, he gives it a factor greater than 100—say, 110, 115 or 120.

It is the usual practice to round off ratings to the nearest multiple of five on the scale; that is to say, if the rate is judged to be 13 per cent above standard, it would be put down at 115. During the first weeks of their training, studymen are unlikely to be able to rate more closely than the nearest ten.

If the studyman's ratings were always impeccable, then however many times he rates and times an element the result should be that—

$$\text{Observed Time} \times \text{Rating} = \text{A Constant}$$

provided that the element is of the type described as a constant element in section 6 of the previous chapter, and that it is always performed in the same way.

An example, expressed numerically, might read as follows:

Cycle	Observed time (decimal minutes)		Rating		Constant
1	0.20	×	100	=	0.20
2	0.16	×	125	=	0.20
3	0.25	×	80	=	0.20

and so on.

The reader may be puzzled that, in the figures above, 0.20×100 is shown as equal to 0.20 rather than 20. It must be remembered, however, that rating does not stand by itself: it is always a comparison with the standard rating (100) so that, when the amended time is being calculated, the assessed rating is the numerator of a fraction of which the denominator is the standard rating. In the case of the 100 standard this makes it a percentage which, when multiplied by the observed time, produces the constant known as the "basic time" for the element.

$$\text{Observed Time} \times \frac{\text{Rating}}{\text{Standard Rating}} = \text{Basic Time}$$

For example—

$$0.16 \text{ min} \times \frac{125}{100} = 0.20 \text{ min}$$

This basic time (0.20 minutes in the example) represents the time the element would take to perform (in the judgement of the observer) if the operative were working at the standard rate, instead of the faster one actually observed.

If the operative was judged to be working more slowly than the standard, a basic time less than the observed time would be arrived at, for example—

$$0.25 \text{ min} \times \frac{80}{100} = 0.20 \text{ min}$$

In actual practice, the multiple Observed Time × Rating is very rarely exactly constant when taken over a large number of readings, for various reasons such as—

☐　　　Variations in the work content of the element.

☐　　　Inaccuracies in noting and recording observed times.

☐　　　Inaccuracies in rating.

☐　　　Variations due to rating to the nearest five points.

9.　Recording the rating

We have discussed the theory of rating at some length and are now in a position to undertake the complete study.

In general, each element of activity must be rated during its performance **before the time is recorded,** without regard to previous or succeeding elements. No consideration should be given to the aspect of fatigue, since the allowance for recovery from fatigue will be assessed separately (see Chapter 18).

In the case of very short elements and cycles this may be difficult. If the work is repetitive, it is possible to rate every cycle or possibly the complete study. This is done when the short cycle study form (figure 77, page 212) is used.

It is most important that the rating should be made while the element is in progress and that it should be noted before the time is taken, as otherwise there is a very great risk that previous times and ratings for the same element will influence the assessment. For this reason the "Rating" column on the time study sheet in figures 75 and 76 is placed to the left of the "Watch Reading" column. It is, perhaps, a further advantage of the cumulative method of timing that the element time does not appear as a separate figure until the subtractions have been made later in the office. If it did, it might influence the rating or tempt the studyman to "rate by the watch".

Since the rating of an element represents the assessment of the average rate of performance for that element, the longer the element the more difficult it is for the studyman to adjust his judgement to that average. This is a strong argument in favour of making elements short, subject to the conditions discussed in Chapter 16. Long elements, though timed as a whole up to the break points, should be rated every half-minute.

Rating to the nearest five is found to give sufficient accuracy in the final result. Greater accuracy than this can be attained only after very long training and practice.

We may now refer back to the time study form in figures 75 and 76. We have discussed the filling-in of two columns, namely "Watch Reading" (WR) and the "Rating" (R), both entries being made on the same line.

These readings are continued for a sufficient number of cycles, at the end of which the watch is allowed to run on until compared with the clock with which it was synchronised when started. The "time after" can then be noted and recorded. The study is then at an end. The next step, after thanking the operative for his co-operation, is to work out the basic time for each element. How to do this is described in the next chapter.

Chapter 18
Time study: From study to standard time

1. Summarising the study

At the stage we have now reached, the studyman has completed his observations at the workplace and has returned to the work study office with his study. No doubt he will later be making further studies on the same job or operation as performed by different operatives, but for the moment we shall consider how he works up the study he has just taken and enters the results obtained on the **analysis of studies sheet** for the operation. Later in the chapter we shall see how standard times are compiled from the entries on the analysis of studies sheet.

All the entries made so far on the time study top steet (figure 75) and the continuation sheets (figure 76) have been written in pencil. As well as the heading details shown in the data block on the top sheet, there will be the "time before", the first entry on the study proper; the "time after", which will be the last entry; and two entries for each watch reading made—the rating and the watch reading itself. The ratings will all be in the column headed "R" and will consist of numbers such as 95, 115, 80, 100, 75, 105, etc., though until the studyman has had considerable practice he should confine his ratings to steps of ten, such as 80, 90, 100, etc. In the next column, that headed "WR", will be the watch readings in decimal minutes. Since watch readings will have been made at intervals of half-a-minute or less (long elements being rated and timed every half-minute during the element as well as at the break point which signals its end), most of the entries will consist of two figures only, with a three-figure entry occurring whenever a full minute has been crossed. It is usual to omit the decimal points. This saves the studyman a certain amount of writing and in practice gives rise to no ambiguity.

Let us assume that the "time before" was 2.15 minutes. The first entry on the study proper will thus be 215. The next may be 27, indicating that the watch was read 2.27 minutes after it was started. If the next three entries are 39, 51 and 307, these will signify that the watch was read at 2.39, 2.51 and 3.07 minutes after it was started. Two- and three-figure entries will continue in this way down the sheet until ten minutes have elapsed, when the next entry will be a four-figure one. Most studymen then revert to three-figure and two-figure entries again until another ten minutes have passed, using four figures only for the first entries after the ten-minute intervals. The study will close with the "time after" entry, at which time also the "time off" will be noted in the data panel on the study top sheet. Every now and then in the study there may be watch readings without accompanying ratings, when some delay or stoppage has occurred. These of course cannot be rated, for they are not work.

It should be made a working rule that none of these pencil entries may ever be erased and replaced. Occasionally a study may contain a very obvious error, of a sort which may be corrected without invalidating the study. If so, the correction should be made in ink, over the original pencil entry, so that it may always be seen later as a change made in the study office, not at the place where the study was made. Whenever there is an error about which there is doubt as to how it should be corrected, that part of the study should be ignored. It may be necessary to scrap the study and make another.

It is good practice to carry out all subsequent work on the study sheets either in ink or in pencil of a different colour from that used for the initial recordings. Many study departments make this a standing rule also. There is then no doubt whatever about what was actually recorded from direct observation and what represents subsequent calculation. Quite apart from its merits in obtaining orderly processing of the data recorded, the practice helps also to maintain the confidence of workers and their representatives that nothing improper is permitted in the working up of studies.

2. Preparing the study summary sheet

As will be seen a little later, much of the work necessary before the study summary sheet can be completed consists of quite simple routine calculations which may be done by a clerk while the studyman gets on with something else. In the beginning, however, the studyman should do everything himself, until he is so thoroughly familiar with all the procedures involved that he can not only instruct the clerk on what has to be done but can also check the calculations easily and quickly. It is also a good idea to provide the clerk with a calculator to help to reduce the number of mistakes and increase the amount of useful information that can be extracted from the study.

The first step is to complete the data at the head of the study summary sheet (figure 80), copying the details neatly, in ink, from the study sheets. From the time off and the time on, the elapsed time may be calculated and entered. When cumulative timing is being practised, the elapsed time should of course agree with the final watch reading. If it does not, there is an error which must at once be investigated. It is no use doing further work on the study until this is cleared up, for a serious error may be cause for scrapping the study and starting again. Deducting from the elapsed time the total "check time"—the sum of the "time before" and the "time after"—yields the net time. This should agree with the sum of all the observed times when using flyback timing, or the sum of all the subtracted times with cumulative timing. If flyback timing has been used, this check should be made before proceeding further, by adding up all the element times recorded and seeing how the total compares with the net time. It is unlikely that there will be exact agreement, for the reasons noted earlier, but the discrepancy should be within ± 2 per cent. If it is greater than this, some departments make it their practice to ignore the study and make another.

When cumulative timing has been used, the check cannot be made until the subtracted times have been obtained and totalled. The comparison then serves as a check on the accuracy with which the subtractions have been made. Any error should be investigated and corrected before the work of extension is undertaken.

On the body of the study summary sheet the studyman next lists in order all the repetitive elements observed, in order of their occurrence, noting the break points used on the reverse of the sheet.

Some of these repetitive elements may be variable elements, which will have to be treated in a different way from the constant elements. These variable elements are therefore listed again in a fresh tabulation below the full list of repetitive elements. Below the variable elements the studyman next lists any occasional elements observed, including with them any contingency elements of work which actually occurred during the study. Below these again are listed any foreign elements and in-effective time. When these entries have been made, the sheet should provide for a summarised record of everything that has been observed during the study.

ENTER FREQUENCIES

The next step is to enter against each element listed on the study summary sheet the frequency with which that element occurred. Repetitive elements, by defini-tion, occur at least once in every cycle of the operation so the entry to be made against a repetitive element will read 1/1, or 2/1, etc., indicating that the element concerned occurs once in every cycle (1/1), twice (2/1), or whatever may be the case. Occasional elements (for example, the element "sharpen tools") may occur only once every 10 or 50 cycles, when the entry would be 1/10, 1/50, or as appropriate. The entries are made in the column headed "F" on the study summary sheet.

3. Extension: the calculation of basic time

The studyman has now completed the entries in the heading block of the study summary sheet, listed the elements, entered frequencies and (if necessary) made a clear sketch of the workplace layout on the reverse on the sheet (when appropriate, the use of a simple instant-print-type camera can save a great deal of time and money; it is usually necessary to include in the photograph a simple scale, such as a square rod painted in 1 cm bands). He must turn next to the calculations which have to be made on the time study sheets themselves before he can go any further with his study summary. The results of his calculations will be entered on the time study sheets in ink or pencil of a different colour from that used when recording observations at the workplace.

If flyback timing has been used, the studyman may proceed direct to exten-sion. When using cumulative timing, however, it is first necessary to subtract each watch reading from the one **following** it, in order to obtain the observed time for each element. The entries obtained in this way should properly be styled "subtracted times" rather than "observed times"; they are entered in the third column on the time study sheets, that headed "ST". The subtracted times derived when using cumulative timing are of course exactly equivalent to the observed times entered directly at the

253

workplace when using flyback timing, so for the sake of simplicity the single term "observed time" is used during the rest of this chapter to mean both directly observed and subtracted times.

The next step is to convert each observed time to a basic time, entering the result in the column headed "BT" on the time study sheets.

> **Basic Time is the time for carrying out an element of work at standard rating, i.e.**
>
> $$\frac{\textbf{Observed Time} \times \textbf{Observed Rating}}{\textbf{Standard Rating}}$$
>
> **Extension is the calculation of basic time from observed time**

The effect of extending an observed time for an element to the basic time is shown graphically in figure 85.

Figure 85.   Effect of extension on the time of an element

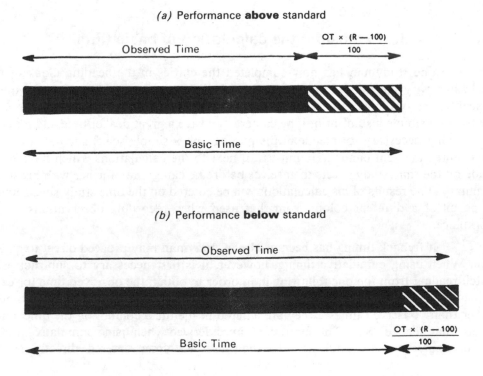

(a) Performance **above** standard

$$\frac{OT \times (R - 100)}{100}$$

Observed Time

Basic Time

(b) Performance **below** standard

Observed Time

Basic Time

$$\frac{OT \times (R - 100)}{100}$$

254

4. The selected time

> **The selected time is the time chosen as being representative of a group of times for an element or group of elements. These times may be either observed or basic and should be denoted as selected observed or selected basic times**

CONSTANT ELEMENTS

In theory the results of all the calculations of the basic time for any single constant element should be the same, but for the reasons given in Chapter 17 this is rarely so. It is necessary to select from all the basic times which have been entered on the time study sheets a representative time for each element. This will be recorded against the element description on the study summary sheet and will later be transferred to the analysis of studies sheet as the end result of the study, at least in so far as that particular element is concerned.

The calculations necessary to arrive at the selected basic time are carried out on the working sheet. As was noted in Chapter 15, it is quite common to use simple lined sheets for making the analysis (or, for variable elements, squared paper), without having any special forms printed. The working sheets, when completed, are stapled to the time study sheets and filed with them. Much time can be saved and accuracy can be greatly improved by using a small calculator or computing equipment.

There are various methods of examining and selecting the representative basic time for a constant element. Perhaps the most common, and in many ways often the most satisfactory, is by making a straight average of the element times arrived at, adding all the calculated basic times together and dividing the total by the number of occasions on which the element was recorded. Before doing this, however, it is usual to list all the basic times for the element and scrutinise the list, ringing out any times which are excessively high or low, well outside the normal range. These ringed times are sometimes styled "rogues". They should be examined carefully.

An exceptionally high time may be due to an error in timing. If cumulative timing is being used, an error of this sort will be revealed by examining the study, because an excessively long time for one element will cause shortening of the recorded time for the next. A high time may also be due to an error having been made in extension. But perhaps the most common cause, apart from errors, is that there has been some variation in the material being worked on or in some other aspect of the working method, which has caused a higher work content on the particular occasion recorded. If so, it is necessary to establish the cause and to consider whether it is likely to recur frequently or only very rarely. If the latter, it is usual to exclude the element basic time from the total from which the average is derived and then, having calculated the average time for the element, to carry the excess-over-average time contained in any ringed times down to contingencies, adding it to any other contingency time which

255

may have been observed and recorded during the study. In this way the extra time is fully accounted for, but it is treated as an exceptional event or contingency, which it properly is. On the other hand, if minor variations in the work content of an element are at all common, it will be much better not to exclude any calculations at all when calculating the average. Frequent minor variations should always be treated as signals to alert the studyman. If they are unavoidable, they at least indicate that studywork will have to be continued until a large number of observations have been taken on the element concerned, so that the resulting average of all the basic times may be sufficiently representative. Very often, however, they indicate that a further study should be made of the operation to find out the reason for them, and, if possible, to eliminate it.

Exceptionally short times should also be examined with great care. They too may be due to the studyman's error. On the other hand, they may indicate that a minor method improvement was adopted on the occasion during which the much shorter time than usual was noted. If so, it will be well to study the job again, giving special and more detailed attention to the working methods used.

The approach outlined above is valid so long as the exceptional times are either very infrequent, or, if frequent, only minor in character. Frequent large variations indicate that the element is not constant but variable, and it must be treated as such.

During a time study made on the operation of inspecting and jacketing a book, one element was described as: "Pick up one book, inspect, initial back end paper (break point: book closed)". This element was observed 31 times, and the basic minutes calculated were as shown below:

	Basic minutes	
27	26	28
26	25	25
27	29	27
27	28	27
26	28	26
27	27	25
26	27	26
25	26	26
26	27	(49) (Faulty part)
27	26	26
		28

It will be seen that one figure has been ringed—the basic time of 0.49 minutes which arose when a faulty book was encountered, examined and rejected. Excluding this figure, the total of the remaining 30 basic times is 7.97 minutes, which yields an average of 0.266 minutes per occasion. At this stage in the studywork the figure 266 would be entered on the study summary sheet and be carried to the analysis of studies sheet; but at the end of the calculations for the element, the basic time finally selected would be rounded off to the nearest two figures—in this case 0.27 minutes. The excess work observed in the ringed observation (0.49–0.27 = 0.22) would be carried down to the contingencies record.

Selection by averaging in this way is simple to teach and to understand, and is readily accepted by both studymen and workers. When the total number of observations made on an element is relatively small, averaging usually gives a more accurate result than is obtainable with other methods of selection. It does, however, give rise to a great deal of clerical work when many observations have been recorded, particularly when short elements have been observed very many times. Consequently, other methods of selection have been devised to reduce the calculation effort required.

One method, which obviates the necessity for extending observed times to basic times, is to tabulate the observed times for the element under the ratings recorded as corresponding to each observation, so as to form a distribution table against ratings. The table can be compiled direct from the entries made on the time study sheets at the workplace. For the element in the example above, the distribution table would appear as follows:

Rating:	80	85	90	95	100	105	
Observed times	31	32	30	28	28	27	
		31	30	30	27		
		30	30	27	27		
		31	26	28	26		
		31	27	27	27		
			28	26	28		
			29	29	27		
			29				
			29				
	31	155	258	195	190	27	Totals of observed times
Basic times	**25**	**132**	**232**	**185**	**190**	**28**	**Total = 792**

In the tabulation above, all the 30 observed times from which the basic times shown in the earlier example were calculated are listed, the one ringed observation having been excluded. The observed times are then totalled under each rating, and these totals are then extended by multiplying by the corresponding ratings, to yield the basic times (totals) shown in the line below. The grand total of all these basic times comes to 7.92 minutes, which, when divided by 30 (the number of observations) given the selected basic time for the element—0.264 minutes. This may be compared with the result of 0.266 minutes achieved by averaging the individual basic times.

A third method also avoids the need to extend each observed time, the selection being made by constructing a plot as shown in figure 86. In this method there are two sections to the plot, and two entries are made for each observation, but the entries are crosses or dots. The left-hand axis contains the time scale and shows the range of times observed for the element, in this case from 26 to 32. The scale at the top of the right-hand part of the plot shows the ratings observed, from 80 to 105. To make the plot, the studyman runs down his study, and each time the element is recorded he makes a cross against the time observed, and a second cross, also against the observed time but under the rating observed, on the right-hand side of the plot.

When all these entries are made, the left-hand side of the diagram will exhibit a frequency distribution of observed times. On the right-hand side, the best

Figure 86.   A graphical method of selecting basic time

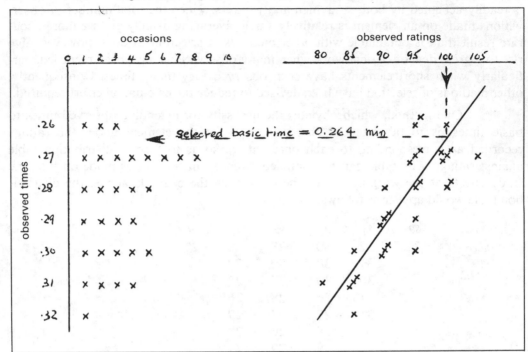

straight line is through the points plotted. The selected basic time for the element can then be read off by entering the right-hand plot under 100 rating, going vertically down until the line through the points is reached, and then reading on the scale at the left the time which corresponds to the intersection.

It is essential that the plot on the left-hand side be completed, in order to check whether the distribution follows the normal pattern. If it does not, the method should not be used. Distributions which are irregular—lopsided, skewed, or having two humps—should be treated as signals that the method will not be reliable, at any rate in the simple form here described. The different distribution patterns which can be produced each have significant meanings, indicating different variations in the work itself, in the operative's rate of working, or in the studyman's rating efficiency; but it will be better not to get involved in sophisticated analyses of this sort until considerable experience has been gained. The method is illustrated briefly here because it is typical of several which make use of graphical means to select representative basic times without extending each observation. Most of them are valid only when the distribution is normal or when the precise significance of any abnormality is thoroughly understood. It is recommended that the graphical methods be avoided unless expert guidance is available. The first two methods described will suffice for all normal needs, and have the merit that they are more easily understood by workers or their representatives.

Before leaving the subject of constant elements, the reader may like to refer again to the comments made in Chapter 17 about certain manual elements when the worker is heavily loaded, so that in all probability he normally performs the element at his best natural pace. Such elements are comparatively rare, but when they occur it may be sufficient to calculate the selected basic time by simply averaging observed times, without recourse to extension. It is essential, however, to have a large number of observations if this is to be done.

VARIABLE ELEMENTS

The analysis of variable elements presents more difficulty. It is necessary to find out what it is that causes the basic time to vary, and quite often there may be several variables to take into account at once. For example, consider the operation of cross-cutting wooden planks with a handsaw. The basic time needed to make the cut will vary with the width of the plank, which establishes the length of cut that has to be made, and also with the thickness of the planks and the hardness of the wood being cut. If the saw needs sharpening, the cut will take longer; however, this would be considered to be the use of an incorrect method, and any observations made while the operative is using a blunt saw would therefore be disregarded.

The first step in the treatment of variable elements is almost always to extend observed times to basic times. The basic times will then be plotted on squared paper against the known variables. Thus for variable elements the analysis of studies sheet takes the form of graph paper, and the graph constructed at the time of summarising the study will probably be attached to the analysis of studies sheet, in place of the entries made on this sheet for constant elements.

Whenever possible, the basis chosen for the plot should be some variable which yields a straight line when the basic times are entered. Sometimes this can be done by using logarithmic paper, when analysis of the operation suggests that the variability with time may not be arithmetically linear. Quite often, however, it is not possible to discover a straight-line relationship between time and the main variable, or with any combination of variables which is tried. In these cases the end product will be a curved line, drawn as smoothly as possible between all the plots made from all the studies on the element. Basic times for the element will then be selected by reading off the curve at the appropriate point on each occasion on which a standard time has to be compiled.

The treatment which the studyman would accord to the times derived from studying the cross-cutting of planks would depend on whether the operation is an incidental one, performed only rarely, or whether it is an element performed many times each day, forming a substantial proportion of the total work done. In the latter case he will probably need to build up a series of graphs, each for a different hardness of wood, with each graph having a family of lines on it, one for each thickness of plank. Basic times would be plotted on these graphs against length of cut. The relationship should be linear, so that once it has been discovered the lines can be expressed as formulae, with factors to take into account the variables, thus dispensing with the graphs for the calculation of basic times. If the element is not of sufficient importance to warrant so much detail, the studyman would probably try plotting basic times against the product: width of plank × thickness of plank, thus combining two of the main variables. He would also try to establish a factor by which to multiply the relationship discovered to take account of different hardnesses of wood. The statistical technique of multiple regression analysis is highly suitable for the calculation of variable times. However, a full explanation of this technique falls outside the scope of this book.

259

It will be evident that, in general, many more observations of a variable element than of a constant element will be necessary before reliable representative basic times can be established. It is well to recognise this at the outset, so that the studywork can be planned to span all the different conditions and variables which are likely to be encountered in practice. It is well also to give close attention from the beginning to discovering the best basis against which to plot the times, essaying trial plots against different possibilities until some satisfactory indicator of the cause of the variable times is revealed. When the basis of the relationship has been discovered, further studywork can be directed to filling any gaps in the information so far compiled. If the essential analysis is left until a later stage, many of the studies taken may turn out to be needless duplication.

It is not possible to prescribe any one method of approach which will yield satisfactory results in the analysis of all variable elements. Each must be treated on its merits. It is here, perhaps more than anywhere else in time study, that close attention to the detailed methods of working is amply repaid; otherwise it will rarely be possible to discover just what it is that causes basic times to vary. Even when the causes are known, there is often scope for considerable ingenuity in devising a simple basis which will reflect the major variables and reveal a definite and repeatable relationship.

5. Completing the study summary sheet

Having completed his calculations, the studyman is now ready to enter on the study summary sheet the information which will make it a clear and concise record of all the results obtained from his observations at the workplace. Against each of the constant elements listed on the sheet he will enter the selected basic time for the element and the number of occasions on which the element was observed. The frequencies of occurrence have already been entered. Against the variable elements he will note the relationship between basic time and the controlling variable, if he has discovered this, or will record a reference to the graph sheet or other study analysis sheet on which the basic times derived have been analysed.

To complete the summary, he must enter a record of any occasional elements observed which have not already been included, and also any foreign elements which may have appeared during the study. Contingency elements and any contingency time extracted during the calculations must be shown. It is usual to express the contingency basic minutes as a percentage of the total basic minutes of repetitive work observed during the whole of the study, so that there may be a basis for comparing the contingencies occurring during one study with those in another.

All the entries which have so far been made represent work, in one form or another. All except any foreign elements will figure later in the calculation of a standard time for the operation, and since they are all work they will all attract relaxation allowances (see section 11). Besides the elements of work, however, there may well have been periods when no work was done during the study, either because the operative was resting or because he was engaged on one or other of the activities which were described earlier in this book as "ineffective time". The time so spent must now be totalled and entered on the summary. It is useful to break down such time into a few main categories, such as "relaxation", "ineffective time", etc. The entries will all be in terms of observed times, of course—periods when no work is done cannot be rated.

6. How many studies?

We dealt with this problem in Chapter 16, outlining a statistical and a conventional method for determining the number of elements and cycles to be studied. When the working conditions vary, studies must be made in each of the different sets of conditions which will be met with in practice: at different times of day if atmospheric conditions change markedly during the shift, for instance, and on all the types of material which have to be processed if the material is not rigidly standard.

The studyman must be prepared to study all the work involved in starting up at the beginning of a shift and in shutting down at the end of it. Start-up and shutdown times are part of the work and may need a separate work value, or they may be taken into account (if appropriate) by making an allowance for them when calculating the standard times for individual jobs. In industries such as printing, presses are not normally left inked up overnight, as the ink would dry before morning. Time may have to be allowed for cleaning machines and the workplace, and for changing clothes in industries where special clothing is required. Activities of this sort are not usually taken into account in the calculation of standard times for individual jobs but are more often dealt with by time allowances. Allowances are discussed later in this chapter: at this point it is sufficient to note that studies will have to be made on all the ancillary and incidental activities which are undertaken during the working day before the matter of allowances can be properly considered.

A simple method of determining when enough cycles of a constant element have been observed—enough, that is, to permit a representative basic time for the element to be selected—is to plot the **cumulative** average basic time for the element each time a study is made on it and summarised. The plot is started with the basic time derived from the first study. When the second study comes in, the figure then plotted is the average, calculated by adding the basic time from the first study times the number of observations during the first study to the product (basic time × observations) from the second study, and then dividing by the total number of observations made during both studies. Further plots are made in the same fashion as successive studies are worked up. When the line on the graph ceases to "wag" and settles down at a constant level, enough studies have been made on this element. An example is shown in figure 87.

With variable elements it is convenient to start by making several short studies which together span the full range of variability, so that an early attempt may be made to establish the relationship between basic time and the indicative variable. Subsequent studywork may then be directed to obtaining the information needed to complete, modify or validate the apparent relationship suggested by the first studies.

7. The analysis of studies sheet

An example of an "analysis of studies sheet" is shown in figure 81 (Chapter 15). The results obtained in each study on an operation are entered on this sheet by

261

Figure 87. *Cumulative average basic times for a constant element*

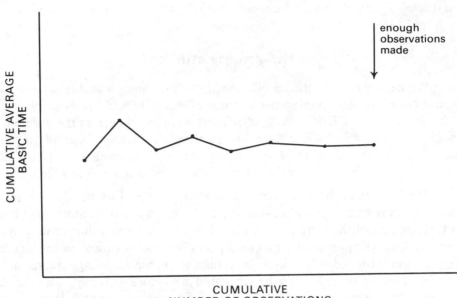

copying from the study summary sheet, as soon as the study has been worked up. A form of the type illustrated provides for a list of all the elements which make up a job or operation, and also for full details in respect of repetitive and occasional elements, together with a record of the contingency and ineffective times observed. Graphs are appended to the sheet to record the results obtained from studying variable elements.

When it is considered that enough observations have been made, the next step is to calculate the final representative basic times for each element. This is done on the analysis of studies sheet. The process of selection is essentially similar to that described in section 4 of this chapter, the usual method being to calculate the over-all weighted average of all the basic times recorded for each element, disregarding any entries which subsequent studywork has shown to be erroneous. The weighted average is obtained by multiplying the basic time recorded from a study by the number of observations of the element made in that study, adding up the products so derived for all the studies, and dividing the total by the sum of all the observations made in all the studies.

When these final representative basic times have been calculated for each constant element, it is a simple matter to calculate the basic time per cycle, per job or per operation for these elements, by multiplying the time per occasion by the frequency per cycle with which each element recurs. Variable elements cannot be dealt with in this way, of course. For them, the basic time may have to be read off the appropriate graph, or, if a straight-line relationship has been established, be calculated from the formula which expresses the line in algebraic terms, or be derived by regression analysis.

If it is considered appropriate to make provision in the job time for contingencies, the allowance necessary is also calculated on the analysis of studies sheet. The first step in doing this is to calculate the percentage which the total observed contingencies represent of the total other work observed. Time spent on contingencies is just as much work as that devoted to repetitive and occasional elements, so contingency time will also be recorded in basic minutes. If the percentage is a very small one, it will probably be convenient to adopt the figure as the percentage allowance to be made; but if it comes out at more than about 4 or 5 per cent, the better course is to inquire into the causes of the contingencies so as to eliminate or reduce them as far as possible. When action of this sort has been taken as a result of the studies, the percentage observed during the earlier studywork will no longer be valid and it will be necessary to make fresh observations.

At the stage now reached, a basic time has been built up for the job or operation, including all repetitive and occasional elements and also any small amount of extra work which may be met with occasionally as a contingency. The compilation has been done element by element, so that, if at any time in the future the job is changed slightly by deleting or changing an element or by adding a fresh one, it will not be necessary to restudy the whole job. The entries on the analysis of studies sheet will still hold good for all the unchanged elements in the new job sequence, and therefore it will be possible to make a fresh compilation after studying the new elements only.

The basic time, however, forms only a part of the standard time which has to be established for the job or operation. Certain allowances must be added before the standard time can be derived. These allowances must now be discussed; before doing so, however, it is necessary to state clearly what is meant by two terms which have been mentioned frequently in the preceding pages but which have not yet been precisely defined: namely **work content** and **standard time.**

8. Work content

In the chapters at the beginning of this book, the term "work content" was used frequently to describe what the words themselves suggest: the amount of work which has to be done to complete a job or operation, as distinct from any ineffective time which may occur. In time study practice, however, the word "work" is accorded a meaning which is slightly different from its usual meaning in ordinary English usage. An observer who was familiar with the word only in its usual sense would say, when watching an operative at his job, that when the worker was actually doing something he was working, and that when he was resting or doing nothing he was not working. In time study practice, however, we are concerned with measuring work in numerical terms, and for this purpose the word "work" is extended to include not only the physical labours performed but also the proper amount of relaxation or rest necessary to recover from the fatigue caused by those labours. We shall see later that relaxation allowances are made for other purposes besides recovery from fatigue; but for the moment the important point is that, when in time study we speak of "work" and set out to measure it, we define work to include the appropriate relaxation allowance, so that the amount of work in a job is taken to be not only the time needed at standard performance to do whatever the job requires but also the additional time which is considered necessary for relaxation.

263

> **The work content of a job or operation is defined as: basic time + relaxation allowance + any allowance for additional work—e.g. that part of contingency allowance which represents work**

9. Allowances

We have seen that, during the method study investigation which should be carried out before any job is timed, the energy expended by the worker in performing the operation should be reduced to a minimum through the development of improved methods and procedures, in accordance with the principles of motion economy and, wherever practicable, by mechanisation. Even when the most practical, economic and effective method has been developed, however, the job will still require the expenditure of human effort, and some allowance must therefore be made for recovery from fatigue and for relaxation. Allowance must also be made to enable a worker to attend to his personal needs; and other allowances (e.g. contingency allowances) may also have to be added to the basic time in order to give the work content.

The determination of allowances is probably the most controversial part of work study. For reasons that will be explained later, it is very difficult to determine precisely the allowances needed for a given job. What should therefore be attempted is an objective assessment of the allowances that can be consistently applied to the various elements of work or to various operations.

The fact that the calculation of allowances cannot be altogether accurate under all circumstances is no excuse for using them as a dumping ground for any factors that have been missed or neglected in making the time study. We have seen how the studyman can go to great lengths to arrive at fair and accurate time standards. These should not be spoilt by the hasty or ill-considered addition of a few percentage points here and there "just in case". Above all, allowances should not be used as "loosening" factors.

The difficulty experienced in preparing a universally accepted set of precise allowances that can be applied to every working situation anywhere in the world is due to various reasons. The most important among them are—

(1) **Factors related to the individual.** If every worker in a particular working area were to be considered individually, it might well be found that a thin, active, alert worker at the peak of physical condition required a smaller allowance to recover from fatigue than an obese, inept worker. Similarly, every worker has a unique learning curve which can affect the manner in which he conducts his work. There is also some reason to believe that there may be ethnic variations in the response to the degree of fatigue experienced by workers, particularly when engaged on heavy manual work. Undernourished workers take a longer time than others to recover from fatigue.

(2) **Factors related to the nature of the work itself.** Many of the tables developed for the calculation of allowances give figures which may be acceptable for light and

medium work in industry but which are inadequate when applied to operations involving very heavy and strenuous work, such as work beside furnaces in steel mills. Moreover, every working situation has its own particular attributes which may affect the degree of fatigue experienced by the worker or may lead to unavoidable delay in the execution of a job. Examples of these factors are: whether a worker has to perform his work standing up or sitting down, and his posture during work; whether he has to exert force to move or carry loads from one place to another; whether the work itself results in undue eye or mental strain, and so on. Other factors inherent in the job can also contribute to the need for allowances, although in a different way—for example, when protective clothing or gloves have to be worn, or when there is constant danger, or when there is a risk of spoiling or damaging the product.

(3) **Factors related to the environment.** Allowances, in particular relaxation allowances, have to be determined with due regard to various environmental factors such as heat, humidity, noise, dirt, vibration, light intensity, dust, wet conditions, and so on. Each of these will affect the amount of relaxation allowances needed. Environmental factors may also be seasonal in nature. This is particularly so for those who work in the open air, such as workers in the construction industry or in shipyards.

It should now be more clear to the reader why it is so difficult to devise an internationally accepted scheme of allowances to meet every working situation. It should also be stated here, in very clear terms, that **the ILO has not adopted, nor is it likely to adopt, any standards relating to the determination of allowances.** The following discussion quotes examples of the calculation of allowances under different conditions. They are quoted here as examples for training purposes and not as an ILO stand on the matter.

It should also be mentioned that this particular aspect of work study has been the subject of extensive research by various organisations which have put forward their own recommendations for the calculation of allowances. Of the more important research carried out, mention should be made of the work of the Max Planck Institut für Arbeitsphysiologie,[1] of REFA Verband für Arbeitsstudien[2] and of G. C. Heyde in Australia.[3]

10. Calculation of allowances

The basic model for the calculation of allowances is shown in figure 88. It will be seen from this model that relaxation allowances (which are intended to aid recovery from fatigue) are the only essential part of the time added to the basic time. Other allowances, such as contingency, policy and special allowances, are applied under certain conditions only.

---

[1] G. Lehmann: *Praktische Arbeitsphysiologie* (Stuttgart, Georg Thieme Verlag, 1953).
[2] REFA: *Methodenlehre des Arbeitsstudiums,* Vol. 2: *Datenermittlung* (Munich, Carl Hanser Verlag, 1971), pp. 299–335.
[3] Chris Heyde: *The sensible taskmaster* (Sydney, Heyde Dynamics, 1976).

Figure 88.   Allowances

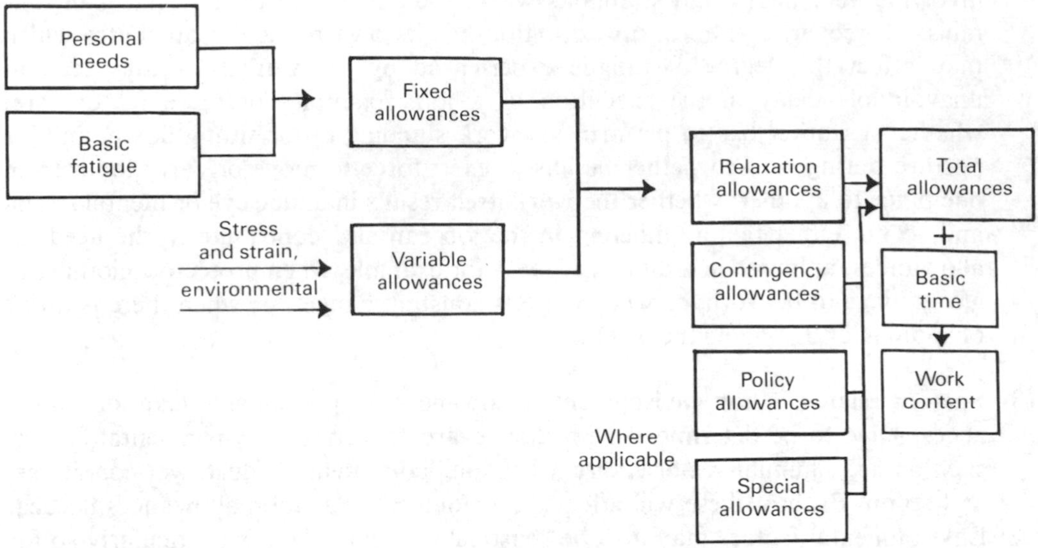

11. Relaxation allowances

> **Relaxation allowance is an addition to the basic time intended to provide the worker with the opportunity to recover from the physiological and psychological effects of carrying out specified work under specified conditions and to allow attention to personal needs. The amount of allowance will depend on the nature of the job**

Relaxation allowances are calculated so as to allow the worker to recover from **fatigue.** Fatigue may be defined as a physical and/or mental weariness, real or imagined, existing in a person and adversely affecting his ability to perform work. The effects of fatigue can be lessened by rest pauses, during which the body recovers from its exertion, or by slowing down the rate of working and thus reducing the expenditure of energy.

Allowances for fatigue are normally added **element by element** to the basic times, so that a work value for each element is built up separately, the element standard times being combined to yield the standard time for the whole job or operation. In this way it is possible to deal with any extra allowance which may be required to compensate for severe climatic conditions, since the element may sometimes be performed in cool weather and sometimes when it is very hot. Allowances for climatic conditions have to be applied to the **working shift** or **working day** rather than to the element or job, in such a way that the amount of work which the worker is expected to produce over the day or the shift is reduced. The standard time for the job remains the

266

same, whether the job is performed in summer or winter, since it is intended to be a measure of the work that the job contains.

Relaxation allowances have two major components: **fixed allowances** and **variable allowances.**

Fixed allowances are composed of—

(1) Allowances for **personal needs.** This allowance provides for the necessity to leave the workplace to attend to personal needs such as washing, going to the lavatory and getting a drink. Common figures applied by many enterprises range from 5 to 7 per cent.

(2) Allowances for **basic fatigue.** This allowance, always a constant, is given to take account of the energy expended while carrying out work and to alleviate monotony. A common figure is 4 per cent of basic time. This is considered to be adequate for a worker who carries out the job while seated, who is engaged on light work in good working conditions, and who is called upon to make only normal use of hands, legs and senses.

Variable allowances are added to fixed allowances when working conditions differ markedly from those stated above, for instance because of poor environmental conditions that cannot be improved, added stress and strain in performing the job in question, and so on.

As was mentioned above, a number of important studies have been carried out by various research organisations to try to develop a more rational approach to the calculation of variable allowances. Most management consultants in all countries have their own tables. In Appendix 3, we give an example of relaxation allowances tables using a points system. Many of these tables appear to work satisfactorily in practice; however, recent evidence indicates that, although many of the fatigue allowance scales established empirically in a laboratory are satisfactory on physiological grounds for work involving normal or moderately intensive effort, they provide inadequate allowances when applied to very heavy operations such as those connected with furnaces.

For the various reasons mentioned earlier in the chapter, when using one of the standard scales it is always preferable to check the amount of relaxation time they yield by carrying out whole-day studies at the workplace, noting the amount of time which the workers actually spend in relaxation (in one form or another) and comparing this with the calculated allowance. Checks of this sort do at least show whether the scale is, in general, too tight or too loose.

Relaxation allowances are given as percentages of the basic time. As mentioned earlier, they are normally calculated on an element-by-element basis. This is particularly the case when the effort expended on different elements varies widely (for example, where a heavy workpiece has to be lifted on or off a machine at the beginning and end of an operation). If, on the other hand, it is considered that no one element of a job is any more or any less fatiguing than any of the other elements, the simplest course is to add up all the elemental basic time first and then add the allowance as a single percentage to the total.

267

REST PAUSES

Relaxation allowances can be taken in the form of rest pauses. While there is no hard and fast rule governing rest pauses, a common practice is to allow a 10 to 15 minute break at mid-morning and mid-afternoon, often coupled with facilities for tea, coffee or cold drinks and snacks, and to permit the remainder of the relaxation allowance to be taken at the discretion of the worker.

Rest pauses are important for the following reasons:

☐ They decrease the variation in the worker's performance throughout the day and tend to maintain the level nearer the optimum.

☐ They break up the monotony of the day.

☐ They give workers the chance to recover from fatigue and to attend to personal needs.

☐ They reduce the amount of time off taken by workers during working hours.

12. Other allowances

It is sometimes necessary to incorporate allowances other than relaxation allowances in the compilation of standard time. Three such allowances are described below.

CONTINGENCY ALLOWANCES

> **A contingency allowance is a small allowance of time which may be included in a standard time to meet legitimate and expected items of work or delays, the precise measurement of which is uneconomical because of their infrequent or irregular occurrence**

Contingency allowances have already been mentioned when we described the calculations which have to be made to complete the study summary sheet and the analysis of studies sheet. The allowance provides for small unavoidable delays as well as for occasional and minor extra work, and so it would be proper to split the allowance into these components, the contingency allowance for work being allowed to attract fatigue allowance, just as any other item of work does, and the delay part of the allowance being given with only a personal needs increment. In practice this is a distinction which is often ignored. Contingency allowances are always very small, and it is usual to express them as a percentage of the total repetitive basic minutes in the job, adding them to the rest of the work in the job and adding a relaxation percentage to the whole contingency allowance. Contingency allowances should not be greater than 5 per cent, and should only be given in cases where the studyman is absolutely satisfied that the contingencies cannot be eliminated and that they are justified. On no account should such allowances be used as "loosening" factors or to avoid carrying out proper time study practice. The duties for which the contingency allowance is given should be specified. However, in fairness, it may be necessary to give contingency allowances as a matter of course in enterprises where the production work is not well organised. This further stresses the need to make the conditions and organisation of work as good as possible **before** setting time standards and is an incentive to the management to do so.

POLICY ALLOWANCES

> A policy allowance is an increment, other than bonus increment, applied to standard time (or to some constituent part of it, e.g. work content) to provide a satisfactory level of earnings for a specified level of performance under exceptional circumstances

Policy allowances are not a genuine part of time study and should be used with the utmost caution and only in clearly defined circumstances. They should always be dealt with quite separately from basic times, and, if used at all, should preferably be arranged as an addition to standard times, so as not to interfere with the time standards set by time study.

The usual reason for making a policy allowance is to line up standard times with the requirements of wage agreements between employers and trade unions. In several enterprises in the United Kingdom, for example, the incentive performance is generally set at such a level that the average qualified worker, as defined, can earn a bonus of $33^1/_3$ per cent of his basic time rate if he achieves standard performance. There is no need to apply a policy allowance to achieve this state of affairs; it is simply necessary to arrange for the rate paid per standard minute of work produced to be $133^1/_3$ per cent of the basic time rate per minute, and in general it is better to accommodate any special wage requirements in this way, by adjusting the rate paid per unit of work rather than the standard time.

There are, however, certain employer-union agreements under which higher bonuses can be earned, and it may not be politic to seek a revision of the terms of these agreements to permit the achievement of their terms by modifying the rates paid rather than the times set. In these circumstances a policy allowance is given to make up the difference. It may be applied as a factor to the work content or to the standard time.

This might be an appropriate course to take when standard times are being introduced to only a small proportion of the total workforce covered by the agreement. Similar policy allowances are sometimes made as temporary additions to cover abnormal circumstances, such as the imperfect functioning of a piece of plant or disruption of normal working caused by rearrangements or alterations.

269

SPECIAL ALLOWANCES

Special allowances may be given for any activities which are not normally part of the operation cycle but which are essential to the satisfactory performance of the work. Such allowances may be permanent or temporary; care should be taken to specify which. Wherever possible, these allowances should be determined by time study.

When time standards are used as the basis for a payment-by-results scheme, it may be necessary to make a **start-up allowance** to compensate for time taken by any work and any enforced waiting time which necessarily occurs at the start of a shift or work period before production can begin. A **shut-down allowance** may similarly be given for work or waiting time occurring at the end of the day. A **cleaning allowance** is of much the same character: it is given when the worker has to give attention from time to time to cleaning his machine or workplace. **Tool allowance** is an allowance of time to cover the adjustment and maintenance of tools.

It would be possible, after the time necessary to perform any or all of these activities has been studied, to express the result as a percentage of the total basic time for the operations expected to be performed during a day and to give the allowance as an increment included in the compilation of standard times. Indeed, this is sometimes thought to be the better course with tool allowance; but, in general, it is preferable to give all these allowances as periods of time *per day* rather than embodying them in the standard times. Usually this is fairer to the operatives, and it has the signal advantage of bringing to the attention of the management the total amount of time which has to be devoted to these activities, thus prompting thoughts about how it could be reduced.

Some allowances are normally given *per occasion* or *per batch*. One such allowance is **set-up allowance,** given to cover the time required for preparing a machine or process for production, an operation which is necessary at the start of production on a batch of fresh products or components. Set-up time is sometimes called make-ready time: its opposite is tear-down or dismantling time, for which a **dismantling allowance** may be given, to cover the time needed for making alterations to machine or process settings after completing a run of production. Very similar is **change-over allowance,** usually given to operatives who are not actually engaged in setting-up or dismantling, to compensate them for time on necessary activities or waiting time at the start and/or the end of a job or batch. These allowances should be denoted as "job change-over allowance" or "batch change-over allowance", as appropriate.

A **reject allowance** may be included in a standard time when the production of a proportion of defective products is *inherent* in the process, but is perhaps more usually given as a temporary addition to standard times, per job or per batch, if an occasional bad lot of material has to be worked. An **excess work allowance,** if necessary, would also be given as an addition to the standard time, to compensate for extra work occasioned by a temporary departure from standard conditions.

Learning allowances may be given to trainee operatives engaged on work for which standard times have been issued, as a temporary benefit while they develop their ability. A **training allowance** is a similar allowance given to an experienced worker to compensate him for the time he is required to spend instructing a trainee, while both are working on jobs for which standard times have been set. These allow-

270

ances are often given as so many minutes per hour, on a declining scale so that the allowances taper off to zero over the expected learning period. Very similar is an **implementation allowance,** given to workers asked to adopt a new method or process to encourage them to attempt an enthusiastic implementation of the new ways and prevent their losing earnings by doing so. In fact, it is sometimes arranged that their earnings will actually be increased during the change-over period, so as to give the new method every chance of success. One system of implementation allowances credits the workers with ten minutes per hour on the first day, nine on the second, and so on down to zero.

A **small batch allowance** is required to enable a worker working on small batches to decide what to do and how to go about it (from instructions, by experience, or by trial and error) and then to work up to a standard performance by practice and repetition. The calculation of this allowance will depend on whether it is a one-of-a-type batch or not, on the length and batch size or run length and on the frequency of similar work and its degree of complexity.

13. The standard time

It is now possible to obtain a complete picture of the **standard time** for a straightforward manual job or operation, one which is considered to attract only the two allowances which have so far been discussed in detail: contingency allowance and relaxation allowance. The standard time for the job will be the sum of the standard times for all the elements of which it is made up, due regard being paid to the frequencies with which the elements recur, plus the contingency allowance (with its relaxation allowance increment). In other words—

> **Standard time is the total time in which a job should be completed at standard performance**

The standard time may be represented graphically as shown in figure 89.

Figure 89.   How the standard time for a simple manual job is made up

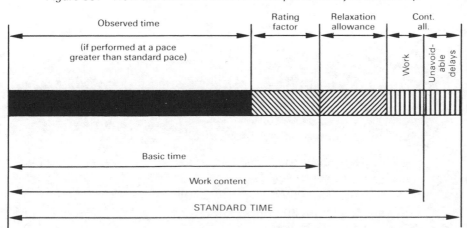

In a case where the observed time is rated at less than standard pace, the rating factor will, of course, be shown inside the observed time. The contingencies and relaxation allowances, however, are still percentages of the basic time. The standard time is expressed in standard minutes or standard hours.

In Chapter 19 we shall discuss the application of time study to operations involving the use of machinery, in which part of the operation time is taken up by work done by the machine while the operative stands by. An example of a fully worked time study is shown in Chapter 20.

Chapter 19
Setting time standards for work with machines

In Chapters 15 to 18 the basic procedures of time study as applied to manual operations were described. Through the use of the techniques and methods which were discussed, time standards can be compiled for all jobs in which the operative works with hand tools or with power tools which he himself manoeuvres, as distinct from machines which perform part of the operation automatically. Such work is known an **unrestricted work,** because the output of the worker is limited only by factors within his control. A man grinding a cutting tool on an electrically operated grindstone is engaged on unrestricted work, and so is a worker polishing a metal component by holding it against a power-driven polishing mop, for in neither of these cases does the worker clamp the workpiece securely in position and leave the machine to get on with the work.

However, it is becoming increasingly common for industrial jobs to be made up partly of elements performed manually by the worker and partly of elements carried out automatically by machines or process equipment, with the worker either being necessarily idle meanwhile or attending to something else. In order to set time standards for such operations, it is necessary to apply somewhat different methods, in extension of the basic time study procedures. For some highly complex operations special techniques have been devised. In the present chapter, only the more generally applicable methods will be described.

1. Plant and machine control

> **Plant and machine control is the name given to the procedures and means by which efficiency and utilisation of units of plant and machinery are planned and checked**

In many enterprises the machines, plant and equipment together account for by far the greatest proportion of the total capital invested in the undertaking. When this is so, the costs incurred in servicing capital, in maintaining the machines, and in providing against depreciation and for the replacement of the equipment may well amount in total to more than any other factory expense (excluding the cost of raw materials and bought components, which is an external rather than a factory expense). Very often these machinery costs are much greater than the total wage bill for the plant, so that it is of the utmost importance to make the most intensive use possible of the machinery and equipment installed, even though this be done at the expense of labour productivity. Indeed, it may be very sound policy to increase the manning complement on the machines, if by so doing greater machine utilisation can be achieved.

Before turning his attention to individual jobs, therefore, the work study man will do well to examine first the over-all utilisation of the machinery in the business; in the enterprise as a whole; in the different departments; and machine by machine in the case of particularly expensive items. He will then be better placed to decide the proper objectives for the application of work study in the plant, and will see clearly whether labour productivity or machine utilisation is of primary importance.

The terms and concepts used in the study of machine utilisation (or plant or process utilisation) are described below. They are largely self-explanatory. The relationship between them is shown graphically in figure 90.

Machine maximum time is the maximum possible time during which a machine or group of machines could work within a given period, e.g. 168 hours in one week or 24 hours in one day.

Machine available time is the time during which a machine could work based on attendance time—i.e. working day or week plus overtime.

Machine idle time is the time during which a machine is available for production or ancillary work but is not used owing to shortage of work, materials or workers, including the time that the plant is out of balance.

Machine ancillary time is the time when a machine is temporarily out of productive use owing to change-overs, setting, cleaning, etc.

Machine down time is the time during which a machine cannot be operated on production or ancillary work owing to breakdown, maintenance requirements, or for other similar reasons.

Machine running time is the time during which a machine is actually operating, i.e. the machine available time **less** any machine down time, machine idle time, or machine ancillary time.

The machine running time is a matter of fact, observable by direct study at the workplace. It does not follow, however, that the machine, though running, is actually operating in the manner in which it should, or has been set so as to perform in the very best manner of which it is capable. It is useful therefore to introduce another concept—

Machine running time at standard. This is the running time that should be incurred in producing the output if the machine is working under optimum conditions.

Figure 90. Explanatory diagram of machine time

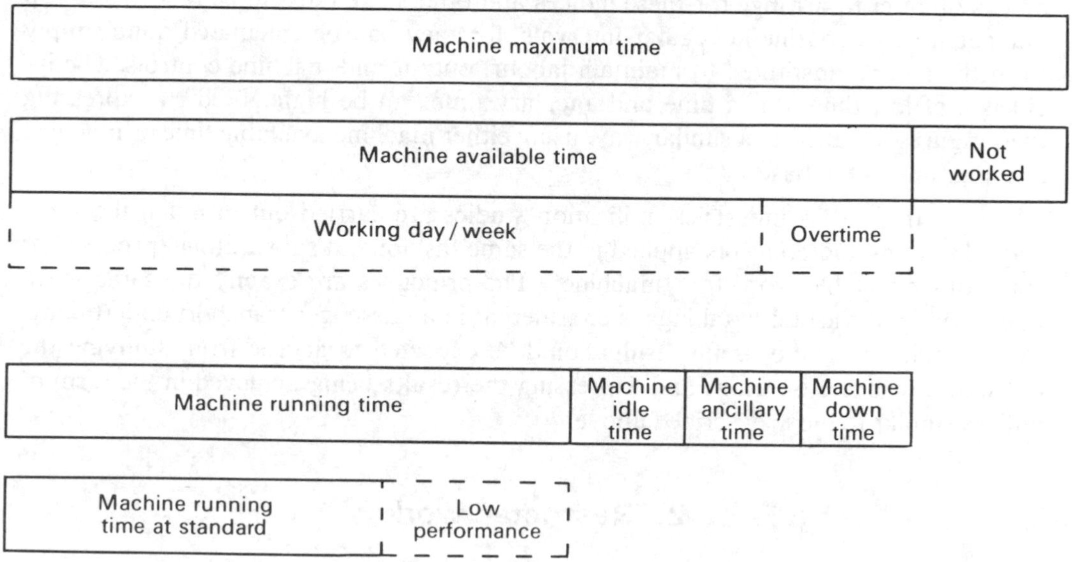

Machine maximum time

Machine available time	Not worked

Working day / week	Overtime

Machine running time	Machine idle time	Machine ancillary time	Machine down time

Machine running time at standard	Low performance

Source: Based on a diagram contained in the B. S. *Glossary, op. cit.*

The most useful work measurement method for studying machine utilisation is **work sampling,** as described in Chapter 14. This technique gives the information required with much less effort than would be needed with time study, especially when many machines are involved.

It is convenient to express the results obtained from studies on machine utilisation in the form of ratios or indices. For this purpose three indices are commonly used.

(1) **Machine utilisation index,** which is the ratio of
    machine running time to
    machine available time
and thus shows the proportion of the total working hours during which the machine has been kept running.

(2) **Machine efficiency index,** the ratio of
    machine running time at standard to
    machine running time
A ratio of 1.0 (or 100 per cent, as it would usually be expressed) would indicate the ideal state, with the machine always performing to the best of its capability whenever it is running.

(3) **Machine effective utilisation index,** the ratio of
    machine running time at standard to
    machine available time
This ratio can be used to provide an indication of the scope for cost reduction that would be available if the machine were operated at full efficiency for the whole of the working time.

275

When work measurement has been applied throughout an organisation, it is an easy matter to arrange for these indices and others like them to be reported to top management as routine at regular intervals, for they can be calculated quite simply from the records instituted to maintain labour, output and machine controls. The incidence of idle time, down time and ancillary time can be highlighted by expressing these figures as ratios in a similar way, using either machine available time or machine running time as the base.

In process industries, utilisation studies are carried out in much the same way, the terms and concepts applied in the same fashion but substituting "process" or some other suitable word for "machine". The principles are exactly the same when utilisation in service undertakings is considered: in a passenger transport undertaking, for example, the same useful results could be expected to accrue from studying the utilisation of buses or trains and expressing the results being achieved in the form of indices similar to those described above.

2. Restricted work

> **Restricted work is work in which the output of the worker is limited by factors outside the control of the worker**

A common example of restricted work occurs when an operative is running a single machine and the machine works automatically for part of the work cycle. The operative may perform the manual elements of his task at standard pace, or faster, or slower; but while this will influence the rate at which the operation is completed, it will not govern it, because the time during which the machine is working automatically will remain the same whatever the worker does.

This does not mean, of course, that nothing can be done to shorten the cycle time. The example of finish-milling a casting on a vertical milling machine which was discussed in Chapter 10 (pages 139-142, figures 46 and 47) shows what can be achieved by arranging for some of the manual elements which were formerly carried out while the machine was stopped to be done while the machine is running automatically, cutting the next casting. The reduction in cycle time achieved is shown graphically in figure 91, which compares the situation before and after the method study. (A time study on this operation is shown fully worked out in the next chapter.)

In this example the machine element remains the same in both cases and takes 0.80 minutes, but the cycle time has been reduced from 2 minutes to 1.36 minutes, a reduction of 32 per cent. In the improved method the operative needs 1.12 minutes at standard pace to perform the manual elements of the job, but some of these are carried out while the machine is working. Even if the operative were to do all his manual work at *twice* the standard pace, this would not reduce the cycle time by half, but only by some 20 per cent. Thus the output of the worker is limited by factors outside his control: the work is "restricted".

Figure 91. Result of method study on milling operation

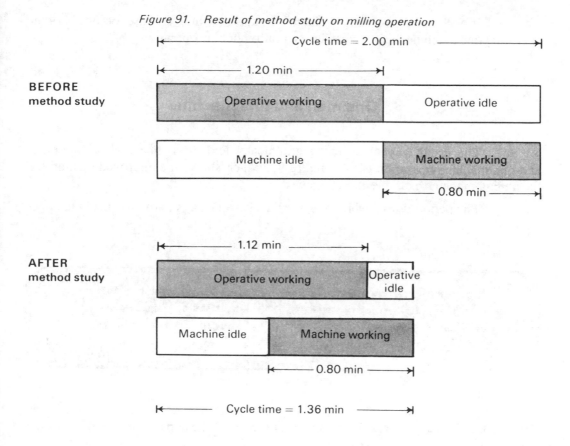

Other examples of restricted work occur when—

(1) One or more operatives are running several machines under conditions similar to those described above.

(2) Operatives are in control of processes, their principal duties being to observe the behaviour of the processes or instruments recording their behaviour and to take action only in response to changes in behaviour, state or reading.

(3) Two or more operatives are working as a team, dependent on one another, and it proves impossible completely to balance the work load of each, with the result that some workers are left with periods of idleness within the work cycle.

Team working can give rise to restricted work even when no machines are used. Assembly work carried out in conjunction with moving conveyors usually does. Even if the conveyor is used simply to transport pieces from one work station to the next, with each operative taking a component off the belt to work on it and returning it when he has finished, a restriction may be imposed by having to wait for the next piece. Again, when assembly operations are carried out directly on the moving conveyor, as is done in motor vehicle manufacture, the conveyor produces conditions equivalent to those imposed by a static production machine.

277

It will be convenient to examine first the simpler case of one worker operating one machine, before considering multi-machine operation.

3. One man and one machine

The usual way of depicting graphically and on a time scale a one-man-and-one-machine operation is as in figure 92, which shows the improved method for the milling machine example quoted above.

The period during which the machine is working is known as the "machine-controlled time".

> **Machine-controlled time (or process-controlled time) is the time taken to complete that part of the work cycle which is determined only by technical factors peculiar to the machine (or process)**

It will be seen that the operative carries out part of his manual work while the machine is stopped, and part while it is running. These parts are called "outside work" and "inside work", respectively.

> **Outside work comprises elements which must necessarily be performed by a worker outside the machine-(or process-)controlled time**
>
> **Inside work comprises those elements which can be performed by a worker within the machine (or process-)controlled time**

Finally, there is the time during which the operative is waiting for the machine to complete the cut, i.e. his "unoccupied time".

> **Unoccupied time comprises the periods during machine-(or process-)controlled time when a worker is neither engaged on inside work nor taking authorised rest**

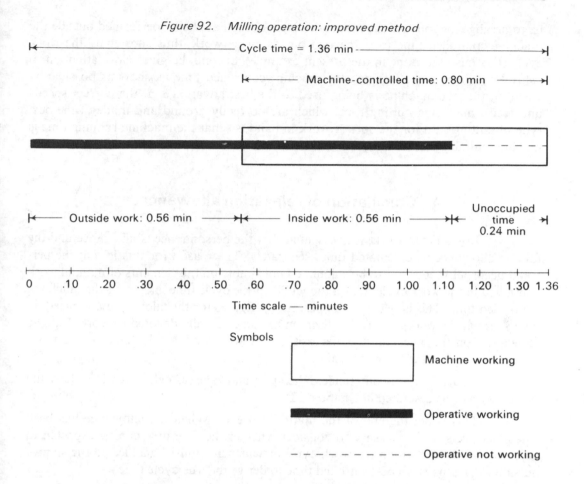

Figure 92.   *Milling operation: improved method*

In diagrams of this sort, the periods of time during which the operative is working (and hence the periods of outside and inside work) are calculated and drawn at standard performance. In figure 92 no account has so far been taken of relaxation or other allowances: manual work has been calculated at standard pace and is thus shown in basic minutes. Machine-controlled time is of course shown in actual minutes, and so, using the 0-100 rating scale advocated in this book, basic minutes for manual work and actual minutes of machine operation are comparable and can be drawn to the same scale.

When unoccupied time is calculated, the working time must first have been calculated at standard performance, that is at standard pace and with proper allowance made for relaxation (the calculation of relaxation allowances is discussed below). In special circumstances the work elements associated with machine operation may be calculated at some defined rate other than standard, but we shall not be concerned with these in this book.

The diagram in figure 92 looks rather like a schematic representation of a bicycle pump, and indeed work study men often refer colloquially to such drawings as "pump diagrams". When seeking to improve the method, the work study man follows two main approaches. First, he tries to "push the handle down into the pump"—that is, to arrange for some of the manual elements which are being performed outside the machine-controlled time to be carried out as inside work, thus shortening the work cycle (this has been done in the present example). Second, he gives close attention to "shrinking the pump"—making the machine-controlled time as short as possible by ensuring that the machine is being used to the best advantage, at the correct speeds and feeds, and using cutting tools which are correctly ground and made of the best type of cutting steel for the sort of work in hand, so that the machine running time is machine running time at standard.

4. Calculation of relaxation allowances

In restricted work, it is essential that the personal needs allowance and the fatigue allowance be calculated quite separately. The reason for this is that the personal needs allowance has to be calculated not simply on the elements of manual work contained in the work cycle but on the whole of the cycle time, including the machine-controlled time. This is because the percentage figures for the allowance are based on time spent at the workplace rather than on the time actually devoted to work. Fatigue allowance, on the other hand, is necessitated by work and is calculated on the basic minutes of work actually performed.

Apart from this difference, relaxation allowance is calculated in exactly the same way as was described in Chapter 18.

This is not the end of the matter, however. When the allowance has been calculated, it is next necessary to consider whether the operative can be expected to take any or all of it within the work cycle or whether it must be added to the sum of outside work plus machine-controlled time to derive the true cycle time.

If the work cycle is a very long one, and there are lengthy periods of unoccupied time within it, it may be possible in certain circumstances for the whole of the personal needs allowance and the fatigue allowance to be taken within the cycle, during the time when the operative is not working. Such periods can only be considered adequate for personal needs allowance if they are long enough (say, 10 or 15 minutes), if they occur in an unbroken stretch, and if it is possible for the operative to leave his machine unattended meanwhile. This may be done safely if the machine has an auto-stop mechanism and needs no attention whatever while it is running; alternatively, when groups of operatives work together it is sometimes possible to arrange for a neighbour to use some of his own unoccupied time in giving attention to the absent worker's machine. In textile factories and in other industries in which the processing machinery is run continuously, perhaps 24 hours a day, it is common to provide "floating" workers who can fill in at work stations for odd moments and can help to keep the machines running during short meal breaks if these are taken at staggered times.

It is much more usual, however, especially with cycles of short duration, for the whole of the personal needs allowance to be taken outside the working cycle. In the milling example which has been illustrated above and which has a cycle time of 1.36 minutes, it would obviously be impossible for the operative to take any of his personal needs allowance within the cycle.

Fatigue allowance is a rather different matter. Quite short periods of unoccupied time can be used for recovery from fatigue, provided that the operative can truly relax during them and is not required to be constantly on the alert or to give attention to the machine during them, and that he has a seat nearby. It is generally considered that any period of 0.50 minutes or less is too short to be counted as available for relaxation, and that any unbroken period of 1.5 minutes or longer can be reckoned as fully available for recovery from fatigue. Periods of 0.50 minutes or less would thus be disregarded. For periods of between 0.50 and 1.50 minutes, it is common to calculate the time which may be considered as effectively available for relaxation by deducting 0.50 minutes from the actual length of the period and multiplying the result by 1.5. The effect of applying this calculation to four periods between 0.50 and 1.50 minutes is shown below—

Actual unbroken period of unoccupied time	Time calculated as effectively available for recovery from fatigue
0.50 min	nil
1.00	0.75 min
1.25	1.12
1.50	1.50

In the milling machine example, the length of time during which the operative was not working was only 0.24 minutes, which is too short to be taken into account for relaxation. In this particular example, the inside work was performed in one unbroken stretch of 0.56 minutes, but it is quite common in machine operations for the workers to have to make adjustments or attend to the machine at intervals, or perhaps carry out manual elements on other workpieces from time to time while the machine is working, so that within the machine-controlled time there will be separated periods of inside work and unoccupied time.

The length of the cycle and the manner in which any inside work occurs thus both affect the way in which relaxation allowance must be treated. Four cases can be distinguished:

1. All the personal needs allowance and all the fatigue allowance must both be taken outside the working cycle.

2. The personal needs allowance must be taken outside the cycle, but all the fatigue allowance can be taken within it.

3. The personal needs allowance and some of the fatigue allowance must be taken outside the cycle, but the rest of the fatigue allowance can be taken within it.

4. All the personal needs allowance and all the fatigue allowance can be taken within the working cycle.

The effect of these four cases for four different operation sequences is illustrated in figure 93. All the four operations have the following characteristics in common:

Figure 93.   Four operations with machine elements

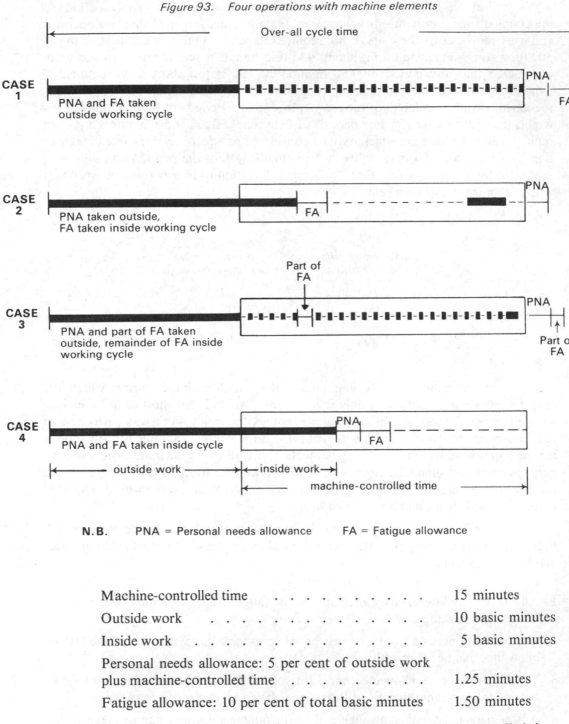

N.B.   PNA = Personal needs allowance   FA = Fatigue allowance

Machine-controlled time	15 minutes
Outside work	10 basic minutes
Inside work	5 basic minutes
Personal needs allowance: 5 per cent of outside work plus machine-controlled time	1.25 minutes
Fatigue allowance: 10 per cent of total basic minutes	1.50 minutes

In case 3 there is a period of 1.0 minute within the machine-controlled time when the operative is not working. By using the method of calculation described above, 0.75 minutes of this is considered to be available for recovery from fatigue, so that the remaining 0.75 minutes of the fatigue allowance has to be taken outside the working cycle. In case 4 the assumption has been made that a neighbouring worker

282

could attend to the operation if it should be necessary for the operative to leave his work station for longer than the ten minutes of non-working time available during the machine element.

It will be seen that the **over-all cycle time** differs in each of the four cases, so that the number of units of output which could be expected over an eight-hour day also differs:

	Over-all cycle time (min)	Anticipated daily output (units)
Case 1	27.75	17.3 say, 17
Case 2	26.25	18.3 say, 18
Case 3	27.00	17.7 with overtime, 18
Case 4	25.00	19.2 say, 19

The **over-all cycle time** is the total time in which the job should be completed at standard performance, and is made up (in the case of operations of the types so far discussed) of outside work at standard pace, machine-controlled time, and any portion of the relaxation allowance which has to be allowed outside the machine-controlled time. If there are no other allowances to be taken into account (e.g. contingency allowance), and an allowance is made for unoccupied time in actual minutes, the over-all cycle time will be numerically equal to the standard time for the operation.

5. Unoccupied time allowance

In the construction of scale diagrams representing restricted work cycles, such as those illustrated in figures 92 and 93, it is usual to show all the manual elements at the times they would take if performed at standard pace. This is convenient for method study, and for the calculations needed to determine relaxation allowances and how they may properly be allocated, after which over-all cycle times and hence anticipated outputs may be calculated.

The next step is to calculate the total period of any unoccupied time, in actual minutes. For operations of the types discussed, unoccupied time is calculated by subtracting from the machine-controlled time the sum of all periods of inside work, in basic minutes, plus any part of the relaxation allowance which may be taken within the machine-controlled time. It should be particularly noted that for the calculation of unoccupied time all work elements must be calculated at standard pace.

Standard times for jobs or operations are calculated on the basis of the work done by operatives—that is, the manual work content of the job—not that done by machines. For a job made up solely of manual elements (unrestricted work), the standard time is essentially a measure of the work which the job contains. With restricted work, however, the standard time expresses something more than this. It will be recalled that the definition of standard time is as follows:

> **Standard time is the total time in which a job should be completed at standard performance**

In order to compile the standard time for a restricted operation, therefore, it is not sufficient simply to calculate the work content (inclusive of relaxation allowances, and the work portion of any contingency allowance considered appropriate), adding to this perhaps some small further contingency allowance for delays. It is necessary to add an allowance for any unavoidable unoccupied time which may be experienced during the machine- (or process-)controlled time.

> **Unoccupied time allowance is an allowance made to a worker when there is unoccupied time during machine- (or process-)controlled time**

Before the allowance is made, the work study man must first have satisfied himself that the unoccupied time is truly unavoidable, and cannot be reduced further by method improvement or by a reallocation of work or machines. It was noted earlier that it may be sound management practice to accept a certain amount of unoccupied time if, by so doing, costly machines can be kept more fully employed, because in restricted work machine utilisation is often more important than labour productivity.

Unoccupied time allowance is made in actual minutes.

PAYMENT FOR UNOCCUPIED TIME

When standard times are used as a basis for payment-by-results schemes, the inclusion of unoccupied time allowances in standard times for restricted work may give rise to payment anomalies, unless special measures are taken to deal with the problems which arise.

The sort of difficulty which can occur is most easily seen by considering an example. Let us assume that in a given enterprise there are three jobs, for each of which the standard time has been calculated as 100 minutes. The first job is made up wholly of manual elements. The other two are both restricted operations, and for both the standard times include allowances for unoccupied time—say, 15 minutes in one case, and 45 minutes in the other.

If all three workers perform the manual elements of their tasks at standard pace and all take exactly the allotted relaxation periods, all three jobs will be completed in the same time (100 minutes). But the operative on unrestricted work will have been working all the time (except, of course, for the relaxation period) while the other two will have been idle for 15 and 45 minutes respectively. If payment is made for unoccupied time at the same rate as that for working time, the more heavily loaded workers will soon become discontented; jobs will become known as "good" jobs or "bad" jobs according to the amount of unoccupied time they contain; and there will be reluctance to undertake tasks with the higher work contents.

Usually this difficulty is dealt with not by modifying the standard times but by establishing different rates of payment for work and for idle time. To enable this to be done, it is usual to express standard times not only as totals but also as work credits plus idle time credits (or in similar terms).

Thus, in the example cited above, the standard time (100 minutes in each instance) would be shown as being made up of 100, 85 and 55 work credits plus 0, 15 and 45 idle time credits respectively. It may be noted in passing that idle time credits included in a standard time may be allocated for reasons other than unoccupied time as discussed above. Idle time credits may sometimes be necessary to compensate for delays caused by waiting for work or for instructions, or by machine breakdowns.

The scheme to be adopted to make differential payments for work and for idle time in a particular enterprise is properly a matter of wages administration, rather than of time study practice, and is thus outside the scope of this introductory book. It may be noted, however, that any such scheme should be simple to understand, so that the workers may readily comprehend why jobs taking the same time to complete attract different payments. The scheme should be negotiated and agreed with the workers' representatives before it is applied. In a typical scheme, idle time credits amounting in total to less than 5 per cent of the work credits may be paid for at the same rate as work credits; idle time amounting to 40 per cent or more of the work credits at three-quarters of the rate of working; and idle times between 5 per cent and 40 per cent at varying rates in between.

The scheme which will be most appropriate for a particular organisation will depend on local circumstances, and especially on whether jobs with large amounts of unoccupied time are exceptional or common. Sometimes variable rates which have to be read off a curve are adopted, but in general a linear relationship is to be preferred, and always one which is simple.

The time study man is concerned primarily with measuring the amount of time needed to complete a job or operation, rather than with whatever arrangements are agreed for making payment for that time. It is common in industrial wage agreements to take account of different levels of skill required for different operations, by paying differing rates per minute or per hour of work. Other factors may also be taken into account in setting payment rates. None of these matters will affect the calculation of any unoccupied *time* allowance which may be necessary to compile the standard time for a job. The time allowance will be in minutes or hours: payment for those minutes or hours will be negotiable quite separately.

In the scheme mentioned above, relatively long periods of unoccupied time are paid for at lower rates than those paid for working. In some circumstances, however, it may be appropriate to pay for both working time and unoccupied time at very high rates indeed, in which case the payment actually made to a particular operative for a minute of unoccupied time may be greater than that paid to another for a minute spent working.

An example is the final machining of a shaft for a turbine-driven electricity generating set. Such a shaft may be several metres in length, and by the time that the last stages of machining are undertaken the component will represent a large investment, in terms of both labour and the costly materials of which it is made. A faulty cut may result in a diameter becoming undersize, with the result that the whole shaft would have to be scrapped. The operative is thus burdened with a very heavy responsibility, although the actual operation itself is not particularly complex. Because of this responsibility the rates paid to the operative, both for working and for any necessarily

285

unoccupied time, may be higher than those for the general run of turning operations. Similar "key" operations or tasks occur in many industries.

6. Multiple machine work

> **Multiple machine work is work which requires the worker to attend two or more machines (of similar or different kinds) running simultaneously**

In section 3 the simple case of one man and one machine was examined. Frequently, however, workers are called upon to look after more than one machine—perhaps many machines—and this poses special problems in time study work. A common example is that of the weaving shed in a textile mill, where a worker may attend anything from 4 to 40 looms (perhaps even more), depending on the type of loom installed and the characteristics of the cloth being woven. Similar circumstances are often encountered in engineering industries, for example when workers operate batteries of screw-making or coil-winding machines. It is usual in work situations of this sort for the machines to be equipped with automatic cut-out devices which bring them to a standstill when their tasks are completed or when breaks or malfunctioning occur.

Tasks of this sort are all examples of restricted work, as the output of the worker may be limited by factors outside his control. So too are team operations, whether the team of workers is concerned with the operation of a single machine (as sometimes occurs in drop-forging), with several machines (a frequent occurrence in textile operations) or indeed with no machines at all, since restrictions can be imposed by lack of balance in the amounts of manual work which have to be performed by different members of the team.

LOAD FACTOR

> **The load factor is the proportion of the over-all cycle time required by the worker to carry out the necessary work at standard performance, during a machine- (or process-)controlled cycle**

The **load factor** is sometimes known by the alternative terms "extent occupied" or "work load". In the simplest case of one man operating one machine, as illustrated in figures 92 and 93, if the over-all cycle time is ten minutes and the amount of manual work contained within the cycle totals only one standard minute, the load factor would be one-tenth, or 10 per cent.

The reciprocal of the load factor therefore indicates the number of machines which the worker could theoretically tend: in this example, ten machines. In practice, other factors have to be taken into account, so that the load factor can be taken only as a very rough first indication of the number of machines which can usefully be allocated to a worker. It does sometimes occur that the work elements consist solely of unloading finished pieces from machines which have stopped automatically, loading fresh pieces and restarting the machines; and if all the machines are alike and are working on exactly similar pieces, it may be possible to achieve the ideal sequence of operation, with the worker able to operate the number of machines indicated by the reciprocal of the load factor. Much more commonly, however, differences occur in the machines or in the work, and frequently attention has to be given to the machines while they are running, with the result that the worker cannot always get to a machine at the exact moment when attention is needed. The delays which then occur are known as **machine interference.**

MACHINE INTERFERENCE

> **Machine interference is the queuing of machines (or processes) for attention—e.g. when one worker is responsible for attending to more than one machine. Similar circumstances arise in team work where random delays at any point may affect the output of the team**

When studying multiple machine working or team working (with or without machines), the work study man has first to examine the methods of working with the object of devising a sequence of operations which will result in the best balance and thus the least interference, and then to use time study techniques to measure the amount of interference which will occur even when the best sequence has been determined. These tasks may sometimes be extremely complicated. They often call for the use of specialised methods which are beyond the scope of this book.

If there are only a few workers in the team, or if one or two workers are operating only a few machines between them, simpler methods will suffice. Operation sequences can be plotted and examined on multiple activity charts (described in Chapter 10), supplemented by cycle diagrams similar to those shown in figures 92 and 93. The diagrams for each machine are drawn one below the other, to the same time scale. A simple example, that of an operative working three machines, is shown in figure 94.

In this example there is no inside work, so that when a machine has been started the operative can turn his attention to another. The sequence in which he does so is indicated by the small vertical arrows. It will be seen that, with this particular routine, machine C is operated without any delays occurring; but the result of doing this is that both machine A and machine B switch themselves off at the end of their

287

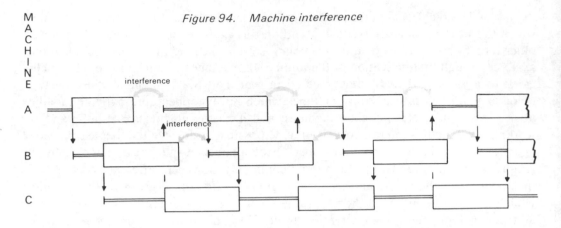

Figure 94. Machine interference

respective operations and then have to wait a while before the operative can get to them. The interference is indicated on the cycle diagrams for machines A and B by grey arcs.

INTERFERENCE ALLOWANCE

> **An interference allowance is an allowance of time for production unavoidably lost through synchronisation of stoppages on two or more machines (or processes) attended by one worker. Similar circumstances arise in team work**

By extending the methods so far described, using the same charting conventions and principles, it is possible to establish work sequences and to calculate interference for a fairly wide range of multiple machine operations, including many which will be met with in the engineering and allied industries, and especially those in which machine stoppages occur in regular, predictable fashion rather than at random. In coil-winding, for example, the winding machines switch themselves off when the coil is completed, and contingencies (such as wire breaks) are rare.

For these simpler forms of multiple machine operation, when an operative has only a few machines to look after and the work being done is of a cyclic nature, with definite beginnings and ends of the work cycles, standard times may be calculated and expressed exactly as for unrestricted work: that is, as so many standard minutes (or hours) per piece, per job or per operation. This is quite common in engineering machine shop operations, especially when workers operate several machines in sequence. For these situations standard times are compiled as described earlier in this book, on the basis of the work content for each job or operation. **There is no need to consider machine interference when compiling the standard times,** though it may be necessary to take this into account when making output predictions and other production control calculations. It will be necessary, however, to provide

288

allowances in the standard times for any **unavoidable unoccupied time** which may be experienced as a result of working with the machines, and this too may be done as described above.

When output is continuous rather than cyclic, and especially in process industries, it is more usual to establish standard times for some convenient **volume, weight,** or **length of output,** rather than per piece or per operation. Thus, in weaving, the standard times may be compiled and expressed as so many standard minutes per 100 metres of cloth woven (this is in fact one of several ways of stating time standards for weaving). When this is done, the focus is shifted from the amount of manual work contained in the operation to the output which may be expected from the machines, though output calculations must of course take into account the quantity of manual work involved in tending the machines. Unoccupied time is of interest, and almost always has to be determined, not for the purpose of making an allowance in the standard time but rather as an indication of the number of machines which a worker can attend. **For the calculation of standard times the allowance which has to be taken into account is interference allowance**—the times during which some of the machines will be stopped while waiting for the operative to get to them.

A case in point is that of a weaver looking after a set of looms. Stoppages in the weaving operation depend upon many circumstances. The strength of the yarn, and hence the frequency of breakages, is influenced by the way the materials forming the warp and weft have been prepared, and also by the temperature and humidity within the weaving shed, both of which may change markedly from time to time during a shift. The state of maintenance of the looms also affects stoppages, while the speed and skill of the weaver have a further influence, since a skilled operative can often prevent stoppages by anticipating trouble and taking preventive action.

In circumstances such as these, it is necessary to evaluate unoccupied time (for work loading and team balancing) and interference (for compiling standard times) by extended studies on the shop floor, covering all the different working conditions and all the different counts of yarn (in weaving) or different materials which have to be worked on. Studies may have to continue for days or weeks, or sometimes extend over several months. Work sampling is an appropriate technique to use for this purpose, and was originally developed expressly for textile operations. It is much more economical than time study, which would be much too long-winded and detailed for this type of observation in any but the smallest shops. Using work sampling, for example, a studyman in a weaving shed can record all the information needed while observing the operation of 10 or 12 looms, which would be impossible with ordinary time study practice.

In an introductory book of this nature it is not possible to cover in detail the specialised methods which are adopted in advanced work study practice to evaluate interference and to calculate interference allowances in complex multiple machine situations. For the most part, these methods are based on statistical procedures and probability theory, and are intended to permit reliable predictions to be made without recourse to either time study or work sampling. For this purpose a number of formulae, curves and sets of tables have been compiled to assist in the determination of interference, and hence probable output, for various worker/machine combinations. The systems, if used with care, offer the prospect of considerable economy of study

289

time in certain specialised, but complex, multiple machine and teamwork situations. It is essential, however, that any predictions made on the basis of formulae and tables should be validated by direct study at the workplace, so that full account may be taken of local working conditions.

The time study methods described earlier in this chapter, together with work sampling (as described in Chapter 14), will usually be found adequate for the calculation of reliable time standards for the majority of the machine working situations likely to be encountered in general industrial practice. Those readers who are faced with the task of determining standards for complex multiple machine operations may find it useful to consult more advanced texts. It is recommended, however, that the more specialised methods should not be attempted until the work study man has had sufficient experience of both time and work sampling to be sure that he can use these techniques to verify any statistical predictions made.

*

*   *

In the next chapter an example of a fully worked time study is shown. The study is one taken on the operation of milling a casting, which was the subject charted on a multiple activity chart in Chapter 10, and for which a cycle diagram appears in section 3 of the present chapter.

Chapter 20

Example
of a time study

In discussing the making of a time study throughout the previous four chapters, we referred to the example based on the milling of a casting which was the subject of the multiple activity chart described in Chapter 10. The complete time study is shown in this chapter. A careful study of the forms shown in the illustrations should enable the reader to follow in detail the processes by which a time study is worked up and a standard time is compiled.

This particular example has been chosen because—

(a) it is simple;

(b) it has already been the subject of a method study;

(c) it includes both manual and machine elements;

(d) it is typical of the sort of operation met everywhere in the engineering industry and in other industries using machines and semi-automatic processes.

The forms used are simple general-purpose forms such as those illustrated in Chapter 15. Although all the entries made on the forms will be handwritten, it is usual to space the lines for use with a typewriter because occasions may arise on which it is required to produce fair copies of original studies for discussion or circulation.

The study illustrated in this chapter was not the first one on this operation. The elements and break points were defined at the time the method study was undertaken, and were then set out on a card prepared and filed by the work study department. This is a useful practice when it is expected that an operation will be studied several times, perhaps by different studymen. It ensures that the recordings made on all the studies are comparable. The elements and break points are shown in figure 95.

Although the example which has been studied in detail is a simple one for a manufacturing industry, exactly the same procedure is carried out for non-manufacturing operations or for any other work which is time-studied for the purpose of setting time standards. Entirely manual operations, such as assembly, would be treated in exactly the same way.

291

Figure 95. *Card giving details of elements and break points*

Card No. 1264

Part: B.239 Gear case.   *Drawing:* 239/1
Material: ISS 2 Cast iron.
Operation: Finish-mill second face.
Machine: No. 4 Cincinnati vertical miller.
Fixture: F.239.
Cutter: 25 cm. TLF
Gauge: 239/7.   Surface plate.

Elements and Break Points

A. Pick up casting, locate in fixture, lock two nuts, set guard, start machine and auto feed. Depth of cut 2.5 mm. Speed 80 r.p.m. Feed 40 cm/min.
Break point: Machine commences cut.

B. Hold casting, break milled edge with file, clean with compressed air.
Break point: Air gun dropped on to hook.

C. Move depth gauge to casting, check machined surface, move gauge away.
Break point: Left hand releases gauge.

D. Pick up machined casting, carry to finished parts box and place aside, pick up next part and position on machine table.
Break point: Casting hits table.

E. Wait for machine to complete cut.
Break point: Machine ceases to cut.

F. Stop machine, return table, open guard, unlock fixture, remove machined casting and place on surface plate.
Break point: Casting hits surface plate.

G. Clear swarf from machine table with compressed air.
Break point: Air gun dropped on to hook.

Note: Elements B, C and D are inside work, and are performed on a casting which has already been machined while the milling machine is cutting the next casting. Element D includes bringing up into a handy position a fresh casting which will be machined after the one now in the machine.

292

Figure 96. *Sketch of part and of workplace layout*
(on reverse of time study top sheet)

A sketch of the workplace layout is generally more necessary in assembly or material-handling studies than in studies of machine shop operations where workplaces are likely to be the same for all jobs on the machines. The part should be sketched showing the surfaces machined; in the case of capstan lathes, tool set-ups should be included. This is best done on squared paper and may be on the back of the time study top sheet, if desired, in order to keep all the information relevant to the study on one sheet. To facilitate sketching, the reverse of the top sheet is often printed as squared paper.

(a) Sketch of gear-case casting showing surface to be machined and dimension

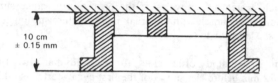

(b) Layout of workplace

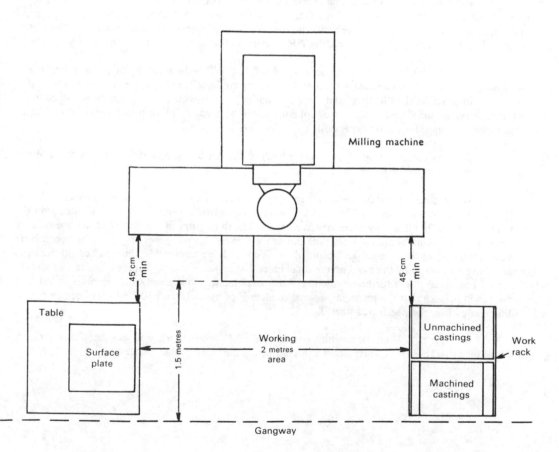

Figure 97.   Time study top sheet

All the information in the heading block at the top of the form (except time off and elapsed time) was entered before the stop-watch was started and study commenced.

If the study had been the first one on this operation, the studyman would have entered in full the element descriptions and break points in the column headed "Element description" on the left-hand side of the page. In the present instance this was not necessary, as the card shown in figure 95 listed all the details. The studyman should watch a few cycles of the operation to make sure that the listed method is being used, and to familiarise himself with the break points, before starting to record. The elements were identified simply by the letters A to G.

At exactly 9.47 a.m. by the study office clock (or the studyman's wrist-watch) the stop-watch was started. It ran for 1.72 min before element A of the first cycle started, so this time is entered at the beginning of the study as the "Time before". Since this was a study using cumulative timing, the watch ran continuously throughout. When the study was broken off after observing 18 cycles, the studyman allowed his stop-watch to run on until the study office clock reached the next full minute (at 10.25 a.m.), noted the "Time after", and stopped his stop-watch. These terminal entries will be found at the end of the recordings in figure 99.

The four columns used in cumulative timing are respectively "Rating" (R), "Watch reading" (WR), "Subtracted time" (ST) and "Basic time" (BT). The placing of the rating column first is logical and encourages the observer to rate while the element is in progress and not to wait for the watch reading. If flyback timing had been used, the WR column on the form would not be necessary.

Only the entries in the two columns headed R and WR were made during observations at the workplace. The other two columns were completed in the study office after observations had been discontinued. In practice, the "Rating" and "Watch reading" entries would be made in pencil while those in the "Subtracted time" and "Basic time" columns would be made in ink or with a pencil of a different colour from that used for the observations.

The studyman numbered the cycles observed, from 1 to 18, with ringed figures at the left of the "Element description" column.

When entering watch readings there is no need to use decimal points. The first entry (Time before, 172) indicates a time of 1.72 minutes. The next watch reading was made 1.95 minutes after the watch was started, but it is only necessary to enter 95. The third entry of 220 indicates that the reading was made at 2.20 minutes after starting; the entries then revert to two figures only until the next minute is passed. During cycle number 15 (recorded on figure 99) the total study time passed 30 minutes, which is the time taken by the hand on the small inner dial on the watch to complete one revolution. As the study continued into a further revolution of the small hand, subsequent watch readings revert to 1 again. It will be seen that the recording against element F of cycle 15 was 106, which of course means 31.06 minutes after the watch was started.

Element E—"Wait for machine to complete cut"—is not work, and was therefore not rated. It will be seen that there is no entry against this element in the "Basic time" column.

TIME STUDY TOP SHEET

DEPARTMENT: *Machine Shop – Milling Section*					STUDY No. *17*			
OPERATION: *Finish-mill second face* M.S. No. *9*					SHEET No. *1* OF *5*			
PLANT/MACHINE: *Cincinnati No. 4 vertical miller* No. *26*					TIME OFF: *10.25 a.m.* TIME ON: *9.47 a.m.* ELAPSED TIME: *38.00*			
TOOLS AND GAUGES: *Fixture F 239 · Cutter 25 cm TLF Gauge 239/7 · Surface plate*					OPERATIVE: CLOCK No. *1234*			
PRODUCT/PART: *B. 239 Gear Case* No. *239/1*					STUDIED BY:			
DWG. No. *B. 239/1* ISS. *2* MATERIAL: *Cast iron*					DATE:			
QUALITY: *As drawing*					CHECKED:			

NOTE: Sketch the WORKPLACE LAYOUT/SET-UP/PART on the reverse or on a separate sheet and attach

ELEMENT DESCRIPTION		R	WR	ST	BT	ELEMENT DESCRIPTION		R	WR	ST	BT
Time before		–	172	–	–	④	A	80	622	32	26
①	A	110	95	23	25		B	85	50	28	24
	B	100	220	25	25		C	85	63	13	11
Elements & B.P.	C	100	32	12	12		D	85	83	20	17
as Card No. 1264	D	95	52	20	19		E	–	703	20	–
	E	–	77	25	–		F	105	26	23	24
	F	110	300	23	25		G	85	38	12	10
	G	110	08	08	09						
						⑤	A	80	70	32	26
②	A	110	31	23	25		B	85	97	27	23
	B	95	58	27	26		C	85	810	13	11
	C	95	71	13	12		D	85	30	20	17
	D	100	89	18	18		E	–	53	23	–
	E	–	412	23	–		F	105	76	23	24
	F	105	37	25	26		G	85	88	12	10
	G	100	47	10	10						
						⑥	A	95	915	27	26
③	A	105	72	25	26		B	95	42	27	26
	B	105	97	25	26		C	105	54	12	13
	C	95	510	13	12		D	80	77	23	18
	D	110	28	18	20		E	–	97	20	–
	E	–	53	25	–		F	95	1020	23	22
	F	100	78	25	25		G	100	30	10	10
	G	95	90	12	11						
				418						440	

Figure 98.   Time study continuation sheet

The recordings covered three sheets in all. Figure 98 shows the first of the two continuation sheets, and it will be seen that it is numbered in the top right-hand corner: Sheet No. 2 of 5. The analysis sheet and study summary sheet eventually completed the set of five sheets, all of which were stapled together after the study was worked up.

Besides the element ratings and timings, continuing as on the top sheet, two interruptions were recorded on this sheet: "Talk to foreman", and "Break for tea". Neither of these was rated, of course. The first was taken account of when considering contingencies, while the second was covered by the relaxation allowance made when the standard time for the operation was compiled.

STUDY No.: 17	TIME STUDY CONTINUATION SHEET					SHEET No. 2 OF 5			
ELEMENT DESCRIPTION		R	WR	ST	BT	ELEMENT DESCRIPTION	R	WR	ST	BT

ELEMENT DESCRIPTION		R	WR	ST	BT	ELEMENT DESCRIPTION		R	WR	ST	BT
⑦	A	105	55	25	26	⑪	A	115	86	25	29
	B	115	78	23	26		B	95	1713	27	26
	C	95	91	13	12		C	75	28	15	11
	D	85	1113	22	19		D	85	50	22	19
	E	–	36	23	–		E	–	68	18	–
	F	80	68	32	26		F	115	90	22	25
	G	95	80	12	11		G	80	1803	13	10
⑧	A	75	1218	38	28	⑫	A	95	30	27	26
	B	110	40	22	24		B	95	55	25	24
	C	105	52	12	13		C	100	67	12	12
	D	100	70	18	18		D	95	87	20	19
	E	–	1300	30	–		E	–	1902	15	–
	F	115	25	25	29		F	95	30	28	27
	G	105	35	10	10		G	75	42	12	09
Talk to foreman		–	75	40	–	Break for tea		–	2554	612	–
⑨	A	105	1400	25	26	⑬	A	85	86	32	27
	B	100	25	25	25		B	80	2618	32	26
	C	95	38	13	12		C	85	33	15	13
	D	95	56	18	17		D	100	53	20	20
	E	–	81	25	–		E	–	68	15	–
	F	100	1509	28	28		F	85	96	28	24
	G	85	21	12	10		G	95	2708	12	11
⑩	A	95	43	22	21	⑭	A	80	40	32	26
	B	80	75	32	26		B	100	65	25	25
	C	95	88	13	12		C	85	80	15	13
	D	95	1608	20	19		D	95	2800	20	19
	E	–	25	17	–		E	–	22	22	–
	F	105	48	23	24		F	80	54	32	26
	G	85	61	13	11		G	105	64	10	10
				631						1203	

297

Figure 99.   Second continuation sheet

The first entry on this sheet recorded another interruption—the patrol inspector, having checked three workpieces, drew the operative's attention to some feature of them and discussed them with him. The time taken to do this, like that recorded on the previous sheet against "Talk to foreman", was later entered as a contingency.

After cycle number 16, a fresh element of work occurred—helping the labourer to move boxes of work off and on to the truck. This was an occasional element, in contrast with elements A to G which were repetitive. The studyman rated and timed the element, and it will be noted that, since the element ran on for rather over a minute in all, the studyman made a rating and a watch reading at the end of each of the first two half-minutes, as well as during the last part of the element. This practice, which makes for greater accuracy, was referred to in section 9 of Chapter 17.

Back in the study office after breaking off observations, the studyman first completed the "Time off" and "Elapsed time" entries in the heading block on the top sheet, and then set about calculating the subtracted times, by deducting each watch reading from the one which follows it and entering the result in the third column, headed ST. It will be seen that he totalled these subtracted times at the foot of each page, and carried forward the subtotals to the sheet shown opposite, where they were added up to yield 35.20 minutes. When the time before and the time after were added to this figure, the result was 38.00 minutes, which agreed with the elapsed time and thus afforded a check that the work of subtraction had been done correctly.

The next step was "extension": multiplying each subtracted time by the percentage rating recorded against it to yield the basic time, entered in the fourth column. Extension is easily and quickly done with the aid of a pocket calculator. The calculation is made to the nearest second decimal place: that is, to the nearest one-hundredth of a minute. Thus 0.204 would be shown as 20, and 0.206 minutes as 21—which leaves the problem of what to do with 0.205. Evidently, in this study office the standing rule was to take half-hundredths of a minute down rather than up, as can be seen by the entry against element G of cycle 15. Here, the rating was 105 and the subtracted time 10, so that the extension yields 0.105 minutes to three places. This has been shown as 10, the half-hundredth having been taken down. Other instances will be found in the study. Most study offices apply the reverse rule: that is, taking middle times up.

STUDY No.: *17*	**TIME STUDY CONTINUATION SHEET**					SHEET No. *3* OF *5*		
ELEMENT DESCRIPTION	R	WR	ST	BT	ELEMENT DESCRIPTION	R	WR	ST	BT
Patrol inspector checks					⑱ *A*	100	71	27	27
3 pieces: discuss	–	2966	102	–	*B*	100	96	25	25
					C	95	609	13	12
⑮ *A*	95	93	27	26	*D*	75	34	25	19
B	80	3023	30	24	*E*	–	52	18	–
C	100	36	13	13	*F*	100	77	25	25
D	100	56	20	20	*G*	75	92	15	11
E	–	74	18	–					
F	80	106	32	26				148	
G	105	16	10	10					
⑯ *A*	80	49	33	26	*Watch stopped 10.25*		800		
B	85	77	28	24	*a.m. (elapsed time*				
C	105	89	12	13	*38.00)*				
D	100	207	18	18	*Time after*			108	
E	–	30	23	–					
F	95	57	27	26					
G	85	70	13	11					
Help labourer unload	85	320	50	43					
boxes of new castings	95	70	50	48					
and load finished work	95	90	20	19	*Check on* subtracted			418	
on truck (30 new + 30					*times*			440	
fin. in boxes of 10)								631	
⑰ *A*	100	417	27	27				1203	
B	85	49	32	27				680	
C	85	64	15	13				148	
D	85	86	22	19				3520	
E	–	509	23	–					
F	100	34	25	25	*Time before*			172	
G	105	44	10	10	*Time after*			108	
					Elapsed			3800	
			680						

Figure 100. Working sheet

The repetitive elements A, B, C, D, F and G were all constant elements, and selected basic times for them were obtained by averaging. As was noted in Chapter 15, study analyses take several forms and for this reason it is not usual to have specially printed sheets for them. Ordinary lined or squared paper serves very well, and when the time study top sheet has been printed on the reverse as squared paper (to facilitate sketching), it will do well enough to use the back side of a top sheet, entering at the top the study and sheet numbers. For a simple study the analysis is often made straight on to the study summary sheet, a few extra columns being ruled in the space headed "Element description".

Methods of obtaining the selected basic times are discussed in Chapter 18. In this instance, inspection of the basic times tabulated under elements A, B, C, D, F and G showed no anomalies, and therefore no need to ring out "rogue" times. For each of these elements the basic times have been totalled, and the selected basic time was calculated by dividing the total by the number of observations (18).

No figures were listed under element E, "Wait for machine to complete cut". This was unoccupied time, which was not rated in the study. The actual length of unoccupied time experienced in the various cycles observed depended on the speed with which the operative carried out the inside work which he performed on another casting while the machine was cutting automatically.

The time the machine took to make the cut, while on automatic feed, did not vary from cycle to cycle because it was determined by the rate of feed at which the machine was set and the length of cut to be made. It could thus be calculated quite easily. In this study the machine-controlled time started at the end of element A and ended with the conclusion of element E. The machine-controlled time can therefore be obtained from the study sheets by subtracting the watch reading against element A from that against E. This has been done, the results being tabulated under "MCT" at the right-hand side of the working sheet. These times are of course actual minutes, not basic times.

It will be seen that two of the MCT entries have been ringed out. The studyman did not enter any explanation of unusual events on his record, and inspection of the observations for the cycles in which these rogue times occurred does not provide any conclusive explanation. Possibly the explanation for the shorter time is to be found in the fact that the operative can start the cut on hand-feed before locking on the auto-feed, and on this occasion, unnoticed by the studyman, he spent longer on hand-feed than usual. The explanation for the longer time in cycle 17 may be that the operative failed to switch the machine off quite as quickly as usual on this occasion, and again this escaped notice. The two ringed times were excluded from the total of 13.05 actual minutes for the machine-controlled times, so that this total was divided by 16 instead of 18 to derive the average MCT of 0.816.

Element E, the unoccupied time, was dealt with by subtracting the total of the selected basic times for elements B, C and D, the inside work elements, from the average MCT. The resulting figure for the average unoccupied time was 0.257 minutes.

At this stage in the calculations, it is usual to make use of three decimal places for the selected basic times, and to retain the third place on the study summary sheet and the analysis of studies sheet.

300

Study No. *17*	WORKING SHEET						Sheet *4* of *5*

Element:	A	B	C	D	E	F	G	MCT
		(Basic times)						(Actual minutes)
Cycle No.								
1	25	25	12	19		25	09	82
2	25	26	12	18		26	10	81
3	26	26	12	20		25	11	81
4	26	24	11	17		24	10	81
5	26	23	11	17		24	10	83
6	26	26	13	18		22	10	82
7	26	26	12	19		26	11	81
8	28	24	13	18		29	10	82
9	26	25	12	17		28	10	81
10	21	26	12	19		24	11	82
11	29	26	11	19		25	10	82
12	26	24	12	19		27	09	(72)
13	27	26	13	20		24	11	82
14	26	25	13	19		26	10	82
15	26	24	13	20		26	10	81
16	26	24	13	18		26	11	81
17	27	27	13	19		25	10	(92)
18	27	25	12	19		25	11	81
Totals	4.69	4.52	2.20	3.35		4.57	1.84	13.05
Occasions	18	18	18	18		18	18	16
Average	0.261	0.251	0.122	0.186		0.254	0.102	0.816

$$\text{MCT} = 0.816 \quad \text{Actual minutes}$$
$$\text{B} + \text{C} + \text{D} = 0.559 \quad \text{Basic minutes}$$
$$\text{Element E (unoccupied)} = 0.257$$

Figure 101.   Study summary sheet

The study summary sheet, when completed, was stapled on top of the other four study sheets and was eventually filed with them. The sheets which have been used for recording observations at the workplace often become somewhat dirty as a result of the conditions in which they have to be used. Moreover, because of the speed with which the observations have to be written down, the studyman may have used many abbreviations, and perhaps his hurried writing may be difficult for anyone except the studyman himself to read. The study summary sheet therefore not only presents concisely all the results obtained from the study but also records in the heading block, in ink and neatly written, all the information about the operation which was originally entered on the time study top sheet.

The repetitive elements A to G, excluding E, were entered first, and it has been noted that three of these were inside work and the other three outside work. The entries in the column headed BT are the basic times per occasion, and were taken from the working sheet shown in figure 100. For each of these elements the frequency of occurrence is shown as 1/1, indicating that each occurred once in every cycle of the operation. The time calculated for the machine element, and hence the unoccupied time (element E), is shown below. The column headed Obs. shows the number of observations of the element which have been taken into account in deriving selected basic times. This information will be carried to the analysis of studies sheet where it will be of use when the final selected basic times are derived for the compilation of the standard time.

Under the heading "Occasional elements and contingencies" is shown the basic time for the element of helping the labourer to load and unload boxes of castings. It is noted that this element was observed once only, and that its frequency ought to be 1/30 since three boxes of ten fresh castings were brought, and three boxes of finished castings loaded. The other two non-repetitive occurrences observed were "Talk to foreman", and "Inspector checks three pieces and discusses". Neither of these periods was rated, so the times are shown in actual minutes (a.m.).

Finally, the studyman recorded, in actual minutes, the amount of relaxation taken during the period of the study.

Basic times were entered to the third decimal place, and have been carried forward in this form to the analysis of studies sheet. It may be thought that this is a degree of refinement which is not warranted in view of the accuracy of the data on which the entries are based. There is a good reason for the practice, however. If it is eventually decided to make the final selection of basic times, on the analysis of studies sheet, by the process of averaging, each of the entries from this study will be multiplied by the corresponding number of observations to yield the total basic minutes observed for the element. The totals from all the studies taken on this operation will be added, and an average obtained by dividing by the aggregate number of observations. At that stage, when the whole chain of arithmetical calculations has been completed, the final selections will be expressed to the nearest second decimal place only, that is to the nearest one-hundredth of a minute.

STUDY SUMMARY SHEET

DEPARTMENT: *Machine Shop*	SECTION: *Milling*	STUDY No.: *17*
OPERATION: *Finish mill second face*	M.S. No.: *9*	SHEET No.: *5* OF *5*

PLANT/MACHINE: *Cincinnati No. 4*	No.: *26* *25 cm TLF*	DATE:	
Vertical Miller	*Cutter*	TIME OFF:	*10.25 a.m.*
TOOLS AND GAUGES: *Fixture F. 239* *Gauge 239/7 Surface plate*		TIME ON:	*9.47*
PRODUCT/PART: *B. 239 Gear Case* No.:		ELAPSED TIME:	*38.00*
		CHECK TIME:	*2.80*
DWG. No.: *B. 239/1*	MATERIAL: *Cast Iron*	NET TIME:	*35.20*
	to I.S.S. 2	OBS. TIME:	*35.20*
QUALITY: *as dwg.*	WORKING CONDITIONS:	UNACC. TIME:	*–*
	m/c 9 cutter OK: light good	U.T. AS %:	*–*
OPERATIVE: M/F CLOCK No.: *1234*		STUDIED BY:	
		CHECKED BY:	

Sketch and notes on back of sheet 1

El. No.	ELEMENT DESCRIPTION	BT	F	Obs.	
	Repetitive				
A	*) Outside work*	*0.261*	*1/1*	*18*	
B	*| Inside work*	*0.251*	*1/1*	*18*	
C	*{ As card No. 1264 .. ..*	*0.122*	*1/1*	*18*	
D	*| ..*	*0.186*	*1/1*	*18*	
F	*| Outside work*	*0.254*	*1/1*	*18*	
G	*) .. ..*	*0.104*	*1/1*	*18*	
	Machine element	*0.816*	*1/1*	*16*	
E	*Unoccupied time within MCT*	*0.257*	*1/1*	*18*	
	Occasional elements and contingencies				
	Help unload boxes of new castings				
	and load boxes of finished castings				
	to truck	*1.100*		*1*	*Freq. 1/30 castings*
	(outside work)				*(Boxes hold 10 castings)*
	Talk to foreman (OW) (a.m.)	*0.400*	*1/18*	*obs.*	
	Inspector checks 3 pieces and				
	discusses (a.m.)	*1.020*	*1/18*	*obs.*	
	(OW)				
	Relaxation time (a.m.)	*6.120*			

Figure 102.   Extract from the analysis of studies sheet

As each time study on the operation was worked up and summarised, the entries from the study summary sheet were transferred to an analysis of studies sheet of the type illustrated in figure 81. These sheets are often printed on paper of A3 or double foolscap size or larger, and so only a portion of the whole sheet is reproduced opposite.

It will be seen that five studies were made in all on this operation, a total of 92 cycles being observed. The work of three different operatives was studied, by four different studymen. Standard times for regular machine shop operations are usually compiled from predetermined time standards (see Chapter 21), and when a considerable body of data has been built up it is often possible to derive accurate time standards with fewer studies, or by observing a smaller number of cycles of the operation.

Inspection of the study results for the elements A, B, C, D, F and G indicated normal consistency, with no reading suggesting a need for further investigation. The work of proceeding to the final selected basic times for the elements was therefore undertaken next. The selection was made by taking the weighted average for each element. All the repetitive elements were constant elements, so that there was no need for graphical presentation. In the first of the four columns in the block at the right-hand side of the sheet, the total basic time was entered against each element. Dividing these totals by 92, the aggregate number of cycles, yielded the figures for basic minutes per occasion, entered in the next column. These are now shown to the second decimal place only; that is, to the nearest one-hundredth of a minute.

The third column records the frequency of occurrence per cycle—for all the repetitive elements 1/1—and thus the entries in the last column, which show the basic minutes per cycle, are for this operation the same as those in the second column of the right-hand block. The unoccupied time, element E, has been arrived at in the same manner as on the study summary, by deducting the sum of the inside work basic minutes from the machine-controlled time. Usually the unoccupied time would not be evaluated until after relaxation allowance had been added to the work elements, but in this instance, as is indicated when discussing these allowances on the next page, there was no need for such a refinement.

The occasional element "Help labourer" was observed on three occasions only, in three different studies. Since it is known that the truck carries three boxes each containing ten castings, it is clear that the frequency with which this element will occur is once every 30 castings, or cycles. The average basic time per occasion was therefore divided by 30 to yield the basic time per cycle of 0.04 minutes.

"Talk to foreman" was dealt with by dividing the total time observed by the 92 cycles observed, giving a time of 0.01 minutes per cycle. The "Inspector checks" element was treated similarly, though in this instance as it was learned from the foreman that the inspector's duty was to check three castings in every 100 the frequency has been taken as 1/100. These two very small periods of time, both entered in actual minutes, were eventually considered to be best dealt with as contingencies and were covered by the contingency allowance given.

Study No.:	3	9	17	25	28		TOTALS	SELECTED BASIC TIME PER OCCASION	FREQUENCY OF OCCURRENCE PER CYCLE	BASIC MINUTES PER CYCLE
Date:	27/4	1/5	4/5	7/5	11/5					
Operative:	CAA	TBN	CAA	TBN	CRW					
Clock No.:	1234	1547	1234	1547	1846					
Machine No.:	26	34	26	127	71					
Study taken by:	BDM	CEP	MN	DFS	BDM		Cycles			
No. of cycles studied:	15	26	18	13	20		92			

M. No.	ELEMENTS	BASIC TIME PER OCCASION						B.T.	B.M.		B.M.
A	P/U casting, locate, lock, set on	0.276	0.257	0.261	0.270	0.281		24.645	0.27	1/1	0.27
B	Hold, break milled edge, clean	0.240	0.266	0.251	0.252	0.244		23.305	0.25	1/1	0.25
C	Gauge	0.114	0.127	0.122	0.128	0.111		11.089	0.12	1/1	0.12
D	Aside finished part, position new	0.197	0.196	0.186	0.191	0.180		17.485	0.19	1/1	0.19
E	Wait m/c (actual minutes)	0.264	0.222	0.257	0.253	0.275				1/1	0.26
F	Stop m/c, unlock, aside part	0.271	0.270	0.254	0.250	0.245		23.820	0.26	1/1	0.26
G	Clear swarf	0.096	0.112	0.104	0.090	0.092		9.240	0.10	1/1	0.10
	Machine-controlled time (actual minutes)	0.821	0.811	0.816	0.824	0.810		75.000	0.82	1/1	0.82
	Help labourer U/L and load boxes of castings	—	—	1.100 (1 occ.)	1.420 (1 occ.)	1.310 (1 occ.)		3.830	1.28	1/30	0.04
	Talk to foreman (actual minutes)	1.140	—	0.400	0.870	—		2.410	0.80	1/92	0.01
	Inspector checks, discuss (a.m.)	—	1.470 (1 occ.)	1.020 (1 occ.)	—	1.770 (1 occ.)		4.260	1.42	1/100	0.01

Figure 103. Calculation of relaxation allowance

A form such as that shown in the figure reproduced below is often used for the compilation of relaxation allowances. It provides a convenient way of ensuring that no item of relaxation allowance is omitted. The derivation of the allowances is based on the data given in the tables reproduced in Appendix 3. In this example the weight in kgs has been converted into lbs so that the points can be derived from these tables. The total figure for relaxation allowances (which represents both fixed and variable allowances) has also an added 5 per cent personal needs allowance. By deducting this figure for each element from the total allowances figure, one can arrive at fatigue allowances alone.

Since this is an example of restricted work the fatigue allowance has been calculated separately.

RELAXAT

PRODUCT: *B. 239 Gear Case*
WEIGHT : *6.8 kg each (15 lbs)*

OPERATION: *Finish-mill second face*

WORKING CONDITIONS: *Good*

PHYSICAL STRAINS

El. No.	ELEMENT DESCRIPTION	AVERAGE FORCE		POSTURE		VIBRATION		SHORT CYCLE		RESTRICTIVE CLOTHING		
		Strain²	Pts.	Strain	Pts.	Strain	Pts.	Strain	Pts.	Strain	Pts.	Stra
A	*Pick up casting, locate in fixture, lock 2 nuts, set guard, start machine*	M	20	L	1	—	—	—	—	—	—	
B	*Break edges with file, and clean*	L	—	L	1	—	—	—	—	—	—	
C	*Gauge*	L	—	L	1	—	—	—	—	—	—	
D	*Pick up casting, place in box, pick up new casting and place near machine*	M	20	L	1	—	—	—	—	—	—	
E	*Wait for machine (unoccupied time)*	—	—	—	—	—	—	—	—	—	—	—
F	*Stop machine, open guard, unlock nuts, remove casting, place on surface plate*	M	20	L	1	—	—	—	—	—	—	
G	*Clean fixture with compressed air*	—	—	L	3	—	—	—	—	—	—	—
Occasional Element	*Help labourer load and unload boxes of castings (10 per box = 68 kg/2 men, 1/30 cycles)*	H	89	H	12	—	—	—	—	—	—	—

¹ The percentages of total allowances, as derived from the points conversion table in Appendix 3, cover both basic and variable allowances and a built personal needs allowance of 5 per cent.   ² Severity of strain: L = low; M = medium; H= high.

The only period of unoccupied time during the machine-controlled time totalled 0.26 actual minutes. This was considered to be too short a period for recovery from fatigue (see Chapter 19, section 4), so the whole of the relaxation allowance, both the personal needs part and the fatigue allowance, was considered as an addition to outside work and was added to the cycle time.

The personal needs allowance of 5 per cent was calculated on the sum of the outside work **plus** the machine-controlled time. Fatigue allowance was calculated on the work elements only.

It will be seen from figure 104 that the total relaxation allowance amounted to 0.17 minutes. This is less than the period of unoccupied time (0.26 minutes), but is nevertheless to be added outside the machine-controlled time as periods of 0.50 minutes or less of unoccupied time are ignored for fatigue allowance purposes.

LLOWANCE

JTAL STRAINS					WORKING CONDITIONS															TOTAL POINTS	TOTAL RELAXATION ALLOWANCE[1] (percentage)	FATIGUE ALLOWANCE (Relaxation Allowance less 5 per cent)
MONOTONY	EYE STRAIN		NOISE		TEMPERATURE/HUMIDITY		VENTILATION		FUMES		DUST		DIRT		WET							
Pts.	Strain	Pts.	Strain	Pts.	Strain	Pts.	Strain	Pts.	Strain	Pts.	Strain	Pts.	Strain	Pts.	Strain	Pts.						
1	L	2	L	1	M	6	L	1	—	—	—	—	—	—	—	—				33	16	11
1	L	2	L	1	M	6	L	1	—	—	—	—	—	—	—	—				13	11	6
1	L	2	L	1	M	6	L	1	—	—	—	—	—	—	—	—				13	11	6
1	L	2	L	1	M	6	L	1	—	—	—	—	—	—	—	—				33	16	11
—	—	—	—	—	—	—	—	—	—	—	—	—	—	—	—	—				—	—	—
1	L	2	L	1	M	6	L	1	—	—	—	—	—	—	—	—				33	16	11
—	—	—	L	1	M	6	L	1	—	—	—	—	—	—	—	—				11	11	6
—	—	—	L	1	M	6	L	1	—	—	—	—	—	—	—	—				109	74	69

Figure 104.   Final calculation of relaxation allowance

The allowance which resulted from applying the percentage figures built up in figure 103 is shown opposite. It will be seen that a contingency allowance of 2.5 per cent, inclusive of relaxation, was included under the heading of outside work, to cover the periods spent in discussions with the foreman and the inspector.

Fatigue allowance

		Basic time	Fatigue per cent	Allowance min
Inside work elements:	B	0.25	6	0.015
	C	0.12	6	0.007
	D	0.19	11	0.0209
		0.56		0.0429
Outside work elements:	A	0.27	11	0.0297
	F	0.26	11	0.0286
	G	0.10	6	0.006
Occasional element help labourer		0.04	69	0.0276

Contingency allowance –
2.5 per cent of total basic time,
inclusive of relaxation allowance

		Basic time	Fatigue per cent	Allowance min
		0.03	–	–
		0.70		0.0919
Total fatigue allowance . . .				0.1348

Personal needs allowance

5 per cent of Outside work plus
machine-controlled time:
5 per cent of $(0.70 + 0.82)$ 0.076

Total relaxation allowance

Fatigue allowance plus personal needs allowance . .   0.2108
i.e.   0.21 min

Figure 105.   Calculation and issue of the standard time

The method of calculation shown opposite is that appropriate to restricted work. When standard times for jobs made up wholly of manual elements are compiled, it is common to add the appropriate relaxation allowances element by element, thus building up standard times for each element, the sum of which of course represents the standard time for the whole job. In such instances it is usual to show the final calculations on a job summary sheet which lists the elements in full, with their descriptions, and all relevant details of the job for which the standard time has been built up. This would be done also for restricted work such as that in the present example, though inside and outside work would be shown separately. It is good practice to add a cycle diagram to the job summary sheet.

The methods adopted to issue—or publish—standard times vary according to the circumstances of the work situation. In jobbing shops, and for non-repetitive work (such as much maintenance work) jobs may be studied while they are in progress and the time standards be issued directly to the workers concerned, by annotation on the job sheet or other work instruction, after approval by the shop foreman. When the work is mainly repetitive, with the same operations being performed many times over, for perhaps weeks or months on end, tables of values, derived after extensive studywork, may be issued by the work study department.

Figure 106.   Over-all cycle time

The over-all cycle time is of course the same as the standard time. The final cycle diagram is shown opposite.

*
*   *

The use to which time standards may be put is discussed in Chapter 23. It should be noted that, although the example which has been studied in detail is a simple one for a manufacturing industry, a very similar procedure is carried out for non-manufacturing operations or for any other work which is time-studied for the purpose of setting time standards.

Computation of Standard Time

Outside work.	0.70 basic min
Inside work	0.56 basic min
Relaxation allowance	0.21 min
Unoccupied time allowance . .	0.26 min
Standard time.	1.73 **standard min**

Alternatively:

Outside work.	0.70 basic min
Machine-controlled time . . .	0.82 min
Relaxation allowance	0.21 min
	1.73 **standard min**

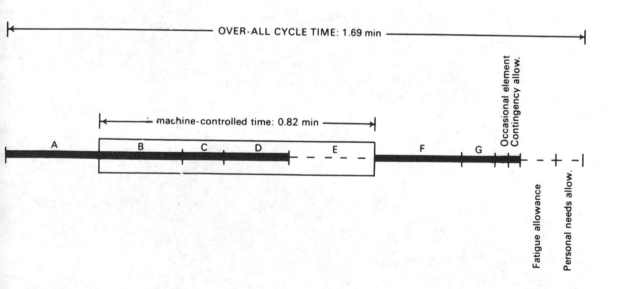

Chapter 21
Predetermined time standards

1. Definition

Predetermined time standards (PTS) are advanced techniques which aim at defining the time needed for the performance of various operations by derivation from pre-set standards of time for various motions and not by direct observation and measurement. They are not normally considered suitable for the trainee to use until he has gained a real understanding of and considerable experience in work study practice. He will also require specialised PTS training. The essential nature of these standards will be explained in this chapter.

> A predetermined time standard is a work measurement technique whereby times established for basic human motions (classified according to the nature of the motion and the conditions under which it is made) are used to build up the time for a job at a defined level of performance

As the definition indicates, PTS systems are techniques for synthesising operation times from standard time data for basic motions. Synthesis and standard data are discussed more fully later in this book.

The nature of PTS systems can be easily illustrated by reference to a simple work cycle, such as putting a washer on a bolt. The operator will **reach** to the washer, **grasp** the washer, **move** the washer to the bolt, **position** it on the bolt and **release** it.

Many operations consist, broadly speaking, of some or all of these five basic motions. To these are added other body motions and a few other elements. Table 18 illustrates the components of a basic PTS.

By examining a given operation and identifying the basic motions of which it is composed, and by referring to PTS tables which indicate standard times for each type of motion performed under given circumstances, it is possible to derive a standard time for the operation as a whole.

313

Table 18.   Components of a basic PTS

Motion	Description
REACH	Move hand to destination.
GRASP	Secure control of object with fingers.
MOVE	Move object.
POSITION	Line up and engage objects.
RELEASE	Let go of object.
BODY MOTIONS	Leg, trunk movements.

2. Origins

The pioneer of motion classification was Frank B. Gilbreth whose "therblig" (see Chapter 11, section 9) subdivisions of hand or hand and eye motions were the key concept in the development of motion study. Two main ideas underlying Gilbreth's approach were that the act of making a detailed critical analysis of work methods stimulates ideas for method improvement; and that the evaluation of alternative work methods can be achieved by a simple comparison of the number of motions, the better method being the one requiring fewer motions.

The credit for adding the time dimension to motion study is attributed to A. B. Segur, who in 1927 stated that "within practical limits the time required for all experts to perform true fundamental motions is a constant".[1] Segur developed the first predetermined time standards, calling his system Motion Time Analysis. Little is known publicly about the system since he exploited it as a management consultant and bound his clients to secrecy.

The next important development was the work of J. H. Quick and his associates, who originated the Work Factor system in 1934. Like Segur's system, this was exploited on a management consultancy basis and little information was published about it. However, it was eventually adopted by a large number of companies and is now in active use.

A considerable number and variety of PTS systems were produced during and following the Second World War. Among these was a system which has become very widely used throughout the world, Methods-Time Measurement (MTM). Because of its importance MTM will be used here to illustrate the way in which predetermined time standards are arrived at.

MTM was first developed by three men working on the system at the Westinghouse Electric Corporation in the United States: H. B. Maynard, G. J. Stegemerten and J. L. Schwab. Their findings were published, and thus, for the first time, full details of a PTS system were made freely available to everyone. MTM has also set up, in various countries, independent non-profit-making MTM associations to control the standards of training and practice and to continue research into and the

---

[1] A. B. Segur: "Labour costs at the lowest figure", in *Manufacturing Industries* (New York), Vol. 13, 1927, p. 273.

development of MTM. These associations have established an international co-ordinating body, the International MTM Directorate. In 1965, a simplified form of MTM known as MTM-2 was developed, and this led to a rapid increase in the use of the system.

3. Advantages of PTS systems

PTS systems offer a number of advantages over stop-watch time study. With PTS systems one time is indicated for a given motion, irrespective of where such a motion is performed. In stop-watch time study it is not so much a motion as a sequence of motions making up an operation that is timed. Timing by direct observation and rating can sometimes lead to inconsistency. A PTS system, which avoids both rating and direct observation, can lead to more consistency in setting standard times.

Since the times for the various operations can be derived from standard-time tables, it is possible to define the standard time for a given operation even before production begins, and often while the process is still at the design stage. This is one of the great advantages of PTS systems, as they allow the work study man to change the layout and design of the workplace and of the necessary jigs and fixtures in such a way that the optimum production time is achieved. They also make it possible, even before starting the operation, to draw up an estimate of the cost of production, and this could obviously be valuable for estimating and tendering purposes or for budgeting. PTS systems are not too difficult to apply and can be less time-consuming than other methods when time standards for certain operations are being determined. They are particularly useful for very short repetitive time cycles such as assembly work in the electronics industry.

4. Criticisms of PTS systems

In view of the value of PTS systems, it is surprising that it took so long for them to become part of general work study practice. The main reason for this delay is probably the considerable number and variety of systems that have been produced, together with the fact that many of them could be obtained only by employing consultants. At present, over 200 such systems exist. This proliferation has led to complaints from management, trade unions and work study men.

Furthermore, any PTS system is rather complicated. It is not easy to learn, and a work study man needs a good deal of practice before he can apply it correctly. The task of learning enough about the various systems to be able to judge their claims and their relative merits is an almost impossible one. For example, some systems do not go into sufficient detail in defining a certain motion. They might, for instance, give the same time for the movement both of an empty cup and of one full of water, or for the movement of a dry brush and of one laden with paint, which must be moved with care. The situation was made more complicated by the lack of freely available information on many systems, whose tables were considered to be the property of their developers and were thus not available for publication.

315

Some work study researchers also questioned the basic assumptions of PTS systems. In part, these criticisms were justified, although some appear to have arisen through misinformation or misunderstanding. PTS systems do not, as was claimed, eliminate the need for the stop-watch, any more than they eliminate method study or work sampling. Machine time, process time and waiting time are not measurable with PTS systems, and occasional or incidental elements are often more economically measured by using other techniques. In fact, it is difficult to obtain 100 per cent coverage in a plant using only a PTS system, and for certain operations such as batch production or non-repetitive jobs the use of such a system can be an expensive proposition.

One type of criticism stems from a too literal interpretation of the basic assumption of Segur, quoted above. In fact, absolute constant times are **not** implied. The times indicated in PTS tables are **averages,** and the limits associated with the averages are small enough to be neglected in all practical circumstances.

Another common criticism is that it is invalid to add up times for individual small motions in the way required by PTS systems because the time taken to perform a particular motion is influenced by the motions preceding and following it. It is unfair to criticise the more important PTS systems on these grounds, because not only were these relationships clearly recognised by their originators but also special provision was made to ensure that the essential correlations were maintained. In the case of MTM, for example, this was achieved by establishing subdivisions of the main classes of motions and by creating special definitions and rules of application to ensure their essential linking. The relationships are also preserved in simplified systems such as MTM-2.

It has also been declared that the direction of the motion influences the time—for example, that it takes longer to cover the same distance when moving upwards than when moving downwards—and that no PTS system isolates this variable. MTM researchers would agree that the direction of the motion is an important variable. However, they argue that in a single work cycle the operative will not be reaching only upwards, nor always away from the body, nor making only anti-clockwise turns: he will reach downwards or towards the body or make clockwise turns also, and so justify the use of average values.

5. Different forms of PTS systems

The work study man is likely to encounter a number of different forms of PTS systems, and it will therefore be useful for him to understand the main ways in which the systems vary. He will find differences as regards levels and scope of application of data, motion classification and time units.

DATA LEVELS

Figure 107 illustrates data levels by means of the official international MTM systems: MTM-1, MTM-2 and MTM-3.

Figure 107.   PTS data levels: basic motions

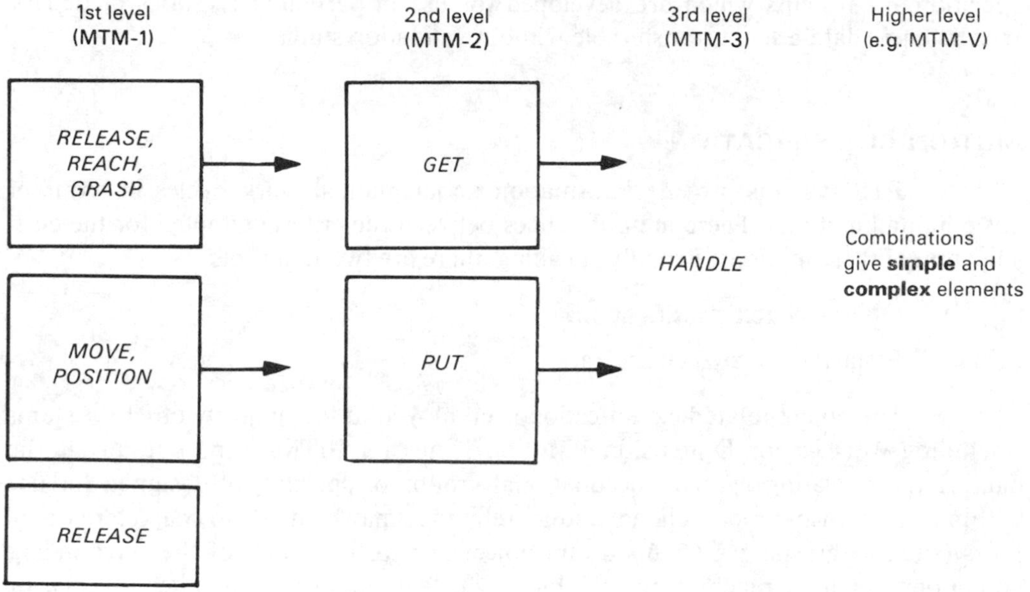

1st level (MTM-1)	2nd level (MTM-2)	3rd level (MTM-3)	Higher level (e.g. MTM-V)

```
 ┌──────────────┐        ┌──────────────┐
 │   RELEASE,   │        │              │
 │    REACH,    │───────▶│     GET      │──────▶
 │    GRASP     │        │              │
 └──────────────┘        └──────────────┘
                                               HANDLE      Combinations
                                                           give simple and
                                                           complex elements
 ┌──────────────┐        ┌──────────────┐
 │              │        │              │
 │    MOVE,     │───────▶│     PUT      │──────▶
 │  POSITION    │        │              │
 └──────────────┘        └──────────────┘

 ┌──────────────┐
 │   RELEASE    │
 └──────────────┘
```

The first level comprises the motions *RELEASE, REACH, GRASP, MOVE, POSITION, RELEASE.* At the second level these motions are combined: in MTM-2, for instance, the motions are *GET* and *PUT.* At the third level, the motions have been further combined as *HANDLE,* to give a description of the complete work cycle. Beyond the third level there are as yet no completely clear-cut rules, and methods of classification vary according to the work area for which the data are intended.

SCOPE OF APPLICATION OF DATA

PTS systems vary as regards the universality of their application. It is difficult to explain this concept exactly, but table 19 attempts some clarification.

First of all there are systems of universal application, which cover all work anywhere. This is so for motion data at the MTM-1, 2 or 3 levels and for the Work Factor systems. Second, there are data which relate to a main occupation, for example office work, maintenance work or some kinds of production work. Examples of these are Master Clerical Data for the office and MTM-V, the Swedish MTM

Table 19.   Scope of application of data

Degree	PTS system	Scope of application
1 - Universal	MTM-1, 2, 3; Work Factor	Transferable throughout the world and applicable in all manual work areas.
2 - General	Master Clerical Data (office); MTM-V (machine shops)	Transferable but within a work area.
3 - Specific	Standard data for particular departments in a plant	Not transferable without validation studies.

317

Association data for machine shops. Finally, there is the least general category: the specific data systems which are developed for use in particular factories or departments. These data are not transferable without validation studies.

MOTION CLASSIFICATION

PTS systems provide information about manual work cycles in terms of basic human motions. There are differences between the criteria adopted for the classification of these motions. Broadly speaking, there are two main sets:

☐   Object-related classification.

☐   Behaviour-related classification.

The object-related classification is employed in the majority of PTS systems (including Work Factor, Dimensional Motion Times and MTM-1) and virtually all the data systems relating to main occupational groups or specifically designed for use within a plant. In an object-related system, reference may be made to characteristics of parts (such as grasping a $6 \times 6 \times 6$ mm object), or to the nature of the surrounding conditions (such as reaching to an object which is jumbled with other objects, or reaching to an object which is lying flat against a surface). The classification is, however, not entirely object-related since motions such as Release Load or Disengage have behavioural definitions.

Unlike most systems, MTM-2 employs exclusively behavioural concepts. This is also true of MTM-3, Master Standard Data and a few less well known systems. The behaviour-related systems classify motions according to what they look like to an observer: for example, a movement of the empty hand for a distance of between 5 and 15 cm followed by a grasping action made by a simple closing of the fingers defines the *GET* motion in the MTM-2 system (see below).

TIME UNITS

No two PTS systems have the same set of time values. This is partly due to the fact that different systems have different motion classes and the time data therefore refer to different things. Again, the choice of the basic unit (fractions of a second, minutes, hour) may vary, and some systems follow the practice of adding contingency allowances to motion times, whereas others do not. A final major cause of variations arises from the differences in the performance level implied in the time data. The methods adopted for standardising, normalising or averaging the motion times are not uniform. Consequently PTS time data are divided into one of two sets: Work Factor systems, which express their data in minutes; and MTM systems, expressed in time measurement units (tmu) which represent one hundred-thousandth of an hour or about one twenty-eighth of a second. The MTM time values, which were derived mainly from film analysis of a variety of industrial operations (the method was to count the number of "frames" occupied by each motion), were standardised using the well known "Westinghouse" or "Levelling" system. The times are stated to be those which are achieved by an experienced operative of average skill, working with average effort and consistency under average conditions. The performance level, MTM 100, is therefore

318

somewhat less than BSI 100. A public statement on this by the United Kingdom Institute of Work Study Practitioners and the MTM Association suggests that MTM 100 equals BSI 83.[1]

OTHER CONSIDERATIONS

Some important properties of PTS systems are much less easy to establish and to compare than the aspects discussed in the previous subsections. Examples of these are the precision and accuracy of the time data, speed of application, methods description capability, and learning time. The lack of reliable, detailed information and, to some extent, the lack of agreed design criteria hamper comparison of these properties.

6. Use of PTS systems

The system most likely to be used by the work study man is MTM-2. The following categories constitute the MTM-2 system. Each will be explained in detail in the following subsection.

Category	Code
GET	GA
	GB
	GC
PUT	PA
	PB
	PC
REGRASP	R
APPLY PRESSURE	A
EYE ACTION	E
FOOT MOTION	F
STEP	S
BEND AND ARISE	B
WEIGHT FACTORS	GW
	PW
CRANK	C

The MTM-2 system provides time standards ranging from 3 to 61 tmu. These are shown on the data card reproduced in table 20. As stated above, one tmu equals one hundred-thousandth of an hour.

---

[1] "MTM and the BSI rating scale", in *Work Study and Management Services* (London), Feb. 1969, p. 97.

Table 20. MTM-2 data card

	Time in tmu					
Code	GA	GB	GC	PA	PB	PC
− 5	3	7	14	3	10	21
−15	6	10	19	6	15	26
−30	9	14	23	11	19	30
−45	13	18	27	15	24	36
−80	17	23	32	20	30	41

GW: 1 per 1 kg   PW: 1 per 5 kg

A	R	E	C	S	F	B
14	6	7	15	18	9	61

Warning: Do not attempt to use these data unless you have been trained and qualified under a scheme approved by the International MTM Directorate.

MTM-2 CATEGORIES

☐   *GET* (G)

GET is an action with the predominant purpose of reaching with the hand or fingers to an object, grasping the object and subsequently releasing it.

The scope of *GET* starts: with reaching to the object;

includes: reaching to, gaining control and subsequently releasing control of the object;

ends: when the object is released.

Selection of a *GET* is done by considering three variables:

(1) case of *GET*—distinguished by the grasping action employed;

(2) distance reached;

(3) weight of the object or its resistance to motion.

Cases of *GET* are judged by the following decision model:

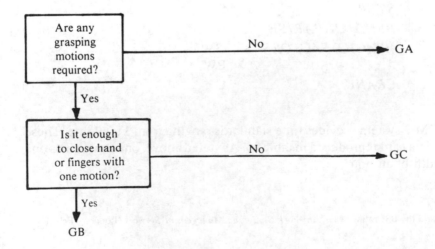

320

An example of GA is putting the palm of the hand on the side of a box in order to push it across a table.

An example of GB is getting an easy-to-handle object, such as a one-inch cube, which is lying by itself.

An example of GC is getting the corner of a page of this book in order to turn it over.

Distance is a principal variable in *GET,* and five distance classes are provided. Distances are judged by the upper limits of the classes, which are 5, 15, 30, 45 and over 45 cm. The code 80 is assigned to the highest class. Distances are estimated from the path of travel of the hand, less any body assistance.

cm		Code
Over	Not over	
0.0	5.0	− 5
5.0	15.0	− 15
15.0	30.0	− 30
30.0	45.0	− 45
45.0	—	− 80

□   *GET WEIGHT* (GW)

GET WEIGHT is the action required for the muscles of the hand and arm to take up the weight of the object.

The scope of *GET WEIGHT* starts:	with the grasp on the object completed;
	includes:	muscular force necessary to gain full control of the weight of the object;
	ends:	when the object is sufficiently under control to permit movement of the object.

GET WEIGHT occurs after the fingers have closed on the object in the preceding *GET*. It must be accomplished before any actual movement can take place. When the weight or resistance is less than 2 kg per hand, no GW is assigned. When resistance exceeds 2 kg, 1 tmu is assigned for every kg including the first two.

□   *PUT* (P)

PUT is an action with the predominant purpose of moving an object to a destination with the hand or fingers.

The scope of *PUT* starts: with an object grasped and under control at the initial place;

includes: all transporting and correcting motions necessary to place an object;

ends: with object still under control at the intended place.

Selection of a *PUT* is done by considering three variables:

(1) case of *PUT*—distinguished by the correcting motions employed;

(2) distance moved;

(3) weight of the object or its resistance to motion.

Cases of *PUT* are judged by the following decision model:

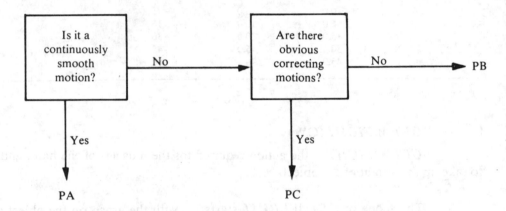

An example of PA is tossing aside an object.

An example of PB is the action of putting a 12 mm ball in a 15 mm diameter hole.

An example of PC is inserting a Yale or similar key in a lock.

A correction is not likely to be confused with a short PA. A correction is a very short unintentional motion at the terminal point; a PA is purposive, usually of easily discernible length.

The motion distance is handled in a similar manner to *GET*.

When there is an engagement of parts following a correction, an additional *PUT* will be allowed when the distance exceeds 2.5 cm.

□   *PUT WEIGHT* (PW)

PUT WEIGHT is an addition to a *PUT* motion depending on the weight of the object moved.

The scope of *PUT WEIGHT* starts: when the move begins;

    includes: the additional time, over and above the move time in *PUT,* to compensate for the differences in time required in moving heavy and light objects over the same distance;

    ends: when the move ends.

PW is assigned when resistance to movement exceeds 2 kg per hand. Weights are calculated as in *GET WEIGHT.* Between 2 kg and 5 kg, 1 tmu is allowed and coded PW5; between 5 kg and 10 kg 2 tmu are allowed and coded PW10; and so on.

☐   *REGRASP* (R)

REGRASP is a hand action with the purpose of changing the grasp on an object.

The scope of *REGRASP* starts: with the object in the hand;

    includes: digital and hand muscular readjustment on an object;

    ends: with the object in a new location in the hand.

A single *REGRASP* consists of not more than three fractional movements.

Digital and muscular readjustments, while performing an *APPLY PRESSURE,* are included in *APPLY PRESSURE.* A *REGRASP* should not be assigned in combination with *APPLY PRESSURE.*

If the hand relinquishes control and then secures another grasp on the object, the action will be a *GET,* not a *REGRASP.*

An example of R is changing the grasp on a pencil in order to get into the position for writing.

☐   *APPLY PRESSURE* (A)

APPLY PRESSURE is an action with the purpose of exerting muscular force on an object.

The scope of *APPLY PRESSURE* starts: with the body member in contact with the object;

    includes: the application of controlled increasing muscular force, a minimum reaction time to permit the reversal of force and the subsequent releasing of muscular force;

    ends: with the body member in contact with the object, but with muscular force released.

The minimum dwell time covers mental reaction time only. Longer dwells, in holding actions, must be separately evaluated.

APPLY PRESSURE applies to the action of exerting muscular force on an object to achieve control, to restrain or to overcome resistance to motion. The object is not displaced more than 6 mm during the action of *APPLY PRESSURE*.

APPLY PRESSURE, which can be performed by any body member, is recognised by a noticeable hesitation while force is applied.

An example of A is the final tightening action made with a screwdriver or spanner.

□   *EYE ACTION* (E)

EYE ACTION is an action with the purpose of

either: recognising a readily distinguishable characteristic of an object;

or: shifting the aim of the axis of vision to a new viewing area.

The scope of *EYE ACTION* starts: when other actions must cease because a characteristic of an object must be recognised;

includes:

either: muscular readjustment of the lens of the eyes and the mental processes required to recognise a distinguishable characteristic of an object;

or: the eye motion performed to shift the aim of the axis of vision to a new viewing area;

ends: when other actions can start again.

A single eye focus covers an area 10 cm in diameter at 40 cm from the eyes. Recognition time included is sufficient only for simple binary decision.

An example of E is the action of determining whether a coin is showing head or tail.

□   *FOOT MOTION* (F)

FOOT MOTION is a short foot or leg motion when the purpose is not to move the body.

The scope of *FOOT MOTION* starts: with the foot or leg at rest;

includes: a motion not exceeding 30 cm that is pivoted at the hip, knee or instep;

ends: with the foot in a new location.

FOOT MOTION is judged by the decision model for *FOOT MOTION* and *STEP*.

☐ *STEP* (S)

STEP is

either: a leg motion with the purpose of moving the body;

or: a leg motion longer than 30 cm.

The scope of *STEP* starts: with the leg at rest;

includes:

either: a motion of the leg where the purpose is to achieve displacement of the trunk;

or: a leg motion longer than 30 cm;

ends: with the leg at a new location.

STEP or *FOOT MOTION* is judged by the following decision model:

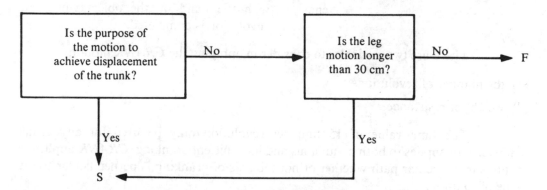

To evaluate walking, count the number of times the foot hits the floor.

An example of F is depressing a foot pedal in a car.

An example of S is making a single step to the side to enable the arm to reach further.

☐ *BEND AND ARISE* (B)

BEND AND ARISE is a lowering of the trunk followed by a rise.

The scope of *BEND AND ARISE* starts: with motion of the trunk forward from an upright posture;

includes: movement of the trunk and other body members to achieve a vertical change of body position to permit the hands to reach down to or below the knees and the subsequent arise from this position;

ends: with the body in an upright posture.

The criterion for *BEND AND ARISE* is whether the operative is able to reach to below the knees, not whether he actually does so.

Kneeling on both knees should be analysed as 2B.

☐   *CRANK* (C)

CRANK is a motion with the purpose of moving an object in a circular path of more than half a revolution with the hand or finger.

The scope of *CRANK* starts: with the hand on the object;

includes: all transporting motions necessary to move an object in a circular path;

ends: with the hand on the object when one revolution is completed.

There are two variables to consider in applying the *CRANK* motion:

(1) the number of revolutions;

(2) weight or resistance.

The time value of 15 tmu per revolution may be used for any crank diameter and applies to both continuous and intermittent cranking. *CRANK* applies to motions in a circular path whether or not the axis of cranking is perpendicular to the plane of rotation.

The number of revolutions should be rounded to the nearest whole number.

The weight or resistance influences the time for moving an object. The rules of adding GW and PW to *PUT* motions also apply to *CRANK*. PW applies to each revolution, whether continuous or intermittent. GW is applied once only to a continuous series of revolutions, but to each revolution where these are intermittent.

No correcting motions as applied to *PUT* are included in *CRANK*. If correcting motions occur in putting the object at the intended place an extra *PUT* must be allowed.

An example of C is turning a hand wheel through one revolution.

TRAINING REQUIREMENTS

In the preceding subsection the essentials of the MTM-2 system were outlined. To obtain an adequate understanding of the system, however, a trainee will require at least two weeks of formal training in MTM-2 theory and practice, followed by guided application on the shop floor with an MTM instructor. A trainee who is already competent in work study practice should reach a reasonable standard in the use of MTM-2 after about a month of guided application. MTM-1 will require a longer training period. It is helpful if part of this training can be carried out in a plant where MTM standards are already in use. When a trainee finds that his own analyses compare closely with established standards his confidence is rapidly built up. Without guidance it is very difficult for a trainee to learn how to use MTM adequately.

7. Application of PTS systems

PTS systems can be applied in two main ways:

(1) direct observation of the motions used by the operative;

(2) mental visualisation of the motions needed to accomplish a new or alternative work method.

The over-all approach adopted when one of the PTS systems, such as MTM-2, is used for direct observation is not very different from that adopted for making a time study (see Chapter 16, especially page 224). Indeed, a person experienced in the procedures described in that chapter—selecting the job, approach to the worker, recording job information, breakdown into elements, allowances, compiling total job times—is well equipped to become a good PTS practitioner. The main difference in the approach is that at the point in the total time study procedure where the observer is ready to time and rate the work cycle, he will instead make an MTM-2 analysis and then enter the motion times on his analysis sheet from the MTM-2 data card. The calculation of allowances, completion of the documentation and issuing of the job times are then done in much the same way as in a time study. If the same type of summary sheets can be used, so much the better. The study summary sheet shown as figure 80 (page 216) and the short cycle study form (figures 78 and 79, pp. 213 and 214) can be adapted to summarise the information from the MTM-2 analysis sheets.

CHOOSING THE OPERATIVE

In the choice of operative to be observed, it is just as desirable to have a co-operative, good-average worker for PTS analysis as it is for time study. Exceptionally fast or abnormally slow performances are difficult for time study men to rate, and they present problems for PTS analysts too. The super-skilled operative combines and overlaps motions in a manner beyond the capabilities of the average worker, while an abnormally slow or reluctant operative will make separate, one-handed, hesitant motions which the average operative will perform smoothly and simultaneously. The rules and motion combination tables of the MTM system, like those of other systems such as Work Factor, do provide information for adjusting the observed motion pattern to that applicable to the good-average worker; this additional work can, however,

327

be avoided by an intelligent choice of operative in the first place. Of course, the very experienced PTS analyst may also study extreme performances with advantage. The performance of an exceptionally fast operative may give clues as to how all operatives might be trained to reach a higher-than-average performance level, and the study of slow operatives would show where difficulties are being encountered and whether further training might eliminate these.

RECORDING JOB INFORMATION

In recording job information, it is important to remember that distance is a significant variable in PTS systems. The plans for the workplace layout should therefore be accurately drawn to scale. This will help in judging or checking the length of motions shown in the analyses.

BREAKDOWN INTO ELEMENTS

In PTS systems the division of the operation into work elements follows the same principles as for time study. The breakdown can be made very much finer, if required, because the difficulty of timing short elements does not arise. If necessary, the break points can also be changed easily and without having to retime the cycle. This flexibility is illustrated in table 21, which shows a very common work cycle—that of fitting a nut and washer on a stud. For example, if a change of method eliminates the need for a washer, the appropriate motions (GC30, PC30, PA5) and time (56 tmu) can easily be removed from the analysis. Finger turns can also be readily separated from spanner turns and, indeed, from the fitting actions and subsequent turns.

Table 21.   Fitting a nut and washer on a stud

Element	tmu	Code	Description
Fit washer.	23	GC30	Washer.
	30	PC30	To stud.
	3	PA5	On stud.
Fit nut and turn down by hand.	10	GB15	Nut.
	26	PC15	To stud.
	6	2PA5	Engage threads.
	42	6GB5	Turn down nut.
	18	6PA5	
Tighten nut using spanner.	23	GB30	Spanner.
	30	PC30	To nut.
	6	PA15	Turn nut.
	14	A	Tighten.
	231		

ALLOWANCES AND JOB TIMES

There is no problem of rating with a PTS system such as MTM-2, since the times have been rated once and for all. All that needs to be done is to add up the motion times and transfer the totals to the study summary sheet. If times are to be issued at BSI 100 and not MTM 100, the tmu total from the study summary sheet should be multiplied by 0.83. (This means that, if times are issued in standard minutes, the total tmu can be divided by 2,000.) It should be understood that the general relationship between the scales applies only to the time totals, and most definitely not to the individual motion times shown on the MTM data cards. Converting individual motion times is quite improper since these are not improved uniformly when a higher performance of a cycle time is achieved.

The times for low control motions (such as GA and PA) are improved only a little compared with those for the highly complex motions (such as GC and PC). The issue is, however, more complicated than this because one would also need a different set of motion combinations when considering a different performance level. Sophisticated MTM users, such as those in the Scandinavian countries, prefer to issue values at MTM 100.

Relaxation and other allowances are added in exactly the same way as for time study, in order to give the total job time.

VISUALISATION

When the work study man does not have the opportunity of observing the work cycle, for example when he is designing a new work method or constructing alternative methods during method study of an existing job, he must mentally visualise the motions needed. Figures 108 and 109 give an example of a PTS problem which can be solved by visualisation of the various motions involved. as can be seen from figure 110.

The ability to visualise motion patterns depends on the studyman's intelligence and on his practical experience. The more familiar he is with work study, the more readily he can picture in his mind the motions necessary to pick up and fit parts together, as well as visualising which motions can be performed together easily and which motions are difficult to carry out simultaneously.

In designing work methods, it can be helpful to use a methods laboratory (see Chapter 11, section 14). However, when motion analysis is undertaken there is a need for caution, just as there is with time standards. The experiments with new methods will probably be performed by the work study man himself or by his colleagues, and it is important that they should bear in mind that their own performances will generally fall far short of those which will be achieved by the regular shop floor operatives. Even where a shop floor operative is assisting in the methods laboratory, his performance of a new work cycle will fall short of the standard he will achieve when he has had sufficient practice in working the cycle under shop floor conditions.

In both these instances the rules for work design, particularly those of the motion combination possibilities expected of the average experienced operative, must be used to arrive at a correct shop floor method.

It is in the work design process that a work study man who chooses to use an MTM-2 system, for example, will reap the benefit of a full training in the detailed MTM-1 system on which MTM-2 was founded. However, at the very minimum he must understand the classification details of MTM-1, the basic motions which make up the MTM-2 motions and the rules covering the motion combination possibilities of the basic motions, particularly in relation to practice opportunity, area of normal vision and difficulty of handling. With this knowledge he will know, for example, that

329

Figure 108. Base assembly

MEASUREMENTS
IN MILLIMETRES

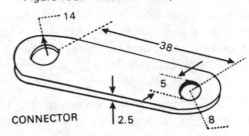

CONNECTOR

14

38

5

2.5

8

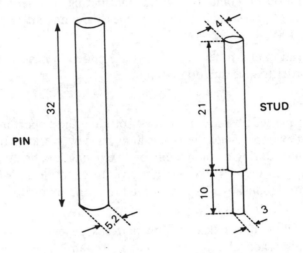

PIN

32

5,2

STUD

4

21

10

3

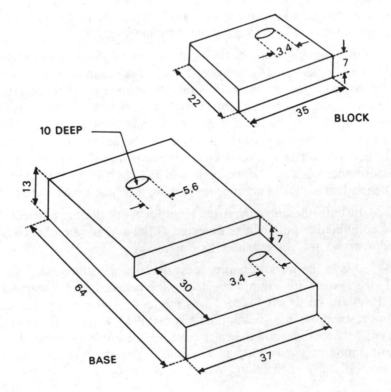

3,4

7

22

35

BLOCK

10 DEEP

13

5,6

7

64

30

3,4

BASE

37

Figure 109.   Base assembly workplace layout

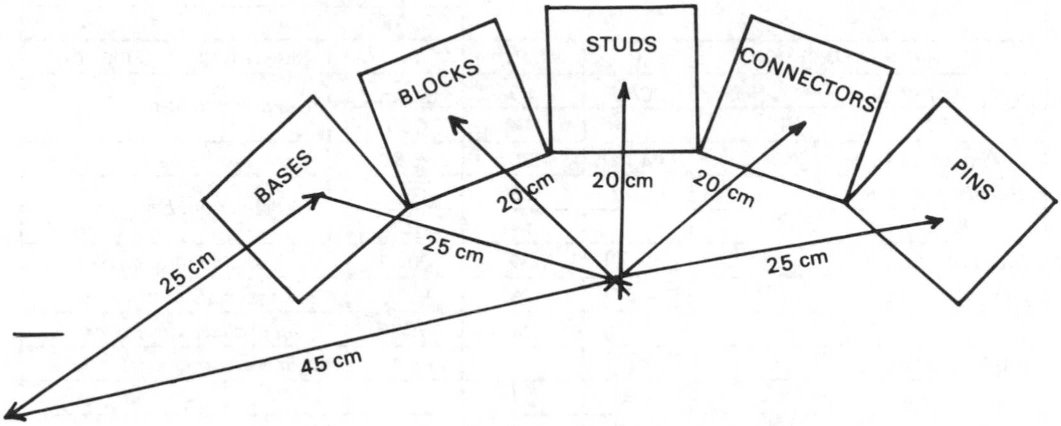

if he designs the workplace for the parts to be kept in tote pans, this will require a separate GC with either hand. He will know that even expert operatives cannot perform these motions simultaneously, because each motion involves a kind of minute searching and selecting activity, because the objects are jumbled together. Similarly, he will know that putting loose-fitting round plugs into round holes can be done with both hands simultaneously, provided that he has designed the workplace so that the targets are within the area of normal vision as defined above under *EYE ACTION*. The rules provide many such guidelines.

PTS SYSTEMS AND THE BROADER TECHNIQUES

The nature and value of PTS systems should now be reasonably clear. If a work study man intends to become a specialist, for example in MTM, he will need full training in MTM-1 and MTM-2 and in all the advanced techniques outlined in this book. In the more general case, where he will probably undertake both work study and other jobs as well (such as production planning and control—a common combination in small plants, particularly in the developing countries), an MTM-2 training may be sufficient.

However, it is most important that the studyman should not lose sight of the fact that the PTS technique is a fine precision tool. Before getting down to minute detail, he should first have seen what can be accomplished by using the broader, simpler approaches. In companies where work study practice has not yet been introduced, intelligent broad thinking will usually reveal ways of bringing about considerable initial improvements in productivity.

331

Figure 110. MTM-2 analysis sheet, base assembly

JOB DESCRIPTION:			REF.:	
Assemble base			SHEET No. *1* of *1*	
(see sketches of parts and layout)			ANALYST:	
			DATE:	

LEFT-HAND DESCRIPTION	LH	TMU	RH	RIGHT-HAND DESCRIPTION
Get base from box	GC30	23	G—	Get pin from box
		14	GC5	
Put base on bench	PA30	30	PC30	Locate pin to base
Get block from box	GC30	23	G—	Get stud from box
		14	GC5	
Move block stud	P—	30	PC30	Locate stud through block
Assist location	P—	26	PC15	Fit assembly to base
		23	GC30	Get connector from box
Assist location	GB—	30	PC30	Locate to stud
Locate to pin	PC5	21		
Pick up assembly	GB15	10		
Place on conveyor	PA80	20		
		264		

Table 22. Methods-Time Measurement application data in tmu
(Based metric weights and measures)

OFFICIAL INTERNATIONAL MTM-1 DATA

© INTERNATIONAL MTM DIRECTORATE
AND
MTM ASSOCIATION FOR
STANDARDS AND RESEARCH

Tables reproduced by kind permission of the International MTM Directorate.

TABLE I – REACH – R

Distance (cm)	Time (tmu)				Hand in motion		Case and description
	A	B	C or D	E	A	B	
2 or less	2.0	2.0	2.0	2.0	1.6	1.6	A Reach to object in fixed location, or to object in other hand or on which other hand rests.
4	3.4	3.4	5.1	3.2	3.0	2.4	
6	4.5	4.5	6.5	4.4	3.9	3.1	
8	5.5	5.5	7.5	5.5	4.6	3.7	
10	6.1	6.3	8.4	6.8	4.9	4.3	
12	6.4	7.4	9.1	7.3	5.2	4.8	B Reach to single object in location which may vary slightly from cycle to cycle.
14	6.8	8.2	9.7	7.8	5.5	5.4	
16	7.1	8.8	10.3	8.2	5.8	5.9	
18	7.5	9.4	10.8	8.7	6.1	6.5	
20	7.8	10.0	11.4	9.2	6.5	7.1	
22	8.1	10.5	11.9	9.7	6.8	7.7	C Reach to object jumbled with other objects in a group so that search and select occur.
24	8.5	11.1	12.5	10.2	7.1	8.2	
26	8.8	11.7	13.0	10.7	7.4	8.8	
28	9.2	12.2	13.6	11.2	7.7	9.4	
30	9.5	12.8	14.1	11.7	8.0	9.9	
35	10.4	14.2	15.5	12.9	8.8	11.4	D Reach to a very small object or where accurate grasp is required.
40	11.3	15.6	16.8	14.1	9.6	12.8	
45	12.1	17.0	18.2	15.3	10.4	14.2	
50	13.0	18.4	19.6	16.5	11.2	15.7	
55	13.9	19.8	20.9	17.8	12.0	17.1	
60	14.7	21.2	22.3	19.0	12.8	18.5	E Reach to indefinite location to get hand in position for body balance or next motion or out of way.
65	15.6	22.6	23.6	20.2	13.5	19.9	
70	16.5	24.1	25.0	21.4	14.3	21.4	
75	17.3	25.5	26.4	22.6	15.1	22.8	
80	18.2	26.9	27.7	23.9	15.9	24.2	

333

TABLE II – MOVE – M

| Distance (cm) | Time (tmu) | | | | Wt allowance | | | Case and description |
	A	B	C	Hand in motion B	Wt (kg) up to	Static constant (tmu)	Dynamic factor	
2 or less	2.0	2.0	2.0	1.7	1	0	1.00	
4	3.1	4.0	4.5	2.8				
6	4.1	5.0	5.8	3.1	2	1.6	1.04	A Move object against stop or to other hand.
8	5.1	5.9	6.9	3.7				
10	6.0	6.8	7.9	4.3				
					4	2.8	1.07	
12	6.9	7.7	8.8	4.9				
14	7.7	8.5	9.8	5.4				
16	8.3	9.2	10.5	6.0	6	4.3	1.12	
18	9.0	9.8	11.1	6.5				
20	9.6	10.5	11.7	7.1	8	5.8	1.17	
22	10.2	11.2	12.4	7.6	10	7.3	1.22	
24	10.8	11.8	13.0	8.2				
26	11.5	12.3	13.7	8.7				B Move object to approximate or indefinite location.
28	12.1	12.8	14.4	9.3	12	8.8	1.27	
30	12.7	13.3	15.1	9.8				
					14	10.4	1.32	
35	14.3	14.5	16.8	11.2				
40	15.8	15.6	18.5	12.6				
45	17.4	16.8	20.1	14.0	16	11.9	1.36	
50	19.0	18.0	21.8	15.4				
55	20.5	19.2	23.5	16.8	18	13.4	1.41	
60	22.1	20.4	25.2	18.2				C Move object to exact location.
65	23.6	21.6	26.9	19.5	20	14.9	1.46	
70	25.2	22.8	28.6	20.9				
75	26.7	24.0	30.3	22.3	22	16.4	1.51	
80	28.3	25.2	32.0	23.7				

TABLE IIIA – TURN – T

| Weight | Time (tmu) for degrees turned | | | | | | | | | | |
	30°	45°	60°	75°	90°	105°	120°	135°	150°	165°	180°
Small 0 to 1 kg	2.8	3.5	4.1	4.8	5.4	6.1	6.8	7.4	8.1	8.7	9.4
Medium 1 to 5 kg	4.4	5.5	6.5	7.5	8.5	9.6	10.6	11.6	12.7	13.7	14.8
Large 5.1 to 16 kg	8.4	10.5	12.3	14.4	16.2	18.3	20.4	22.2	24.3	26.1	28.2

TABLE IIIB – APPLY PRESSURE – AP

Full cycle			Components		
Symbol	tmu	Description	Symbol	tmu	Description
APA	10.6	AF + DM + RLF	AF	3.4	Apply force
			DM	4.2	Dwell, minimum
APB	16.2	APA + G2	RLF	3.0	Release force

TABLE IV – GRASP – G

Case	Time (tmu)	Description
1A	2.0	Pick Up Grasp—Small, medium or large object by itself, easily grasped.
1B	3.5	Very small object or object lying close against a flat surface.
1C1	7.3	Interference with grasp on bottom and one side of nearly cylindrical object. Diameter larger than 12 mm.
1C2	8.7	Interference with grasp on bottom and one side of nearly cylindrical object. Diameter 6 to 12 mm.
1C3	10.8	Interference with grasp on bottom and one side of nearly cylindrical object. Diameter less than 6 mm.
2	5.6	Regrasp.
3	5.6	Transfer Grasp.
4A	7.3	Object jumbled with other objects so search and select occur. Larger than $25 \times 25 \times 25$ mm.
4B	9.1	Object jumbled with other objects so search and select occur. $6 \times 6 \times 3$ mm. to $25 \times 25 \times 25$ mm.
4C	12.9	Object jumbled with other objects so search and select occur. Smaller than $6 \times 6 \times 3$ mm.
5	0	Contact, sliding or hook grasp.

335

TABLE V – POSITION* – P

Class of fit		Symmetry	Easy to handle	Difficult to handle
1 Loose	No pressure required	S	5.6	11.2
		SS	9.1	14.7
		NS	10.4	16.0
2 Close	Light pressure required	S	16.2	21.8
		SS	19.7	25.3
		NS	21.0	26.6
3 Exact	Heavy pressure required	S	43.0	48.6
		SS	46.5	52.1
		NS	47.8	53.4

* Distance moved to engage—max. 25 mm.

TABLE VI – RELEASE – RL

Case	Time (tmu)	Description
1	2.0	Normal release performed by opening fingers as independent motion.
2	0	Contact release

TABLE VII – DISENGAGE – D

Class of fit	Easy to handle	Difficult to handle
1 Loose—Very slight effort, blends with subsequent move.	4.0	5.7
2 Close—Normal effort, slight recoil.	7.5	11.8
3 Tight—Considerable effort, hand recoils markedly.	22.9	34.7

TABLE VIII – EYE TRAVEL AND EYE FOCUS – ET AND EF

Eye travel time $= 15.2 \times \dfrac{T}{D}$ tmu, with a maximum value of 20 tmu.

where T = the distance between points from and to which the eye travels.

D = the perpendicular distance from the eye to the line of travel T.

Eye focus time = 7.3 tmu.

TABLE IX – BODY, LEG AND FOOT MOTIONS

Description	Symbol	Distance	Time (tmu)
Foot motion—Hinged at ankle.	FM	Up to 10 cm.	8.5
With heavy pressure.	FMP		19.1
Leg or foreleg motion.	LM-	Up to 15 cm.	7.1
		Each add'l cm.	0.5
Sidestep—Case 1 - Complete when leading leg contacts floor.	SS-C1	Less than 30 cm.	Use REACH or MOVE time
		30 cm	17.0
		Each add'l cm.	0.2
Case 2 - Lagging leg must contact floor before next motion can be made.	SS-C2	Up to 30 cm	34.1
		Each add'l cm.	0.4
Bend, stoop, or kneel on one knee.	B.S. KOK		29.0
Arise.	AB.AS. AKOK		31.9
Kneel on floor—Both knees.	KBK		69.4
Arise.	AKBK		76.7
Sit.	SIT		34.7
Stand from sitting position.	STD		43.4
Turn body 45 to 90 degrees—			
Case 1 - Complete when leading leg contacts floor.	TBC1		18.6
Case 2 - Lagging leg must contact floor before next motion can be made.	TBC2		37.2
Walk.	W-M	Per metre	17.4
Walk.	W-P	Per pace	15.0
Walk—Obstructed.	W-PO	,, ,,	17.0

337

TABLE X – SIMULTANEOUS MOTIONS

REACH			MOVE			GRASP			POSITION			DISEN-GAGE		CASE	MOTION
A, E	B	C, D	A, Bm	B	C	G1A G2 G5	G1B G1C	G4	P1S	P1SS P2S	P1NS P2SS P2NS	D1E D1D	D2		
		*	*	*	*		*	*	**	**	**		**		
		W·O	W·O	W·O	W·O		W·O	W·O	E·D	E·D	E·D	E	E·D		
						X X			X X X					A, E	REACH
	X		X X ■			X X ■ X X X	■ ■ ■						X	B	
		X X ■ X ■ ■ ■				X ■ ■ ■ ■ ■ ■ ■ ■					X	■ ■		C, D	
								■ ■ ■				■ ■		A, Bm	MOVE
						X X ■ X X X	■ ■ ■						X	B	
				X ■		X ■ ■ ■ ■ ■ ■ ■ ■					X	■ ■		C	
								■ ■ ■				■ ■		G1A, G2, G5	GRASP
						■ ■ X ■ ■ ■ ■ ■ ■ ■ ■		■			■	■ ■		G1B, G1C	
						■ ■ ■ ■ ■ ■ ■ ■		■			■	■ ■		G4	
						X ■ ■ ■ ■ ■ ■		■			■	■ ■		P1S	POSITION
						■ ■ ■ ■		■			■	■ ■		P1SS, P2S	
						■ ■		■			■	■ ■		P1NS, P2SS, P2NS	
												X	X X		D1E, D1D	DISENGAGE
													X X		D2	

□ = EASY to perform simultaneously.

X = Can be performed simultaneously with PRACTICE.

■ = DIFFICULT to perform simultaneously even after long practice. Allow both times.

MOTIONS NOT INCLUDED IN ABOVE TABLE: TURN—Normally EASY with all motions except when TURN is controlled or with DISENGAGE.

APPLY PRESSURE | May be EASY, require PRACTICE, or DIFFICULT.
CRANK | Each case must be analysed.

POSITION—Class 3—Always DIFFICULT. DISENGAGE—Class 3—Normally DIFFICULT. RELEASE—Always EASY. DISENGAGE—Any class may be DIFFICULT if care must be exercised to avoid injury or damage to object.

*W = Within ⎰ the area of normal vision. i.e.: $r = 10$ cm
 O = Outside ⎱ $d = 40$ cm

**E = EASY to handle
  D = DIFFICULT to handle

Chapter 22
Standard data

Many operations in a given plant have several common elements. The element "walking", for example, is a component of many different jobs. Diverse activities such as painting, handling or working on a site invariably involve an element of "walking". When these activities are timed, the same common element is in fact timed again and again. The job of a work study man would therefore be made much easier if he had at his disposal a set of data from which he could readily derive standard times for these common work elements without necessarily going into the process of timing each one. If, for instance, a standard time could be derived for the particular element "walking" and could be read directly from a table, this would not only reduce effort and cost but also lead to greater consistency in time estimations.

One can therefore see that there is an advantage in building up a **standard data** bank for various elements which occur repeatedly at the workplace. If such data existed for a wide range of elements and were reliable, there would be no need to carry out a time study for a new job. Instead, by breaking down the job into elements and referring to the data bank to derive the normal times for each element, one could calculate the total time needed to perform this new job and determine its standard time by adding the appropriate allowances in the usual way.

1. Major considerations

It is, however, difficult to visualise a situation where all the possible elements making up any and every job could be timed and stored for future retrieval. We may therefore conclude that in practice it is better to **restrict the number of jobs** for which standard data are derived—normally to one or more departments in a plant, or to all the processes involved in manufacturing a certain product. In this way the coverage becomes more manageable.

The **reliability of the data** can be increased if as many common elements as possible that are performed in the same way are grouped together for analysis, and if a sufficient amount of accumulated or collected data on each element has been analysed by a trained studyman.

Reliability can be further increased by making sure that all the factors affecting a certain element have been taken into consideration. For example, the time taken to move a sheet of a given size will vary depending on whether it is a solid sheet (of metal, for instance) or a malleable one (of rubber, for instance). The weight will also be an important factor. The time taken to move an iron sheet will be different from the time taken to move one of foam or cardboard. Again, the thickness will affect the timing in each case. Consequently, the description of the element must be as precise as possible and the various factors affecting the timing (in this case, nature of material, thickness and weight) will also have to be indicated.

Another basic consideration concerns the **source of the time data.** Should this be observed time based on stop-watch readings (what might be called "macroscopic" timing systems) or "microscopic" systems such as predetermined time standards? The first alternative may be more acceptable to the factory personnel in certain cases, and is sometimes cheaper. However, for certain elements it is not always possible to have on record enough readings to enable reliable data to be derived. Several months or even a year or more may elapse before sufficient data are accumulated in this way. The choice of a microscopic system such as MTM may make for better coverage, but its use also depends on whether sufficient experience has been acquired in using the system and on its applicability. Even in this case, one has to decide whether to use detailed systems such as MTM-1 (which can be more precise but are expensive) or MTM-2 or MTM-3 (which are less expensive but less precise).

Again, standard data have to be built up with due regard to **users' needs.** They are indeed invaluable for a variety of purposes, among them production planning, cost estimation, incentive payments and budgetary control. However, the "level of confidence" in the developed data base which can be tolerated by those who use standard data for these purposes varies considerably: for example, the requirements for production planning allow for much greater potential deviation in the standards than the requirements for individual bonus schemes. Since one cannot produce a different set of data for each user, it is necessary to build a data system that produces the maximum benefit for each user at the same time.

2. Developing the standard data

The following steps should be taken to develop standard data:

1. **Decide on coverage.** As indicated above, the coverage should be restricted to one or more departments or work areas or to a limited range of processes within a plant (for example, those involved in manufacturing a specific product) in which several similar elements, performed by the same method, are involved in carrying out the jobs.

2. **Break the jobs into elements,** through job analysis. In this case try to identify as many elements as possible that are common to the various jobs. Let us assume, for example, that we have a worker in a fruit-packing plant who works at the end of the operation and whose job is to remove a carton of fruit from a conveyor belt, stencil the name of the customer on the carton and carry it to a nearby skid. Such an operation may be broken down into elements in various ways, but if the studyman proceeds as indicated below he may find that several of the component elements also occur elsewhere in the plant. The suggested breakdown is—

(a) lifting the carton from the conveyor and positioning it on the table;

(b) positioning a stencil on the carton;

(c) applying a 10 cm brush and tar to stencil the name and address of the client;

(d) lifting the carton;

(e) walking with the carton; and

(f) placing on the skid.

The elements "lifting and positioning of carton" and "walking with carton" may occur in various other jobs in the plant, although not necessarily in the same manner. Depending on the size and type of fruit, the carton may vary in size and weight. These are important considerations and will influence the time for these elements. Furthermore, in other parts of the operation the element "walking with carton" may recur but the distance covered during the walk may not be the same. These variations should not deter the work study man from collecting the necessary information for building up his standard data. This will become clear as we proceed with our step-by-step approach.

3. **Decide on type of reading,** i.e. whether you will use readings based on stop-watch time study (macroscopic systems) or derived from PTS systems such as MTM (microscopic systems). As explained earlier, the nature of the job and the cost of applying each system will be the major determining factors. If stop-watch time study is chosen, sufficient time must be allowed to collect the readings necessary to produce statistically reliable data.

4. **Determine the factors** that are likely to affect the time for each element, and classify them into major and minor factors. Let us take a simple example: the case of a worker walking. If the time for this activity is calculated, it will be found that there is always a variation in the readings. This is due to several factors, some major and others which may be considered minor. In this particular case the factors may be indicated as follows:

Activity

Restricted walking starting at dead point and ending at a dead stop.

Factors influencing the time

Major	*Minor*
Distance covered.	Physical make-up of worker.
	Temperature.
	Humidity.
	Lighting.
	External attraction.
	Variation due to time study man.

It is clear here that the time for walking will be affected mainly by the distance covered; nevertheless, other minor factors will exert a small influence as well, and these may cause slight variations from reading to reading.

5. When using macroscopic systems, **measure the time taken to perform the activity from actual observations.** Here the studyman can choose arbitrary distances and time the worker for each distance. If it is found that in most cases a worker walks either 10, 20, 30 or 40 metres, readings for these distances can be timed and entered in standard tables. However, this is rarely the case. A worker may walk any distance between 10 and 40 metres. The studyman will then find it more appropriate to draw a curve to indicate the relationship between time and distance covered. Let us proceed with our example of walking and assume that the readings reproduced in table 23 were recorded.

It is now possible to plot base time against distance. The curve using the line of best fit will appear as shown in figure 111. For greater accuracy one may also use the method of least squares to determine the slope and the line of best fit for the curve. From the curve it will now be possible to derive standard times for values lying anywhere between 10 and 40 metres. Occasionally the relationship between the two variables may be curvilinear rather than linear; in such cases logarithmic graph paper should be used.

Table 23.   Restricted walking

Distance (m) x	Actual time (min) a	Rating r	Base time (min) ($a \times r =$) t	Average (min) y
10	0.13	85	0.1105	
	0.13	90	0.1170	
	0.13	85	0.1105	
	0.11	95	0.1045	
	0.12	90	0.1080	
	0.15	80	0.1200	0.1118
20	0.21	105	0.2205	
	0.21	105	0.2205	
	0.22	95	0.2090	
	0.22	100	0.2200	
	0.26	80	0.2080	
	0.22	90	0.1980	0.2127
30	0.29	110	0.3190	
	0.30	100	0.3000	
	0.32	90	0.2880	
	0.30	100	0.3000	
	0.30	100	0.3000	
	0.33	95	0.3135	0.3034
40	0.38	110	0.4180	
	0.37	110	0.4070	
	0.38	110	0.4180	
	0.43	90	0.3870	
	0.42	90	0.3780	
	0.37	110	0.4070	0.4025

Figure 111. Restricted walking

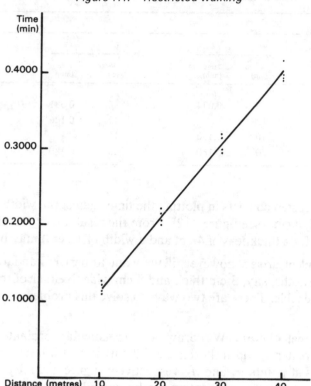

In several cases, however, the work study man may be faced with a problem where more than one major factor affects the time of operation. Let us therefore assume that we have a case where a motor-driven circular saw is used for cross-cutting wood (of the same type). When we analyse the major and minor factors as we did in the previous example, we may reach the following conclusions:

Activity

Cross-cutting wood of the same type by hand feed.

Factors influencing the time

Major	Minor
Variation in the thickness of the wood.	Physical make-up of worker.
	Temperature.
Variation in the width of the wood.	Humidity.
	Lighting.
	Method of holding wood.
	Degree of physical force applied.
	Machine in good working order.
	Experience of worker.

We are assuming here that we are dealing with skilled workers. After a period of time, it proves possible to calculate the base time for some, but not all, thicknesses and widths of wood. The results are shown in table 24.

343

Table 24. Base times for cross-cutting wood of varying width and thickness

Thickness (cm)							
2		4		6		8	
Width (cm)	Time (min)	Width (cm)	Time (min)	Width (cm)	Time (min)	Width (cm)	Time (min)
6	0.064	6	0.074	6	0.081	6	0.093
12	0.088	12		12	0.126	12	0.146
16	0.104	16	0.130	16		16	0.181
20	0.120	20	0.160	20	0.180	20	

The first step consists in plotting the time against the width of wood for each thickness (2, 4, 6, 8 cm) (see figure 112). From the resulting curves the missing values in the table (say, for a thickness of 4 cm and a width of 12 cm) may be derived.

A problem arises, however, if we want to derive standard times for other thicknesses and widths, say, 3 cm thick and 8 cm wide. Neither of these dimensions is represented in the table. There are two ways to solve this problem.

1. By **calculation.** We draw a perpendicular ordinate from the point representing the required width (in this case, 8 cm) and let it intercept the appropriate lines of thickness at points a_1 and a_2 respectively (figure 112). By "appropriate" we mean the thickness curves representing the lower and upper values on either side of the desired thickness. In our example, the required thickness is 3 cm; therefore the two appropriate curves are those representing a thickness of 2 and 4 cm.

We can then apply the following equation:

$$T = a_1 + (a_2 - a_1) f$$

where

T = time we wish to calculate;

a_1 = time at the thickness of 2 cm (lower limit curve) (in this case it is 0.072);

a_2 = time at the thickness of 4 cm (upper limit curve) (in this case it is 0.086);

f = a decimal fraction representing the required thickness in relation to a_2 and a_1 (in this case it is halfway between the two, or $f = 0.5$);

By applying the equation we obtain the following result:

$$T = 0.072 + 0.5 (0.086 - 0.072) = 0.079 \text{ min.}$$

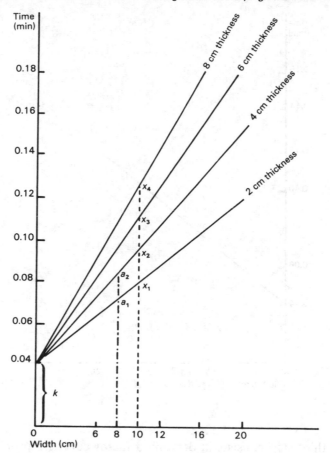

Figure 112.   Base times for cross-cutting wood of varying width and thickness

2. By **graphical factor comparison.** The first step in this method is to plot the four curves representing the various thicknesses of wood with width as the independent variable and time as the dependent variable (the curves shown in figure 112).

Looking again at table 24, we see that the data for width and time for the 2 cm thickness are complete, and that the points fit well on the curve drawn in figure 112 for that thickness. This curve is then reproduced separately and called a **base curve** (see figure 113).

For the second step, we go back to figure 112 and choose an arbitrary point representing the width anywhere between the values of 6 and 20 cm on the horizontal axis. Let us assume that we have selected a point representing 10 cm. From this point we draw a perpendicular ordinate which will intercept the four curves at points x, x_2, x_3 and x_4 respectively.

345

Figure 113. Base curve for cross-cutting wood of 2 cm thickness and of varying width

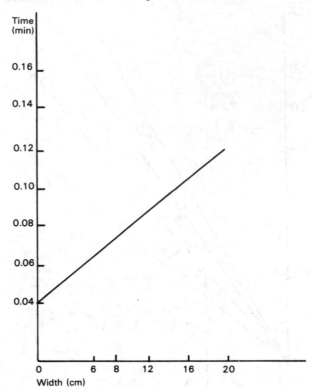

The third step consists in drawing a **factor curve** from points that may be calculated as follows:

Thickness:	2	4	6	8
Factor:	$\dfrac{x_1}{x_1} = 1$	$\dfrac{x_2}{x_1}$ or $\dfrac{96}{80} = 1.2$	$\dfrac{x_3}{x_1}$ or $\dfrac{112}{80} = 1.4$	$\dfrac{x_4}{x_1}$ or $\dfrac{128}{80} = 1.6$

From these figures it is now possible to plot the factor curve (figure 114). The time can now be readily calculated from both the base curve and the factor curve, using the following equation:

$$\text{total time} = \text{base time} \times \text{factor}$$

to calculate the time needed for cutting a piece of wood 8 cm wide by 3 cm thick:

$$T = 0.072 \times 1.1 = 0.079 \text{ min.}$$

In this case, the time needed for a width of 8 cm (read from the base curve) is multiplied by the factor for a thickness of 3 cm (read from the factor curve).

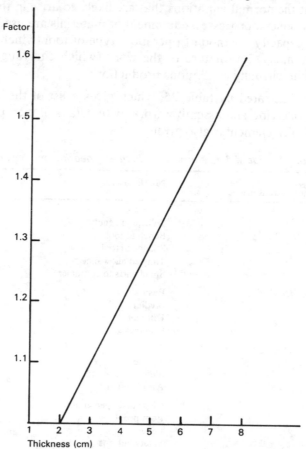

It can be seen, therefore, that the data required to derive standard times can be obtained from either tables or graphs. To these data the work study man can then add any allowances in the usual way. If a firm decides that the same allowance factor is applicable to every job in a given class of work, it can then express its standard data in terms of the standard time for each element, instead of using the normal times as we did.

A word of caution is necessary here. The data collected usually cover a certain range of readings. It is not advisable to extrapolate these data for values that fall outside this range. For example, in our previous example the readings covered pieces of wood ranging from 6 to 20 cm wide and from 2 to 8 cm thick. We know what happens within this range; but there is no way of knowing whether the same type of linear relationship will continue if we go beyond this range by exceeding the widths and thicknesses actually studied and by projecting our curves beyond the points for which we have time study data.

3. Use of PTS systems to develop standard data

The method used for developing standard data outlined above assumed that the work study man based his calculations on data derived from stop-watch time study. As was mentioned earlier, standard data may also be developed from PTS

347

systems such as MTM or Work Factor. In this case the data derived for each element take into account the normal variations that are likely to arise in the execution of the job when other products, processes, equipment or materials are used. These variations result from size, capacity, method of operation, type of tool (which may be simple or elaborate, few or many) and nature of the work (which can range from jobbing or small batch work to virtually continuous production).

This is illustrated by table 25, which gives a list of the most common elements in light engineering and assembly work, with details of their possible variations. The definition of each element is also given.

Table 25. Standard data elements in light engineering and assembly work

General elements (can be used in several departments)	Possible variations	Code
GET	Stillage to bench	GSB
	Bench to tool	GBT
	Stillage to tool	GST
	Tangled allowance	GTA
	Small parts to container	GSP
POSITION IN TOOL	Easy	PE
	Medium	PM
	Difficult	PD
	Complex	PC
CLAMP AND UNCLAMP	Fingers	CF
	Toggle	CT
	Slide	CS
	Air-operated	CA
OPERATE	Close and open guard	OCG
	Foot pedal	OP
	Lever	OL
	Safety buttons	OSB
	Flypress	OFP
	Machine type	OMT
REMOVE FROM TOOL	Automatic	RA
	Easy	RE
	Medium	RM
	Difficult	RD
	Complex	RC
	Lever out component	RLC
TURN (IN) TOOL	Turn in tool	TIT
	Turn tool	TT
ASIDE	Automatic	AA
	Tool to bench	ATB
	Bench to stillage	ABS
	Tool to stillage	ATS
MISCELLANEOUS	Count parts	MCP
	Mark or score parts	MSP
	Work area to tool	WAT
INSPECT OR CHECK	Component in fixture or gauge	CCF

Element Definitions

GET — Covers picking up and moving an object, or handful of objects, to a destination.

POSITION IN TOOL — Covers positioning an object, or handful of objects, in a tool fixture, etc.; or between electrodes.

CLAMP AND UNCLAMP	Covers all the motions necessary to close and *later* open a clamp of the type that operates by *pressure* on the object held; or to hold an object in a tool or fixture, by a clamping action of the fingers.
OPERATE	Covers all the time and all the manual motions necessary to—

— close and later open a guard (OCG);
— grasp or contact an operating control, and *later* return the hand to the working area, or the foot to the ground;
— operate the controls and initiate the machine cycle (OMT).

REMOVE FROM TOOL	Covers removing an object from a tool, fixture, etc.; or a part, component or fixture from under a drill; or from between electrodes.
TURN (IN) TOOL	Occurs when two "Operate" elements follow each other, *and* the object must be removed from the tool, turned, and repositioned in the tool; *or* the fixture or jig must be turned or moved, in or under the tool.
ASIDE	Covers moving and putting down an object or handful of objects, already held.

Word Definitions

Object	Any object handled; such as parts, hand-tools, sub-assemblies or completed articles. Also, any jig, fixture or other holding device.
Handful	The optimum number of objects which can be conveniently picked up, moved and placed as required.
Bench	The term "bench" includes any table, tote pan or other storage area, convenient to the tool or workplace.
Stillage	A storage box or container on legs, for moving by a hand-lifting or fork-lift truck. The term "stillage" includes a pallet, the floor or any other storage device at floor level.
Tool	A general term to cover any fixture, jig, electrode, press or other tool used to hold or operate on an object or objects.
	One tool can be positioned in another—for example, a parts-holding fixture under a drill or a welding electrode.

Figure 115 illustrates a typical operation in a light engineering plant. Many operations, including the one shown here, contain one or other of the following sequences of elements (note that other sequences are also possible):

(a) get material; position in tool; operate machine; remove part; aside; or

(b) get material; position in tool; position fixture in machine; operate machine; remove fixture; remove part; aside.

In figure 116, sequence *(a)* is shown as applied in power press work, and in figure 117 the element *TRANSPORT* has been further analysed and the distances indicated.

To develop standard data from a PTS system, each sequence of elements is now analysed, using MTM-2, for example. It is also possible to build up from MTM-2 and other PTS systems a **data bank** for certain standard operations, with their possible variations. Standard data developed in this way may be presented either as a table (as in figure 118) or algorithmically (as in figure 119). Figure 120 reproduces a form which can then be used to record the time for a particular activity using data derived from either figure 118 or figure 119.

349

Figure 115. Sequence of elements

(a)

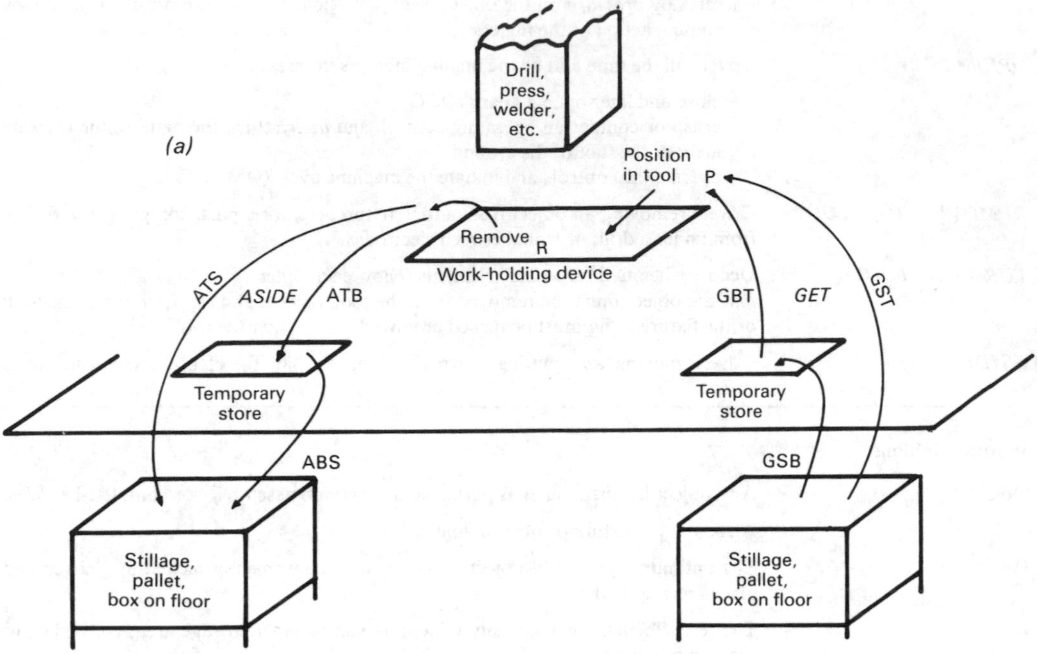

(b)

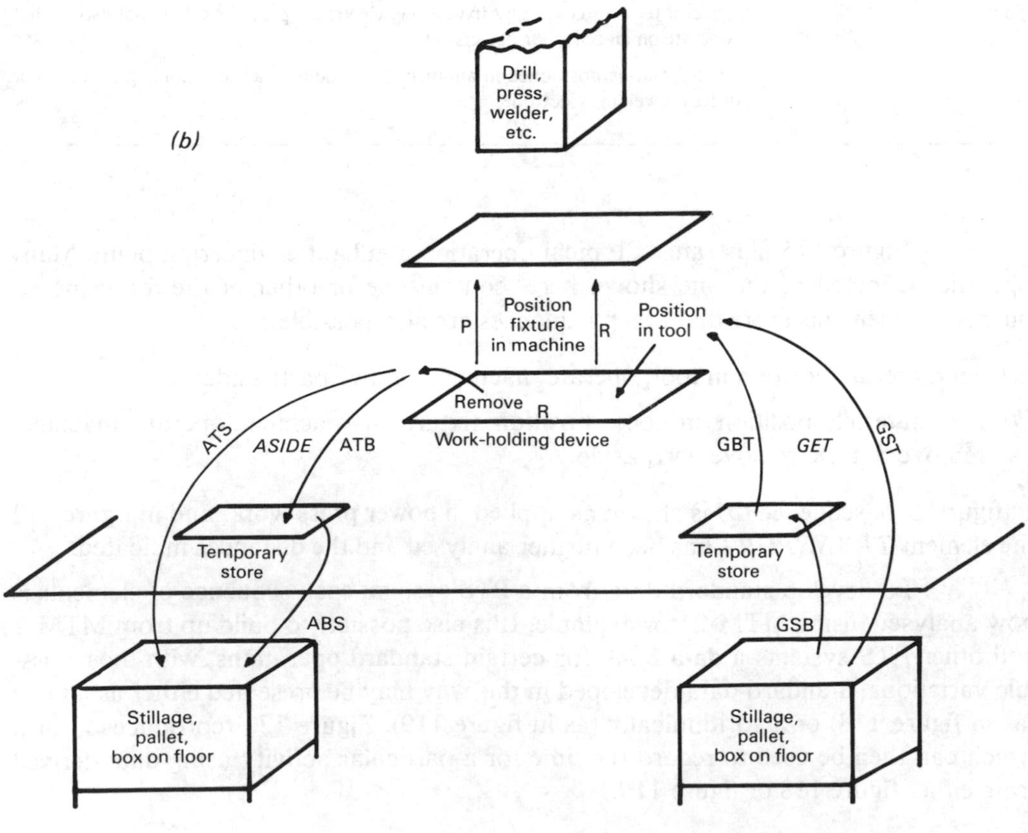

Figure 116. Basic elements of power press work

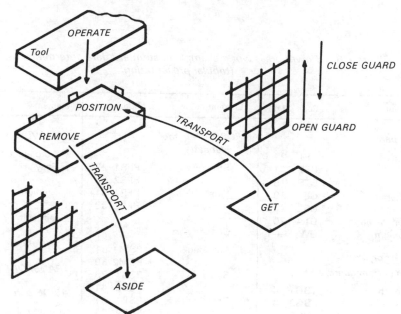

Figure 117. Power press work: example of TRANSPORT elements and distances

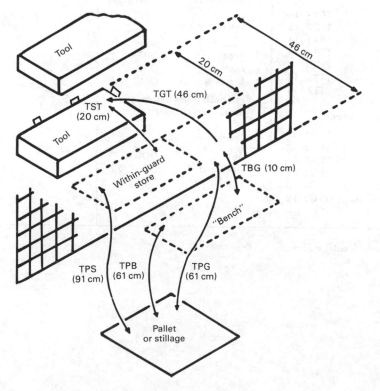

Figure 118.   Power press work: example of standard data determined by MTM-2 (tabular presentation)

Element	Code	tmu	Element	Code	tmu	Element	Code	tmu
GET part			*POSITION in tool*			*REMOVE from tool*		
			Flat part			Auto eject	RA-	0
Flat	GF1	21	Stops	PFS1	27	Easy	RE1	17
	GF2	31		PFS2	30		RE2	17
Use tool	GTS	15	Pins	PFP1	31	Medium	RM1	36
Shaped	GS1	19		PFP2	33		RM2	52
	GS2	28				Difficult	RD1	50
Tangle, add	GTA	20	*Shaped part*				RD2	50
Weight	GW	—	Moulded	PSM1	31	*Weight*	GW	—
				PSM2	39			
TRANSPORT			Stops	PSS1	38	*TRANSPORT* (as above)		
To or from guard, and				PSS2	41			
Bench	TBG1	4	Pins	PSP1	31	*ASIDE part*		
	TBG2	4		PSP2	35	Auto aside	AA-	0
Pallet,	TPG1	18	*Weight*	PW	—	Throw	AT1	7
etc.	TPG2	18					AT2	7
Tool	TGT1	18	*OPERATE PRESS*			Lay aside	AL1	10
	TGT2	18	*Close guard*				AL2	10
Bend, add	TB-	61	Auto	OCGA	0	Stack aside	AS1	11
Step, add	TS-	18	One hand	OCG1	21		AS2	19
			Two hands	OCG2	30	*Weight*	—	—
To or from tool and								
Guard	TGT1	18	*Operate press*					
	TGT2	18	Auto	OPA	*			
Store	TST1	11	Foot	OPF	*			
	TST2	11	Buttons	OPB	*			
Hand	THT1	4	Machine cycle	OMC	*			
2nd tool	TTT1	14	* For each press use machine					
	TTT2	14	data or time study					
To or from pallet and			*Open guard*					
Bench	TPB1	32	Auto	OOGA	0			
	TPB2	32	One hand	OOG1	22			
Store	TPS1	42	Two hands	OOG2	31			
	TPS2	42						
Guard	TPG1	18						
	TPG2	18						
Weight	PW	—						

Note: Last character in code indicates: 1 — One-handed
2 — Two-handed

Figure 119. Power press work: example of standard data determined by MIM-2 (algorithmic presentation)

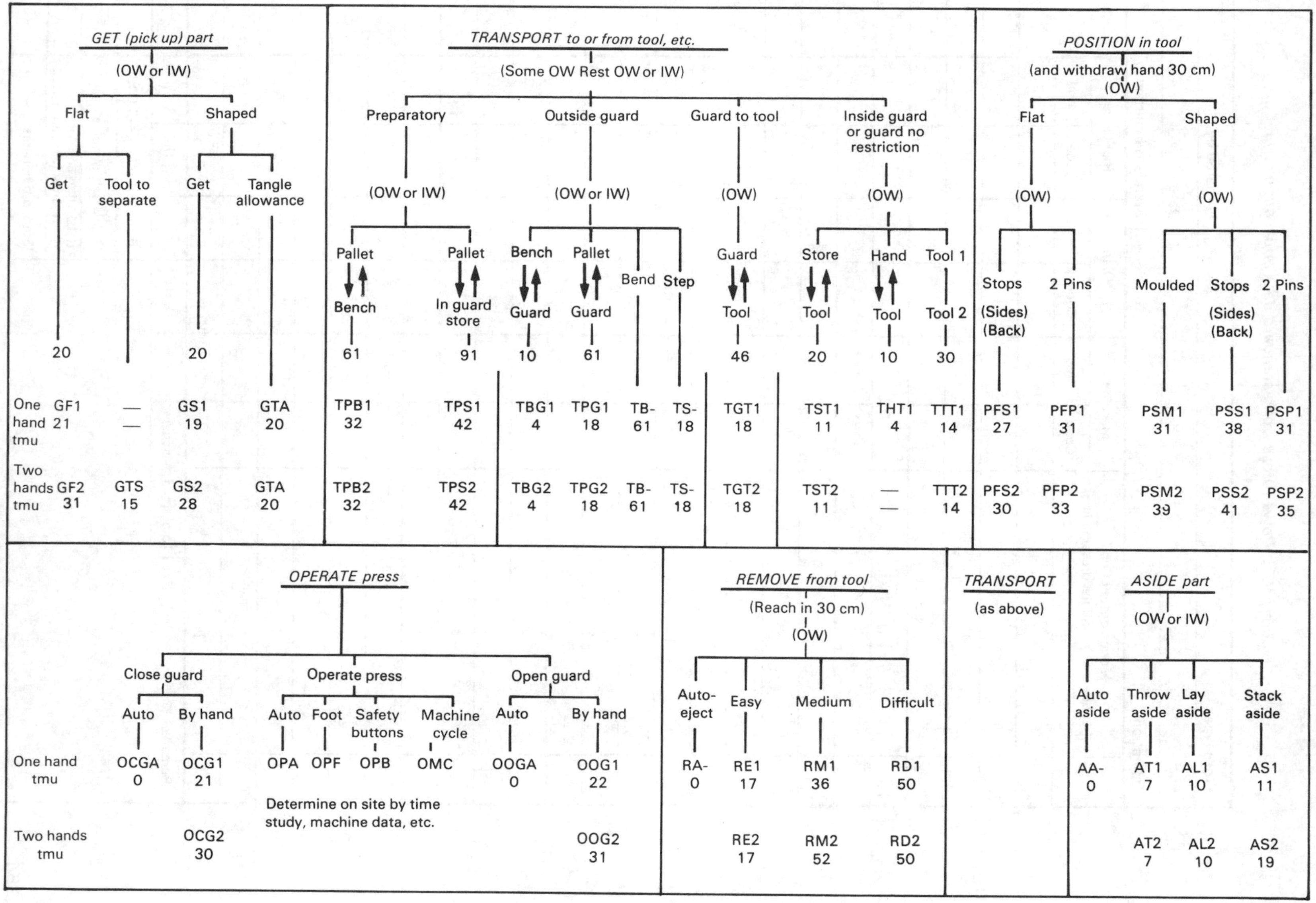

Figure 120.   Power press work: standard data application form

Press type:							Prepared by:	
Part:							Date:	
Operation:							Standard minutes:	

Seq. no.	Motion description (Simultaneous motions on same line)	Machine		Left hand		Right hand		Charge
		Code	tmu	Code	tmu	Code	tmu	tmu

Remarks		Total tmu	Machine		L.H.		R.H.	
			Basic minutes ($\div$ 2,000)					
			Total basic minutes					
			Relaxation and contingency allowance (%)					
			Standard minutes					

4. Use of computing equipment to calculate time standards

It is evident that the design and the development of standard data and time study in general involve a great deal of calculation. Computing equipment is now being used more and more to make the task easier. In particular, mini-computers and small programmable calculators (see figures 121, 122 and 123) have proved invaluable and have brought about considerable savings. Several programmes have been developed for use with these calculators, for instance for time study analysis, for system error and control and for the control of drift.

In a typical case using a "Time Study Analysis Programme", the first and most time-consuming step consists, as usual, in multiplying each observed time by the relevant rating (see figure 124). The programme now produces a histogram of observations for each of the three elements in figure 124. This is probably the most important feature of the programme, as it enables the work study man to see whether the element he has selected is, for example, normally distributed (as is the case for element 1—see figure 125); or skewed (as for element 2—see figure 126), in which case more readings may be needed; or bimodal (as for element 3—see figure 127), which shows that the element has been incorrectly selected and that new break points must be selected as two activities appear to overlap. The calculator automatically produces the highest value of the histogram, its lowest value, and the intervals and the frequency of each column.

When the basic and standard times have been calculated for each element, the calculator produces various items of information to help to determine whether the study is reliable. First, the **total standard time** for all the elements is calculated as well as the **total effective time.** Second, after the **total ineffective time** and **check times** are entered, the programmed calculator produces the **total recorded time.** Third, it compares this with the **total elapsed time** to give the **percentage error,** and calculates the **number per standard hour.** The definition of all these terms is given in table 26. Figure 128 shows this sequence of calculation as computed by the calculator. By reading the percentage error, the work study man can then decide whether to accept or reject the study.

It can be seen that programmes such as the one described above permit the calculation of a wide range of values in a very short time. The programmes are supplied on magnetic cards or magnetic cassettes with a complete listing and with operating instructions. Consequently, they can be used with a minimum of instruction.

Figure 121. *A small hand-held programmable calculator, the Hewlett-Packard 67, showing the programme cards. Similar machines are available from several other manufacturers*

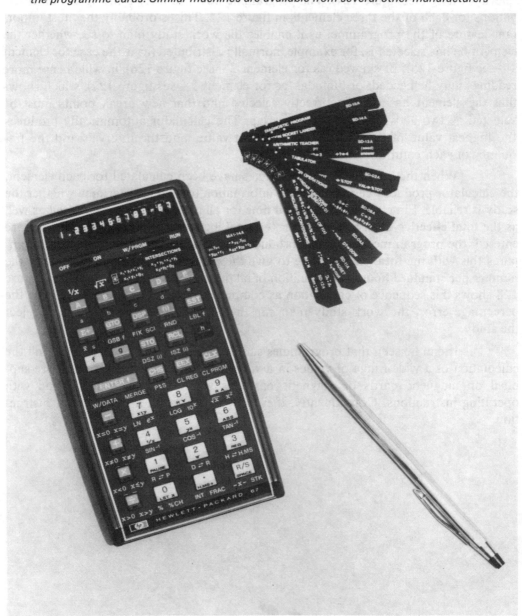

Figure 122. A small programmable calculator, the Hewlett-Packard 97, providing a printed output. Similar machines are available from several other manufacturers

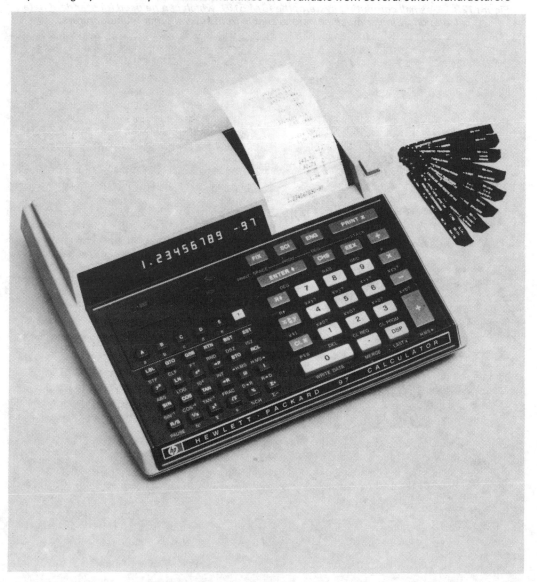

Figure 123.   A small computing system, the IBM 5110, which can be used for standard data calculations. Similar machines are available from several other manufacturers

Figure 124.   Time study analysis programme

OBSERVED DATA - ELEMENT 1

Watch reading (centiminutes[1])	20.50	1.00	8.50	12.40	12.50	2.50	4.00	6.00	8.80
Rating 0-100	75	100	95	85	100	120	110	115	85
Watch reading (centiminutes)	10.40	15.70	7.60	7.20	6.40	15.30	8.80	5.20	8.40
Rating 0-100	95	75	65	100	75	75	95	105	110
Watch reading (centiminutes)	9.00	10.50	9.90	9.40	10.80	14.90	6.60		
Rating 0-100	65	85	110	75	85	65	110		

OBSERVED DATA - ELEMENT 2

Watch reading (centiminutes)	20.80	1.00	14.60	2.91	4.30	7.10	13.00	13.10	6.92
Rating 0-100	75	100	95	110	120	100	75	95	65
Watch reading (centiminutes)	13.60	9.52	7.70	8.42	8.46	7.56	3.78	10.20	10.94
Rating 0-100	85	105	100	95	65	75	95	100	95
Watch reading (centiminutes)	8.52	8.47	6.50	5.16	5.18				
Rating 0-100	95	105	100	120	110				

OBSERVED DATA - ELEMENT 3

Watch reading (centiminutes)	26.10	1.00	3.36	16.30	3.42	9.50	6.00	5.42	14.80
Rating 0-100	65	100	95	80	105	100	120	70	75
Watch reading (centiminutes)	14.60	17.20	21.60	5.10	14.20	17.00	13.30	5.57	8.90
Rating 0-100	95	70	65	100	100	90	60	95	100
Watch reading (centiminutes)	6.00	6.10	5.90						
Rating 0-100	90	100	110						

[1] 1 centiminute = $^1/_{100}$th minute.

Figure 125.   Time study analysis programme for element 1

```
AUTO START
ENTER FILE NO.
TIME STUDY
PROGRAM
XXXXXXXXXXXXXXXX           7.200
DO YOU WANT TO              100
ENTER-                      0.072
2)TIME(CMS) R/S
  RATING R/S
1)BASIC(CMS) R/S           0.400
XXXXXXXXXXXXXXXX            75
ELEMENT       1            0.048

     20.500                15.300
        75                    75
     0.154                 0.115

      1.000                 8.800
       100                    95
      0.010                 0.084

      8.500                 5.200
        95                   105
      0.081                 0.055

     12.400                 8.400
        85                   110
      0.105                 0.092

     12.500                 9.000
       100                    65
      0.125                 0.059

      2.500                10.500
       120                    85
      0.030                 0.089

      4.000                 9.900
       110                   110
      0.044                 0.109

      6.000                 9.400
       115                    75
      0.069                 0.071

      8.800                10.800
        85                    85
      0.075                 0.092

     10.400                14.900
        95                    65
      0.099                 0.097

     15.700                 6.600
        75                   110
      0.118                 0.073

      7.600         ENTER
        65          1 ERRORS
      0.049         0 NONE
```

Histogram shows
normal distribution
for this element

↓

```
----------------------------
+X
+XX
+XXXX
+XXXXXX
+XXXXXX
+XXXX
+X
+X
OS 5%
BT=            0.080

FRQ2
                 1
                 1
REST ALLOW
                12
OTHER ALLOW
                 3
STD TIME=   0.093

MORE ELEMENTS
1 YES
2 NO
```

↑

The standard time for
the element is automatically
determined from basic time,
relaxation and other allowances.

Figure 126.   Time study analysis programme for element 2

```
XXXXXXXXXXXXXXX
ELEMENT         2

    22.800
       75
     0.171

     1.000
      100
     0.010

    14.600                         10.200
       95                            100
     0.139                          0.102

     2.910                         10.940
      110                            95
     0.032                          0.104

     4.300                          8.520
      120                            95
     0.052                          0.081

     7.100                          8.470
      100                            105
     0.071                          0.089

    13.000                          6.500
       75                            105
     0.098                          0.068

    13.100                          5.160
       95                            120
     0.124                          0.062

     6.920                          5.180
       65                            110
     0.045                          0.057

    13.600             ENTER
       85              1 ERRORS
     0.116             0 NONE
                       -----------------
     9.520             +X
      105              +XXX
     0.100             +XXXXXX
                       +XXXXX
     7.700             +XXXX
      100              +XX
     0.077             +X
                       +X
     8.420             OS 5%
       95              BT=          0.079
     0.080
                       FRQ2
     8.460                          1
       65                           1
     0.055             REST ALLOW
                                    12
     7.060             OTHER ALLOW
       75                           3
     0.053             STD TIME=  0.091

     3.780             MORE ELEMENTS
       95              1 YES
     0.036             2 NO
```

← The histogram
    shows the data
    to be slightly
    skewed.

    More observations
    may be needed.

361

Figure 127.   Time study analysis programme for element 3

```
ELEMENT              X
                     3
      26.100
          65
       0.170

       1.900
         100
       0.010

       3.360                         13.300
          95                            60
       0.032                         0.080

                                      5.570
      16.300                             95
          80                          0.053
       0.130
                                      8.900
       3.420                            100
         105                          0.089
       0.036
                                      6.000
       9.500                             90
         100                          0.054
       0.095
                                      6.100
       6.000                            100
         120                          0.061
       0.072
                                      5.900
       5.420                            110
          70                          0.065
       0.038
                              ENTER
      14.800                  1 ERRORS
          75                  0 NONE
       0.111                  ----------------
                              +X
      14.600                  +XXX
          95                  +XXXXX
       0.139                  +XXX
                              +X
      17.200                  +XXX
          70                  +XXXX
       0.120                  +X
                              DUAL MAX
      21.600                  OS 5%
          65                  BT=           0.086
       0.140
                              FRQ2
       5.100                              1
         100                              3
       0.051                  REST ALLOW
                                          12
      14.200                  OTHER ALLOW
         100                              3
       0.142                  STD TIME=   0.033

      17.000                  MORE ELEMENTS
          70                  1 YES
       0.119                  2 NO
```

This element has been incorrectly selected resulting in a bimodal distribution.

New break points for the element need to be selected. This could not have been detected if the normal practice of finding the arithmetical average of observed data had been carried out.

*Figure 128.   Time study analysis programme calculating various
time factors and percentage errors*

```
XXXXXXXXXXXXXXX
TOT STD MIN
          0.217

EFF TIME=  6.529
INEFF TIME?
          0.125
          0.146
          0.255
          0.178
          0.198
TOT       0.902
CHK TIME?
          1.250
          2.690
TOT       3.940
TOT REC TIME=
          11.371
START FIN ?
          12.12
          12.12

          12.12
          12.00

ELAPSED TIME=
          12.00
ERROR=        5%
NO./STD HOUR=
          276.16
```

*Table 26.   Definition of terms, time study analysis programme
(from B.S. 3138/1959)*

Term	Definition
CHECK TIME	The time intervals between the start of a time study and the start of the first element (TEBS: "time elapsed before starting") and the finish of the last element and the finish of the study (TEAF: "time elapsed after finishing").
SELECTED BASIC TIME	The basic time chosen as being representative of a group of times for an element or combination of elements.
EFFECTIVE TIME	That portion of the elapsed time, excluding the check time, during which the worker is engaged in the proper performance of a prescribed job.
INEFFECTIVE TIME	That portion of the elapsed time, excluding the check time, spent on any activity which is not a specified part of the job.
ELAPSED TIME	The total time from start to finish of a time study.
UNACCOUNTED TIME	The difference between the elapsed time and the sum of the separate times, including check times, recorded during a time study.
PERCENTAGE ERROR	The difference between the elapsed time and the recorded time, expressed as a percentage of the elapsed time.

363

Chapter 23
The use
of time standards

1. Define the work covered by the time standards

When the studywork has been completed, it is important that a detailed record be made of the methods, tools and equipment used and of every feature of the operations which could possibly have a bearing on the time. This is necessary because changes in the work content of an operation affecting the time will also affect planning and costing; it is doubly important where the time standard is to be used in setting rates of pay under an incentive scheme. It is a cardinal principle of all sound incentive schemes based on time study that the time standards set should not be changed except when the work content of the job is changed, when there is a change in the organisation of the work, or to correct a clerical error.[1]

When time standards are to be used as the basis for an incentive scheme, it is usual to prepare two documents to describe and define completely the way in which time standards are compiled and the working conditions to which the standards refer. These two documents are known respectively as the **technical set-up** and the **work specification.**

The technical set-up is essentially a work study document, having no reference to rates of pay, control of workers or other matters of contract between employers and employees. It shows in summary form, in suitably presented tables and graphs, the main results of the studywork undertaken in the section and how all the time standards which have been set have been derived. It contains all the information necessary to calculate fresh time standards, should the jobs or the working conditions change, in so far as these fresh standards can be compiled from the studywork already undertaken. It is thus in effect a manual from which time standards can be built up.

It will be necessary to compile a separate set-up for each technically different section of an enterprise, since the methods by which time standards are compiled will differ from section to section. Thus in a vitreous enamelling shop there would probably be one set-up for the sprayers, another for the operators of the shot-blast machines, a third for the furnacemen, and so on.

Summaries of all the data on which the technical set-up is based should be attached to it, including—

---

[1] ILO: *Payment by results*, op. cit., p. 183.

flow process charts showing the improved methods developed;

analysis of studies sheets;

relaxation allowance calculation sheets;

data from predetermined time standards (PTS);

curves and graphs relating to standard data.

The greatest care should be taken of the technical set-up and of all the original documents attached to it, since they are essential evidence in any disputes which may arise. They are also of great value in compiling time standards for similar work in the future. Technical set-ups are normally filed in the work study department, where they are available to the management or to the workers' representatives whenever they may be needed.

2. The work specification

> **A work specification is a document setting out the details of an operation or job, how it is to be performed, the layout of the workplace, particulars of machines, tools and appliances to be used, and the duties and responsibilities of the worker. The standard time or allowed time assigned to the job is normally included**

The work specification thus represents the basic data on which the contract between employer and employee for the operation of an incentive scheme rests.

The amount of detail necessary in a work specification varies greatly according to the nature of the operation concerned. In machine shop work in the engineering industry, where a large number of different jobs are done on machines whose methods of operation are broadly similar, general conditions governing all jobs can be established for the whole shop and only variations in detail need be specifically recorded.

On the other hand, where an operation involves a whole shop or department and will run for an indefinite period substantially unchanged, as is the case in parts of the textile industry, the work specification may be lengthy and detailed. For instance, the work specification for draw-frame tenting in one spinning mill is 18 pages long and includes specifications for the alternatives of cotton or artificial fibre.

Generally speaking, the following points should be covered by a work specification, which should, of course, embrace the standard method laid down as a result of the method study:

A.   **Details of the workpieces or products, including—**

drawing, specification or product number and title;
material specification;
sketch, where necessary, of parts or surfaces to be treated.

366

B.   **Details of the machine or plant on which the operation is performed, including—**

make, size or type, plant register number;
speeds and feeds, pulley sizes or other equivalent data;
jigs, tools and fixtures;
other equipment;
sketch of workplace layout (where not available on the method study).

C.   **Operation number and general description of the work covered.**

D.   **Quality standards, including—**

quality grade;
finish and/or tolerances, where applicable;
checking and gauging requirements, gauges and other inspection apparatus;
frequency of inspection.

E.   **Grade and sex of labour, including—**

direct and indirect labour;
part-time assistance by inspectors or supervisors.

F.   **Detailed description of all work involved, including—**

repetitive elements, constant and variable;
occasional elements;
indirect work: setting up and breaking down;
cleaning, greasing, etc., and frequency with which such operations are carried out.

G.   **Details of time standards, including—**

standard time for each element, job or operation, as appropriate;
allowed time for all indirect work, with a note on how it has been assessed;
percentage relaxation allowance included in each element time;
other allowances.

H.   **Clerical procedure to be carried out by operatives in recording output and booking waiting time.**

I.   **Conditions under which the time standard is issued, and any special provisos.**

It may be necessary to supply copies of the work specification to the management and to the departmental and shop supervisors and, in the case of specifications affecting a large number of workers, to the workers' representatives.

The manner in which the time standards are made known to the operatives depends largely on the nature of the work. If the job is one that is done only by a single worker (the one who was timed), it is usually enough for the work study man to tell him personally, in the first instance. When work study has been accepted, workers do not usually want lengthy explanations: what they are interested in are the targets at which they must aim in order to earn a reasonable bonus. Time standards are likely to be better understood if they are put in the form: "You will need to do 12 pieces an hour for time-and-a-third", or "17 hanks a shift for time-and-a-third" than in the form: "13 standard minutes per piece". If anything appears to be wrong with the time standard, further details will very soon be sought. If a whole shop is on the same type of work, as is often the case in certain process industries, including textile spinning, summaries of time standards should be posted on the notice boards in the department. It may also be desirable to read relevant parts of the work specification at a departmental meeting. This will have to be done where most of the people affected by the time standards are illiterate. In batch production the standard time is generally written or printed on the work ticket, job card or process layout.

3. The standard unit of work

Standard times are generally set down in the following forms:

x minutes per piece;

y minutes per 100 (or per 1,000) pieces; or

z minutes per ton, metre, square metre, etc.

They are sometimes calculated or translated into hours. These time values represent the output at standard performance, that is, at 100 rating.

The minutes or hours allowed for any given job are not minutes or hours of continuous work. Each unit of time contains within it an element of relaxation.

The proportions of relaxation and work will vary according to the heaviness of the work. In extremely heavy, hot work such as furnace tending, the proportion of relaxation may be 50 per cent or more.

Since the standard minute is a measure of output it can be used in measuring and comparing productivity, which may be represented by the ratio—

$$\text{Performance} = \frac{\textbf{output of work in standard minutes}}{\textbf{input of labour time or machine time in clock minutes}} \times 100$$

A particular advantage of the standard minute is that it can be used to measure and compare outputs in dissimilar types of work, the accuracy of the comparison being limited by the consistency of the time standards.

4. Production planning and the utilisation of plant and labour

One of the causes of ineffective time due to management shortcomings mentioned in Chapter 3 is failing to plan the flow of work and of orders, with the result that one order does not immediately follow on another and plant and labour are not continuously employed.

In order to plan a programme of work effectively, it is necessary to know precisely—

1. What is to be made or done.

2. The quantity involved.

3. What operations are necessary to carry out the work.

4. What plant, equipment and tools are needed.

5. What types of labour are needed.

6. How long each operation may be expected to take.

7. How much plant and equipment of the types necessary are available.

8. How much labour of the types necessary is available.

The information on items 1 and 2 is generally supplied by the sales office or commercial department.

The information for determining items 3, 4 and 5 is supplied by process planning and **method study.**

The information on item 6 is supplied by **work measurement.**

The information on item 7 is supplied from plant department records or those of the department concerned.

The information on item 8 is supplied from personnel office records or those of the department concerned.

Once this information is available, it is a matter of simple arithmetic to match the requirements with the available capacity. Both the requirements and the capacity available to fulfil them must be stated in terms of time.

Requirements will be stated as—

number of operations of each type to be performed × expected time for each operation.

This must be matched against the total time available on each type of plant and with each type of labour necessary to perform the operations.

When a programme is being planned, only the actual times which the operations may be expected to take are of interest. These will depend, among other things, on whether the general conditions in the plant—including the state of labour-management relations and the system of remuneration in use—are such that the workers are working at their best rate. Where this is the case and the work study application has had time to settle down, these times should be those of the average performance of the shop or department as given by the production records over a period. This may even apply to an individual machine or process. It is the only realistic basis for such calculations. The times are arrived at by multiplying the standard times by

$$\frac{100}{\text{Average performance}}$$

The plant and labour capacity available is expressed in "man-minutes" or "machine-minutes", due regard being paid to any time it is necessary to allot for cleaning, setting up, dismantling, change-overs, repairs, etc.

369

The matching of production or operational requirements to capacity in this way makes it possible to—

(a) show whether there is an insufficiency of any type of plant or labour likely to hold up the programme or cause bottlenecks in the course of production and, if so, its extent;

(b) show whether there is an excess of capacity in any type of plant or labour and its extent;

(c) give accurate estimates of delivery dates.

If the management can have such information, compiled from realistic standards of performance, available well before production is due to start, it can take steps to prevent hold-ups from occurring. Alternatively, it can start looking for work to fill up spare capacity. Without such standards it has no sure basis for doing either of those things.

5. Estimating production costs

The success or failure of a firm in a competitive market may depend on the accuracy with which it is able to price its products. Unless the manufacturing time of the product is accurately known, the labour cost cannot be estimated, and many indirect costs dependent on time—such as plant depreciation, fuel and power consumption, rent, and the salaries of staff and supervision—cannot be accurately determined.

If the management can rely on the accuracy of the costing, economic prices can be fixed. If these are below those of the firm's competitors, the management can be happy in the knowledge that it is underselling them in safety; if they are above, the cutting of costs can be undertaken with more assurance than would otherwise be the case and with a knowledge of the margins available to be cut.

Standard and actual labour costs per 100 or per 1,000 standard minutes of production are frequently calculated each week from the weekly control statements. Since the actual labour cost per 100 standard minutes takes into account both direct and indirect labour costs, it is the more useful figure to use for estimating production costs.

6. Standard costing and budgetary control

Work measurement provides the basic information for setting standards of labour costs and the means of controlling them. These standards can also be used as the basis of the labour budgets for **budgetary control;** they provide certain elements of the information necessary for the production and indirect expense budgets and, related to the sales budget, indicate the plant and labour capacity likely to be available over the period of the budget.

Besides providing the standards, work measurement also provides, accurately, the actual performance figures. The need for such accurate standards cannot be overstressed. The absence of complete cost information is at the root of much bad management and of many failures of industrial enterprises. Labour costs will, as usual, be based on standard times, with appropriate provision being made for deviations from standard performance.

370

7. Incentive schemes

Direct incentive schemes based on output do not necessarily follow on an application of work measurement. There are many enterprises where time studies are made but direct incentives are not employed. One of the reasons why a good deal of attention has been paid in previous chapters to features of time study particularly related to its use in connection with incentives is that no discussion of time study would be complete without them; moreover, in practice the installation of an incentive scheme is generally one of the principal objects of a time study application.

The merits of work measurement as a basis for incentive schemes lie in several features inherent in the techniques, namely—

(1) The times are based on direct observation and on recording by the most accurate practicable means.

(2) Enough observations are taken of all elements of work, both repetitive and occasional, to ensure that the times finally selected to make up the standard time are truly representative and that random occurrences are taken into account.

(3) Full records are made and retained so as to be available for examination by either management or workers, should the occasion arise.

(4) The recorded times and associated data give a factual basis to any management-labour negotiations on performance standards, as opposed to the bargaining based on opinion which must take place when times are estimated.

(5) Properly applied method study followed by work measurement enables the management to guarantee the time standards with reasonable assurance that it is not exposing itself to risks of perpetuating uneconomic rates.

It is important for the success for any incentive scheme that the workers should know as quickly as possible the bonus they have earned. Wherever possible, this information should be made available the day after the one to which it refers. It may be shown in money units, as a percentage of the standard performance, or as the average number of standard minutes produced per hour. In these latter ways the figures can be posted on the notice board without workers actually seeing each other's earnings. In many firms it is the practice for the shop clerk or foreman to tell each operative his performance, which enables him to raise any queries on the spot. When workers get used to thinking in standard minutes, they generally know at the end of each day what they have earned and tend to regard the daily figures as confirmation.

The value of this practice to an incentive scheme is as follows:

(1) The effect of the operative's own actions on his earnings is brought home to him while the events concerned are still fresh in his mind.

(2) Any queries on the amount of bonus due can be taken up and corrections made, if necessary, **before** the wages are made up.

(3) The posting of the figures daily on the notice board, where this has been agreed to by the workers and their representatives, adds interest and may stimulate a competitive spirit.

(4) Repeated confirmation of their own calculations by the management's figures, or clear explanations where they differ, tend to increase the confidence of the workers in the fairness of the system. Conversely, repeated mistakes by the wages staff can rapidly undermine their confidence.

8. Organisation of the recording system associated with work measurement and labour control

A full application of work measurement, when associated with an incentive scheme, has to be backed by a system of recording operatives' times and output of work. These times and output figures must then be assembled at a central point—usually the accounts department once the work study application is running properly—where they can be worked out and put into forms suitable for use in compiling the bonus earned by each worker and providing the management with compact and easily understandable statistics for the control of factory performance and costs.

Devising a system suitable for use in the organisation in which he is employed is generally one of the jobs of the work study man. Any such system must have certain characteristics. It should—

(a) provide accurate and full information;

(b) ensure that all the necessary information is recorded as a matter of routine and transmitted with the minimum delay to the central office;

(c) be **simple to understand and to operate** and as nearly as possible foolproof, so that all the routine work can be carried on by comparatively unskilled clerical staff;

(d) be economical of staff;

(e) be economical of paper.

Working out a system to fulfil all these requirements for any but the smallest works engaged on the simplest type of manufacturing is not easy, and a chapter could well be devoted to the subject. Space does not permit this, however, and the variety of systems for different applications is such that any set of examples given here would run the risk of being too complicated for some enterprises and insufficient for others. Comment will therefore be confined to some general notes and to the basic data required together with their probable source.

The sheets on which output and performance information is summarised and reported to the management are known as **control statements.** In a fully developed labour control system there will probably be three different labour control statements, prepared at different intervals and for different purposes. A daily statement may be prepared each morning, separately for each section of the organisation, to indicate to the foreman or supervisor in charge of the section the results of the previous day's working. Once a week the weekly control statement will be compiled, usually on a departmental rather than a section-by-section basis. The weekly statement will go to both foremen and departmental heads. A single sheet frequently has space for the record of 13 weeks of work, a fresh line being used each week, so that

Table 27.   Minimum data required for work measurement and labour control records

Information	Source
(1) Hours of attendance of each operative	Clock card or time sheet
(2) Standard time for each operation	Job card or work study office
(3) Times of starting and finishing each operation	Job card or work sheet (via shop clerk)
(4) Quantities produced	Job card or work sheet (via work checker)
(5) Scrap or rectification: quantities and times	Scrap note or rectification slip (via inspector and shop clerk)
(6) Waiting time and non-productive time	Waiting time slips or daily work sheet (via shop clerk)

the current week's results can be compared with those of earlier weeks during the same quarter. The control statement which goes to the top management is usually made up monthly, on either a departmental or a whole-works basis.

In any system of recording associated with work measurement and an incentive system, the minimum data given in table 27 must be recorded and eventually transmitted to the wages and cost offices.

It should be noted that the application of work measurement will almost certainly entail an increase in clerical staff. The idea of this frightens many managers, who fear increases in their overhead expenses, forgetting that the increased cost is likely to be very small compared with the savings which the techniques of work study can make in their total costs of production or operation.

The design of labour control statements varies according to the needs of the organisation, but the usual form is divided into two parts. In the first part, the labour utilisation and effectiveness are expressed in terms of time; in the second part, the figures are translated into costs. In addition to the output (in standard minutes) and the clock minutes worked, from which the productivity of the department may be calculated, waiting time and additional allowances are analysed by causes, so that the manager can at once question and take action on any cause of excessively high waiting time, and can see the cost of it.

This concludes the section of the book devoted to work measurement.

Part four

From analysis to synthesis: New forms of work organisation

Chapter 24
Combined methods and tasks: New forms of work organisation

1. Method study and work measurement: basic tools for job design

In the preceding chapters we have thoroughly discussed modern work study techniques. Since the introduction of these techniques at the beginning of this century, work study has become an effective tool in improving the performance of enterprises. Few developments have contributed so much towards attaining that goal. Moreover, the underlying principles of these methods will, for the foreseeable future, continue to be of immense importance in the great majority of enterprises, regardless of their size or area of economic activity.

Let us briefly summarise the basic significance of systematic work study for the development of better methods of work.

METHODS: SYSTEMATIC v. HAPHAZARD

The first rule of work study is that each task must be systematically analysed in advance and the ways of carrying it out must be thought through. If the task in question is to be carried out only once, perhaps this preliminary analysis is of no great importance—indeed, there might be no point in paying too much attention to it. But if the task is to be carried out repeatedly, we can easily see that much is to be gained by carefully scrutinising the manner in which the task is executed. Every movement that can be eliminated or improved, every time span that can be shortened will produce economies—and if each task is repeated many times, as happens with mass production or long runs, the saving of even tiny movements or of a few seconds here and there can be of crucial economic importance.

It can thus readily be seen that if **systematic** analyses of this kind are not carried out, preferably before production is begun, inefficiency will in effect be built into the job.

WORK ANALYSIS: STEP-BY-STEP EXAMINATION

An important feature of work study is therefore the systematic analysis of the job, that is the division of a task into its various component parts followed by a careful examination and discussion of each part. By thus breaking down a complex problem into its underlying elements, a clearer and more readily understandable picture of the task can be obtained, and a good method of carrying it out can be deduced.

377

In Chapter 8 we examined various methods of breaking down work processes into small parts. In the same chapter we went over the questioning technique—a method of questioning everything that is done and taking nothing for granted, with the aim of finding new alternatives, new combinations and new ideas.

PRE-SET TIMES FOR VARIOUS MOVEMENTS

One of the most important features of modern work study is that it is possible to fix in advance, with moderate margins of error, the times necessary to carry out different movements. There are many different methods of doing this, ranging from summary estimates to highly refined PTS systems. One point that these methods have in common, however, is that they all contain a more or less established method of determining, on the basis of the characteristics of the work in question, the "normal" time that a task should require.

This process of pre-setting times for various tasks is of overwhelming importance in production management. Most important, it makes it possible to test alternative methods and combinations of methods of performing a certain job and to determine which alternative is the most time-saving. Furthermore, with the help of these systematic time guidelines, it becomes feasible to distribute work assignments among different individuals and groups in order to plan production more efficiently and to construct a foundation for discussing production-linked wages and similar incentives.

Again, this is an element of modern work study that is virtually indispensable in normal industrial activities. Without the help of work study methods and systematic time formulae, the determination of guidelines would be pure guesswork.

THE LATEST ROLE OF WORK STUDY: FROM ANALYSIS TO SYNTHESIS

So far we have discussed the basic role of work study in the design of individual jobs and of work organisation. Before we go into more detail, it should be emphasised that the development of method study and work measurement has been continuous, so that it is now possible to apply work study to any kind of activity. Furthermore, the workers' understanding of and active involvement in work study has increased rapidly.

With this point clear in our minds, let us now turn to the question of how the basic "building blocks" of method study and work measurement can be put together in designing jobs, and how work organisation can best be shaped in other respects. We shall divide this discussion into three parts, corresponding to three organisational levels—

1. Design of individual work roles.
2. Design of group work in production.
3. Design of product-oriented organisations.

A detailed examination of these topics falls outside the scope of this introductory book, and we shall limit ourselves here to a discussion of some of their basic features.

2. Design of individual work roles

GUIDELINES IN THE DESIGN OF JOBS: SOME EXAMPLES

In putting together an individual work role with the help of the fundamental building blocks we have been discussing (that is, the component parts of each task and the description of methods), we may adopt a number of criteria as guidelines for satisfactory job design.

Most important are the economic aspects. With the help of systematic work study the component parts of a task are put together in such a way that as little time as possible is required to carry it out. In this book we have so far confined our discussion to this point.

However, the design of individual work roles is too complex to be effected with the aid of a single criterion—that is, what appears on paper to be the shortest time needed to carry out a task. In practice, numerous different factors must be considered.

Some of these are purely practical considerations, such as the need for different types of machinery, the nature of the different components of each job, and so on. For example, if it takes ten minutes to carry out a particular component part of the task and if this component part is repeated 1,000 times within a 50-man work group, it is easy to see that the results of this study must be combined with other information about the work situation in order to arrive at a reasonable division of the task among the various members of the group. This example is given merely to indicate the problem, which we shall not examine here. There is, however, one special group of factors that we must look at more closely: namely, the worker's needs and preferences, his experience of the work and his reaction to different kinds of work organisation. This is a new and important dimension, since it implies the need to adapt work design to the individual's wishes and capacities, to create jobs in industry that offer a reasonable challenge, and to provide the worker with the chance of a working climate that offers some degree of satisfaction. The reader will no doubt recall that this point was made earlier, in Chapter 5. Here we can identify three important factors that can lead to increased job satisfaction—

(1) A moderate amount of variety in the work done.

(2) Decoupling of man/machine processes, that is, freedom from being tied to a machine during the entire working day.

(3) The opportunity to integrate various service and auxiliary tasks into a production job.

These three topics will be treated separately below.

Variety at work

If work is to be done well, there must be a reasonable correlation between the job and the person doing that job. A job that consists of only a few simple movements and takes only a few seconds to do can certainly be easy to learn. At first sight, it may seem that this is an efficient way of organising the work. But this type of job is hardly efficient from a more practical viewpoint. It will rapidly become monotonous

379

and tiring, and such extreme specialisation requires long runs, plus a degree of structural stability and production volume that is not often found in reality. It is much better to create work roles that display a reasonable amount of variety, that require something from the worker in terms of learning and that are adapted to reality in terms of the true length of runs, a stable product mix and infrequent production disturbances.

There is no complete, clear answer to the question of how a task cycle that gives just the right amount of variety should be designed. However, a study of the following factors offers some guidance in bringing about improvements:

the basic structure of the technical system;

the pattern of the physical load;

the information content of the task;

the balance between physical and intellectual task components;

the demand for learning and the need for individual development opportunities.

In many production technologies the basic structure of the technical system is the determining factor. For example, on a motor car assembly line the length and content of the job cycle are wholly dictated by the technical system. If 500 cars are to be produced in 500 minutes, each operative has one minute in which to do his job. There is nothing that can be done about it. In other words the job cycle can be changed only if the concept of the technical system itself (i.e. the assembly line as a working arrangement) is changed. We shall come back to this question of assembly system design later.

But the fixed-speed assembly line is not the only technical system that prevents the introduction of a time cycle of reasonable length. Short-cycle man/machine operations, such as those carried out with eccentric shaft presses, offer another example of the need to reshape the entire technical system in order to apply time cycles that are of a comfortable length for the operative. This also will be discussed later.

It should be emphasised that variety in the time cycle is primarily a subjective concept and therefore cannot be precisely defined, either technically or mathematically. However, it is more or less closely related to other factors such as—

length of the time cycle;

size of the run;

frequency of recurrence of a product (that is, the time that passes before the same product is worked on again);

amount and distribution, in repetitive jobs, of non-repetitive tasks;

differences in work structure and job content between different series.

Example. In an enterprise manufacturing electrical circuit breakers, two alternatives for the organisation of the work were identified. The first would require that assembly be done in four separate jobs, each carried out at a specially built and specially equipped work station. At the last of these work stations the assembly work is completed and a control check is made. In this type of arrangement the cycles are about ten seconds in length. Variations within cycles are virtually non-existent.

The second alternative would require that the entire circuit breaker assembly be done at each of the work stations (i.e. one job at each work station). In order to arrive at this solution, the materials supply system would have to be completely reorganised. By planning the work in this way the cycle is lengthened to 40 seconds. In addition, opportunities for varying the cycles increase markedly.

After an analysis of the practical consequences of the two choices at the workplace, the second alternative was chosen. The decision is significant, since it exemplifies the efforts that have been made in recent years to limit monotony in jobs and to achieve a practical balance of working conditions.

One important point in an analysis of this kind is the fact that people are different. At any one time the people at the same workplace will present quite different characteristics. And if we study the same person at different times during his working life, we shall find significant differences in his performance. This is an important, indeed fundamental element in the design of individual work roles. Jobs should be different, and should present different degrees of difficulty to those who execute them. Thus different people can find a work role and a level of difficulty that match their own aptitudes and preferences. In addition, an individual can begin working in a particular job that has a particular level of difficulty, and can then move steadily to more challenging jobs as he develops further.

Decoupling man/machine systems

The rigidity of the links on a worker in a man/machine system may be due to several factors. The person can be tied to the workplace in a geographical sense—it may be impossible for him to be absent from his station for even a short time. He can also be tied by the method—it may be impossible to vary the order in which operations are carried out. And he can be tied in terms of time—he may be required to carry out certain operations at fixed times.

The degree of rigidity with which he is tied can be "planned"—that is, the man and the machine are consciously and deliberately tied together in a man/machine system—but in many cases the rigidity is quite "unplanned". In some cases this unplanned rigidity arises from a fault in the technical system; the operational stability of the machines may be so poor that the machines must be continuously tended, usually with only simple movements. Unplanned rigidity can, however, be reduced through the use of more operationally reliable technology.

Three different types of solution may be offered for this problem of rigid man/machine links—

(1) Complete decoupling through increased mechanisation.

(2) Use of technical auxiliary equipment to free the operative from the machine.

(3) Decoupling through contact and co-operation among operatives.

Let us examine more closely each of these three choices.

381

Complete decoupling through mechanisation

Decoupling of this kind requires heavy capital investment. Therefore, production processes that are to be handled in this way must be characterised by mass production, extremely short cycles and severe rigidity and monotony. In such cases mechanisation means the complete elimination of all human intervention.

Technical auxiliary equipment for the operator

This principle can be put into effect by establishing **buffers** and **magazines** in an integrated man/machine system in order to reduce dependence relationships between men and machines. (A buffer is a waiting point located between two consecutive operations in the production flow; a magazine is a point of accumulation located within an operation and providing automatic feeding of material to the machine.) The key is to create processes that can accept variations in the speed at which different sections of the line move.

Both buffers and magazines are characterised by an "accumulation of products for continued processing" which can be completely identical in their technical design.

Since buffers and magazines are placed at different points in the man/ machine system, their characteristics as accumulators of time are influenced by different types of time gaps in the process.

A buffer makes it possible to accumulate:

(a) the waiting times created when two operatives on opposite sides of the buffer work at different speeds; and

(b) the waiting times created because the quantities of work done at two stations are not absolutely identical.

A magazine makes it possible to accumulate:

(a) waiting times created because an operative works at a different speed from the over-all speed of the technical process; and

(b) waiting times created because an operative is forced to wait while a machine does its part of the work.

Decoupling through contact and co-operation

Finally, decoupling can be achieved if, through job rotation and mutual co-operation and in agreement with the management, workers are able to interchange tasks and assignments.

Integration of production and auxiliary tasks

In the design of individual work roles it can often be advantageous to include various service and auxiliary tasks in production jobs. This leads to greater variety for the individual in his job.

　　　　Auxiliary tasks that are most often combined in this way are:

maintenance of machines and tools;

setting-up of machines;

handling of materials near the work station;

inventory work;

quality control.

Let us discuss some of these auxiliary tasks further.

When we speak of maintenance in production positions, we are referring to measures that can be taken to reduce the number and extent of production errors. Maintenance can include a regular inspection of the system in order to find errors and take remedial measures. Maintenance can also include repairs of parts so as to make it possible to achieve the established precision norms required in production. In addition, it can include a statistical follow-up in order to improve the capacity utilisation of equipment.

The possibility of including machine setting-up and similar preparatory functions in the ordinary operative's role depends on a number of factors, among which are the following:

degree of difficulty and time available for the setting-up operation;

frequency of setting-up operations;

degree of rigidity in other production tasks;

need for special auxiliary equipment to undertake this work.

Example. A metalworking enterprise conducts its operations with the help of advanced computer-controlled equipment. In one department the operative was trained to programme the computer equipment himself. He was thus able to handle the traditional job as well as the programming of the machine tool's computer equipment. He therefore works both as a programmer and as a machine operator. This example shows that even moderately difficult and specialised tasks can sometimes be integrated into a normal production job.

Regarding the possible integration of material-handling work near the work station, the following factors are some of the more decisive:

character of the product;

volume of materials to be handled;

design of the transport system;

degree of rigidity in the production operation.

These are some examples showing how direct production jobs can be supplemented with various auxiliary and service tasks. There are no simple, standard solutions in this area; each case must be examined in the light of its special characteristics. However, the guiding principle in making these decisions is that a practical and smoothly functioning arrangement must be feasible, that jobs can be broadened sufficiently to include everyday variations and that they must not be excessively monotonous.

3. Design of group work in production

ADVANTAGES OF GROUP WORK

Once individual jobs have been designed, the next logical step is to co-ordinate these roles. One method of co-ordination that has attracted increasing interest in recent years is the tying together of individual jobs into work groups. Organisational descriptions of a complete work group specify which roles are included in the group and the principles according to which these roles should be co-ordinated. Group work in production can have many advantages. Here we shall touch only on some of the more important of them.

The most important advantage is the way in which objectives are established and the results measured. In this connection it must be borne in mind that it is much easier to formulate appropriate objectives for a group than for an individual job, and this is an important advantage.

Another advantage is that the leeway for variations in the individual's activities increases and that a stronger sense of participation in the larger process can be experienced than when each person is tied to a limited individual task. People working in a group have a better chance to co-operate continuously in improving methods and eliminating unnecessary work. Attitudes can change as team spirit develops.

A further merit of group organisation is that the organisation's capacity to adapt itself to change increases. An enterprise is in a state of continuous change. The management alone cannot completely control, manage and follow up this process of adaptation to change; the organisation itself must possess a strong built-in capacity for self-adaptation.

These are some of the most important reasons why ideas of group work in production have been gaining ground in the design of work organisation. But group work is not suitable everywhere. In certain types of production systems it is an excellent concept, while in others it is completely unworkable. Let us look at some models of production systems and see how group work might fit with specific working conditions.[1]

SEVEN PRODUCTION SYSTEM MODELS: WHERE DOES GROUP WORK FIT?

We shall divide these production systems schematically into seven main types, and then use this classification to discuss where group production is most suitable as an organisational concept. We may refer to these seven models as follows:

(1) The machine-paced line.

(2) The man-paced line.

(3) The automated process.

(4) The concentrated operation.

---

[1]These models are taken from Hans Lindestad and Jan-Peder Norstedt: *Autonomous groups and payment by result* (Stockholm, Swedish Employers' Confederation, 1973). For further details see also George Kanawaty (ed.): *Managing and developing new forms of work organisation* (Geneva, ILO, 2nd ed., 1981).

(5) The diversified line group.

(6) The service group.

(7) The construction group.

Let us study briefly the requisite characteristics for group work in each of these categories.

The machine-paced line

This type of arrangement is most often found in situations where material handling is an important factor and where the material-handling function occupies a dominant role. The classical example of this type is the motor car factory's final assembly on a fixed-speed assembly line.

Figure 129.   Machine-paced line

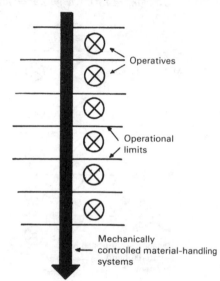

In this type of production system a high degree of mechanised handling is chosen. The flow of materials and the organisation of work are therefore completely under the control of the technical system. Until only a few years ago this was the only assembly arrangement used in situations where a high volume of materials was the rule. The disadvantage of this system is that the individual's work role is strictly limited and that the work pace is completely controlled by the technical system. In systems of this type, where operatives are tightly tied to a short task cycle, no genuine group work is possible. Consequently, the most important disadvantage of such production systems is the way in which operatives experience their work. Other disadvantages include the extreme sensitivity of such lines to disturbances. These production chains are only as strong as their weakest link, and it requires only a small influenza epidemic in the region where the factory is located to upset the whole system. Moreover, it is difficult to make changes in such production lines.

385

The advantages are short through-put times, the efficient utilisation of space, machines and auxiliary equipment and, consequently, the efficient operation that is achieved through the extreme division of work and specialisation. However, these advantages apply only when the production system is in operation.

During recent years a considerable number of attempts to "loosen up" the assembly line have been made with the help of different innovative arrangements—a point to which we shall return later.

The man-paced line

If we imagine an assembly line from which we have removed the mechanised control and flow speed and introduced some inventories between work stations, we have a type of functional arrangement that is common in many companies (in the clothing and metalworking industries, for example).

Figure 130.   Man-paced line

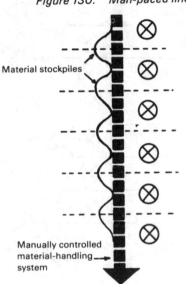

In this sort of production system the control is less rigorous and the existence of buffers makes it possible to adapt the individual work pace in a completely different way from work on an assembly line. In such a system work organisation based on production groups is an excellent arrangement. Within a group made up of individual work roles, operatives can help each other, take care of work disturbances, even out peaks and valleys of work flows and strive for a good common work result.

The automated process

If it were possible to mechanise all the manually executed tasks on a conventional assembly line, the result would be a kind of process line where the individual's work would be concerned primarily with supervision and control. Process lines of this type are extensively used, particularly in the steel, chemical and paper and pulp industries.

On a process line the possibilities of creating meaningful group work are often excellent. Operatives rely greatly on one another and possess a common goal. Working together to attain this goal is a clear-cut necessity. One factor that may sometimes make group co-operation difficult is an excessive distance between group members. A key question in this type of production system is the relationship of direct production tasks and maintenance tasks executed in the work organisation. The higher the degree of mechanisation, the fewer production workers there are; but the number of maintenance workers normally increases at almost the same rate as the number of production workers decreases.

Figure 131.   Automated process

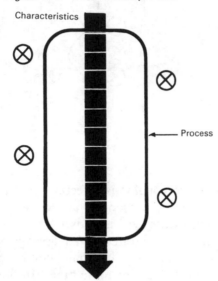

The concentrated operation (functional layout)

A constant element in the three types of system that we have discussed up to now is the grouping together of production equipment along the production flow so that different types of machines are placed in the correct order along the direction of flow. However, if we group the machines in such a way that all machines of a certain type are concentrated in one department, all machines of another type in another department, and so on, we obtain a concentration of each type of operation in one place (this is the "functional layout" referred to earlier in the book). In this layout the product to be worked is sent through the various departments in turn—the drilling department, the turning department, the milling department, and so forth.

This type of concentrated operation often occurs in batch production, where series are short and the products varied.

In this type of production system it is extremely difficult to organise meaningful group work. In everyday reality each individual is bound to his own individual job and work station. Genuine group work with spontaneous interaction between different roles and role occupants is virtually impossible to bring about.

387

Figure 132.   Concentrated operation

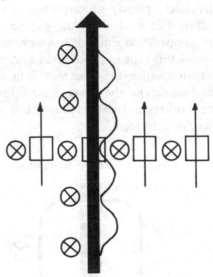

The diversified line group

In many cases the conditions affecting production are such that neither highly developed line grouping nor an advanced degree of operation grouping is suitable. Instead, an intermediate type is chosen—what we may call the "diversified line group". Production is concentrated in an arrangement that is primarily flow-oriented, but in order that it may carry out many combinations of tasks, some critical operational stages are repeated two or more times. In this way a system is obtained that can, with a high degree of efficiency, combine the capacity of the flow group to accept and channel a large volume of materials with the capacity of the functional layout to execute all conceivable production assignments.

In this type of production system, group work is often an excellent organisational concept. With this arrangement the division of work between various individuals must be adapted continuously to varying conditions. But this cannot be done entirely by the management, and a substantial proportion must occur spontaneously at the initiative of the members of the group. In a group organisation the capacity for such spontaneous self-adaptation can gradually be generated.

The service group

Conditions within service-producing organisations differ in several respects from the types of activity we have discussed earlier. Various forms of services are produced in large sectors, such as commerce, transportation, hotels and restaurants and motor vehicle repair shops. But service functions also occur in manufacturing industry, a good example being repair and maintenance activities.

The service functions of a production unit must be highly adaptable to varying demands. Generally, the tasks to be done vary in nature. The work load is uneven and it is difficult to plan the work in detail.

Figure 133.   Service group

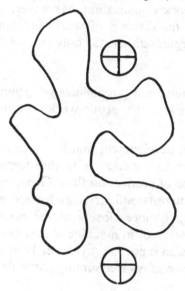

Group organisation is a good concept in this type of situation also. The work group can itself handle much of the variation that shows up in the inflow of tasks, in routine work planning and in other circumstances that tend to vary.

The construction group

For the final type in our classification, let us see how construction operations are carried out. In this case the product itself is the centre for the whole organisation, which is built up around the construction object itself. Work organisations of this type are also found in industry, for example in manufacturing very large products (e.g. turbines, ships, process machinery).

Figure 134.   Construction group

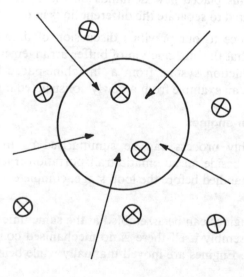

389

In production work of this type, group work is not only a good idea: it is the only conceivable type of work organisation. Moreover, the work is varied, and the spontaneous adaptation of the division of work and planning is such an essential feature that flexible group organisation is the only possible solution.

We have now briefly examined the possibilities of group work in different types of production system. We have seen that group work is more suitable in some cases than in others.

One of the lines of development that has been particularly advocated in discussions about group work in production is the degree to which groups can be organised **along** the direction of production flow. Grouping of this type makes it possible to direct the group's interests and strivings toward a good common production result. We might look rather more closely at the possibilities of organising such groups, either in assembly work or in machine shops. Our purpose in taking up these examples for special discussion is not to provide ready-made solutions but to point out a line of development that nowadays is assuming particular importance.

FLOW GROUPS IN ASSEMBLY WORK: SOME TRENDS AND EXAMPLES

In assembly work, flow groups have always been the most natural arrangement. Let us take final assembly of a motor car, for example. When this arrangement was first conceived it was quite natural to introduce an assembly system that moved beside a materials inventory, with the different components being assembled on the car as it moved past. This is an extreme example of flow orientation in assembly work. The flow of materials was completely decisive in arranging the work.

But an arrangement of this type can also have its disadvantages. The work is strictly controlled and the cycle time is normally very short.

At subsequent stages of development, efforts were made to introduce buffers in the production line in order to create greater freedom in different parts of the production system. This placed new demands on the system, and various technical solutions were advocated to separate the different links in the chain from each other.

With reference to our previous discussion of different production system models, we may say that the introduction of buffer arrangements in motor car assembly changes the production system from a "machine-paced line" to a "man-paced line". The following is an example from a newly constructed motor car engine factory.

Assembly of motor car engines

The assembly process can be summarised as follows. Seven assembly groups are organised beside an automatic transportation track loop. Except for certain steps which are handled before the loop stage, complete engines are assembled in each group.

Up to six engines can be assembled at the same time within each production group. During the assembly itself there is no mechanised control of the flow as in a moving assembly line. Engines are moved manually while being assembled. When an

390

Figure 135. *Assembly of motor car engines*

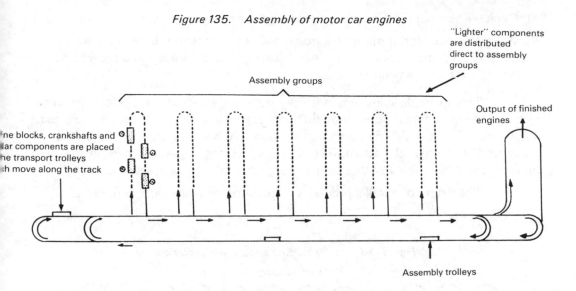

"Lighter" components
are distributed
direct to assembly
groups

Assembly groups

Output of finished
engines

ne blocks, crankshafts and
lar components are placed
he transport trolleys
h move along the track

Assembly trolleys

engine has been completely assembled in a group, it is transported automatically to a testing station which is common to all groups. At the same time it is automatically registered that an engine has left the group and a new assembly trolley is moved forward to that group on the transport track.

The advantages and disadvantages of this type of assembly process, as compared with the traditional assembly line, are as follows:

(1) This arrangement is more flexible and less susceptible to interruptions and fluctuations in the production flow.

(2) It offers good possibilities for job expansion and a more stimulating kind of group work. Each of the small loops contains a production group, a "gang" whose members co-operate closely in everyday tasks and themselves take care of such chores as the adaptation of work to changing conditions. One of the seven groups is a training group. In this group there is a fairly strict and extensive division of tasks based on detailed instructions. In the other groups the division of work is made on the basis of the abilities of individual members. There is therefore an opportunity to adapt the design of jobs within the group to the workers' knowledge and experience.

(3) It is not necessary to carry out an extensive and costly reconstruction of the line every time the production volume has to be increased or decreased. Capacity can be expanded to a certain extent by varying the numbers of members in the groups, up to six. Further increases in capacity can be achieved by increasing the number of groups.

(4) Job design is better adapted to the individual and should therefore lead to better recruiting possibilities, reduced personnel turnover and less absenteeism.

(5) The new arrangement requires greater floor space and higher goods-in-process inventories than a moving assembly line.

391

(6) Capital investment is somewhat higher for the new arrangement.

(7) Work efficiency (primarily as regards speed of movement) is lower than on a moving assembly line, because of the lower degree of specialisation and the fragmentation of work assignments.

This example illustrates not only how buffer arrangements can be introduced between different jobs and different capacities for work of different individuals but also how different parts of an assembly line—or an entire line—can be rearranged in a parallel pattern. The assembly of the engines is carried out at a number of stations, with an entire engine being assembled at each station.

The nature of parallel production operations is made clear in figure 136.

Figure 136.   Line grouping and parallel grouping

Line grouping

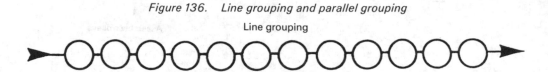

Parallel grouping

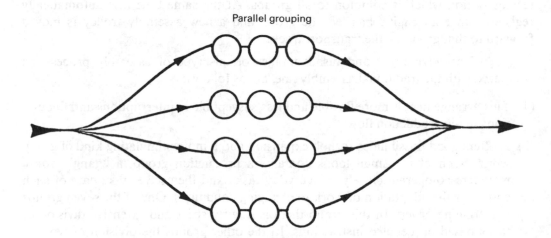

The most important advantages offered by the parallel arrangement of an assembly operation (or parts of an assembly operation) are as follows:

(1) Production reliability—it is naturally less likely that several subsystems will all be simultaneously affected by disturbances than that one large system will be so affected.

(2) Flexibility—it is easier to handle different product models, as well as changes in production volume, in a parallel system.

(3) Work content and work organisation—the possibility of creating tasks with a richer content, and of finding natural dividing lines between groups, is considerably greater. Opportunities for production groups to accept responsibility for quality and the division of work, for example, are also greater.

Flow-oriented machine groups in batch production

In a traditional layout in batch production, machines and personnel are grouped in departments, with each department carrying out its own separate function. For example, one department may handle turning, another drilling, a third milling, and so on. The advantage of this arrangement is that it results in great flexibility and a high degree of utilisation of machine capacity. A major disadvantage is that the volume of goods-in-process, and therefore the amount of working capital tied up in these goods, is always substantial. Moreover, the work in a plant of this kind is highly fragmented. It is difficult for an individual or a group of individuals to see the connection between their own work roles and the over-all activity of the company. It is therefore difficult for individuals and groups to participate actively in work planning and in attaining the established goals of the company.

During recent years, interest has grown in finding ways of grouping machinery and equipment around flow-oriented groups in batch production, that is, groups formed around the manufacture of entire products or complex product components. We shall discuss these trends briefly here.

What is a **flow-oriented group?** Figure 137 illustrates the basic principle.

With the help of a standard classification method, we have selected an assortment of different components, such as axles and flanges. In each of these groups there are subgroups that resemble each other as regards the types of work required. Machines, personnel and other resources needed for the components—from metal supplies to finished parts—are collected in one unit. Through the choice of suitable components, methods and equipment we can create a simple flow pattern.

With this manufacturing arrangement through-put times, and therefore also the working capital tied up in the system, can both be reduced. Production can be carried out with a minimum of supplies of materials on hand—this applies particularly to the work stations themselves. The lower the supply of materials on hand, the shorter and surer the through-put times become.

In a functional organisation, each operative's task at "his" machine and the job planned for the machine are fixed in advance. A flow-oriented group is a machine group for the finished manufacture of a mix of components. It contains more machines or work stations than there are operatives, and each operative should preferably master several types of job. This means that all the members of the group must be able to work relatively independently. The group members themselves have the responsibility for dividing the work between them and seeing that material flows through the group as it should. Thus the work of a flow group relies heavily on teamwork and co-operation.

Unlike a functional grouping of machines, a flow group makes heavy demands on individuals. But a flow group also makes possible the creation of more attractive work roles for group members, because—

(1) They have a better over-all view of their contribution to the larger production process.

(2) They have more variety in their work because they can move between various tasks.

393

Figure 137.   Schematic diagram of a flow-oriented group

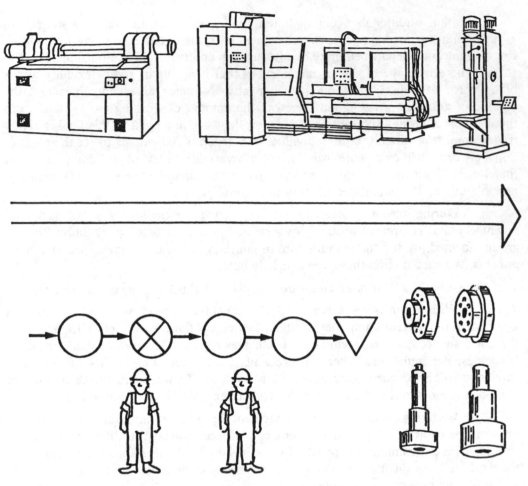

(3) They have the chance of being trained for new jobs.

(4) They have increased contact with their colleagues at work as well as with the management.

Example. In figure 138, a flow group has been created for the manufacture of pump axles in a metalworking company. In this group approximately 150 types of axle are produced; however, these are based on about ten general methods, of which the most widely used account for about 65 articles.

The simplest components are manufactured from pre-cut metal pieces during a single trip through the group. The most complicated components must go through the group three times. Operatives can easily return parts to the incoming station with the help of roller conveyor tracks. Two men work in this group; their work is delineated by the shape of the conveyor.

However, flow-oriented manufacturing in short series requires certain definite conditions and cannot be used in all situations. For example, a systematic structuring of the product mix must be made, to make it possible to channel certain

394

Figure 138.   Flow group for the manufacture of pump axles

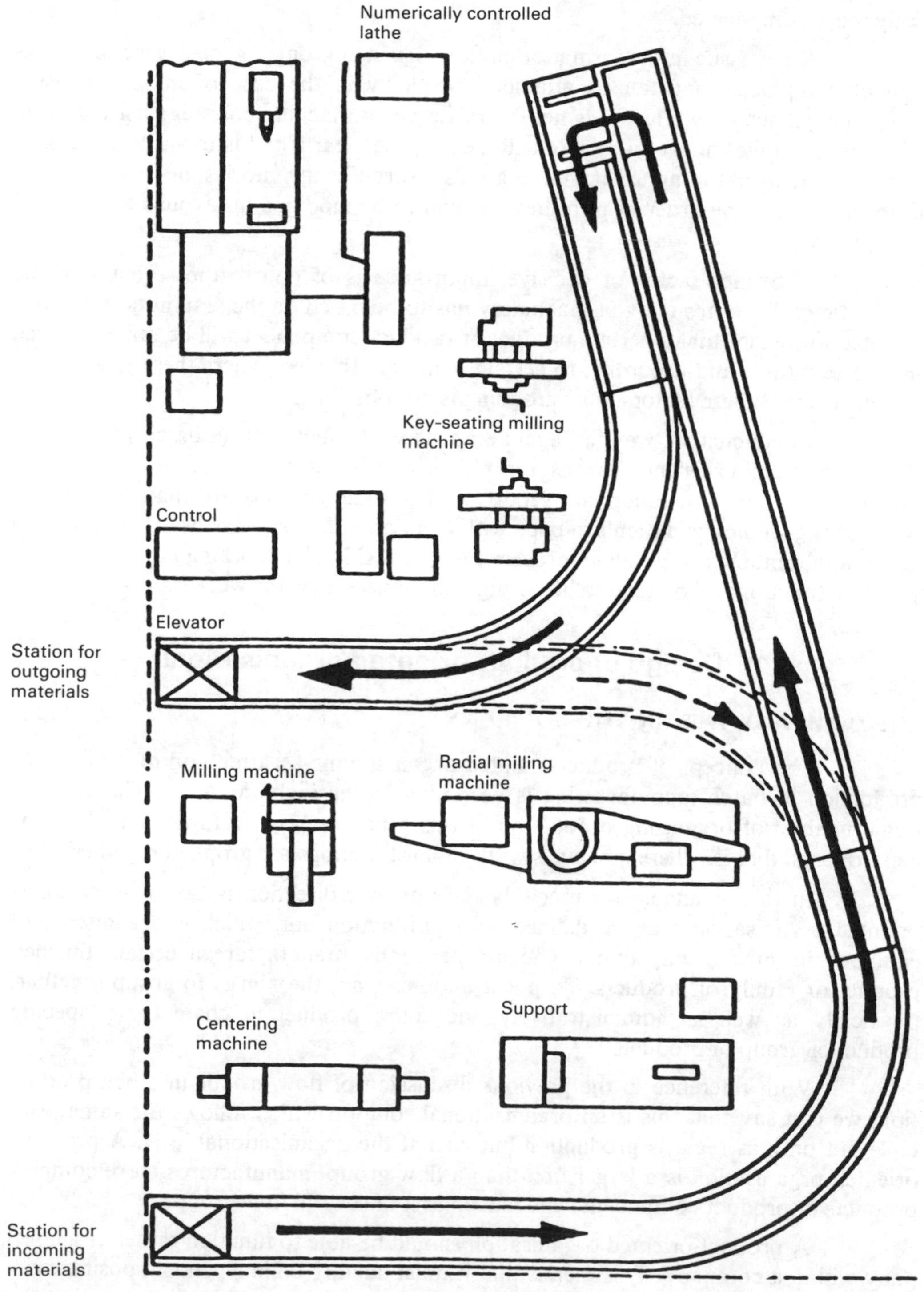

Numerically controlled
lathe

Key-seating milling
machine

Control

Elevator

Station for
outgoing
materials

Milling machine

Radial milling
machine

Centering
machine

Support

Station for
incoming
materials

main types of product in a homogeneous flow. Moreover, production must be of such a nature that an "unbroken flow principle" can be applied. If it is necessary to break the material flow within the flow group at a certain operational step and to send components outside the group for working, the planning will naturally become substantially more complicated.

A key issue in the formation of flow-oriented groups is the degree of utilisation of equipment that can be attained, especially in the case of more expensive production machinery. Here it is necessary to weigh machine costs against the costs of tying up capital in everyday work. Recently, the clear trend is towards a recognition of the fact that tying up capital in goods-in-process inventories has reached such proportions that the order of priorities has had to be modified in favour of the use of flow groups.

A further factor of decisive importance is of course the stability of the product mix. Flow grouping of machinery has to be based on the assumption that it is possible to foresee that a certain product or product component will be manufactured in a certain form and according to certain methods. In cases where there is some uncertainty about these factors, flow grouping is not possible.

In conclusion, we may again emphasise the fact that, in batch production, there are often excellent reasons for choosing flow grouping of machinery and operatives rather than functional grouping. The main reasons are that, in practice, functional grouping is difficult to cope with from an administrative point of view, that substantial amounts of goods-in-process tie up considerable working capital and that jobs in a functional shop tend to be boring and monotonous for workers.

4. Design of product-oriented organisations

THE COMPANY WITHIN THE COMPANY

The concept of product-oriented organisations as a method of structuring production in batch manufacturing is becoming increasingly common. The conventional method of organising production of this type has been in functional shops or departments, that is, where machines with similar functions are grouped together.

In this arrangement, precisely the opposite direction is taken. A product-oriented organisation may be defined as a production unit which is organised and equipped in such a way that it can independently manufacture a certain finished product or family of products. To put it another way, the aim is to group together, physically as well as administratively, the entire production chain for a specific product or group of products.

With reference to the previous discussion of flow groups in batch production, we can say that this is an organisational solution which follows the same principle not only as regards production but also at the organisational level. A product-oriented organisation is a larger unit than a flow group, manufactures more complex products or product components and can consist of several flow groups.

A product-oriented organisation should be able to function rather as a company within a company. This means that it must occupy an independent position vis-à-vis its environment. Complete manufacturing resources should be found so that the complete manufacturing chain can be handled from beginning to end for a certain product or product component. It should also have its own administrative resources and its own operating services, such as maintenance, material handling, and so on.

By locating complete manufacturing resources within the plant so that the entire production chain can be held together in one place, there is very little dependence on other units and the co-ordination of products can be taken care of within the organisation. In this way a simple planning process and short through-put times can be attained. The unit can also be truly independent with regard to other working areas in the immediate vicinity.

If this method is to work properly, however, all the machinery necessary to carry out the complete production operation must be available. In general, the capacity of utilisation of most machines will be lower than in a functional shop. The possible machine utilisation will thus be a key factor in examining the feasibility of this organisational concept, and should be weighed against its other advantages, especially as regards lower working capital tied up in inventories and simpler administration.

FLOW PATTERNS IN A PRODUCT-ORIENTED ORGANISATION: AN EXAMPLE

By definition, the product-oriented organisation refers to a certain flow of production. Within the unit itself, however, this flow can be more or less divided, and machine grouping can vary from very pronounced line grouping to a more operationally grouped functional arrangement. Let us look at two examples of the organisation of a product shop.

In the first example, a heat exchanger unit, a systematic attempt has been made to build the production structure on the basis of flow groups. It proved possible to do so for the main part of the manufacturing process despite the fact that it is heavily influenced by customer orders and that batches are small. Figure 139 shows how an attempt was made to come as near as possible to a "straight-line" arrangement. This simplifies material handling and gives all operatives a good over-all view of the manufacturing process.

However, it will be seen that the flow is divided between two areas in the manufacturing chain. There is a materials buffer for assembly, and there is also a buffer between the pressing of plates and finishing of products (see figure 139). The reason for this is to achieve reasonable batch sizes and to reduce change-over times in production.

In our second example, relating to the manufacture of electric motors, figure 141 shows a product-oriented organisation consisting of a number of flow groups in which different components are manufactured. Among the principles on which the arrangement was based are the following:

(1) Manufacture of components in units from raw materials, each in its own component flow or flow group.

(2) Co-ordination of component flow directly with the main flow without material buffers or interim inventories.

(3) Completion of main flow with delivery of finished motors.

397

Figure 139.   Layout for a heat exchanger unit

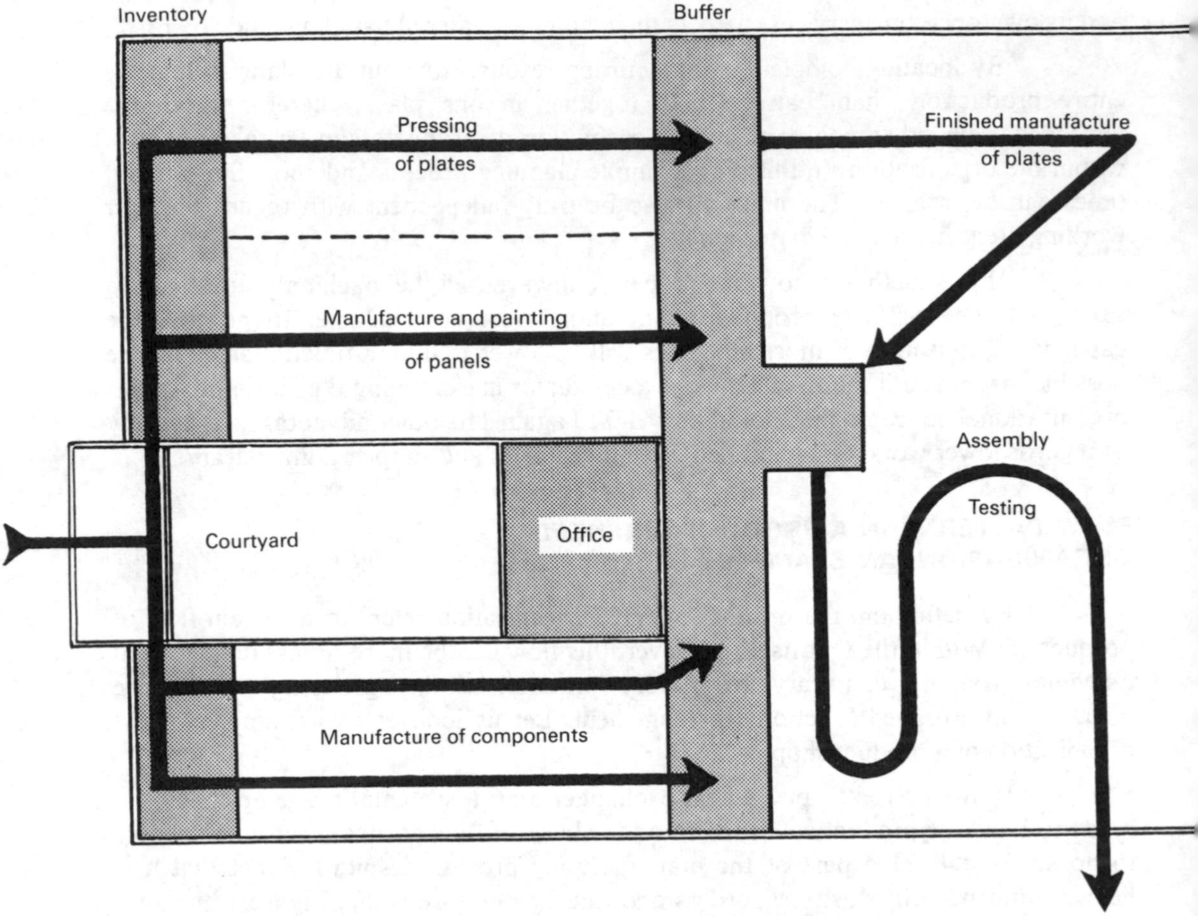

This arrangement of the flow means that the quantity of goods-in-process is very small, and the through-put times from the first operation to the finished motor is only two or three days. Furthermore, no interim inventories are needed for assembly.

5. Criteria of good work organisation: some concluding remarks

EFFICIENCY

The first and most fundamental criterion of good work organisation is, of course, that it should be effective—that the use of resources should be maximised and that the largest possible output should be obtained from the smallest possible input. The various chapters of this book have dealt extensively with this criterion, because this factor will always be of fundamental significance—in all types of technology, in all stages of development and at every workplace.

Naturally, there are situations in which considerations other than those of a purely economic nature are of paramount importance. If, for example, there are evident safety or health risks at a workplace, and if additional investment is required to

Figure 140.   Some examples of the building of buffer stock in manufacturing operations

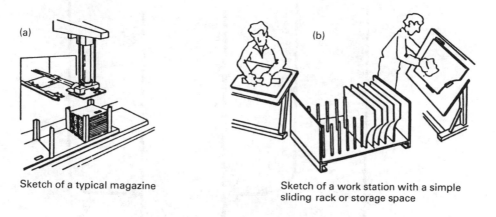

(a)

Sketch of a typical magazine

(b)

Sketch of a work station with a simple sliding rack or storage space

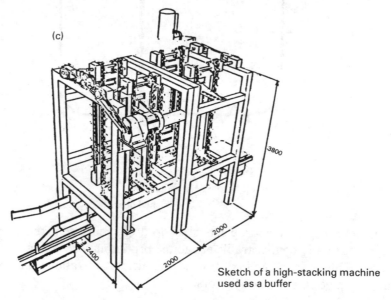

(c)

Sketch of a high-stacking machine used as a buffer

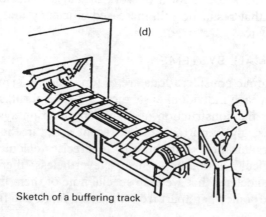

(d)

Sketch of a buffering track

399

Figure 141.   Manufacture of electric motors

Raw materials

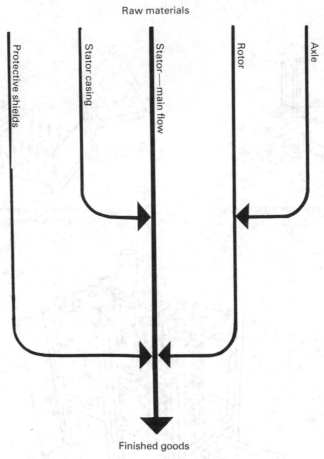

Finished goods

eliminate them, the appropriate steps to do so must be taken even if it is not possible to point to any demonstrable economic profitability resulting directly from such measures. This is an example of how economic considerations (at least in the short term) have to give way to other factors.

But, notwithstanding special cases such as this where particular circumstances obtain, economic considerations must inevitably be of fundamental importance in the choice of a suitable form of work organisation. The organisational principles and solutions that result both in increased efficiency **and** in better jobs for the workers are naturally to be preferred.

AUTONOMY OF SMALL SYSTEMS

Even if economic considerations are of fundamental significance and must be carefully analysed in each individual case, there are several rules of thumb, or general lines of thinking, for the construction of a good production system—guidelines that have become increasingly important during recent years in the development of new forms of work organisation but in which precise calculations of short-term profitability are difficult, if not impossible. Nevertheless, there has been so much emphasis on these guidelines that we take special note of them here; but we must also stress that they stand somewhat apart from the basic economic factors.

The first of these criteria for constructing good production systems is the **search for greater independence for small systems** in company organisation. By this we mean production systems that consist of moderately large production units and can function with a relatively high degree of independence within the larger company. The underlying intention is to create a production arrangement that emphasises local independence within smaller units. Breaking down the company into these smaller units reduces the need for co-ordination, and therefore management problems too become simpler to deal with.

The decentralisation that results from this type of production arrangement is also of great value in stimulating local initiative and in increasing the ability to adapt to the changing conditions and needs that arise in different parts of the company. It has also been shown that workers are often more satisfied and more involved in their work if they are members of smaller and more independent production units.

If we wish to create production systems based on this principle, four points are particularly significant—

(1) The possibility of dividing up larger systems into smaller systems.

(2) The possibility of arranging finished manufacturing units into smaller units so that the need for contacts with adjacent units is reduced.

(3) The possibility of arranging for self-sufficiency as regards production resources, operational service, and so on.

(4) The possibility of arranging for less direct management control from high levels, so that the independence of the smaller units is not eroded too much by control from the upper levels of the hierarchy.

STABILITY OF THE PRODUCTION SYSTEM

One further rule of thumb or criterion of a good production system which has received increasing interest in recent years is the desire to arrange for stable production activity with a minimum of disturbance. The following requirements in particular arise in this connection:

(1) A simple flow pattern, so that as far as possible the workers have an over-all view and that it becomes easier to plan the work.

(2) An operationally reliable technology with an optimum level of mechanisation, so that technical disturbances are held within reasonable limits.

(3) A disturbance-resistant work arrangement, so that all production stages that are critical for production are organised in parallel and that those that are particularly sensitive to disturbance are surrounded with buffers of different kinds.

ATTRACTIVE JOBS

It is important to be able to offer people jobs that they find attractive and in which they can feel personally involved. Personal aspirations vary from individual to individual and from situation to situation, and depend not only on a person's ambitions and desires but also on his or her abilities, knowledge and capacity to develop. A production organisation must therefore offer a variety of jobs, so that the desires of as

401

many people as possible can be satisfied and so that a particular individual can progress from simple jobs to more complex work roles.

Among the factors that should be considered in any endeavour to create sufficiently attractive jobs are the following:

(1) The creation of jobs with different degrees of difficulty through flow orientation, different degrees of subdivision of work and different degrees of integration of auxiliary tasks. Variations of this kind make it possible to offer to different individuals at different times jobs that correspond to their abilities and wishes.

(2) The creation of individual jobs and group arrangements that bring about a degree of independence in work, through finished manufacturing of entire products, self-sufficiency of production service functions and buffering vis-à-vis adjacent systems. This independence is of value both in terms of the production results obtained and for the way the work is experienced by individuals in the group.

(3) The design of a work organisation that is suitable for teamwork, as a result of flow grouping and similar arrangements that are compatible not only with more attractive jobs and work situations but also with greater efficiency.

(4) Provision of over-all views from inside the organisation. In order for a person to find his work attractive, he must also be able to view the larger context of which his work is a part. It is also important that he should be involved, if possible, in the design of his work and be able to feel some sense of "belonging" with his group of fellow workers and with the over-all production process in which he performs his function.

GOOD WORKING ENVIRONMENTS

An important criterion of a good job is the quality of the working environment. In Chapter 6 we indicated the basic factors that have to be considered with respect to safety at the workplace.

In addition, however, a working environment should also be pleasant to work in—in other words, it should be so designed that it becomes easier to adopt ergonomically correct working positions.

CONCLUSION

We have briefly touched on some of the trends leading towards new forms of work organisation. We have given some principles and general guidelines. We have provided some examples and emphasised certain current lines of development. Finally, we have given some criteria to be borne in mind when designing good working environments.

It is important, however, to stress the fact that there are **no standard solutions** to these problems. Our aim has been merely to put forward a few ideas, tendencies and general indications of solutions to problems. It must be remembered that the best solution to a problem can be found only in the specific circumstances of the particular case—when the actual conditions are known, when local values are considered and when the persons involved are able to find their own solutions.

Part five
Appendices

I.   Glossary of terms used

A. Work study

Activity Sampling *(Chapter 14)*

>   See *Work Sampling*.

Basic Time *(Chapter 18)*

>   The time for carrying out an element of work at standard rating, i.e.—

$$\frac{\text{Observed Time} \times \text{Observed Rating}}{\text{Standard Rating}}$$

Break Point *(Chapter 16)*

>   The instant at which one element in a work cycle ends and another begins.

Check Time *(Chapter 18)*

>   The time intervals between the start of a time study and the start of the first element observed, and between the finish of the last element observed and the finish of the study.

Chronocyclegraph *(Chapter 11)*

>   A cyclegraph in which the light source is suitably interrupted so that the path appears as a series of pear-shaped dots, the pointed end indicating the direction of movement and the spacing indicating the speed of movement.

Contingency Allowance *(Chapter 18)*

>   A small allowance of time which may be included in a standard time to meet legitimate and expected items of work or delays, the precise measurement of which is uneconomical because of their infrequent or irregular occurrence.

Cumulative Timing *(Chapter 16)*

>   See *Timing*.

Cyclegraph *(Chapter 11)*

>   A record of a path of movement, usually traced by a continuous source of light on a photograph, preferably stereoscopic.

Cycle Time *(Chapter 20)*

>   The total time taken to complete the elements constituting the work cycle.

Elapsed Time *(Chapter 16)*

>   The total time from the start to the finish of a time study.

Element *(Chapter 16)*

A distinct part of a specified job selected for convenience of observation, measurement and analysis.

Constant Element

An element for which the basic time remains constant whenever it is performed.

Foreign Element

An element observed during a study which, after analysis, is not found to be a necessary part of the job.

Governing Element

An element occupying a longer time than that of any other element which is being performed concurrently.

Machine Element

An element automatically performed by a power-driven machine (or process).

Manual Element

An element performed by a worker.

Occasional Element

An element which does not occur in every work cycle of the job, but which may occur at regular or irregular intervals.

Repetitive Element

An element which occurs in every work cycle of the job.

Variable Element

An element for which the basic time varies in relation to some characteristics of the product, equipment or process, e.g. dimensions, weight, quality, etc.

Extension *(Chapter 18)*

The calculation of basic time from observed time.

Fatigue Allowance *(Chapter 18)*

A subdivision of the relaxation allowance intended to cater for the physiological and psychological effects of carrying out specified work under specified conditions.

Film Analysis *(Chapter 11)*

The frame-by-frame examination of a ciné film of an operation to determine the state of activity of the subject during each exposure.

Flow Diagram *(Chapter 7)*

A diagram or model, substantially to scale, which shows the location of specific activities carried out and the routes followed by workers, materials or equipment in their execution.

Flow Process Chart *(Chapter 8)*

A process chart setting out the sequence of the flow of a product or a procedure by recording all events under review using the appropriate process chart symbols.

Equipment Type Flow Process Chart

A flow process chart which records how the equipment is used.

Man Type Flow Process Chart

A flow process chart which records what the worker does.

Material Type Flow Process Chart

A flow process chart which records how material is handled or treated.

Flyback Timing *(Chapter 16)*

See *Timing*.

Idle Time *(Chapter 2)*

That part of attendance time when the worker has work available but for various reasons does not do it.

Ineffective Time *(Chapter 2)*

That portion of the elapsed time, excluding the check time, spent on any activity which is not a specified part of a job.

Inside Work *(Chapter 19)*

Elements which can be performed by a worker within the machine- (or process-)controlled time.

Interference Allowance *(Chapter 19)*

An allowance of time for production unavoidably lost through synchronisation of stoppages on two or more machines (or processes) attended by one worker. Similar circumstances arise in team work.

Interference Time *(Chapter 19)*

The time when the machine (or process) is idle awaiting attention, while the worker attends to another machine (or process). Similar circumstances arise in team work.

Job Breakdown *(Chapter 16)*

A listing of the content of a job by elements.

Load Factor *(Chapter 19)*

The proportion of the over-all cycle time required by the worker to carry out the necessary work at standard performance, during a machine- (or process-)controlled cycle.

Machine Ancillary Time *(Chapter 19)*

The time when a machine is temporarily out of productive use owing to change-overs, setting, cleaning, etc.

Machine Available Time *(Chapter 19)*

The time during which a machine could work based on attendance time—i.e. working day or week plus overtime.

Machine Capacity *(Chapter 19)*

The potential volume of a machine, usually expressed in physical units capable of being produced in any convenient unit of time, e.g. tons per week, pieces per hour, etc.

Machine-Controlled Time *(Chapter 19)*

The time taken to complete that part of the work cycle which is determined only by technical factors peculiar to the machine.

Machine Down Time *(Chapter 19)*

The time during which a machine cannot be operated on production or ancillary work owing to breakdown, maintenance requirements, or for other similar reasons.

Machine Effective Utilisation Index *(Chapter 19)*

The ratio of: Machine Running Time at Standard
           to: Machine Available Time.

Machine Efficiency Index *(Chapter 19)*

The ratio of: Machine Running Time at Standard
           to: Machine Running Time.

Machine Hour *(Chapter 22)*

The running of a machine or piece of plant for one hour.

Machine Idle Time *(Chapter 19)*

The time during which a machine is available for production or ancillary work but is not used owing to shortage of work, materials or workers, including the time that the plant is out of balance.

Machine Interference *(Chapter 19)*

The queuing of machines (or processes) for attention—e.g. when one worker is responsible for attending to more than one machine. Similar circumstances arise in team work where random delays at any point may affect the output of the team.

Machine Maximum Time *(Chapter 19)*

The maximum possible time during which a machine or group of machines could work within a given period, e.g. 168 hours in one week or 24 hours in one day.

Machine Running Time *(Chapter 19)*

The time during which a machine is actually operating, i.e. the machine available time *less* any machine down time, machine idle time, or machine ancillary time.

Machine Running Time at Standard *(Chapter 19)*

The running time that should be incurred in producing the output if the machine is working under optimum conditions.

Machine Utilisation Index *(Chapter 19)*

The ratio of: Machine Running Time.
           to: Machine Available Time.

Man-Hour *(Chapter 2)*

The labour of one man for one hour.

Memomotion Photography *(Chapter 11)*

A form of time-lapse photography which records activity by a ciné camera adapted to take pictures at longer intervals than normal. The time intervals usually lie between ½ and 4 seconds.

Method Study *(Chapter 4)*

The systematic recording and critical examination of existing and proposed ways of doing work, as a means of developing and applying easier and more effective methods and reducing costs.

Methods-Time Measurement (MTM) *(Chapter 21)*

408   A system of Predetermined Time Standards (q.v.).

Micromotion Study *(Chapter 11)*

The critical examination of a simo chart prepared by a frame-by-frame examination of a ciné film of an operation.

Multiple Activity Chart *(Chapter 10)*

A chart on which the activities of more than one subject (worker, machine or item of equipment) are each recorded on a common time scale to show their inter-relationship.

Multiple Machine Work *(Chapter 19)*

Work which requires the worker to attend two or more machines (of similar or different kinds) running simultaneously.

Observed Time *(Chapter 17)*

The time taken to perform an element or combination of elements obtained by means of direct measurement.

Outline Process Chart *(Chapter 8)*

A process chart giving an over-all picture by recording in sequence only the main operations and inspections.

Outside Work *(Chapter 19)*

Elements which must necessarily be performed by a worker outside the machine- (or process-)controlled time.

Personal Needs Allowance *(Chapter 18)*

A subdivision of the relaxation allowance intended to cater for attention to personal needs.

Plant and Machine Control *(Chapter 19)*

The procedures and means by which efficiency and utilisation of units of plant and machinery are planned and checked.

Policy Allowance *(Chapter 18)*

An increment, other than bonus increment, applied to standard time (or to some constituent part of it, e.g. work content) to provide a satisfactory level of earnings for a specified level of performance under exceptional circumstances.

Predetermined Time Standards (PTS) *(Chapter 21)*

A work measurement technique whereby times established for basic human motions (classified according to the nature of the motion and the conditions under which it is made) are used to build up the time for a job at a defined level of performance.

Primary Questions *(Chapter 8)*

The first stage of the questioning technique, which queries the fundamental purpose, place, sequence, person and means of every activity recorded, and seeks a reason for each reply.

Principles of Motion Economy *(Chapter 11)*

Characteristics which, when incorporated in the methods adopted, make for easier working.

Process Charts *(Chapter 8)*

Charts in which a sequence of events is portrayed diagrammatically by means of a set of process chart symbols to help a person to visualise a process as a means of examining and improving it.

409

Process-Controlled Time *(Chapter 19)*

The time taken to complete that part of the work cycle which is determined only by technical factors peculiar to the process.

Qualified Worker *(Chapter 16)*

One who is accepted as having the necessary physical attributes, who possesses the required intelligence and education, and who has acquired the necessary skill and knowledge to carry out the work in hand to satisfactory standards of safety, quantity and quality.

Questioning Technique *(Chapter 8)*

The means by which the critical examination is conducted, each activity being subjected in turn to a systematic and progressive series of questions.

Random Observation Method *(Chapter 14)*

See *Work Sampling.*

Rating *(Chapter 17)*

(1)   The assessment of the worker's rate of working relative to the observer's concept of the rate corresponding to standard pace.

(2)   The numerical value or symbol used to denote the rate of working.

   (a) Loose rating: an inaccurate rating which is too high.
   (b) Tight rating: an inaccurate rating which is too low.
   (c) Inconsistent ratings: a mixture of loose, tight and accurate ratings.
   (d) Flat ratings: a set of ratings in which the observer has underestimated the variations in the worker's rate of working.
   (e) Steep ratings: a set of ratings in which the observer has overestimated the variations in the worker's rate of working.

Rating Scale *(Chapter 17)*

The series of numerical indices given to various rates of working. The scale is linear.

Ratio-Delay Study *(Chapter 14)*

See *Work Sampling.*

Relaxation Allowance *(Chapter 18)*

An addition to the basic time intended to provide the worker with the opportunity to recover from the physiological and psychological effects of carrying out specified work under specified conditions and to allow attention to personal needs. The amount of the allowance will depend on the nature of the job.

Representative Worker *(Chapter 17)*

A worker whose skill and performance is the average of a group under consideration. He is not necessarily a qualified worker.

Restricted Work *(Chapter 19)*

Work in which the output of the worker is limited by factors outside the control of the worker.

Secondary Questions *(Chapter 8)*

The second stage of the questioning technique, during which the answers to the primary questions are subjected to further query to determine whether possible alternatives of place, sequence, persons and/or means are practicable and preferable as a means of improvement upon the existing method.

Selected Time *(Chapter 18)*

The time chosen as being representative of a group of times for an element or group of elements. These times may be either observed or basic and should be denoted as selected observed or selected basic times.

Setting-Up Time *(Chapter 19)*

The time required to prepare a machine for work. It includes the removal of tools used for the previous tasks, any necessary cleaning of the machine, and the fixing of tools and fixtures for the new job.

Simultaneous Motion Cycle Chart ("Simo Chart") *(Chapter 11)*

A chart, often based on film analysis, used to record simultaneously on a common time scale the therbligs or groups of therbligs performed by different parts of the body of one or more workers.

Snap-Reading Method *(Chapter 14)*

See *Work Sampling.*

Standard Data *(Chapter 22)*

Tables and formulae derived from the analysis of accumulated work measurement data, arranged in a form suitable for building up standard times, machine process times, etc., by synthesis.

Standard Performance *(Chapter 17)*

The rate of output which qualified workers will naturally achieve without over-exertion as an average over the working day or shift, provided that they know and adhere to the specified method and provided that they are motivated to apply themselves to their work. This performance is denoted as 100 on the standard rating and performance scales.

Standard Time *(Chapter 18)*

The total time in which a job should be completed at standard performance, i.e. work content, contingency allowance for delay, unoccupied time and interference allowance, where applicable.

String Diagram *(Chapter 10)*

A scale plan or model on which a thread is used to trace and measure the path of workers, material or equipment during a specified sequence of events.

Therblig *(Chapter 11)*

The name given by Frank B. Gilbreth to each of the specific divisions of movement, according to the purpose for which it is made. These therbligs cover movements or reasons for absence of movement. Each therblig has a specific colour, symbol and letter for recording purposes.

Time Study *(Chapter 15)*

A work measurement technique for recording the times and rates of working for the elements of a specified job carried out under specified conditions, and for analysing the data so as to obtain the time necessary for carrying out the job at a defined level of performance.

Timing *(Chapter 16)*

The practice of observing and recording, by the use of a watch or other device, the time taken to complete each element. Three alternative methods of timing with a stop-watch are:

Cumulative Timing

A method in which the hands of the stop-watch are allowed to continue to move without returning them to zero at the end of each element, the time for each element being obtained subsequently by subtraction.

Differential Timing

A method for obtaining the time of one or more small elements. Elements are timed in groups, first including and then excluding each small element, the time for each element being obtained subsequently by subtraction.

411

Flyback Timing

A method in which the hands of the stop-watch are returned to zero at the end of each element and are allowed to restart immediately, the time for the element being obtained directly.

Tool Allowance *(Chapter 18)*

An allowance of time, which may be included in a standard time, to cover adjustment and maintenance of tools.

Travel Chart *(Chapter 10)*

A tabular record for presenting quantitative data about the movements of workers, materials or equipment between any number of places over any given period of time.

Two-Handed Process Chart *(Chapter 11)*

A process chart in which the activities of a worker's hands (or limbs) are recorded in their relationship to one another.

Unoccupied Time *(Chapter 19)*

The periods during machine- (or process-)controlled time when a worker is engaged neither on inside work nor in taking authorised rest, the time for carrying out the work being calculated at a defined performance.

Unoccupied Time Allowance *(Chapter 19)*

An allowance made to a worker when there is unoccupied time during machine- (or process-) controlled time.

Unrestricted Work *(Chapter 19)*

Work in which the output of the worker is limited only by factors within the control of the worker.

Work Content *(Chapter 18)*

Basic time + relaxation allowance + any allowance for additional work—e.g. that part of contingency allowance which represents work.

Work Cycle *(Chapter 16)*

The sequence of elements which are required to perform a job or yield a unit of production. The sequence may sometimes include occasional elements.

Work Factor *(Chapter 21)*

A system of Predetermined Time Standards (q.v.).

Work Measurement *(Chapter 4)*

The application of techniques designed to establish the time for a qualified worker to carry out a specified job at a defined level of performance.

Work Sampling *(Chapter 14)*

A method of finding the percentage occurrence of a certain activity by statistical sampling and random observations. (Work sampling is also known as ratio-delay study; observation ratio study; snap-reading method; random observation method; and activity sampling.)

Work Specification *(Chapter 23)*

A document setting out the details of an operation or job, how it is to be performed, the layout of the workplace, particulars of machines, tools and appliances to be used, and the duties and responsibilities of the worker. The standard time or allowed time assigned to the job is normally included.

Work Study *(Chapter 4)*

A generic term for those techniques, particularly method study and work measurement, which are used in the examination of human work in all its contexts, and which lead systematically to the investigation of all the factors which affect the efficiency and economy of the situation being reviewed, in order to effect improvement.

B. Plant layout

Factory Flow Analysis

Part of production flow analysis (q.v.). A technique which uses networks to study and simplify the flow of materials between departments.

Fixture

A device for holding parts which would otherwise have to be held in one hand while the other worked on them.

Group Analysis

Part of production flow analysis (q.v.). A technique used to determine the best division of the machines in a machining department into groups and the best division of the parts made into families.

Group Layout

A layout in which a set of machines, chosen so that it can carry out the complete processing of a given family of products, is laid out together in one area.

Jig

A device which holds parts in an exact position and guides the tool that works on them.

Line Analysis

Part of production flow analysis (q.v.). A technique used to study the flow of materials between the machines in a group, in order to find the best arrangement for their layout.

Line Layout

A layout in which the machines are set out in a line in their sequence of use, with materials flowing along the line.

Plant Layout

The arrangement of the desired machinery and equipment of a plant, established or con-templated, in the way which will permit the easiest flow of materials, at the lowest cost and with the minimum of handling, in processing the product from the receipt of raw materials to the dispatch of the finished product.

Process Layout

A layout in which all machines or processes of the same type are grouped together.

Product Layout

A layout in which all machines or processes concerned in the manufacture of the same product or range of products are grouped together.

Production Flow Analysis

A technique used to study the flow of materials in a factory and to find the best division into groups and families for group layout (q.v.).

Tooling Analysis

Part of production flow analysis (q.v.). A technique used to find the sequence for loading parts on a machine which will give minimum setting time.

Workplace Layout

A convenient term used to describe the space and the arrangement of facilities and conditions provided for a worker in the performance of a specified job.

C. Management

Budgetary Control

A means of controlling the activities of an enterprise by carefully forecasting the level of each activity and converting the estimate into monetary terms. The actual cost of or revenue from each activity is checked against the estimates.

Incentive Scheme

Any system of remuneration in which the amount earned is dependent on the results obtained, thereby offering the employee an incentive to achieve better results.

Inspection

The application of tests with the aid of measuring appliances to discover whether a given item or product is within specified limits of variability.

Maintenance *(in the management sense)*

The systematic inspection, servicing and repair of plant, equipment and buildings with a view to preventing breakdowns while in use.

Market Research

The gathering, recording and analysing of all facts about problems relating to the transfer and marketing of specified goods and services from producer to consumer.

Marketing Policy

The policy of an enterprise regarding the marketing of its products or services. It includes questions relating to the range of goods or services to be offered, markets to be entered, price ranges, selling methods, distribution and sales promotion, and the appropriate policy mix to be followed by management with regard to the marketing of its products.

Material Control

Procedures and means by which the correct quantity and quality of materials and components are made available to meet production plans.

Operator Training

The systematic training or retraining of workers in manual skills with a view to ensuring sound and uniform working methods.

Personnel Policy

The policy of an enterprise towards its employees. It embraces methods of selection, recruitment, training, remuneration, welfare services, consultation, relations with unions, social security and all other matters in which the attitude of the employer can affect the quality of working life and well-being of those employed.

Process Planning

The detailed planning of the processes of manufacture necessary to convert raw material into finished products before commencing operation. The term originated in the engineering industry.

Process Research

Research into the nature and characteristics of a given production process.

Product Development

The stage, usually between design and large-scale production, during which units of the product are tested and studied with a view to improving performance, ease of manufacture and market appeal.

Product Research

Research into the nature and characteristics of a product or potential product in relation to the functions it has to or may have to perform.

Production Control

The planning, direction and control of the supply of materials and processing activities of an enterprise.

Production Planning

The planning of the physical means of production. It is concerned with process planning, with the design of tooling, with the layout of plant and equipment and with the handling of materials and tools in the workshop. Work study is a major technique in production planning.

Productivity

The ratio of output to input.

Progressing

Systematic control procedures designed to ensure that the programmes and orders issued by production control are carried out.

Quality Control

The function of management which controls the quality of products. It includes inspection and other procedures and means (including sampling methods based on statistical principles) of maintaining the quality of products.

Standard Costing

A system of costing in which standard costs are estimated in advance; the actual costs incurred are compared with the standards and any variance is analysed for causes.

Standardisation

The development and application of a standard for a particular product or type of component or range of products or components or a given procedure.

Value Analysis

The systematised investigation of the product and its manufacture to reduce cost and improve value.

Variety Reduction

The systematic reduction of the number of varieties of products made and materials, parts and tools used in a factory.

415

2. Check-list of questions which may be of use in applying the questioning sequence in method study

Most of the questions listed below apply generally to method study investigations. They amplify the questioning procedure described in Chapter 8, and may be of service in suggesting to studymen aspects of the method which might otherwise be overlooked. The questions are listed under the following headings:

A. Operations
B. Design
C. Inspection Requirements
D. Material Handling
E. Process Analysis
F. Material

G. Work Organisation
H. Workplace Layout
I. Tools and Equipment
J. Working Conditions
K. Job Enrichment

A. Operations

1. What is the purpose of the operation?

2. Is the result obtained by the operation necessary?
    If so, what makes it necessary?

3. Is the operation necessary because the previous operation was not performed correctly?

4. Is the operation instituted to correct a condition that has now been corrected otherwise?

5. If the operation is being carried out to improve appearance, does the additional cost give extra saleability?

6. Can the purpose of the operation be obtained in another way?

7. Can the material supplier perform the operation more economically?

8. Is the operation being performed to satisfy the requirements of all users of the product, or is it made necessary by the requirements of one or two customers only?

9. Does a subsequent operation eliminate the necessity for this operation?

10. Is the operation being performed as a result of habit?

11. Was the operation established to reduce the cost of a previous operation, or a subsequent operation?

12. Was the operation added by the sales department as a special feature?

13. Can the part be purchased at a lower cost?

14. Would adding a further operation make other operations easier to perform?

15. Is there another way to perform the operation and still maintain the same results?

16. If the operation has been established to correct a subsequent difficulty, is it possible that the corrective operation is more costly than the difficulty itself?

17. Have conditions changed since the operation was added to the process?

18. Could the operation be combined with a previous or a subsequent operation?

417

B. Design

1. Can the design be changed to simplify or eliminate the operation?
2. Is the design of the part suitable for good manufacturing practice?
3. Can equivalent results be obtained by changing the design and thus reducing cost?
4. Can a standard part be substituted?
5. Would a change in design mean increased saleability, an increased market?
6. Can a standard part be converted to do the job?
7. Is it possible to improve the appearance of the article without interfering with its utility?
8. Would an additional cost caused by improved appearance and greater utility be offset by increased business?
9. Has the article the best possible appearance and utility on the market at the price?
10. Has value analysis been used?

C. Inspection Requirements

1. What are the inspection requirements for this operation?
2. Does everybody involved know exactly what the requirements are?
3. What are the inspection details of the previous and following operations?
4. Will changing the requirements of this operation make it easier to perform?
5. Will changing the requirements of the previous operation make this operation easier?
6. Are tolerance, allowance, finish and other standards really necessary?
7. Can standards be raised to improve quality without unnecessary cost?
8. Will lowering standards reduce cost considerably?
9. Can the finished quality of the product be improved in any way above the present standard?
10. How do standards for this operation/product compare with standards for similar items?
11. Can the quality be improved by using new processes?
12. Are the same standards necessary for all customers?
13. Will a change in standards and inspection requirements increase or decrease the defective work and expense in the operation, shop or field?
14. Are the tolerances used in actual practice the same as those shown on the drawing?
15. Has an agreement been reached by all concerned as to what constitutes acceptable quality?
16. What are the main causes of rejections for this part?
17. Is the quality standard definitely fixed, or is it a matter of individual judgement?

D. Material Handling

1. Is the time spent in bringing material to the work station and in removing it large in proportion to the time used to handle it at the work station?
2. If not, could material handling be done by the operatives to provide a rest through change of occupation?
3. Should hand, electric or fork-lift trucks be used?
4. Should special racks, containers or pallets be designed to permit the handling of material with ease and without damage?
5. Where should incoming and outgoing materials be located in the work area?
6. Is a conveyor justified, and if so, what type would best be suited for the job?

7.   Can the work stations for progressive steps of the operation be moved closer together and the material-handling problem overcome by gravity chutes?

8.   Can material be pushed from operative to operative along the bench?

9.   Can material be dispatched from a central point by means of a conveyor?

10.   Is the size of the container suitable for the amount of material transported?

11.   Can material be brought to a central inspection point by means of a conveyor?

12.   Could the operative inspect his own work?

13.   Can a container be designed to make material more accessible?

14.   Could a container be placed at the work station without removing the material?

15.   Can an electric or air hoist or any other lifting device be used with advantage?

16.   If an overhead travelling crane is used, is the service prompt and accurate?

17.   Can a tractor-trailer train be used? Could this or an individual railway replace a conveyor?

18.   Can gravity be utilised by starting the first operation at a higher level?

19.   Can chutes be used to catch material and convey it to containers?

20.   Would flow process charts assist in solving the flow and handling problem?

21.   Is the store efficiently located?

22.   Are truck loading and unloading stations located centrally?

23.   Can conveyors be used for floor-to-floor transportation?

24.   Can waist-high portable material containers be used at the work stations?

25.   Can a finished part be easily disposed of?

26.   Would a turntable eliminate walking?

27.   Can incoming raw material be delivered at the first work station to save double handling?

28.   Could operations be combined at one work station to save double handling?

29.   Would a container of standard size eliminate weighing?

30.   Would a hydraulic lift eliminate a crane service?

31.   Could the operative deliver parts to the next work station when he disposes of them?

32.   Are containers uniform to permit stacking and eliminate excessive use of floor space?

33.   Could material be bought in a more convenient size for handling?

34.   Would signals, i.e. lights, bells, etc., notifying men that more material is required, save delay?

35.   Would better scheduling eliminate bottlenecks?

36.   Would better planning eliminate crane bottlenecks?

37.   Can the location of stores and stockpiles be altered to reduce handling and transportation?

E. Process Analysis

1.   Can the operation being analysed be combined with another operation? Can it be eliminated?

2.   Can it be broken up and the various parts of the operation added to other operations?

3.   Can a part of the operation being performed be completed more effectively as a separate operation?

4.   Is the sequence of operations the best possible, or would changing the sequence improve the operation?

5.   Could the operation be done in another department to save the cost of handling?

6.   Should a concise study of the operation be made by means of a flow process chart?

7.   If the operation is changed, what effect will it have on the other operations? On the finished product?

8.   If a different method of producing the part can be used, will it justify all the work and activity involved?

9.   Can the operation and inspection be combined?

10. Is the job inspected at its most critical point, or when it is completed?

11. Will a patrol form of inspection eliminate waste, scrap and expense?

12. Are there other similar parts which could be made using the same method, tooling and set-up?

F. Material

1.   Is the material being used really suitable for the job?

2.   Could a less expensive material be substituted and still do the job?

3.   Could a lighter-gauge material be used?

4.   Is the material purchased in a condition suitable for use?

5.   Could the supplier perform additional work on the material that would improve usage and decrease waste?

6.   Is the material sufficiently clean?

7.   Is the material bought in amounts and sizes that give the greatest utilisation and limit scrap, offcuts and short ends?

8.   Is the material used to the best possible advantage during cutting, processing?

9.   Are materials used in connection with the process—oils, water, acids, paint, gas, compressed air, electricity—suitable, and is their use controlled and economised?

10. How does the cost of material compare with the cost of labour?

11. Can the design be changed to eliminate excessive loss and scrap material?

12. Can the number of materials used be reduced by standardisation?

13. Could the part be made from scrap material or offcuts?

14. Can newly developed materials—plastics, hardboard, etc.—be used?

15. Is the supplier of the material performing operations on it which are not necessary for the process?

16. Can extruded materials be used?

17. If the material was of a more consistent grade, could better control of the process be established?

18. Can a fabricated part be substituted instead of a casting to save pattern costs?

19. Is the activity low enough to warrant this?

20. Is the material free from sharp edges and burrs?

21. What effect does storage have on material?

22. Could a more careful inspection of incoming materials decrease difficulties now being encountered in the shop?

23. Could sampling inspection combined with supplier rating reduce inspection costs and delays?

24. Could the part be made more economically from offcuts in some other gauge of material?

G. Work Organisation

1.   How is the job assigned to the operative?

2.   Are things so well controlled that the operative is never without a job to do?

3. How is the operative given instructions?

4. How is material obtained?

5. How are drawings and tools issued?

6. Is there a control on time? If so, how are the starting and finishing times of the job checked?

7. Are there many possibilities for delays at the drawing-room, tool-room and store-room and at the clerk's office?

8. Does the layout of the work area prove to be effective, and can it be improved?

9. Is the material properly positioned?

10. If the operation is being performed continually, how much time is wasted at the start and end of the shift by preliminary operations and cleaning up?

11. How is the amount of finished material counted?

12. Is there a definite check between pieces recorded and pieces paid for?

13. Can automatic counters be used?

14. What clerical work is required from operatives for filling in time cards, material requisitions and the like?

15. How is defective work handled?

16. How is the issue and servicing of tools organised?

17. Are adequate records kept on the performance of operatives?

18. Are new employees properly introduced to their surroundings and do they receive sufficient instruction?

19. When workers do not reach a standard of performance, are the details investigated?

20. Are suggestions from workers encouraged?

21. Do the workers really understand the incentive plan under which they work?

H. Workplace Layout

1. Does the plant layout aid efficient material handling?

2. Does the plant layout allow efficient maintenance?

3. Does the plant layout provide adequate safety?

4. Is the plant layout convenient for setting-up?

5. Does the plant layout help social interaction between the operatives?

6. Are materials conveniently placed at the workplace?

7. Are tools pre-positioned to save mental delay?

8. Are adequate working surfaces provided for subsidiary operations, e.g. inspection and deburring?

9. Are facilities provided for the removal and storage of swarf and scrap?

10. Is adequate provision made for the comfort of the operative, e.g. fan, duckboard or chairs?

11. Is the lighting adequate for the job?

12. Has provision been made for the storage of tools and gauges?

13. Has provision been made for the storage of the operatives' personal belongings?

I. Tools and Equipment

1. Can a jig be designed that can be used for more than one job?

2. Is the volume sufficient to justify highly developed specialised tools and fixtures?

3. Can a magazine feed be used?

421

4.   Could the jig be made of lighter material, or so designed with economy of material to allow easier handling?

5.   Are there other fixtures available that can be adapted to this job?

6.   Is the design of the jig correct?

7.   Would lower-cost tooling decrease quality?

8.   Is the jig designed to allow maximum motion economy?

9.   Can the part be quickly inserted and removed from the jig?

10. Would a quick-acting, cam-actuated mechanism be desirable for tightening the jig, clamp or vice?

11. Can ejectors be installed on the fixture for automatically removing the part when the fixture is opened?

12. Are all operatives provided with the same tools?

13. If accurate work is necessary, are proper gauges and other measuring instruments provided?

14. Is the wooden equipment in use in good condition and are work benches free from splinters?

15. Would a special bench or desk designed to eliminate stooping, bending and reaching reduce fatigue?

16. Is pre-setting possible?

17. Can universal tooling be used?

18. Can setting time be reduced?

19. How is material supply replenished?

20. Can a hand or foot air-jet be supplied to the operative and applied with advantage?

21. Could jigs be used?

22. Could guides or bullet-nosed pins be used to position the part?

23. What must be done to complete the operation and put away all the equipment?

J. Working Conditions

1.   Is the light even and sufficient at all times?

2.   Has glare been eliminated from the workplace?

3.   Is the proper temperature for comfort provided at all times; if not, can fans or heaters be used?

4.   Would installation of air-conditioning equipment be justified?

5.   Can noise levels be reduced?

6.   Can fumes, smoke and dirt be removed by exhaust systems?

7.   If concrete floors are used, are duckboards or matting provided to make standing more comfortable?

8.   Can a chair be provided?

9.   Are drinking fountains with cool water provided and are they located nearby?

10. Has due consideration been given to safety factors?

11. Is the floor safe, smooth but not slippery?

12. Has the operative been taught to work safely?

13. Is the clothing suitable from a safety standpoint?

14. Does the plant present a neat and orderly appearance at all times?

15. How thoroughly is the workplace cleaned?

16. Is the plant unduly cold in winter, or stuffy in summer, especially on the first morning of the week?

17. Are dangerous processes adequately guarded?

K. Job Enrichment

1. Is the job boring or monotonous?
2. Can the operation be made more interesting?
3. Can the operation be combined with previous or subsequent operations to enlarge it?
4. What is the cycle time?
5. Can the operative do his own setting?
6. Can he do his own inspection?
7. Can he deburr his own work?
8. Can he service his own tools?
9. Can he be given a batch of tasks and do his own scheduling?
10. Can he make the complete part?
11. Is job rotation possible and desirable?
12. Can group layout be used?
13. Are flexible working hours possible and desirable?
14. Is the operation machine paced?
15. Can buffer stock be provided to allow variations in work pace?
16. Does the operative receive regular information about his performance?

3. Example of tables used to calculate relaxation allowances

This appendix is based on information supplied by Peter Steele and Partners (United Kingdom). Similar tables have been developed by various institutions, such as REFA (Federal Republic of Germany), and by other consulting firms.

Relaxation allowances may be determined by means of the tables of comparative strains and the points conversion table reproduced in this appendix. The analysis should proceed as follows:

(1) For the element of work under consideration, determine the severity of the strain imposed under each sub-heading of the table of strains below, by reference to the tables of comparative strains.

(2) Allocate points as indicated and determine the total points for the strains imposed by the performance of the element of work.

(3) Read off from the points conversion table the appropriate relaxation allowance.

Table I.   Points allocated for various strains: summary

Type of strain	Severity		
	Low	Medium	High
A. *Physical strains resulting from nature of work*			
1. Average force exerted	0-85	0-113	0-149
2. Posture	0-5	6-11	12-16
3. Vibration	0-4	5-10	11-15
4. Short cycle	0-3	4-6	7-10
5. Restrictive clothing	0-4	5-12	13-20
B. *Mental strains*			
1. Concentration/anxiety	0-4	5-10	11-16
2. Monotony	0-2	3-7	8-10
3. Eye strain	0-5	6-11	12-20
4. Noise	0-2	3-7	8-10
C. *Physical or mental strains resulting from nature of working conditions*			
1. Temperature			
Low humidity	0-5	6-11	12-16
Medium humidity	0-5	6-14	15-26
High humidity	0-6	7-17	18-36

Type of strain	Severity		
	Low	Medium	High
2. Ventilation	0-3	4-9	10-15
3. Fumes	0-3	4-8	9-12
4. Dust	0-3	4-8	9-12
5. Dirt	0-2	3-6	7-10
6. Wet	0-2	3-6	7-10

Note: Allocate points for each strain independently, irrespective of what has been allowed for other strains. If any strain occurs for only a proportion of the time, allocate a similar proportion of the points:

e.g. High concentration: 16 points, 25 per cent of the time;

Low concentration: 4 points, 75 per cent of the time.

Allocate $16 \times 0.25 = 4$ points plus $4 \times 0.75 = 3$ points, which gives a total of $4 + 3 = 7$ points.

TABLES OF COMPARATIVE STRAINS

A. Physical strains resulting from the nature of the work

1. AVERAGE FORCE EXERTED (FACTOR A.1)

Consider the whole of the element or period for which the relaxation allowance is required and determine the **average** force exerted.

Example:

Lift and carry a weight of 40 lb. (time 12 seconds) and return empty-handed (time 8 seconds). In this example, if the relaxation allowance is to apply to the full 20 seconds, the "average force exerted" should be calculated as follows:

$$\left(40 \times \frac{12}{20}\right) + \left(0 \times \frac{8}{20}\right) = 24 \text{ lb.}$$

The number of points allocated for the average force exerted will depend upon the type of stress involved. Stresses are classified as follows:

(a) Medium stress

(i) Where the work is primarily concerned with carrying or supporting loads;

(ii) shovelling, swinging hammers and other rhythmical movements.

This category covers most operations.

(b) Low stress

(i) Where the weight of the body is transferred in order to exert force, e.g. foot-pedal operation; pressing an article, with the body, against a buff;

(ii) supporting or carrying well balanced loads strapped to the body or hung from the shoulders; arms and hands free.

(c) High stress

(i) Where the work is primarily concerned with lifting;

(ii) exerting the force by continued use of certain muscles of fingers and arms;

(iii) lifting or supporting loads in awkward attitudes, manipulation of heavy weights into awkward positions;

(iv) operations in hot conditions, hot metalworking, etc.

Relaxation allowances should be awarded in this category only after every endeavour has been made to improve facilities which will make the physical task lighter.

Table II.   Medium stress: points for average force exerted

lb.	0	1	2	3	4	5	6	7	8	9
0	0	0	0	0	3	6	8	10	12	14
10	15	16	17	18	19	20	21	22	23	24
20	25	26	27	28	29	30	31	32	32	33
30	34	35	36	37	38	39	39	40	41	41
40	42	43	44	45	46	46	47	48	49	50
50	50	51	51	52	53	54	54	55	56	56
60	57	58	59	59	60	61	61	62	63	64
70	64	65	65	66	67	68	69	70	70	71
80	72	72	72	73	73	74	74	75	76	76
90	77	78	79	79	80	80	81	82	82	83
100	84	85	86	86	87	88	88	88	89	90
110	91	92	93	94	95	95	96	96	97	97
120	97	98	98	98	99	99	99	100	100	100
130	101	101	102	102	103	104	105	106	107	108
140	109	109	109	110	110	111	112	112	112	113

Table III.   Low stress: points for average force exerted

lb.	0	1	2	3	4	5	6	7	8	9
0	0	0	0	0	3	6	7	8	9	10
10	11	12	13	14	14	15	16	16	17	18
20	19	19	20	21	22	22	23	23	24	25
30	26	26	27	27	28	28	29	30	31	31
40	32	32	33	34	34	35	35	36	36	37
50	38	38	39	39	40	41	41	42	42	43
60	43	43	44	44	45	46	46	47	47	48
70	48	49	50	50	50	51	51	52	52	53
80	54	54	54	55	55	56	56	57	58	58
90	58	59	59	60	60	60	61	62	62	63
100	63	63	64	65	65	66	66	66	67	67
110	68	68	68	69	69	70	71	71	71	72
120	72	73	73	73	74	74	75	75	76	76
130	77	77	77	78	78	78	79	80	80	81
140	81	82	82	82	83	83	84	84	84	85

Table IV.   High stress: points for average force exerted

lb.	0	1	2	3	3-4	4	5	6	7	8	9
0	0	0	0	3	6	8	11	13	15	17	18
10	20	21	22	24		25	27	28	29	30	32
20	33	34	35	37		38	39	40	41	43	44
30	45	46	47	48		49	50	51	52	54	55
40	56	57	58	59		60	61	62	63	64	65
50	66	67	68	69		70	71	72	73	74	75
60	76	76	77	78		79	80	81	82	83	84
70	85	86	87	88		88	89	90	91	92	93
80	94	94	95	96		97	98	99	100	101	101
90	102	103	104	105		105	106	107	108	109	110
100	110	111	112	113		114	115	115	116	117	118
110	119	119	120	121		122	123	124	124	125	126
120	127	128	128	129		130	130	131	132	133	134
130	135	136	136	137		137	138	139	140	141	142
140	142	143	143	144		145	146	147	148	148	149

A study should be made of the elements in relation to low, medium and high stress conditions. The points to be allocated, according to the type of stress and the average force applied, are set out in tables II to IV.

Example: If the weight carried is 25 lb.—

(i) determine the type of stress involved (medium, low or high);

(ii) in the left-hand column of the table for the type of stress (table II, II or IV), find the line for 20 lb.;

(iii) on this line, move across the table to the right, to column 5;

(iv) read off the points allocation for 25 lb. carried, which is—

table II, medium stress: 30 points;

table III, low stress: 22 points;

table IV, high stress: 39 points.

2. POSTURE (FACTOR A.2)

Consider whether the worker is sitting, standing, stooping or in a cramped position and whether a load is handled easily or awkwardly.

	Points
Sitting easily	0
Sitting awkwardly, or mixture of sitting and standing	2
Standing or walking freely	4
Ascending or descending stairs unladen	5
Standing or walking with a load	6
Climbing up or down ladders, or some bending, lifting, stretching or throwing	8
Awkward lifting, shovelling ballast to container	10
Constant bending, lifting, stretching or throwing	12
Coalmining with pickaxes, lying in a low seam	16

3. VIBRATION (FACTOR A.3)

Consider the impact of the vibration on the body, limbs or hands and the addition to mental effort due to it, or to a series of jars or shocks.

	Points
Shovelling light materials	1
Power sewing-machine Power press or guillotine if operative is holding the material Cross-cut sawing	2
Shovelling ballast Portable power drill operated by one hand	4
Pickaxing	6
Power drill (two hands)	8
Road drill on concrete	15

4. SHORT CYCLE (HIGHLY REPETITIVE) (FACTOR A.4)

In highly repetitive work, if a series of very short elements form a cycle which is continuously repeated for a long period, award points as indicated below, to compensate for the lack of opportunity to vary the muscles used during the work.

Average cycle time (centiminutes)	Points
16-17	1
15	2
13-14	3
12	4
10-11	5
8-9	6
7	7
6	8
5	9
Less than 5	10

5. RESTRICTIVE CLOTHING (FACTOR A.5)

Consider the weight of the protective clothing in relation to effort and movement. Consider also whether ventilation and breathing are affected.

	Points
Thin rubber (surgeon's) gloves	1
Household rubber gloves Rubber boots	2
Grinder's goggles	3
Industrial rubber or leather gloves	5
Face mask (e.g. for paint-spraying)	8
Asbestos suit or tarpaulin coat	15
Restrictive protective clothing and respirator	20

B. Mental strains

1. CONCENTRATION/ANXIETY (FACTOR B.1)

Consider what would happen if the operative relaxed his attention, the responsibility carried, the need for exact timing of movements, and the accuracy or precision required.

	Points
Routine simple assembly Shovelling ballast	0
Routine packing, labourer washing vehicles Wheeling trolley down clear gangway	1
Feed press tool; hand clear of press Topping up battery	2
Painting walls	3
Assembling small and simple batches, performed without much thinking Sewing-machine work, automatically guided	4
Assembling warehouse orders by trolley Simple inspection	5
Load/unload press tool, hand feed into machine Spray-painting metalwork	6
Adding up figures Inspecting detailed components	7
Buffing and polishing	8
Guiding work by hand on sewing-machine Packing assorted chocolates, memorising pattern and selecting accordingly Assembly work too complex to become automatic Welding parts held in jig	10
Driving a motor bus in heavy traffic or fog Marking out in detail with high accuracy	15

2. MONOTONY (FACTOR B.2)

Consider the degree of mental stimulation and if there is companionship, competitive spirit, music, etc.

	Points
Two men on jobbing work	0
Cleaning own shoes for half an hour on one's own	3
Operative on repetitive work Operative working alone on non-repetitive work	5
Routine inspection	6
Adding similar columns of figures	8
One operative working alone on highly repetitive work	11

3. EYE STRAIN (FACTOR B.3)

Consider the lighting conditions, glare, flicker, illumination, colour and closeness of work and for how long the strain is endured.

	Points
Normal factory work	0
Inspection of easily visible faults Sorting distinctively coloured articles by colour Factory work in poor lighting	2
Intermittent inspection for detailed faults Grading apples	4
Reading a newspaper in a motor bus	8
Arc-welding using mask Continuous visual inspection, e.g. cloth from a loom	10
Engraving using an eyeglass	14

4. NOISE (FACTOR B.4)

Consider whether the noise affects concentration, is a steady hum or a background noise, is regular or occurs unexpectedly, is irritating or soothing. (Noise has been described as "a loud sound made by somebody else".)

	Points
Work in a quiet office, no distracting noise Light assembly factory	0
Work in a city office with continual traffic noise outside	1
Light machine shop Office or assembly shop where noise is a distraction	2
Woodworking machine shop	4
Operating steam hammer in forge	5
Rivetting in a shipyard	9
Road drilling	10

C. Physical or mental strains resulting from the nature of the working conditions

1. TEMPERATURE AND HUMIDITY (FACTOR C.1)

Consider the general conditions of atmospheric temperature and humidity and classify as indicated below. Select points according to average temperature within the ranges shown.

Humidity (per cent)	Temperature		
	Up to 75°F	76° to 90°F	Over 90°F
Up to 75	0	6- 9	12-16
76-85	1-3	8-12	15-26
Over 85	4-6	12-17	20-36

2. VENTILATION (FACTOR C.2)

Consider the quality and freshness of the air and its circulation by air-conditioning or natural draught.

	Points
Offices	
Factories with "office-type" conditions	0
Workshop with reasonable ventilation but some draught	1
Draughty workshops	3
Working in sewer	14

3. FUMES (FACTOR C.3)

Consider the nature and concentration of the fumes: whether toxic or injurious to health; irritating to eyes, nose, throat or skin; disagreeable odour.

	Points
Lathe turning with coolants	0
Emulsion paint	
Gas cutting	1
Soldering with resin	
Motor vehicle exhaust in small commercial garage	5
Cellulose painting	6
Moulder procuring metal and filling mould	10

4. DUST (FACTOR C.4)

Consider the volume and nature of the dust.

	Points
Office	
Normal light assembly operations	0
Press shop	
Grinding or buffing operations with good extraction	1
Sawing wood	2
Emptying ashes	4
Linishing weld	6
Running coke from hoppers into skips or trucks	10
Unloading cement	11
Demolishing building	12

5. DIRT (FACTOR C.5)

Consider the nature of the work and the general discomfort caused by its dirty nature. This allowance covers "washing time" where this is paid for (i.e. where operatives are allowed three minutes or five minutes for washing, etc.). Do **not** allow both points and time.

	Points
Office work }	
Normal assembly operations }	0
Office duplicators	1
Dustman	2
Stripping internal combustion engine	4
Work under old motor vehicle	5
Unloading bags of cement	7
Coalminer }	
Chimney-sweep with brushes }	10

6. WET (FACTOR C.6)

Consider the cumulative effect of exposure to this condition over a long period.

	Points
Normal factory operations	0
Outdoor workers, e.g. postman	1
Working continuously in the damp	2
Rubbing down walls with wet pumice block	4
Continuous handling of wet articles	5
Laundry wash-house, wet work, steamy, floor running with water, hands wet	10

POINTS CONVERSION TABLE

Table V. Percentage relaxation allowance for total points allocated

Points	0	1	2	3	4	5	6	7	8	9
0	10	10	10	10	10	10	10	11	11	11
10	11	11	11	11	11	12	12	12	12	12
20	13	13	13	13	14	14	14	14	15	15
30	15	16	16	16	17	17	17	18	18	18
40	19	19	20	20	21	21	22	22	23	23
50	24	24	25	26	26	27	27	28	28	29
60	30	30	31	32	32	33	34	34	35	36
70	37	37	38	39	40	40	41	42	43	44
80	45	46	47	48	48	49	50	51	52	53
90	54	55	56	57	58	59	60	61	62	63
100	64	65	66	68	69	70	71	72	73	74
110	75	77	78	79	80	82	83	84	85	87
120	88	89	91	92	93	95	96	97	99	100
130	101	103	105	106	107	109	110	112	113	115
140	116	118	119	121	122	123	125	126	128	130

Example: If the total number of points allocated for the various strains is 37:

    (i) in the left-hand column of table V, find the line for 30;

    (ii) on this line, move across the table to the right, to column 7;

    (iii) read off the relaxation allowance for 37 points, which is 18 per cent.

EXAMPLES OF CALCULATION OF RELAXATION ALLOWANCES

1. *Power press operation.* As press guard opens automatically, reach in with left hand, grasp piece-part, and disengage it. With left hand move piece-part to tote bin, while right hand places new blank in press tool. Withdraw right hand, while left hand closes guard. Operate press with foot. Simultaneously, with right hand reach to tote bin, grasp blank and orient it in hand, move blank near guard and wait for guard to open.

On 20-ton press. Maximum reach 50 cm (20 in.). Posture somewhat unnatural; seated at machine. Noisy department, adequate lighting.

2. *Carry 50 lb. sack up stairs.* Lift sack on to bench 90 cm (3 ft.) high; transfer to shoulder, carry up stairs, drop sack on floor. Dusty conditions.

3. *Pack chocolates* in three layers of 4 lb. box, according to pattern for each layer, average 160 chocolates. Operative sits in front of straight shelves bearing 11 kinds of chocolates in trays or tins; he must pack the chocolates according to a memorised pattern for each layer. Air-conditioned, good light.

Table VI.   Calculation of relaxation allowances: examples

Type of strain	Job					
	Power press operation		Carrying 50 lb. sack		Packing chocolates	
	Stress	Points	Stress	Points	Stress	Points
A. *Physical strains*						
1. Average force (lb.)	—	—	M	50	—	—
2. Posture	L	4	M	6	L	2
3. Vibration	L	2	L	—	—	—
4. Short cycle	H	10	L	—	—	—
5. Restrictive clothing	—	—	—	—	—	—
B. *Mental strains*						
1. Concentration/anxiety	M	6	L	1	H	10
2. Monotony	M	6	L	1	L	2
3. Eye strain	L	3	—	—	L	2
4. Noise	M	4	L	—	L	1
C. *Working conditions*						
1. Temperature/humidity	—	—	L/L	1	L/L	3
2. Ventilation	—	—	—	—	—	—
3. Fumes	—	—	—	—	—	—
4. Dust	—	—	H	9	—	—
5. Dirt	M	3	L	—	—	—
6. Wet	—	—	L	—	—	—
Total points		38		68		20
Relaxation allowance, including tea breaks (per cent)		18		35		13

4· Conversion factors

(1)	(2)	To convert column (1) into column (2), multiply by
Length		
Inches	Feet	0.083
Inches	Centimetres	2.540
Feet	Yards	0.333
Feet	Metres	0.305
Yards	Feet	3
Yards	Metres	0.914
Poles	Yards	5.502
Poles	Metres	5.029
Furlongs	Miles	0.125
Furlongs	Kilometres	0.201
Miles	Yards	1,760
Miles	Kilometres	1.609
Fathoms	Feet	6
Fathoms	Metres	1.829
Centimetres	Inches	0.394
Metres	Feet	**3.281**
Metres	Yards	1.094
Metres	Poles	0.199
Metres	Fathoms	0.547
Kilometres	Furlongs	4.975
Kilometres	Miles	0.621
Area		
Square inches	Square feet	0.0069
Square inches	Square centimetres	6.452
Square feet	Square yards	0.111
Square feet	Square metres	0.093
Square yards	Square feet	9
Square yards	Square metres	0.836
Acres	Square feet	43,560
Acres	Square miles	0.0016
Acres	Square metres	4047
Acres	Hectares	0.405
Square miles	Square feet	27,878,400
Square miles	Square kilometres	2.590

435

(1)	(2)	To convert column (1) into column (2), multiply by
Square miles	Hectares	259.2
Square miles	Acres	640
Square centimetres	Square inches	0.155
Square metres	Square feet	10.754
Square metres	Square yards	1.196
Square metres	Acres	0.0025
Square kilometres	Hectares	100
Square kilometres	Acres	247.105
Square kilometres	Square miles	0.386
Hectares	Acres	2.471
Hectares	Square kilometres	10^{-2}
Hectares	Square miles	0.0039

Volume

Cubic inches	Cubic feet	5.787×10^{-4}
Cubic inches	Cubic centimetres	16.387
Cubic feet	Cubic yards	0.037
Cubic feet	Cubic metres	0.028
Cubic yards	Cubic feet	27
Cubic yards	Cubic metres	0.765
Cubic centimetres	Cubic feet	3.53×10^{-5}
Cubic centimetres	Cubic inches	0.061
Cubic metres	Cubic yards	1.308
Cubic metres	Cubic feet	35.315

Liquid measure

Fluid ounces (Imperial)	Fluid ounces (US)	0.961
Fluid ounces (Imperial)	Millilitres	28.413
Fluid ounces (US)	Fluid ounces (Imperial)	1.041
Fluid ounces (US)	Millilitres	29.574
Pints (Imperial)	Pints (US)	1.201
Pints (Imperial)	Quarts	0.5
Pints (Imperial)	Gallons (Imperial)	0.125
Pints (Imperial)	Litres	0.568
Pints (US)	Pints (Imperial)	0.833
Pints (US)	Litres	0.473
Gills	Pints	0.25
Gills	Litres	0.142
Gallons (Imperial)	Gallons (US)	1.201
Gallons (Imperial)	Litres	4.546
Gallons (US)	Gallons (Imperial)	0.833
Gallons (US)	Litres	3.785
Cubic centimetres	Litres	10^{-3}
Litres	Pints (Imperial)	1.760
Litres	Pints (US)	2.113

Weight

Grains (avdp.)	Grains (troy)	1.003
	Grams	0.0648

(1)	(2)	To convert column (1) into column (2), multiply by
Grains (troy)	Grains (avdp.)	0.996
	Grams	0.0648
Pennyweight (troy)	Grains (troy)	24
	Grams	1.555
Ounces (avdp.)	Ounces (troy)	0.9115
	Pounds	0.0625
	Grams	28.350
Ounces (troy)	Ounces (avdp.)	1.097
	Grams	31.104
Pounds (avdp.)	Pounds (troy)	1.215
	Ounces (avdp.)	16
	Kilograms	0.454
Pounds (troy)	Pounds (avdp.)	0.823
	Ounces (troy)	12
	Kilograms	0.373
Stones	Pounds (avdp.)	14
	Grams	6350.297
Tons (short)	Pounds (avdp.)	2000.
	Kilograms	907.185
Tons (long)	Pounds (avdp.)	2240.
	Kilograms	1016.047
Grams	Ounces (avdp.)	0.035
	Ounces (troy)	0.032
Kilograms	Pounds (avdp.)	2.205
	Tons (short)	0.0011
	Tons (long)	0.00098

5. Selected bibliography

Agurén, S.; Hansson, R.; Karlsson, K. G.: *The Volvo Kalmar plant: The impact of new design on work organisation* (Stockholm, Rationalisation Council – Swedish Employers' Confederation – Swedish Trade Union Confederation, 1976).

Alford, L. P.; Bangs, J. R.: *Production handbook* (New York, Ronald Press, 2nd ed., 1964).

Allenspach, Heinz: *Flexible working hours* (Geneva, ILO, 1975).

Arscott, P. E.; Armstrong, M.: *An employer's guide to health and safety management: A handbook for industry* (London, Engineering Employers' Federation, 1976).

Ashcroft, H.: "The productivity of several machines under the care of one operator", in *Journal of the Royal Statistical Society* (London), Series B, Vol. XII, 1950, pp. 145-151.

Barnes, Ralph M.: *Work sampling* (New York and London, John Wiley, 2nd ed., 1957).

—: *Motion and time study: Design and measurement of work* (New York and London, John Wiley, 6th ed., 1969).

Benson, F.: "Further notes on the productivity of machines requiring attention at random intervals", in *Journal of the Royal Statistical Society,* Series B, Vol. XIV, 1952, pp. 200-210.

—: Cox, D. R.: "The productivity of machines requiring attention at random intervals", in *Journal of the Royal Statistical Society,* Series B, Vol. XIII, 1951, pp. 65-82.

Biel-Nisen, H. E.: "Universal maintenance standards", in *Journal of Methods-Time Measurement* (Fair Lawn, NJ), Vol. 7, Nos. 4 and 5, Nov. 1960-Feb. 1961.

Bowman, Edmond; Fetter, Robert: *Analysis for production management* (Homewood, Ill., Richard Irwin, 1961).

British Institute of Management: *Classification and coding: An introduction and review of classification and coding systems* (London, 1971).

British Standards Institution: *Glossary of terms used in work study* (London, 1969).

Buffa, E. S.: *Modern production management* (New York and London, John Wiley, 4th ed., 1973).

Burbidge, J. L.: *Principles of production control* (London, Macdonald and Evans, 3rd ed., 1971).

—: *Production planning* (London, Heinemann, 1971).

—: *The introduction of group technology* (London, Heinemann, 1974).

Bureau des temps élémentaires: *Vocabulaire technique concernant l'étude du travail* (Paris, Les Editions d'organisation, 1954).

—: "La préparation scientifique des décisions (recherche opérationnelle) appliquée à l'étude du travail", in *L'étude du travail* (Paris), Jan. 1960, pp. 7-24.

Carpentier, J.; Cazamian, P.: *Night work: Its effects on the health and welfare of the worker* (Geneva, ILO, 1977).

Carroll, P.: *How to chart data* (New York and London, McGraw-Hill, 1960).

Carson, G. B. (ed.) et al.: *Production handbook* (New York, Ronald Press, 3rd ed., 1972).

Cemach, H. P.: *Work study in the office* (Barking, UK, Applied Science Publishers, 4th ed., 1969).

de Chantal, R.: "Etude du travail et théorie des attentes", in *L'étude du travail,* June 1957, pp. 14-20.

439

Cox, D. R.: "Tables on operator efficiency in multi-machine operation", in *Journal of the Royal Statistical Society,* Series B, Vol. XV, 1953.

—: "A table for predicting the production from a group of machines under the care of one operative", in *Journal of the Royal Statistical Society,* Series B, Vol. XVI, 1954, pp. 285-287.

Crossan, R. M.; Nance, H. W.: *Master standard data: The economic approach to work measurement* (New York and London, McGraw-Hill, 2nd ed., 1972).

Currie, R. M.: *Simplified P.M.T.S.* (London, British Institute of Management, 1963).

—: *Financial incentives based on work measurement,* 2nd ed. revised J. E. Faraday (London, British Institute of Management, 1971).

—: *Work study,* 4th ed. revised J. E. Faraday (London, Pitman, 1977).

Edwards, G. A. B.: *Readings in group technology* (Brighton, UK, Machinery Publishing Co., 1971).

Evans, A. A.: *Hours of work in industrialised countries* (Geneva, ILO, 1975).

Grant, E. L.: *Statistical quality control* (New York and London, McGraw-Hill, 4th ed., 1972).

Heyde, Chris: *The sensible taskmaster* (Sydney, Heyde Dynamics, 1976).

Hunter, D.: *The diseases of occupations* (London, Hodder and Stoughton Educational, 6th ed., 1977).

International Labour Office (ILO): *Higher productivity in manufacturing industries,* Studies and reports, New series, No. 38 (Geneva, 3rd. impr., 1967).

—: *Accident prevention: A workers' education manual* (Geneva, 9th impr., 1978).

—: *Encyclopaedia of occupational health and safety,* 2 vols. (Geneva, 5th impr., 1976).

—: *Job evaluation,* Studies and reports, New series, No. 56 (Geneva, 9th impr., 1977).

—: *Payment by results,* Studies and reports, New series, No. 27 (Geneva, 14th impr., 1977).

—: *Protection of workers against noise and vibration in the working environment* (Geneva, 2nd impr., 1980).

—: *Management of working time in industrialised countries* (Geneva, 1978).

—: *New forms of work organisation, 1* (Geneva, 1979).

—: *New forms of work organisation, 2* (Geneva, 1979).

—: *Managing and developing new forms of work organisation,* edited by G. Kanawaty (Geneva, 2nd ed., 1981).

International Occupational Safety and Health Centre (CIS): *CIS Abstracts* (Geneva, ILO–CIS; published periodically).

Ishikawa, Kaoru: *Guide to quality control* (Tokyo, Asian Productivity Organisation, 1976).

Lehmann, J. T.: *La mesure des temps alloués* (Louvain, Librairie universitaire, 1965).

Lindholm, Rolf; Norstedt, Jan-Peder: *The Volvo report* (Stockholm, Swedish Employers' Confederation, 1975).

Mallick, R. W.; Gaudreau, A. T.: *Plant layout and practice* (New York and London, John Wiley, 1966).

Marić, D.: *Adapting working hours to modern needs* (Geneva, ILO, 1977).

Marriott, R.: *Incentive payment systems: A review of research and opinion* (London, Staples Press, 3rd ed., 1969).

Mary, J. A.: *L'expérience Guilliet* (Paris, Union des industries métallurgiques et minières (UIMM), 1975).

Maurice, M.: *Shift work: Economic advantages and social costs* (Geneva, ILO, 1975).

Mayer, Raymond E.: *Production and operations management* (New York and London, McGraw-Hill, 3rd ed., 1975).

Maynard, H. B.: *Production: An international appraisal of contemporary manufacturing systems and the changing role of the worker* (New York and London, McGraw-Hill, 1975).

—; Stegemerten, G. J.: "Universal maintenance standards", in *Factory Management and Maintenance* (London), Nov. 1955.

— (ed.): *Industrial engineering handbook* (New York and London, McGraw-Hill, 3rd ed., 1971).

Miles, L. D.: *Techniques of value analysis and engineering* (New York and London, McGraw-Hill, 2nd ed., 1972).

Milward, G. E. (ed.): *Applications of organizations and methods* (London, Macdonald and Evans, 1964).

—: *Organization and methods* (London, Macmillan, 2nd ed., 1967).

Mitrofanov, S. P.: *Scientific principles of group technology* (Boston Spa, UK, National Lending Library for Science and Technology, 1966).

Mundel, M. E.: *Motion and time study: Principles and practice* (Englewood Cliffs, NJ, and Hemel Hempstead, UK, Prentice-Hall, 4th ed., 1970).

Muther, Richard: *Practical plant layout* (New York and London, McGraw-Hill, 1956).

Neale, F. J.: *Primary standard data* (New York and London, McGraw-Hill, 1967).

Niebel, Benjamin W.: *Motion and time study* (Homewood, Ill., Richard Irwin, 1972).

Norstedt, J. P.: *Work organisation and payment system at Orrefors Glasbruk* (Stockholm, Swedish Employers' Confederation, 1970).

PA Management Consultants Ltd: *Work study manual* (London, 1969).

Peck, T. P.: *Occupational safety and health: A guide to information sources,* Management information guides, No. 28 (Detroit, Mich., Gale Research Co., 1974).

Quick, J. H.; Duncan, J. H.; Malcolm, J. A.: *Work Factor time standards: Measurement of manual and mental work* (New York and London, McGraw-Hill, 1962).

Ranson, G. M.: *Group technology: A foundation for better total company operation* (New York and London, McGraw-Hill, 1972).

Saunders, N. F. T.: *Factory organization and management* (London, Pitman, 5th ed., 1973).

Shaw, Anne G.: *The purpose and practice of motion study* (Buxton, UK, Columbine Press, 2nd ed., 1960).

Singleton, W. T.: *Introduction to ergonomics* (Geneva, World Health Organization, 1972).

Smith, J. Tennant: Series of articles on interference published in *Work Study* (London, Sewell Publications), June-Oct. 1965.

Stansfield, R. G.: *The accuracy of effort rating by time study* (London, City University, Department of Social Studies and Humanities, new impr., Oct. 1969).

—: *Bibliography: Work study and time and motion study* (London, City University, Department of Social Studies and Humanities, Oct. 1969).

Starr, M. K.: *Production management: Systems and synthesis* (Englewood Cliffs, NJ, and Hemel Hempstead, UK, Prentice-Hall, 2nd ed., 1972).

Swedish Employers' Confederation: *Job reform in Sweden* (Stockholm, 1975).

United Kingdom, Civil Service Department: *The design of forms in government departments* (London, HMSO, 3rd ed., 1972).

Valota, A.: "L'interférence réciproque des machines", in *L'industrie textile,* July 1958, pp. 519-523.

Voris, William: *Production control: Text and cases* (Homewood, Ill., Richard Irwin, 1961).

Whitmore, Dennis A.: *Work study and related management services* (London, Heinemann, 3rd ed., 1976).

Other ILO publications

Managing and developing new forms of work organisation. Edited by George Kanawaty

"This new book provides practical guidelines for developing and introducing new forms of work organisation in enterprises. It analyses the implications of such a change for the various areas of enterprise activity and shows how a change in work design in one area – for example shop-floor activity – can trigger off and be reinforced by corresponding changes in other areas of management, such as the areas of accounting or personnel management." (*International Journal of Manpower,* Hull).

"An unusually good collection… most likely to be of use to teachers of management courses, and could be helpful for MBA/DMS courses, as it is not too technical and also rather up-to-date." (*Journal of General Management,* London)

ISBN 92-2-102707-4

The practice of entrepreneurship. By Geoffrey G. Meredith, Robert E. Nelson and Philip A. Neck

Practising managers, would-be entrepreneurs and management advisers interested in developing their entrepreneurial skills will find this book of great value. It is a distillation of the research, reading and personal experience of the three authors, all of whom are professional management consultants and trainers used to dealing with entrepreneurs in a wide range of occupations. *The practice of entrepreneurship* is in three parts, dealing respectively with the personal traits and characteristics of entrepreneurs; the financial aspects of entrepreneurship which most commonly reflect business success; and the external aspects of entrepreneurship, including dealings with those people whose advice and help may be valuable. Anyone using this book can hardly fail to benefit from it.

ISBN 92-2-102846-1 (limp cover); ISBN 92-2-102839-9 (hard cover).

Management consulting: A guide to the profession. Edited by M. Kubr

This book is intended for new or future consultants, firms, educational and professional institutes, public and private organisations and managers who use consultants.

"This is an excellent handbook for anyone involved in management consulting … well written and easy to use …" *(British Institute of Management)*

"A valuable contribution to the literature which compared with some professions is still 'thin on the ground' … comprehensive and informative … written with an eye to present-day conditions …" (*The Training Officer,* Manchester)

"Essential for anyone contemplating entry, reminderful for current practitioners, helpful to users of consulting services …" (*Consultants News*, Fitzwilliam, New Hampshire)

ISBN 92-2-101165-8

Night work: Its effects on the health and welfare of the worker. By James Carpentier and Pierre Cazamian

"This small book is another of the well compiled reviews by ILO experts … A wide ranging introduction which sets the research findings in a historical and industrial context. The material is commendably up to date. [The authors'] conclusions regarding the health effects of night work come down firmly on the side of clear evidence for increased ill health … This is a useful text (and) should interest ergonomists, production engineers and managers and industrial medical personnel for its coverage of a problem area which is becoming more important every day." (*Applied Ergonomics,* Guildford)

ISBN 92-2-101676-5 (limp cover)

Case method in management development: Guide for effective use. By John I. Reynolds

"Real-life case-studies always provide interesting practical examples to illuminate theory, and are particularly useful in business and management studies … The ILO has now produced a manual on the case method with a view to helping managements schools, teachers and trainers, as well as participants in management programmes, to use the method more effectively. The ILO believes that management education and training in the 1980s will use a mix of methods and techniques, with increasing emphasis on live problem analysis and problem solving, practical projects, teamwork, organisation development, and the individual manager's responsibility for his own development. The case method will have an important role to play and teachers will need to master case teaching and case writing … This is a very interesting and clearly written practical guide." (*British Business*, London)

ISBN 92-2-102363-X